The Global Economic Crisis

This meticulous, vital, timely and accessible work unravels the history of a hydra-headed monster: military, media and politics, culminating in "humanity at the crossroads"; the current unprecedented economic and social crisis... From the first page of the preface of "The Global Economic Crisis", the reasons for all unravel with compelling clarity. For those asking "why?" this book has the answers.

–Felicity Arbuthnot, award-winning author and journalist based in London

The current economic crisis, its causes and hopefully its cure have been a mystery for most people. I welcome a readable exposition of the global dimensions of the crisis and hope for some clarity on how to better organize money locally and internationally for the future.

–Dr. Rosalie Bertell, renowned scientist, Alternative Nobel Prize laureate and Regent, International Physicians for Humanitarian Medicine, Geneva

This work is much more than a path-breaking and profound historical analysis of the actors and institutions, it is an affirmation of the authors' belief that a better world is feasible and that it can be achieved by collective organized actions and faith in the sustainability of a democratic order.

–Frederick Clairmonte, distinguished analyst of the global political economy and author of the 1960s classic, *The Rise and Fall of Economic Liberalism: The Making of the Economic Gulag*

Decades of profligate economic policies and promiscuous military interventions reached a critical mass, exploding in the meltdown of globalization in 2008. Today, the economic meltdown is reconfiguring everything – global society, economy and culture. This book is engineering a revolution by introducing an innovative global theory of economics.

–Michael Carmichael, prominent author, historian and president of the *Planetary Movement*

The Global Economic Crisis

The Great Depression of the XXI Century

Michel Chossudovsky and
Andrew Gavin Marshall, Editors

Global Research

The Global Economic Crisis. The Great Depression of the XXI Century
Michel Chossudovsky and Andrew Gavin Marshall (Editors) — First Edition.

Global Research Publishers is a division of the Centre for Research on Globalization (CRG), P.O. Box 55019, 11, rue Notre-Dame Ouest, Montréal, Québec,
H2Y 4A7, Canada.

For more information, contact the publisher at the above address or by email at
our website at **www.globalresearch.ca**

FIRST EDITION

Cover Photo © iStockphoto
Cover graphics by Andréa Joseph © Global Research, 2010
Page layout and book design by Andréa Joseph, pagexpress@videotron.ca

Printed and bound in Canada.
Printed on chlorine-free 100% post-consumer recycled Canadian paper.

ISBN 978-0-9737147-3-9

Legal Deposit:
Bibliothèque et Archives nationales du Québec
Library and Archives Canada

Library and Archives Canada Cataloguing in Publication

Chossudovsky, Michel and Marshall, Andrew Gavin

    The global economic crisis: the great depression of the XXI century /
    Michel Chossudovsky and Andrew Gavin Marshall, editors.
    Includes bibliographical references and index.
    ISBN 978-0-9737147-3-9

1. Global Financial Crisis, 2008-2009. 2. Economic history-21st century.
3. Economic policy. 4. International finance. I. Chossudovsky, Michel, 1942-
II. Marshall, Andrew Gavin, 1987-

HB3717.2008G56 2010   330.9'0511   C2010-902440-0

To the memory of Evgeny Chossudovsky,
who taught me the true meaning of Internationalism. –MC

To Salma, John, Dave and my family
for their continued guidance and constant,
unyielding support, without which I would not be here today. –AGM

Titles by Global Research Publishers

Michel Chossudovsky, *The Globalization of Poverty and the New World Order*, 2003.

Michel Chossudovsky, *America's War on Terrorism*, 2005.

F. William Engdahl, *Seeds of Destruction: The Hidden Agenda of Genetic Manipulation*, 2007.

Table of Contents

PART II
Global Poverty

PART III
War, National Security and World Government

PART IV

The Global Monetary System

PART V

The Shadow Banking System

List of Tables

List of Charts

About the Contributors

Ellen Brown is a prominent economic analyst and attorney based in Los Angeles. In her latest best-selling book, *Web of Debt* (2007), she examines the inside workings of the Federal Reserve and "the money trust". Another best-selling title, *Forbidden Medicine* (2008), traces the suppression of natural health treatments by the same corrupt corporate influences which captured the money system.

Tom Burghardt is an independent writer and researcher based in the San Francisco Bay Area. He has written extensively on issues pertaining to intelligence, covert operations and the Homeland Security state. His writings have documented in detail the derogation of fundamental civil rights in the United States under the Bush and Obama administrations. He is the editor of *Police State America: U.S. Military "Civil Disturbance" Planning* (2002).

Michel Chossudovsky is an award-winning author, Professor of Economics (Emeritus) at the University of Ottawa and Director of the Centre for Research on Globalization (CRG), Montreal. He is the author of *The Globalization of Poverty and The New World Order* (2003) and *America's "War on Terrorism"* (2005). He is also a contributor to the Encyclopaedia Britannica. His writings have been published in more than twenty languages.

Richard C. Cook is an author and analyst focusing on issues of local economic sustainability and monetary reform. As a policy analyst for the U.S. government, Richard Cook's career included service with the U.S. Civil Service Commission, the Food and Drug Administration, the Carter White House, NASA and the U.S. Treasury Department. His most recent book is *We Hold These Truths: The Hope of Monetary Reform* (2008).

Shamus Cooke is an author, trade-unionist and social service worker. His numerous writings on the social impacts of the economic crisis, including health and education, provide a detailed and incisive critique of the workings of U.S. economic and social policy.

John Bellamy Foster is editor of the independent socialist magazine *Monthly Review* and Professor of Sociology at the University of Oregon in Eugene. His writings have focused on political economy, environmental sociology and Marxist theory. His most recent books are *The Great Financial Crisis: Causes and Consequences* (with Fred Magdoff, 2009) and *The Ecological Revolution: Making Peace with the Planet* (2009).

Tanya Cariina Hsu is a British political analyst and specialist in Middle East history based in Riyadh and London. Her research examines the economics and geopolitics of the Middle East and U.S. Saudi relations. She is the author of *Target Saudi Arabia: Essays on the Campaign Against The Kingdom* (2005).

Michael Hudson is a Distinguished Research Professor of Economics at the University of Missouri, Kansas City. For many years he worked as a Wall Street analyst and consultant. He has written extensively on the impacts of the economic crisis both in the United States and the European Union, focusing among other issues on the debt-ridden economies of Greece, Iceland and Latvia. He is currently Chief Economic Advisor to the Reform Task Force Latvia (RTFL).

Fred Magdoff is Professor Emeritus in Plant and Soil Science at the University of Vermont as well as Adjunct Professor at Cornell University. He is also an expert on food and human health, and a director of the Monthly Review Foundation. With co-author John Bellamy Foster, his most recent book is *The Great Financial Crisis: Causes and Consequences* (2009).

Andrew Gavin Marshall is an independent writer both on the contemporary structures of capitalism as well as on the history of the global political economy. He is a Research Associate with the Centre for Research on Globalization (CRG) and is currently studying Political Economy and History at Simon Fraser University, Vancouver.

James Petras, Bartle Professor (Emeritus) of Sociology at Binghamton University, New York, is among America's most prominent social scientists. His political economy writings pertain to the devastating impacts of neoliberalism on developing countries. He is the author of more than sixty books published in 29 languages. He also has a long history of commitment to social justice, working with grassroots organizations in Latin America.

Peter Phillips is Professor of Sociology at the University of California at Sonoma. Peter Phillips has for many years directed the Project Censored Award program at Sonoma. He is the co-author with Dennis Loo of a 2006 bestseller entitled *Impeach the President: The Case Against Bush and Cheney* (2006).

Peter Dale Scott, a former Canadian diplomat and English Professor at the University of California, Berkeley, is a poet, writer and renowned researcher of the New World Order. His latest prose books include *Deep Politics and the Death of JFK* (1993, 1996), *Deep Politics Two* (1994, 1995, 2006), *Drugs Oil and War* (2003), *The Road to 9/11* (2007), and *The War Conspiracy: JFK, 9/11, and the Deep Politics of War* (2008).

Bill Van Auken is a distinguished author and politician. He was presidential candidate in the 2004 U.S. election for the Socialist Equality Party. His recent writings have examined the impacts of the economic crisis, financial fraud as well as the conduct of US foreign policy.

Claudia von Werlhof is Professor of Women's Studies at the Institute of Political Science, University of Innsbruck, Austria. Her research has focused on feminist theories of society, social movements and the impacts of neoliberalism on developing countries. She is one of the pioneers in promoting women's studies as a recognized academic discipline. Her latest book is *There Is An Alternative: Subsistence and Worldwide Resistance to Corporate Globalization* (2009).

Mike Whitney is an independent writer based in Washington State. His numerous articles have analyzed the inner workings of Wall Street, centering on speculative instruments and the role of Shadow Banking. He has also written on issues pertaining to U.S. foreign policy, Homeland Security and Washington's military agenda.

Editors' Note: The abovementioned authors, whose writings are featured in this book, are frequent contributors to the Global Research website at www.globalresearch.ca

Preface

In all major regions of the world, the economic recession is deep-seated, resulting in mass unemployment, the collapse of state social programs and the impoverishment of millions of people. The economic crisis is accompanied by a worldwide process of militarization, a "war without borders" led by the United States of America and its NATO allies. The conduct of the Pentagon's "long war" is intimately related to the restructuring of the global economy.

We are not dealing with a narrowly defined economic crisis or recession. The global financial architecture sustains strategic and national security objectives. In turn, the U.S.-NATO military agenda serves to endorse a powerful business elite which relentlessly overshadows and undermines the functions of civilian government.

This book takes the reader through the corridors of the Federal Reserve and the Council on Foreign Relations, behind closed doors at the Bank for International Settlements, into the plush corporate boardrooms on Wall Street where far-reaching financial transactions are routinely undertaken from computer terminals linked up to major stock markets, at the touch of a mouse button.

Each of the authors in this collection digs beneath the gilded surface to reveal a complex web of deceit and media distortion which serves to conceal the workings of the global economic system and its devastating impacts on people's lives. Our analysis focuses on the role of powerful economic and political actors in an environment wrought by corruption, financial manipulation and fraud.

Despite the diversity of viewpoints and perspectives presented within this volume, all of the contributors ultimately come to the same conclusion: humanity is at the crossroads of the most serious economic and social crisis in modern history.

The meltdown of financial markets in 2008-2009 was the result of institutionalized fraud and financial manipulation. The "bank bailouts" were implemented on the instructions of Wall Street, leading to the largest transfer of money wealth in recorded history, while simultaneously creating an insurmountable public debt.

With the worldwide deterioration of living standards and plummeting consumer spending, the entire structure of international commodity trade is potentially in jeopardy. The payments system of money transactions is in disarray. Following the collapse of employment, the payment of wages is disrupted, which in turn triggers a downfall in expenditures on necessary consumer goods and services. This dramatic plunge in purchasing power backfires on the productive system, resulting in a string of layoffs, plant closures and bankruptcies. Exacerbated by the freeze on credit, the decline in consumer demand contributes to the demobilization of human and material resources.

This process of economic decline is cumulative. All categories of the labor force are affected. Payments of wages are no longer implemented, credit is disrupted and capital investments are at a standstill. Meanwhile, in Western countries, the "social safety net" inherited from the welfare state, which protects the unemployed during an economic downturn, is also in jeopardy.

The Myth of Economic Recovery

The existence of a "Great Depression" on the scale of the 1930s, while often acknowledged, is overshadowed by an unbending consensus: "The economy is on the road to recovery".

While there is talk of an economic renewal, Wall Street commentators have persistently and intentionally overlooked the fact that the financial meltdown is not simply composed of one bubble – the housing real estate bubble – which has already burst. In fact, the crisis has many bubbles, all of which dwarf the housing bubble burst of 2008.

Although there is no fundamental disagreement among mainstream analysts on the occurrence of an economic recovery, there is heated debate as to when it will occur, whether in the next quarter, or in the third quarter of next year, etc. Already in early 2010, the "recovery" of the U.S. economy had been predicted and confirmed through a carefully worded barrage of media disinformation. Meanwhile, the social plight of increased unemployment in America has been scrupulously camouflaged. Economists view bankruptcy as a microeconomic phenomenon.

The media reports on bankruptcies, while revealing local-level realities affecting one or more factories, fail to provide an overall picture of what is happening at the national and international levels. When all these simultaneous plant closures in towns and cities across the land are added together, a very different picture emerges: entire sectors of a national economy are closing down.

Public opinion continues to be misled as to the causes and consequences of the economic crisis, not to mention the policy solutions. People are led to believe that the economy has a logic of its own which depends on the free interplay of market forces, and that powerful financial actors, who pull the strings in the corporate boardrooms, could not, under any circumstances, have willfully influenced the course of economic events.

The relentless and fraudulent appropriation of wealth is upheld as an integral part of "the American dream", as a means to spreading the benefits of economic growth. As conveyed by Michael Hudson, the myth becomes entrenched that "without wealth at the top, there would be nothing to trickle down." Such flawed logic of the business cycle overshadows an understanding of the structural and historical origins of the global economic crisis.

Financial Fraud

Media disinformation largely serves the interests of a handful of global banks and institutional speculators which use their command over financial and commodity markets to amass vast amounts of money wealth. The corridors of the state are controlled by the corporate establishment including the speculators. Meanwhile, the "bank bailouts", presented to the public as a requisite for economic recovery, have facilitated and legitimized a further process of appropriation of wealth.

Vast amounts of money wealth are acquired through market manipulation. Often referred to as "deregulation", the financial apparatus has developed sophisticated instruments of outright manipulation and deceit. With inside information and foreknowledge, major financial actors, using the instruments of speculative trade, have the ability to fiddle and rig market movements to their advantage, precipitate the collapse of a competitor and wreck havoc in the economies of developing countries. These tools of manipulation have become an integral part of the financial architecture; they are embedded in the system.

The Failure of Mainstream Economics

The economics profession, particularly in the universities, rarely addresses the actual "real world" functioning of markets. Theoretical constructs centered on mathematical models serve to represent an abstract, fictional world in which individuals are equal. There is no theoretical distinction between workers, consumers or corporations, all of which are referred to as "individual traders". No single individual has the power or ability to influence the market, nor can there be any conflict between workers and capitalists within this abstract world.

By failing to examine the interplay of powerful economic actors in the "real life" economy, the processes of market rigging, financial manipulation and fraud are overlooked. The concentration and centralization of economic decision-making, the role of the financial elites, the economic think tanks, the corporate boardrooms: none of these issues are examined in the universities' economics programs. The theoretical construct is dysfunctional; it cannot be used to provide an understanding of the economic crisis.

Economic science is an ideological construct which serves to camouflage and justify the New World Order. A set of dogmatic postulates serves to uphold free market capitalism by denying the existence of social inequality and the profit-driven nature of the system is denied. The role of powerful economic actors and how these actors are able to influence the workings of financial and commodity markets is not a matter of concern for the discipline's theoreticians. The powers of market manipulation which serve to appropriate vast amounts of money wealth are rarely addressed. And when they are acknowledged, they are considered to belong to the realm of sociology or political science.

This means that the policy and institutional framework behind this global economic system, which has been shaped in the course of the last thirty years, is rarely analyzed by mainstream economists. It follows that economics as a discipline, with some exceptions, has not provided the analysis required to comprehend the economic crisis. In fact, its main free market postulates deny the existence of a crisis. The focus of neoclassical economics is on equilibrium, disequilibrium and "market correction" or "adjustment" through the market mechanism, as a means to putting the economy back "onto the path of self-sustained growth".

Poverty and Social Inequality

The global political economy is a system that enriches the very few at the expense of the vast majority. The global economic crisis has contributed to widening social inequalities both within and between countries. Under global capitalism, mounting poverty is not the result of a scarcity or a lack of human and material resources. Quite the opposite holds true: the economic depression is marked by a process of disengagement of human resources and physical capital. People's lives are destroyed. The economic crisis is deep-seated.

The structures of social inequality have, quite deliberately, been reinforced, leading not only to a generalized process of impoverishment but also to the demise of the middle and upper middle income groups.

Middle class consumerism, on which this unruly model of capitalist development is based, is also threatened. Bankruptcies have hit several of the most vibrant sectors of the consumer economy. The middle classes in the West have, for several decades, been subjected to the erosion of their material wealth. While the middle class exists in theory, it is a class built and sustained by household debt.

The wealthy rather than the middle class are rapidly becoming the consuming class, leading to the relentless growth of the luxury goods economy. Moreover, with the drying up of the middle class markets for manufactured goods, a central and decisive shift in the structure of economic growth has occurred. With the demise of the civilian economy, the development of America's war economy, supported by a whopping near-trillion dollar defense budget, has reached new heights. As stock markets tumble and the recession unfolds, the advanced weapons industries, the military and national security contractors and the up-and-coming mercenary companies (among others) have experienced a thriving and booming growth of their various activities.

War and the Economic Crisis

War is inextricably linked to the impoverishment of people at home and around the world. Militarization and the economic crisis are intimately related. The provision of essential goods and services to meet basic human needs has been replaced by a profit-driven "killing machine" in support of America's "Global War on Terror". The poor are made to fight the poor. Yet war enriches the upper class, which controls industry, the military, oil and banking. In a war economy, death is good for business, poverty is good for society, and power is good for politics. Western nations, particularly the United States, spend hundreds of billions of dollars a year to murder innocent people in far-away impoverished nations, while the people at home suffer the disparities of poverty, class, gender and racial divides.

An outright "economic war" resulting in unemployment, poverty and disease is carried out through the free market. People's lives are in a freefall and their purchasing power is destroyed. In a very real sense, the last twenty years of global "free market" economy have destroyed, through poverty and social destitution, the lives of millions of people.

Rather than addressing an impending social catastrophe, Western governments, which serve the interests of the economic elites, have installed a "Big Brother" police state, with a mandate to confront and repress all forms of opposition and social dissent.

The economic and social crisis has by no means reached its climax and entire countries, including Greece and Iceland, are at risk. One need only look at the escalation of the Middle East Central Asian war and the U.S.-NATO threats to China, Russia and Iran to witness how war and the economy are intimately related.

Our Analysis in this Book

The contributors to this book reveal the intricacies of global banking and its insidious relationship to the military industrial complex and the oil conglomerates. The book presents an interdisciplinary and multi-faceted approach, while also conveying an understanding of the historical and institutional dimensions. The complex relations of the economic crisis to war, empire and worldwide poverty are highlighted. This crisis has a truly global reach and repercussions that reverberate throughout all nations, across all societies.

In Part I, the overall causes of the global economic crisis as well as the failures of mainstream economics are laid out. Michel Chossudovsky focuses on the history of financial deregulation and speculation. Tanya Cariina Hsu analyzes the role of the American Empire and its relationship to the economic crisis. John Bellamy Foster and Fred Magdoff undertake a comprehensive review of the political economy of the crisis, explaining the central role of monetary policy. James Petras and Claudia von Werlhof provide a detailed review and critique of neoliberalism, focusing on the economic, political and social repercussions of the "free market" reforms. Shamus Cooke examines the central role of debt, both public and private.

Part II, which includes chapters by Michel Chossudovsky and Peter Phillips, analyzes the rising tide of poverty and social inequality resulting from the Great Depression.

With contributions by Michel Chossudovsky, Peter Dale Scott, Michael Hudson, Bill Van Auken, Tom Burghardt and Andrew Gavin Marshall, Part III examines the relationship between the economic crisis, National Security, the U.S.-NATO led war and world government. In this context, as conveyed by Peter Dale Scott, the economic crisis creates social conditions which favor the instatement of martial law.

The focus in Part IV is on the global monetary system, its evolution and its changing role. Andrew Gavin Marshall examines the history of central banking as well as various initiatives to create regional and global currency systems. Ellen Brown focuses on the creation of a global central bank and global currency through the Bank for International Settlements (BIS). Richard C. Cook examines the debt-based monetary system as a system of control and provides a framework for democratizing the monetary system.

Part V focuses on the working of the Shadow Banking System, which triggered the 2008 meltdown of financial markets. The chapters by Mike Whitney and Ellen Brown describe in detail how Wall Street's Ponzi scheme was used to manipulate the market and transfer billions of dollars into the pockets of the banksters.

We are indebted to the authors for their carefully documented research, incisive analysis, and, foremost, for their unbending commitment to the truth: Tom Burghardt, Ellen Brown, Richard C. Cook, Shamus Cooke, John Bellamy Foster, Michael Hudson, Tanya Cariina Hsu, Fred Magdoff, James Petras, Peter Phillips, Peter Dale Scott, Mike Whitney, Bill Van Auken and Claudia von Werlhof, have provided, with utmost clarity, an understanding of the diverse and complex economic, social and political processes which are affecting the lives of millions of people around the world.

We owe a debt of gratitude to Maja Romano of Global Research Publishers, who relentlessly oversaw and coordinated the editing and production of this book, including the creative front page concept. We wish to thank Andréa Joseph for the careful typesetting of the manuscript and front page graphics. We also extend our thanks and appreciation to Isabelle Goulet, Julie Lévesque and Drew McKevitt for their support in the revision and copyediting of the manuscript.

MICHEL CHOSSUDOVSKY AND ANDREW GAVIN MARSHALL,
Montreal and Vancouver, May 2010

PART I

The Global Economic Crisis

CHAPTER 1

The Global Economic Crisis: An Overview

Michel Chossudovsky

We are at the crossroads of the most serious economic crisis in world history.

The economic crisis has by no means reached its climax, as some economists have predicted.

The crisis is deepening, with the risk of seriously disrupting the structures of international trade and investment.

The Nature of the Economic Crisis

In contrast to Roosevelt's New Deal, adopted at the height of the Great Depression, the macroeconomic policy agenda of the Obama administration does not constitute a solution to the crisis. In fact, quite the opposite: it directly contributes to the concentration and centralization of financial wealth, which in turn undermines the real economy.

The crisis did not commence with the 2008 meltdown of financial markets. It is deeply rooted in major transformations in the global economy and financial architecture which unfolded in several stages since the early 1980s. The September-October 2008 stock market crash was the outcome of a process of financial deregulation and macroeconomic reform.

We are dealing with a long-term process of economic and financial restructuring. In its earlier phase, starting in the 1980s during the Reagan-Thatcher era, local and regional level enterprises, family farms and small businesses were displaced and destroyed. In turn, the merger and acquisition boom of the 1990s led to the concurrent consolidation of large corporate entities both in the real economy as well as in banking and financial services.

International commodity trade has plummeted. Bankruptcies are occurring in all major sectors of activity: agriculture, manufacturing, telecoms, consumer retail outlets, shopping malls, airlines, hotels and tourism, not to mention real estate and the construction industry.

What is distinct in this particular phase of the crisis is the ability of the financial giants – through stock market manipulation as well as through their overriding control over credit – not only to create havoc in the production of goods and services, but also to undermine and destroy large and well established business corporations.

This crisis is far more serious than the Great Depression. All major sectors of the global economy are affected. Factories are closed down. Assembly lines are at a standstill. Unemployment is rampant. Wages have collapsed. Entire populations are precipitated into abysmal poverty. Livelihoods are destroyed. Public services are disrupted or privatized. The repercussions on people's lives in North America and around the world are dramatic.

PART I: THE FINANCIAL MELTDOWN

The subprime residential mortgage crisis leading to millions of people losing their homes reached its climax in the last days of August 2008, when financial institutions reported billions of dollars in losses.

Friday, September 12, 2008, Lehman Brothers faced collapse in weekend negotiations behind closed doors on Wall Street. Black Monday descended on September 15, 2008. Following the filing for Chapter 11 Bankruptcy by Lehman on Monday morning, the Dow Jones industrial average declined by 504 points (4.4 percent), its largest drop since September 17, 2001, when trading resumed on Wall Street after the 9/11 attacks.

The following day, it was the turn of AIG, the insurance conglomerate. On the evening of September 16, the Bush administration "granted an $85 billion loan to AIG in exchange for a controlling 79.9% equity share of the company".[1]

The financial slide proceeded unabated throughout September. Barely two weeks later, on Monday, September 29, the

Dow Jones plummeted by 778 points, its largest one-day drop in the history of the New York Stock Exchange. This followed the rejection by the U.S. House of Representatives of the Bush administration's 700 billion dollar bailout plan, which was slated to come to the rescue of the banks affected by the subprime mortgage crisis. In a single day, 1.2 trillion dollars had seemingly evaporated.

The world's stock markets are interconnected around the clock through instant computer link-up. Instability on Wall Street immediately spills over into the European and Asian stock markets, thereby rapidly permeating the entire financial system.

Speculative Onslaught on Black Monday, September 29, 2008

There was something disturbing about the Black Monday, September 29, 2008 collapse of Wall Street, following the decision of the U.S. House of Representatives. Did this paper money "vanish into thin air" as claimed by financial analysts, or was it "appropriated" by institutional speculators in one of the largest transfers of money wealth in American history?

There was prior knowledge on how the Congressional vote would proceed. President Bush's speeches had intimated that a collapse would occur. There was also an expectation that the market would crumble if the proposed 700 billion dollar bailout were to be rejected by the U.S. Congress.

Speculators, including major financial institutions, had already positioned themselves. Powerful financial actors with prior knowledge and access to privileged information prior to the House's rejection of the bill made billions in speculative trade on Black Monday when the market crumbled. And then on Tuesday, September 30, they made billions when the market rebounded, with the Dow jumping up by 485 points, a 4.68 percent increase, compensating in part for Monday's decline. Those financial actors who had foreknowledge and/or who had the ability to influence the vote in the U.S. Congress also made billions of dollars.

Ironically, almost twice as much money was wiped out from the U.S. stock market on Black Monday, September 29 (1.2 trillion dollars) than the value of the Bush administration's bank bailout under the Troubled Assets Relief Program (TARP) (700 billion dollars).

> Even before the opening bell, Monday looked ugly. But by the time that bell sounded again on the New York Stock Exchange, seven and a half frantic hours later, $1.2 trillion had vanished from the U.S. stock market.[2]

This money did not vanish. It was confiscated from the pockets of people who had invested their lifelong savings in the stock market.

While public opinion celebrated the refusal of the U.S. Congress to accept the Bush administration's bailout, the decision of the legislature had fed the speculative onslaught.

Political uncertainty regarding the proposed bailout constituted ammunition for the speculators.

In a bitter irony, the Wall Street banks are "double dippers"; they are the recipients of the bank bailout. And at the same time they made money speculating first on the rejection by the U.S. Congress and subsequently on the later adoption of the bank bailout legislation.

On October 1, Wachovia Bank was taken over by Wells Fargo, overriding a competing bid from Citigroup. The deal was sealed with the support of Warren Buffett, the richest man in the world, according to Forbes, and a major shareholder of Wells Fargo.[3]

The first week in October 2008 represented a crucial turning point. The Dow Jones fell by 21 percent over the week, with Thursday, October 9 suffering its biggest fall since Black Monday, October 19, 1987. The S&P 500 index lost 22 percent of its value. The entire western banking landscape was in disarray. Iceland's banking system was destabilized and the country was put in receivership. The Reykjavik government gave the green light for the forced bankruptcy of the entire banking system.

Following a pledge by G7 finance ministers and central bank governors on the weekend of October 10-11 to prevent further bank collapses, the world's stock markets rebounded on October 13. The G7 had committed itself to "taking all necessary steps to unfreeze credit and money markets". The Dow increased by 936 points (eleven percent) at the close of trading on October 13, its largest one day increase since 1933.[4] Most European exchanges had "recovered", with the Paris CAC index rebounding by an astounding 8.8 percent at the close of trading.

This short-lived "recovery" was part of the speculative game. Two days later, on October 15, Black Wednesday, the Dow Jones plummeted by 7.9 percent.

The sequence of a "one day collapse" followed by a "one day surge" and recovery, followed by another "one day collapse" a few days later, is part of the process of financial manipulation. Day to day instability and swings in stock market values are the source of large windfall profits accruing to "institutional speculators" and hedge funds.

CHART 1.1 Dow Jones Industrial Average (2000-2010)

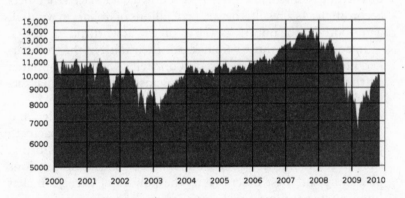

Source: New York Stock Exchange and Wikipedia.org

Financial Warfare: The Powers of Deception

The September-October 2008 financial meltdown was not the consequence of a cyclical downturn of economic activity. It was the result of a complex process of financial manipulation, which included speculative trade in derivatives.

Financial manipulation has a direct bearing on the workings of the market. It potentially triggers instability in market transactions. This snowballing instability then becomes cumulative, leading to an overall slide of market values.

Inside information, high level political connections and fore-knowledge of key policy announcements are crucial instruments in the conduct of large-scale speculative operations.

"Financial intelligence" and the powers of deceit were the driving forces behind the 2008 financial meltdown. Covert undercover financial operations were waged. Those powerful financial institutions, which had the ability to drive the market up at an opportune moment and then drive it down, had placed their bets accordingly. As a result, they reaped billions of dollars in windfall gains both on the upturn as well as on the downturn.

In contrast, for those who had put their faith in the free market, lifelong savings were erased in one fell swoop, appropriated by the shadow banking system. The crash of financial markets had led to a massive concentration of financial wealth.

The weapons used on Wall Street are prior knowledge and inside information, the ability to manipulate with the capacity to predict results and the spreading of misleading or false information on economic occurrences and market trends. These various procedures are best described as the powers of deception that financial institutions routinely use to mislead investors.

The art of deception is also directed against their banking competitors, who are betting in the derivatives and futures markets, stocks, currencies and commodities. Those who have access to privileged information (political, intelligence, military, scientific, etc.) will invariably have the upper hand in the conduct of these highly leveraged speculative transactions, which are the source of tremendous financial gains. The CIA has its own financial institutions on Wall Street.

In turn, the corridors of private and offshore banking enable financial institutions to transfer their profits with ease from one location to another. This procedure is also used as a safety net that protects the interests of key financial actors including CEOs and major shareholders of troubled financial institutions. Companies can be divested from within and large amounts of money can be moved out at an opportune moment, prior to the company's demise on the stock market (e.g. Lehman, Merrill Lynch and AIG, not to mention Bernhard Madoff).

As events unfolded, Merrill Lynch was bought and Lehman Brothers was pushed into bankruptcy. These are not haphazard occurrences. They are the result of manipulation, using highly leveraged speculative operations to achieve their objective, which consists in either displacing or acquiring control over a rival financial institution. The 2008 financial meltdown has nothing to do with free market forces: it is characterized by financial warfare between competing institutional speculators.

The Federal Reserve Bank of New York and its powerful Wall Street stakeholders – which are Wall Street's largest private banks – have inside information on the conduct of U.S. monetary policy. They are therefore in a position to predict outcomes and hedge their bets in highly leveraged operations on the futures and derivatives markets. They are in an obvious conflict of interest because their prior knowledge of particular decisions by the Federal Reserve Board enables them, as private banking institutions, to make multibillion dollar profits.

Links to U.S. intelligence, the CIA, Homeland Security and the Pentagon are crucial in the conduct of speculative trade, since that allows the speculators to predict events through prior knowledge of foreign policy and/or national security decisions which directly affect financial markets. An example: they purchased "put options" on airline stocks in the days preceding the 9/11 attacks.

Who Picks Up the Pieces in the Wake of the Financial Meltdown?

An internal war within the financial system is unfolding. Consider the following: Lehman Brothers goes bankrupt and Merrill Lynch is bought up; mortgage giants Fannie Mae and Freddie Mac are taken over by the government; Bear Stearns collapses; shares for AIG, America's largest insurance company, collapse from $22.19 on September 9, 2008, to less than $4 at the close of trading on September 16, a decline of more than eighty percent of its value.

With the collapse in stock market values, listed companies experience a major collapse in the price of their shares, which immediately affects their creditworthiness and their ability to borrow and/or renegotiate debts (which are based on the quoted value of their assets).

Bankruptcies and foreclosures constitute a money-spinning operation for the financial giants. Among the companies on the verge of bankruptcy are some highly lucrative and profitable operations. The important question is: who takes over the ownership of giant bankrupt industrial corporations?

The institutional speculators, the hedge funds, *et al.* have cashed in on their windfall loot. They are the ultimate creditors. They trigger the collapse of listed companies through short selling and other speculative operations and then cash in on their large scale speculative gains. They transform their paper money wealth into real assets through the purchase of real economy companies.

In this regard, there was evidence that the November 2008 plunge of the U.S. automobile industry was in part the result of financial manipulation, including the short selling of GM shares: "General Motors and Ford lost 31 percent to $3.01 and 10.9 percent to $1.80 despite hopes that Washington may save the industry from the brink of collapse. The fall came after Deutsche Bank set a price target of zero on GM."[5]

The financiers are on a shopping spree and America's Forbes 400 billionaires are waiting in limbo. Once they have consolidated their position in the banking industry, the financial giants (including J.P. Morgan Chase and Bank of America, amongst others) will use their windfall money gains and bailout money provided under the Bush and Obama bank bailouts to further extend their control over the real economy. The next step consists in transforming liquid assets, namely, money paper wealth, into the acquisition of real economy assets.

In this regard, Warren Buffett's Berkshire Hathaway Inc. is a major shareholder of General Motors. Following the collapse in stock values in October and November 2008, Buffett boosted his stake in oil producer ConocoPhillips, not to mention Eaton

Corp, whose price on the NYSE tumbled in late 2008 by 62 percent in relation to its December 2007 high.[6]

The target of these acquisitions is the numerous highly productive industrial and services sector companies, which are on the verge of bankruptcy and/or whose stock values have collapsed. The money managers are picking up the pieces.

Centralization of Bank Power: What Lies Ahead?

The 2008 financial meltdown has been conducive to a massive concentration and centralization of bank power. In a bitter irony, the financial disarray provided Wall Street's largest banks with an opportunity to take over weaker financial institutions. The process of mergers and acquisitions has risen to new heights, leading to an unprecedented centralization of financial power, with Bank of America, J.P. Morgan Chase and the Federal Reserve Bank of New York playing a dominant role. Market manipulation has created financial chaos, which has acquired its own destructive momentum. The meltdown will be conducive to the demise of numerous banking and financial institutions, which will either be driven out of the financial landscape altogether or acquired by the financial giants.

As a case in point, Bank of America acquired Merrill Lynch, leading to the formation of the world's largest financial institution, clashing with Citigroup and J.P. Morgan Chase. It should be noted that while Citigroup and J.P. Morgan Chase are competing institutions, they are nonetheless entwined through intermarriage between the Rockefeller and Stillman families. In the last two decades, Bank of America has developed into a financial giant through a series of mergers and acquisitions. In 2004, Bank of America acquired FleetBoston Financial, in 2005 it purchased credit card giant MBNA, and in 2007 it acquired LaSalle Bank Corporation and Corporate Finance from the Dutch bank ABN AMRO. On September 14, 2008, Bank of America announced its intention to acquire Merrill Lynch for fifty billion dollars.

What we are dealing with is a clash between a handful of major financial institutions that have developed, through mergers and acquisitions, into worldwide financial giants. The financial meltdown on Wall Street largely benefits Bank of America and J.P. Morgan Chase, which is part of the Rockefeller empire. It comes at the expense of Lehman Brothers, Merrill Lynch and Morgan Stanley. Lehman Brothers filed for Chapter 11 bankruptcy on Bloody Monday, September 15. It should be noted that Lehman's assets total approximately 639 billion dollars.

Money Wealth

Paper wealth, namely, billions of dollars in the hands of banks, financial institutions and wealthy individuals, constitutes the means for exercising economic power. Financial paper wealth acquired through speculative trade as well as the multibillion dollar bank bailouts creates purchasing power, not for commodities, but for the acquisition of real economy assets.

Resulting from the multitrillion dollar trade in derivatives, a new generation of powerful financiers has emerged. This purchasing power of the ultimate creditors is virtually unlimited. It enables the financial elites to buy out their weaker competitors in the financial services industry, as well as acquire virtually all forms of real economy assets, including automobile production, airlines, telecoms, etc. Significantly, it also enables the financial establishment to potentially buy out all forms of publicly owned assets, including roads and public utilities, public lands and infrastructure, port facilities, etc.

The financiers are not buying consumer goods, nor is this money being used extensively to invest in new plant and equipment. This increased liquidity, resulting from an unlimited capacity to create *fiat money*, is not driving up prices; instead it is being used to acquire existing real economy assets. The financiers are using worthless paper wealth to acquire real wealth. What we are dealing with is a large scale process of expropriation, unprecedented in history.

As far as state-owned assets are concerned, the process of privatization occurs through the debt overhang and the overriding power of the creditors. The public debt is no longer sovereign debt, and everything under state jurisdiction is up for private acquisition, as occurred under the brunt of the IMF's structural adjustment program in the developing countries.

The developed countries will eventually experience the plight of so-called strong economic medicine, modeled on the IMF's deadly macroeconomic reforms and imposed directly on Western

TEXT BOX 1.1
THE ART OF SHORT SELLING

A stock market meltdown can be a highly profitable operation. With foreknowledge and inside information, a collapse in market values constitutes (through short selling) a lucrative and money-spinning opportunity for a select category of powerful speculators who have the ability to manipulate the market in the appropriate direction at the appropriate time. Short selling consists in massively selling off shares that you do not possess for delivery at a future date in anticipation that the share price will tumble, and then buying back the shares in the wake of the collapse in the spot market, with a view to completing the transaction.

The most notorious case in recent history, requiring advanced knowledge, was the massive short selling of airline stocks, including American Airlines, in the days leading up to the September 11, 2001 attacks on the World Trade Center and the Pentagon. The share prices of United Airlines and American airlines had tumbled when the New York Stock Exchange opened up again on September 17, 2001.

With regard to the 2008 financial meltdown, short selling as well as the spreading of false rumors were used as a strategy to trigger the collapse of selected stocks on Wall Street including Lehman, Morgan Stanley, Goldman Sachs and General Motors:

> Short sellers aim to profit from share declines, usually by borrowing a stock, selling it and buying it back after its price has decreased. In abusive "naked" short selling, the seller does not borrow the stock and fails to deliver it to the buyer.

> Some market participants say abusive short sellers have contributed to the fall of companies such as Lehman Brothers by forcing down share prices.

> John Mack, chief executive of Morgan Stanley, told employees in an internal memo Wednesday: "What's happening out there? It's very clear to me – we're in the midst of a market controlled by fear and rumors, and short sellers are driving our stock down."[7]

> Regulators have acknowledged that the collapse of Bear Stearns in March 2008 was attributable to short selling: "Regulators have been looking into a combination of short-sales, and false rumors are part of the problem."[8]

governments, without the intermediation of the Bretton Woods institutions. The financial establishment ultimately calls the shots on the restructuring and privatization of the State.

September 15, 2008: Temporary Ban on Short Selling

Following the stock market meltdown on Black Monday September 15, the Security and Exchange Commission (SEC) introduced a temporary ban on short selling. In a bitter irony, the SEC listed a number of companies which were "protected by regulators from short sellers". The SEC September 18 ban on short selling pertained largely to banks, insurance companies and other financial services companies.

The effect of being on a protected list was to no avail. It was tantamount to putting those listed companies on a hit list. If the SEC had implemented a complete and permanent ban on short selling coupled with a freeze on all forms of speculative trade, including index funds and options, this would have contributed to reducing market volatility and dampening the meltdown.

The ban on short selling was applied with a view to establishing the protected list. It expired on Wednesday, October 8, at midnight. The following morning, Thursday, October 9, when the market opened up, those companies on the "protected list" became "unprotected" and were the first targets of the speculative onslaught, leading to a dramatic collapse of the Dow Jones on Thursday, October 9 and Friday, October 10.

The course of events was entirely predictable. The lifting of the ban on short selling contributed to accentuating the downfall in stock market values. The companies which were on the hit list were the first victims of the speculative onslaught. The shares of Morgan Stanley dropped 26 percent on October 9, upon the expiry of the short selling ban and a further 25 percent the following day.

The Failures of Mainstream Economics

The financial crisis is not an object of concern by economists in North America's universities. There is at present an absence of in-depth scholarly analysis and understanding. Mainstream economics, taught in graduate schools across America, provides a misleading and one-sided understanding of the workings of financial markets:

> Discussion of investor irrationality, of bubbles, of destructive speculation had virtually disappeared from academic discourse. The field was dominated by the "efficient-market hypothesis," promulgated by Eugene Fama of the University of Chicago, which claims that financial markets price assets precisely at their intrinsic worth given all publicly available information. (The price of a company's stock, for example, always accurately reflects the company's value given the information available on the company's earnings, its business prospects and so on)[12]

TEXT BOX 1.2
THE FATE OF THE ROYAL BANK OF SCOTLAND

The crisis continued into 2009. On "Blue Monday", January 19, 2009, the stock values of British banks collapsed on the London Stock exchange, following the announcement by the Royal Bank of Scotland (RBS) of the largest corporate losses in British history. The price of RBS stock shares plunged by 67 percent in one day.

There was a temporary surge in the stock market in Spring 2009 which, according to government officials and financial analysts, was indicative that "the crisis and the credit crunch are over":

> After contracting sharply over the past year, economic activity appears to be leveling out, both in the United States and abroad, and the prospects for a return to growth in the near-term appear good.
>
> –Federal Reserve Chairman Ben Bernanke[9]

> The worst of the economic crisis is over and, while the situation remains fragile, there are growing signs of a recovery on the horizon.
>
> –Italian economy minister Giulio Tremonti, May 2009[10]

> We are convinced that we can overcome this crisis in a period of 18 months... We have already taken urgent and extraordinary steps to stabilize our financial sectors and strengthen economic growth.[11]
>
> –Asia Pacific Economic Cooperation (APEC) Summit Statement, November 2008

Orthodox economic theory does not acknowledge the amply documented fact that financial actors can not only influence but actually *manipulate* the market, make it move in a particular direction. The market mechanism, in a neoclassical framework, does not take into consideration the actions of large banks, corporations and powerful individuals.

The free market mechanism is said to be characterized by "a continuum of traders (individuals)". Economic agents in a competitive environment are said to be too small and insignificant to have an impact on the movement of key economic variables (e.g. stock market prices). "Atomistic behavior" prevails: consumers, workers and companies are economic agents. There is no asymmetry between a worker or consumer on the one hand, and a company or business entity on the other. They are presented as individuals trading in a competitive market.

Economic theory does not address the structural causes of economic collapse. The presumption is that the free market mechanism will trigger an economic recovery, without the need for active state intervention. The tacit assumption is that once recovery is initiated, economic growth will be cumulative and self-sustaining. "What goes down must eventually go up" is the motto.

We are not dealing with a cyclical process; what is at stake is a major dislocation in the financial, trading and productive structures of the global economy.

The theory of the business cycle, which is characterized by a large literature, broadly posits a number of stages: expansionary economic growth, peak, downward movement marked by economic contraction, trough and economic recovery leading into a new cycle. While relevant to understanding macroeconomic fluctuations, business cycle theory does not apply to the current economic crisis. When examined out of context, it suggests that economic processes are inevitably cyclical and predetermined, and that economic recovery is inevitable irrespective of policy actions.

This vision of the economic process serves to obfuscate the unfolding social crisis. Financial analysts, who are directly linked to Wall Street's major financial institutions, are readily predicting a "recovery":

Goldman Sachs sees growth slipping to 1.5 percent by the third quarter of next year after bouncing to 3 percent by the end of this year. S&P projects 1.5 percent for all of next year. RDQ sees growth hovering between 2 percent and 2.5 percent.

"After this near-term spurt, the economy is likely to slow anew in 2010. In fact, we now expect the second half of 2010 to show a bit less growth than the first," said Goldman economists led by Jan Hatzius in a note Wednesday.[13]

Where do the numbers come from? What are the underlying economic causes? These are Wall Street's self-serving "predictions" emanating from Goldman Sachs and Standard and Poor (S&P). These GDP quarterly extrapolations are mechanical and unrelated to real economic phenomena. They provide a very partial and incomplete measure of what is actually happening.

There is a Great Depression characterized by a string of bankruptcies, rising unemployment and a collapse in purchasing power. These realities are obfuscated by the quarterly upward movement of GDP, which is a composite statistical indicator. A rising GDP can indeed occur alongside a collapse in production and consumer spending.

Mainstream Economics Upholds Financial Deregulation

Sound familiar? The same complacency prevails today as during the frenzy of the late 1920s. Echoing almost verbatim the economic slogans of Irving Fisher, today's economics orthodoxy refutes the existence of an economic crisis.

According to Nobel Laureate Robert Lucas of the University of Chicago, the decisions of economic agents are based on so-called rational expectations, ruling out the possibility of systematic errors which might lead the stock market in the wrong direction. It is ironic that precisely at a time when financial markets were in turmoil, the Royal Swedish Academy announced the granting of the 1997 Nobel Prize in Economics to two American economists for their "pioneering formula for the valuation of stock options [and derivatives] used by thousands of traders and investors,"[15] meaning an "algebraic formula" which is routinely used by hedge funds stock market speculators.

TEXT BOX 1.3
REPLICATING THE POLICY FAILURES OF THE LATE 1920S

Wall Street was swerving dangerously in volatile trading in the months preceding the Wall Street crash on October 29, 1929. *Laissez-faire*, under the Coolidge and Hoover administrations, was the order of the day. The possibility of a financial meltdown had never been seriously contemplated. Professor Irving Fisher of Yale University had stated authoritatively in 1928 that "nothing resembling a crash can occur." The illusion of economic prosperity persisted several years after the Wall Street crash of October 1929. In 1930, Irving Fisher stated confidently, "for the immediate future, at least, the perspective is brilliant." According to the prestigious Harvard Economic Society, "manufacturing activity [in 1930]... was definitely on the road to recovery."[14]

The Global Cheap Labor Economy

The development of world capitalism is predicated on a profit-driven global cheap labor economy. One of the main features of this system has been the development (over the last thirty to forty years) of industrial colonies in the low-wage countries. The relocation of industry to these countries has led to corporate downsizing and layoffs, as well as the outright closing down of a wide range of productive activities in the developed countries.

Mass poverty and a worldwide decline in living standards are largely the result of this global cheap labor economy. The levels of poverty underlying the pre-existing global cheap labor economy have been heightened as a result of the 2008-2009 financial meltdown. In developing countries, including China, which is America's largest industrial colony, the levels of employment are in a freefall. The pre-existing structures of Third World poverty are replaced by social destitution and, in many regions of the developing world, by outright starvation.

In the absence of meaningful state regulation, this relentless process of minimizing labor costs at a world level inevitably leads to a dramatic compression of society's capacity to consume. Low wages create poverty and unemployment, which in turn spearhead the productive system into stagnation.

TABLE 1.1 Annual Collapse in Exports, Selected Countries
(September 2008 – August 2009)

China	23.4 percent
India:	28.4 percent
South Korea	20.6 percent
Malaysia	20.6 percent

Sources: National data, various sources. See Bloomberg, India Exports Fall 28.4 percent, Tenth Monthly Drop in a Row; Alibaba.com, S. Korea Aug exports down 20.6 percent, 31 August 2009; Forbes.com, China exports, imports fall further, September 11, 2009

The 2008-2009 economic crisis extends the boundaries of the global cheap labor economy. The low wage structure is no longer limited to Third World countries. Wages and employment in several developed countries are also in a freefall. Many of the "social safety nets" characteristic of the welfare state, including unemployment insurance and social welfare, are being phased out.

We are not dealing with a scarcity of resources, as posited by mainstream economics. Quite the opposite: the very process of expanding this global cheap labor economy backlashes on the consumption of goods and services. Poverty is not the result of a lack of resources but of an economic system, which inherently compresses the purchasing power of hundreds of millions of people.

The plight of unemployment extends throughout the labor market. It is not limited to "unqualified labor" or to "marginalized" and "underprivileged groups". In the United States, Canada and Western Europe, qualified workers in the upper echelons of the labor market, including engineers, scientists and professionals, are being laid off. Resulting from a massive compression in government spending, public sector workers, including government employees, are being laid off or forced into retirement.

The process of impoverishment and unemployment has extended its grip to the upper echelons of the labor market. Moreover, the collapse in lifelong savings and pension funds, not

TEXT BOX 1.4
COLLAPSE IN THE ASIAN EXPORT ECONOMY

A large share of what is consumed by North American households is produced in China and South East Asia. Resulting from the chaos of financial markets and the concurrent decline in purchasing power in the North America and Western Europe, international trade in manufactured goods has plummeted.

In the year following the September 2008 financial meltdown, worldwide container trade declined by 15.7 percent.[16] Reports from the Asian economies indicate a significant increase in unemployment in export manufacturing assembly lines. Country-level data indicate an annual collapse of the order of 25 percent in commodity exports out of Asia (2008-2009, in the twelve months following the September financial crisis).

In China's Pearl River basin in Southern Guangdong province's industrial export processing economy, some 700 000 workers were laid off in early 2009. In Japan, a decline of industrial output of more than twenty percent was recorded in the immediate wake of the 2008 financial crash. In the Philippines, a country of ninety million people, exports collapsed by more than forty percent in December 2008.[17]

Meanwhile, trade protectionism is unfolding and a trade war largely emanating from the U.S. and the European Union is in the making.

to mention home foreclosures, has contributed to the further impoverishment of a large segment of the middle class.

Collapse in Consumer Spending

Each individual case of bankruptcy results in job losses. In turn, increased unemployment leads to a compression of consumer spending, namely, lower levels of purchasing power. This collapse in spending was referred to by John Maynard Keynes as "a deficiency in aggregate demand." The resulting decline in the demand for commodities leads to lower levels of production, which in turn lead to further plant closures and more unemployment.

We are dealing with a cumulative and destructive process. Plant and equipment are standing idle, assembly plants are closed down and new investments are not carried out. The resulting increase in unemployment is conducive to a dramatic decline in consumer spending which in turn backlashes on the levels of production of goods and services. Bankruptcies trigger unemployment, which in turn contributes to a further decline in purchasing power, resulting in a subsequent string of bankruptcies.

Supply side economics totally disregards this central relationship. No attempt is made by policymakers to break this cumulative and circular cycle, which is well understood by Keynesian economists. This downward spiral is cumulative, ultimately leading to an oversupply of commodities, which triggers bankruptcies in virtually all sectors of economic activity with perhaps the exception of the luxury goods economy and the defense industry, which is fed by lucrative U.S.-NATO contracts for advanced weapons systems.

The Process of Bankruptcy

With plant closures and corporate downsizing, workers become unemployed, inventories of unsold goods pile up and eventually production collapses. The supply of commodities declines through the closing down of production facilities, including manufacturing assembly plants. Thousands of bankrupt firms are virtually driven off the economic landscape, leading to a slump in production.

Official statements as well as media reports will highlight individual bankruptcies, case by case, in specific localities. Bankruptcy is presented as a microeconomic phenomenon limited to particular enterprises. It is not analyzed in relation to the structure of the economic crisis. The broader picture in which thousands of individual enterprises are pushed simultaneously into bankruptcy is rarely mentioned. What we are dealing with is a cumulative macroeconomic process of bankruptcy which is the result of the summation of individual bankruptcies.

Resulting from media disinformation, the detailed impacts of the economic crisis remain unheralded. The broader social consequences of the crisis are not documented. People may be aware of plant closures and layoffs in their home towns, but the broader picture of economic dislocation and bankruptcy at the regional, national and international levels remains vague and

TEXT BOX 1.5
SELECTED LAYOFFS AND BANKRUPTCIES

Immediately following the September 2008 financial crash, "Seventeen of the U.S.'s 29 steel mill blast furnaces have shut down in response to slowing demand... The U.S. auto giants have announced new rounds of job cuts."[18]

The downturn across the manufacturing sector is set to exacerbate the social crisis already affecting wide layers of the working and middle classes. States dependent on industrial employment such as Michigan and Rhode Island, with official jobless rates of 8.7 and 8.8 percent respectively, have been particularly hard hit.

The job cuts have spread from coast-to-coast and affect every industry and many service employers as well. Auto-related production has been hard hit, with Diez Group announcing the closure of three Michigan metal-stamping plants, cutting 352 jobs. DMAX, a joint venture of GM and Isuzu in Moraine, Ohio, cut 300 jobs. B.F. Goodrich cut 500 jobs at its tire plant in Woodburn, Indiana. Thomas-Built cut 205 jobs at its bus plant in High Point, North Carolina.

Other industrial cuts included a combined total of 1,000 jobs at three North Carolina factories now set to close: Silver Line Building Products in Durham, UCO Fabrics in Rockingham, and IWC Direct at Elm City. ADC Telecommunications cut 190 jobs in Minnesota, and Align Technologies 111 jobs in Santa Clara, California.

Healthcare and public services are also beginning to be hit. Cambridge Health Alliance in Massachusetts cut 650 jobs, Blue Cross Blue Shield of Michigan 100, and the University of Pittsburgh Medical Center 500. Lost Angeles County gave layoff notices to 200 workers because of a budget shortfall.

Even greater public service jobs cuts are coming as the recession hits state tax receipts. One of the biggest government employers, the US Postal Service, has informed its unions that 16,000 craft employees are not covered by the no-layoff clause and could face dismissal.[19]

indeterminate. There is no geography of the economic crisis, no attempt by economists and the media to tabulate and analyze the data on individual bankruptcies. The consensus is that the worst of the economic crisis is over and the recovery is under way.

However, it is the aggregation of individual cases of bankruptcy and plant closures which provides us with an understanding of what is happening at both national and international levels. Business enterprises cannot sell their products, because workers have been laid off. Consumers, namely working people, have been deprived of the purchasing power required to fuel economic growth. With their meager earnings, they cannot afford to acquire the goods produced. What occurs is a massive disengagement of productive resources characterized by bankruptcies, plant closures, the curtailment of investment due to cuts in credit and a freeze of public investments in infrastructure and public services.

In turn, the entire commercial wholesale and retail infrastructure that supports the distribution of commodities is in crisis, leading to the collapse of commercial real estate.

No Policy Solutions to the Economic Crisis

The proposed policy solutions are not intended to prevent or reverse the occurrence of individual bankruptcies. In fact quite the opposite: the prevailing environment of deregulation allows firms to be bought up through mergers and acquisitions, downsized or closed down. People are impoverished not as a result of a scarcity of productive resources, which is the mainstream economic explanation. Poverty occurs because productive activities are closed down, following a collapse in aggregate demand. What the economic crisis does is to destroy pre-existing productive capabilities through a process of disengagement: bankrupt industrial and agricultural enterprises are removed from the economic landscape and they no longer produce; plant and equipment are left inactive; agricultural land goes fallow; with the collapse of consumer spending, shopping malls are at a standstill; wholesale and retail outlets are closed down.

In this environment, the proposed policies do not in any way contribute to creating employment and reversing the collapse in purchasing power. In fact, precisely the opposite occurs. The main thrust of state "supply side" macroeconomic policy is to endorse the process of layoffs and plant closures, which directly contributes to increasing the levels of unemployment.

The policy solutions serve the interests of the financial elites. Indebtedness is an overriding and destructive mechanism. It allows the creditors to shut down productive activities, lay off workers as well as acquire ownership of real economy assets.

The "solutions" to the crisis become the cause of further economic collapse. The so-called stimulus package and bailout measures proposed in both the U.S. and the European Union do not constitute a solution to the crisis. The reverse holds true: they unleash an unprecedented concentration of wealth, which in turn contributes to widening economic and social inequalities both within and between nations.

The bailout measures under the Bush and Obama administrations have contributed to a further process of destabilization of the financial architecture. They transfer large amounts of public money, at taxpayers' expense, into the hands of private financiers. These money transfers result in a spiraling public debt and an unprecedented centralization of banking power. Moreover, the bailout money is used by the financial giants to secure corporate acquisitions both in the financial sector and the real economy, including large industrial conglomerates such as General Motors. In turn, this unprecedented concentration of financial power spearheads entire sectors of industry and the services economy into bankruptcy, leading to the layoff of tens of thousands of workers.

The upper spheres of Wall Street overshadow the real economy. The accumulation of large amounts of money wealth by a handful of Wall Street conglomerates and their associated hedge funds is reinvested in the acquisition of real assets. Paper wealth is transformed into the ownership and control of real productive assets, including industry, services, natural resources and infrastructure.

The Process of Indebtedness

The levels of indebtedness have skyrocketed. Industrial corporations are being driven into bankruptcy, taken over by the global financial institutions. Credit, which constitutes the lifeline of production, is controlled by a handful of financial conglomerates. America is the most indebted country on earth.

The financial meltdown inevitably backlashes on consumer markets, the housing market and more broadly on the process of investment in the production of goods and services. There is an almost symbiotic relationship between the real economy and the money economy, or financial system. Central to this relationship is credit, namely, the "supply of loanable funds".

Financial institutions control credit to the real economy. They have the ability to spearhead real economy enterprises into bankruptcy. What we are dealing with is the process of indebtedness, which is by no means limited to businesses and corporations. Financial institutions also control households through residential mortgages and consumers through credit card debt. Bankruptcy permeates the entire fabric of the real economy. We may distinguish between several categories of debt, including:

1) debts incurred by companies, namely, corporate debt
2) debt incurred by state-owned public corporations
3) various categories of public debt including federal debt, state debt and debts of municipalities
4) personal and household debt including mortgage debts, personal debts and credit card debts

A solution to the economic crisis requires tackling the issue of debt by fundamentally modifying the relationship between creditors and debtors, controlling interest rates, erasing certain categories of debt and ultimately challenging the overriding power of the creditors to dictate macroeconomic policy.

The Speculative Onslaught

The worldwide scramble to appropriate wealth through financial manipulation is the driving force behind this crisis. It is the source of economic turmoil and social devastation. What are the underlying causes? What prevails is a deregulated financial environment characterized by extensive speculative trade.

The history of deregulation goes back to the beginnings of the Reagan administration. This new global financial environment has unfolded in several stages since the collapse of the Bretton Woods system of fixed exchange rates in 1971. The debt crisis of the early 1980s (broadly coinciding with the Reagan-Thatcher era) had unleashed a wave of corporate mergers, buyouts and bankruptcies. These changes have, in turn, paved the way for the consolidation of a new generation of financiers clustered around the merchant banks, the institutional investors, stock brokerage firms, large insurance companies, etc. In this process, commercial banking functions have coalesced with those of the investment banks and stock brokers.[20]

While these "money managers" play a powerful role on financial markets, they are, nonetheless, increasingly removed from entrepreneurial functions in the real economy. Their activities (which often escape state regulation) include speculative transactions in commodity futures and derivatives, and the manipulation of currency markets.

What we are facing is the development of a *shadow banking system*, which operates outside the sphere of financial regulation. Major financial actors are routinely involved in "hot money deposits" in the "emerging markets" of Latin America and Southeast Asia, not to mention money laundering and the development of (specialized) "private banks" (which "advise wealthy clients") in the many offshore banking havens. Within this global financial web, money transits at high speed from one banking haven to the next in the intangible form of electronic transfers. Legal and illegal business activities have become increasingly intertwined; vast amounts of unreported private wealth have been accumulated. Favored by financial deregulation, the criminal mafias have also expanded their roles in the spheres of international banking.[21]

The shadow banking system, however, is not a separate and distinct sector of the financial system. The unregulated shadow banking system (hedge funds, offshore private banking, investment funds specializing in speculate trade, etc.) overlaps with the broader banking system, characterized by commercial banks, brokerage firms, etc. The banks are said to be highly indebted, which has justified the governments' multibillion bailout plans. To whom? Who are the ultimate creditors? To whom do they owe money?

Follow the money trail. Through highly leveraged investments involving the trade in derivatives, the shadow banking entities specializing in derivative trade (investment funds, hedge funds, etc.) have become the creditors of the banks. But these financial entities were actually created by the banks themselves in many cases.

Inasmuch as the shadow banking system is an appendage of the global financial system, controlled by the financial elites, this is often money that the large Wall Street banks "owe to themselves", to their unregulated affiliates, hedge funds and related financial entities which they control. This relationship is yet to be firmly established. The shadow banking system and the banking system in general are integrated. They overlap, and the creditors are part of this nexus.

PART II THE HISTORY OF FINANCIAL DEREGULATION

This economic crisis is the outcome of a process of macroeconomic and financial restructuring initiated in the early 1980s. In the developing countries, this restructuring was part of a policy framework: trade and financial sector reforms under WTO auspices, not to mention the imposition of the IMF's deadly macroeconomic reforms, commonly referred to as "the structural adjustment program".

The debt crisis of the early 1980s unleashed a wave of corporate mergers, buyouts and bankruptcies. These changes then paved the way for the consolidation of a new generation of financiers clustered around the large merchant banks, the institutional investors, stock brokerage firms and large insurance companies. In this process, commercial banking functions have coalesced with those of the investment banks and stock brokers, leading to the consolidation of a handful of global financial conglomerates.

The unregulated use of complex speculative instruments has provided Wall Street with the means to extend its global financial empire. The main thrust of this process does not consist in overseeing the stock market *per se*. Rather it resides in controlling the lucrative markets of speculative trade (e.g. derivatives, options, futures and hedges) where the scope for manipulation and insider trade is far greater.

The 1987 Wall Street Crash

Black Monday, October 19, 1987, was the largest one-day drop in the history of the New York Stock Exchange, overshooting the collapse of October 28, 1929, which had prompted the Wall Street crash and the beginning of the Great Depression. In the 1987 meltdown, 22.6 percent of the value of U.S. stocks was wiped out largely during the first hour of trading on Monday morning. The plunge on Wall Street sent a cold shiver through the entire financial system leading to the tumble of the European and Asian stock markets.[22]

CHART 1.2 1987 Financial Meltdown: Dow Jones Industrial Average (June 1987-January 1988)

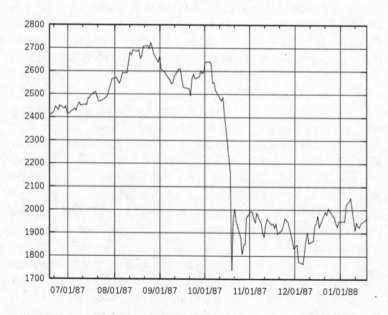

Source: New York Stock Exchange and Wikipedia.org

The Institutional Speculator

The 1987 Wall Street crash served to clear the decks so that only the fittest survive. In the wake of the 1987 crisis, a massive concentration of financial power has taken place. From these transformations, the institutional speculator emerged as a powerful actor overshadowing and often undermining *bona fide* business interests. Using a variety of instruments, these institutional actors appropriate wealth from the real economy. They often dictate the fate of companies listed on the New York Stock Exchange. Totally removed from entrepreneurial functions in the real economy, they have the power of precipitating large industrial corporations into bankruptcy.

The destabilizing role of derivative trade, which triggered the 2008 stock market crash, was known and understood. In 1993, a report of Germany's Bundesbank had already warned that trade in derivatives could potentially "trigger chain reactions and endanger the financial system as a whole."[23]

The Chairman of the U.S. Federal Reserve Board, Alan Greenspan, was acutely aware of the dangers, and had warned:

> Legislation is not enough to prevent a repeat of the Barings crisis in a high tech world where transactions are carried out at the push of the button... The efficiency of global financial markets has the capability of transmitting mistakes at a far faster pace throughout the financial system in ways which were unknown a generation ago.[24]

What was not revealed to public opinion at the time was that these so-called mistakes, resulting from large-scale speculative transactions, were the source of unprecedented accumulation of private wealth.

The 1997 Financial Meltdown

The 1987 crisis had occurred in October. On Monday, October 27, 1997, ten years later almost to the day, stock markets around the world plummeted in turbulent trading. The Dow Jones average nosedived by 554 points, a 7.2 percent decline of its value, its twelfth worst one-day fall in the history of the New York Stock Exchange.[25]

European stock markets were in disarray with heavy losses recorded on the Frankfurt, Paris and London exchanges. The Hong Kong stock exchange had crashed by 10.41 percent on the previous Thursday ("Black Thursday", October 24) as mutual fund managers and pension funds swiftly dumped large amounts of Hong Kong blue chip stocks. The slide at Hong Kong's Exchange Square continued unabated at the opening of trade on Monday morning: a 6.7 percent drop on Monday 27, followed by a 13.7 percent fall on Tuesday (Hong Kong's biggest point loss ever).

The 1997 meltdown of financial markets had been heightened by computerized trading and the absence of state regulation. The NYSE's Superdot electronic order-routing system was able to handle (without queuing) more than 300 000 orders per day (an average of 375 orders per second), representing a daily capacity of more than two billion shares. While its speed and volume had increased tenfold since 1987, the risks of financial instability were significantly greater.[27]

Ten years earlier, in the wake of the 1987 meltdown, the U.S. Treasury was advised by Wall Street not to meddle in financial markets. Free of government encroachment, the New York and Chicago exchanges were invited to establish their own regulatory procedures. The latter largely consisted in freezing computerized program trading through the use of so-called "circuit breakers".[28]

In 1997, the circuit breakers proved to be totally ineffective in averting a meltdown. On Monday, October 27, 1997, a first circuit breaker halted trading for thirty minutes after a 350 point plunge of the Dow Jones. After the thirty minute trading halt, an atmosphere of panic and confusion was installed: brokers started dumping large quantities of stocks, which contributed to accelerating the collapse in market values. In the course of the next 25 minutes, the Dow plunged by a further 200 points, triggering a second "circuit breaker" which served to end the trading day on Wall Street.[29]

The 1997 Asian Crisis: Dress Rehearsal for Things to Come

When viewed historically, the 1997 financial crisis was far more devastating and destructive than previous financial meltdowns.

TABLE 1.2 New York Stock Exchange: Worst Single-Day Declines
(Dow Jones Industrial Average, percentage change)

October 28, 1929	12.8%
October 29, 1929	11.7%
November 6, 1929	9.9%
September 24, 1931	7.1%
August 12, 1932	8.4%
October 5, 1932	7.2%
July 21, 1933	7.8%
October 18, 1937	7.6%
October 19, 1987	22.6%
October 26, 1987	8.0%
October 27, 1997	7.2%
August 31, 1998	6.4%
September 17, 2001	7.13%
September 17, 2008	4.06%
September 29, 2008	6.9 %
October 7, 2008	5.11%
October 9, 2008	7.3%
October 15, 2008	7.9%
December 1, 2008	7.7%

Source: New York Stock Exchange[26]

Both the stock market and currency markets were affected. In the 1987 crisis, national currencies remained relatively stable. In contrast to both the crashes of 1929 and 1987, the 1997-98 financial crisis was marked by the concurrent collapse of currencies and stock markets. An almost symbiotic relationship between the stock exchange and the foreign currency market had unfolded: "institutional speculators" were not only involved in manipulating stock prices, they also had the ability to plunder central banks' foreign exchange reserves, undermining sovereign governments and destabilizing entire national economies.

In the course of 1997, currency speculation in Thailand, Indonesia, Korea and the Philippines was conducive to the transfer of billions of dollars of central bank reserves into private financial hands. Several observers have pointed to the deliberate manipulation of equity and currency markets, including short selling by investment banks and brokerage firms. A member of China's legislature had accused Morgan Stanley of "short selling the market".[30]

Ironically, the same Western financial institutions which looted developing countries' central banks also offered to come to the rescue of Southeast Asia's monetary authorities. ING Baring, for instance, well known for its speculative undertakings, generously offered to underwrite a one billion dollar loan to the Central Bank of the Philippines (CBP) in July 1997. In the months which followed, most of these borrowed foreign currency reserves were reappropriated by international speculators when the CBP sold large amounts of dollars on the forward market in a desperate attempt to prop up the peso.[31]

While the Asian bailout agreements were formally negotiated with the IMF, the major Wall Street commercial banks (including Chase, Bank of America, Citigroup and J. P. Morgan) as well as the "big five" merchant banks (Goldman Sachs, Lehman Brothers, Morgan Stanley and Salomon Smith Barney) were consulted on the clauses to be included in the Asian bailout agreements. It should be noted that these are the 1997 denominations of major financial institutions.

The U.S. Treasury, in liaison with Wall Street and the Bretton Woods institutions, played a central role in negotiating the bailout agreements. Both Larry Summers and Timothy Geithner, respectively Obama's Chairman of the White House National Economic Council (NEC) and Secretary of the Treasury, were actively involved on behalf of the U.S. Treasury in the 1997 bailout of South Korea:

> [In 1997] Messrs. Summers and Geithner worked to persuade [Treasury Secretary] Mr. Rubin to support financial aid to South Korea. Mr. Rubin was wary of such a move, worrying that providing money to a country in dire straits might be a losing proposition.[32]

What happened in Korea under advice from then-Deputy Treasury Secretary Summers *et al.* had nothing to do with financial aid. The country was literally ransacked. Undersecretary of the Treasury David Lipton was sent to Seoul in early December 1997. Secret negotiations were initiated. Washington had demanded the firing of the Korean Finance Minister and the unconditional acceptance of the IMF "bailout".[33]

A new finance minister, who happened to be a former IMF official, was appointed and immediately rushed off to Washington for consultations with his former IMF colleague, Deputy Managing Director Stanley Fischer:

> The Korean Legislature had met in emergency sessions on December 23. The final decision concerning the 57 billion dollar deal took place the following day, on Christmas Eve, December 24th, after office hours in New York. Wall Street's top financiers, from Chase Manhattan, Bank of America, Citicorp and J. P. Morgan had been called in for a meeting at the Federal Reserve Bank of New York. Also at the Christmas Eve venue were representatives of the big five New York merchant banks including Goldman Sachs, Lehman Brothers, Morgan Stanley and Salomon Smith Barney. And at midnight on Christmas Eve, upon receiving the green light from the banks, the IMF was allowed to rush 10 billion dollars to Seoul to meet the avalanche of maturing short-term debts.[34]

The coffers of Korea's central bank had been raided. Creditors and speculators were anxiously waiting to collect the loot. The same institutions which had earlier speculated against the Korean won were cashing in on the IMF bailout money. It was a scam.[35]

"Strong economic medicine" is the prescription of the Washington Consensus. "Short term pain for long term gain" was the motto at the World Bank during Lawrence Summers' term as World Bank Chief Economist.[36] We are looking at an old boys' network of officials, advisers and CEOs at the Treasury, the Federal Reserve, the IMF, World Bank and the Washington think tanks, who are in permanent liaison with leading financiers on Wall Street.

"Economic Contagion": The Asian Flu

Business forecasters and academic economists alike had disregarded the dangers of a global financial meltdown, alluding to "strong economic fundamentals". G7 leaders were afraid to say anything or act in a way which might give the wrong signals. Wall Street analysts continue to bungle on issues of "market correction" with little understanding of the broader economic picture.

The plunge on the New York Stock Exchange on October 27, 1997 was casually blamed on the "structurally weak economies" of Southeast Asia, which barely a few months earlier had been heralded as "upcoming tigers". The seriousness of the financial crisis was trivialized: Alan Greenspan, Chairman of the Federal Reserve Board, reassured Wall Street pointing authoritatively to "the contagious character of national economies, spreading weaknesses from country to country". Following Greenspan's verdict on October 28, the consensus among Manhattan brokers and U.S. academics (without debate or analysis) was that "Wall Street had caught the Hong Kong flu".[37]

The 1998 Stock Market Meltdown

In the uncertain wake of Wall Street's recovery from the 1997 "Asian flu" – largely spurred by panic flight out of Japanese stocks – financial markets backslid a few months later to reach a new dramatic turning point in August 1998 with the spectacular nosedive of the Russian ruble. The Dow Jones plunged by 554 points on August 31, 1998 (its second largest decline in the history of the New York stock exchange) leading, in the course of September 1998, to the dramatic meltdown of stock markets around the world. In a matter of a few weeks, 2 300 billion dollars of paper profits had evaporated from the U.S. stock market.[38]

The ruble's August 1998 freefall had spurred Moscow's largest commercial banks into bankruptcy, leading to the potential takeover of Russia's financial system by a handful of Western banks and brokerage houses. In turn, the crisis had created the danger of massive debt default to Moscow's western creditors, including the Deutsche and Dresdner banks. Since the outset of Russia's macroeconomic reforms, following the first injection of IMF shock therapy in 1992, some 500 billion dollars worth of Russian assets – including plants of the military industrial complex, infrastructure and natural resources – have been confiscated (through the privatization programs and forced bankruptcies) and transferred into the hands of Western capitalists. In the brutal aftermath of the Cold War, an entire economic and social system was being dismantled.

The 1999 Financial Services Modernization Act: Repeal of the Glass-Steagall Act

The 1997 and 1998 financial meltdowns had set the stage for major changes in the global financial architecture. 1999 was a watershed year in the passage of key legislation in the U.S. Congress. The last months of the Clinton administration represented a major turning point in the process of financial deregulation. Under the Financial Services Modernization Act adopted in November 1999 – barely a week before the historic Seattle Millennium Summit of the World Trade Organization (WTO) – U.S. lawmakers had set the stage for a sweeping deregulation of the U.S. banking system.

The Financial Services Modernization Act (Gramm-Leach Bliley Act) was adopted by the U.S. Congress in the wake of lengthy negotiations. Clinton's Secretary of the Treasury Lawrence Summers, who was appointed Chairman of the White House National Economic Council (NEC) by President Barack Obama, played a key role: all regulatory restraints on Wall Street's powerful banking conglomerates were revoked with a stroke of the pen.

Under the 1999 Financial Services Modernization Act ratified by the U.S. Senate and approved by President Clinton, commercial banks, brokerage firms, institutional investors and insurance companies could freely invest in each other's businesses as well as fully integrate their financial operations. The legislation repealed the Glass-Steagall Act of 1933, a pillar of President Roosevelt's New Deal, which was put in place in response to the climate of corruption, financial manipulation and insider trading that resulted in more than 5 000 bank failures in the years following the 1929 Wall Street crash.[39]

The Global Financial Supermarket

The Financial Services Modernization Act (FSMA) should not be viewed in isolation as a domestic procedure, limited to the U.S. financial landscape. The impacts of the legislation extended well beyond the borders of the U.S. financial system. The institutional changes which it brought about, including the concentration and centralization of power in the hands of a small number of financial giants, largely contributed to Wall Street's unswerving quest for global financial domination.

The tendency was towards a worldwide financial supermarket controlled by a handful of global financial institutions which penetrate and permeate the fabric of national economies. The sweeping deregulation of U.S. banking imparted unprecedented powers to Wall Street's financial conglomerates to acquire and take over banking institutions all over the world.

The worldwide scramble to appropriate wealth through financial manipulation was the driving force behind this restructuring of the global financial architecture of which the 1999 U.S. legislation was an integral part, setting the pattern of financial reform in different parts of the world.

The 1999 legislation empowered Wall Street's key players to enter the financial services markets of developing countries and consolidate a hegemonic position in global banking, overshadowing and ultimately destabilizing financial systems in Asia, Latin America and Eastern Europe.

The global financial supermarket created under the FSMA is to be overseen by the Wall Street giants; competing banking institutions are to be removed from the financial landscape. State level banks across America will be displaced or bought up, leading to a deadly string of bank failures. In turn, the supervisory powers of the Federal Reserve Board (which are increasingly under the direct dominion of Wall Street) have been significantly weakened.

Free from government regulation, the financial giants were given the ability to strangle local-level businesses in the U.S. and overshadow the real economy. In fact, due to the lack of competition, the 1999 legislation also entitled the financial services giants (bypassing the Federal Reserve Board and acting in tacit collusion with one another) to set interest rates as they pleased.

In turn, financial deregulation in the U.S. had created an environment which favored an unprecedented concentration of global financial power.

The FSMA had also set the pace of global financial and trade reform under the auspices of the IMF, the World Bank and the WTO. The 1999 banking legislation adopted in the U.S. empowered a handful of banking conglomerates with the ability of destabilizing the domestic financial landscape of developing countries. The legislation was implemented alongside the concurrent reshaping of the global trade and financial architecture under the WTO agenda. Under the General Agreement on Trade in Services (GATS), developing countries have committed themselves to full liberalization of financial services. In other words, national governments, which are already controlled by their external creditors, would be unable to deflect the Wall Street giants from entering and swallowing up national banks and financial institutions.

The provisions of both the WTO General Agreement on Trade in Services and of the Financial Services Agreement (FTA) imply the breaking down of remaining impediments to the movement of finance capital: J.P Morgan Chase, HSBC, Citigroup or Deutsche Bank can go wherever they please, triggering, in country after country, the bankruptcy of national banks and financial institutions.

In practice, this process had already occurred in a large number of developing countries under bankruptcy and privatization programs imposed on an *ad hoc* basis by the Bretton Woods institutions. By the late 1990s, the mega-banks had already penetrated the financial landscape of developing countries, taking control of banking institutions and financial services. In this process, the financial giants were granted *de facto* "national treatment": without recourse to the provisions of the Financial Services Agreement (FTA) of the WTO, Wall Street banks in countries like Korea, Pakistan, Argentina or Brazil became *bona fide* "national banks", operating as domestic institutions and governed by domestic laws established under advice from IMF and the World Bank. The large U.S. and European financial services giants did not require the formal adoption of the GATS to be able to dominate banking institutions worldwide, as well as overshadow national governments.

By early 2000, the process of global financial deregulation was in many regards a *fait accompli*. Wall Street routinely invaded country after country. The domestic banking system was put on the auction block and reorganized under the surveillance of external creditors. National financial institutions were systematically destabilized and driven out of business; mass unemployment and poverty are the invariable results.

Moreover, with the support of the IMF, the Wall Street conglomerates and their European and Japanese partners reinforced and consolidated their roles as the world's major creditor institutions, routinely underwriting the public debt, overseeing the conduct of state budgetary policy, issuing syndicated loans to troubled industrial corporations and overseeing the privatization of state corporations which have been put on the auction block in the context of an IMF bailout agreement.

Assisted by the IMF – which routinely obliges countries to open up their domestic banking sector to foreign investment – retail banking, stock brokerage firms and insurance companies are taken over by foreign capital and reorganized. Citigroup, among other Wall Street majors, has gone on a global shopping spree buying up banks and financial institutions at bargain prices in Asia, Latin America and Eastern Europe. In one fell swoop, Citigroup acquired the 106-branch network of Banco Mayo Cooperativo Ltda., becoming Argentina's second largest bank.

The Merger Frenzy

Following the adoption of the 1999 Financial Services Modernization Act, a new era of intense financial rivalry was set in motion. The New World Order – largely under the dominion of American finance capital – was eventually intent on dwarfing rival banking conglomerates in Western Europe and Japan, as well as sealing strategic alliances with a select club of German and British-based banking giants.

Several mammoth bank mergers (including NationsBank with BankAmerica, and Citibank with Travelers Group) had, in fact, already been implemented and rubber-stamped by the Federal Reserve Board, in violation of the pre-existing legislation, prior to the adoption of the 1999 Financial Services Modernization Act. Citibank, the largest Wall Street bank, and Travelers

Group Inc., the financial services and insurance conglomerate (which also owns Solomon Smith Barney a major brokerage firm) combined their operations in 1998 in a 72 billion dollar merger.[40]

Strategic mergers between American and European banks had also been negotiated, bringing into the heart of the U.S. financial landscape some of Europe's key financial players, including Deutsche Bank AG (linked up with Banker's Trust) and Credit Suisse (linked up with First Boston). The Hong Kong Shanghai Banking Corporation (HSBC), the British-based banking conglomerate – which had already sealed a partnership with Wells Fargo and Wachovia Corporation – had acquired the late Edmond Safra's Republic New York Bank in a nine billion dollar deal.[41]

In the meantime, rival European banks excluded from Wall Street's inner circle were scrambling to compete in an increasingly unfriendly global financial environment. Banque Nationale de Paris (BNP) had acquired Société Générale de Banque and Paribas to form one of the world's largest banks. BNP eventually aspires "to move into North America in a bigger way."[42]

The bank mergers carried out prior to the 1999 legislation in violation of the Glass-Steagall Act were but the tip of the iceberg, the shape of things to come. The repeal of the Glass-Steagall Act had created an environment which favored an unprecedented concentration of global financial power.

Effective control over the entire U.S. financial services industry had been transferred to a handful of financial conglomerates.

1999-2009: The Shape of Things to Come

Supported by the neo-cons in the Bush administration, a process of intense financial rivalry had unfolded. The New World Order, largely under the dominion of American finance capital, was intent on dwarfing rival banking conglomerates in Western Europe and Japan, as well as sealing strategic alliances with a select club of German and British banking giants. This is essentially the direction of the ongoing financial crisis: a worldwide process of concentration and centralization of bank power, which has, by no means, reached its peak.

The evolving global financial supermarket was to be overseen by the Wall Street giants. State level banks across America were displaced or swallowed up by the financial giants, leading to a deadly string of bank failures. This bankruptcy of local and regional level banks, however, has not reached its climax.

What prevails today under the Obama administration is a *de facto* system of private regulation, which favors centralization and concentration of the U.S. banking system. The supervisory powers of the Federal Reserve Board are directly under dominion of Wall Street. The financial giants have the ability to strangle local level businesses in the U.S. and overshadow the real economy.

The 2008 financial meltdown was the result of an advanced system of financial deregulation which was set in motion in 1999:

> Despite impending danger signals, the 1999 legislation seems to totally disregard the history of stock market failures since the onset of the "Asian crisis" in mid-1997. The economic and social repercussions in an integrated worldwide financial system – not to mention the risks of a global financial meltdown resulting from the absence of financial regulation – are far more serious today [1999] than during the years following the 1929 Wall Street crash.[43]

The Architects of Economic Collapse: "Putting the Fox in Charge of the Chicken Coop"

Ironically, the architects of both the 1997 Asian Bailout agreements and the 1999 Financial Services Modernization Act, which paved the way for the 2008-2009 financial meltdown, were put in charge of President Obama's economic stimulus and bank bailout programs.

Lawrence Summers is the current director of the White House National Economic Council (NEC) under the Obama administration, and played a key role in lobbying Congress for the repeal of the Glass-Steagall Act. His timely appointment by President Clinton in 1999 as Treasury Secretary spearheaded the adoption of the Financial Services Modernization Act in November 1999. Upon completing his mandate at the helm of the U.S. Treasury, he became president of Harvard University (2001-2006).

The National Economic Council (NEC) headed by Summers is a White House agency. It is part of the Office of the Presidency, which plays a central role in the formulation of economic policy including financial regulatory measures. The Director of the NEC is also "Assistant to the President for Economic Policy". In other words, one of the main architects of financial deregulation has been appointed to formulate policy "solutions" to the economic crisis.

Larry Summers is also a protégé of David Rockefeller. Prior to his appointment as NEC Director, he was a consultant to Goldman Sachs and managing director of a hedge fund, the D.E. Shaw Group. As a Hedge Fund manager, his contacts at the Treasury and on Wall Street provided him with valuable inside information on the movement of financial markets in the months leading up to the September-October 2008 financial meltdown.

Putting a hedge fund manager (with links to the Wall Street financial establishment) as chairman of the National Economic Council is tantamount to "putting the fox in charge of the chicken coop". Lawrence Summers served as Chief Economist for the World Bank (1991-1993). He contributed to shaping the macroeconomic reforms imposed on numerous indebted developing countries. The social and economic impact of these reforms under the IMF-World Bank sponsored structural adjustment program (SAP) were devastating, resulting in mass poverty. His stint at the World Bank coincided with the collapse of the Soviet Union and the imposition of the IMF-World Bank's deadly "economic medicine" on Eastern Europe, the former Soviet republics and the Balkans.

In 1993, Summers moved to the U.S. Treasury. He initially held the position of Undersecretary of the Treasury for International Affairs and later Deputy Secretary. In liaison with his former colleagues at the IMF and the World Bank, he played a key role in crafting the economic shock treatment reform packages imposed at the height of the 1997 Asian crisis on South Korea, Thailand and Indonesia.

The bailout agreements negotiated with these three countries were coordinated through Summers' office at the Treasury in connection with the Federal Reserve Bank of New York and the Washington based Bretton Woods institutions. Summers worked closely with IMF Deputy Managing Director Stanley Fischer, who was later appointed Governor of the Central Bank of Israel.

Robert E. Rubin, former Treasury Secretary and Chairman of the Council of Economic Advisers, is described as an economic adviser to president Obama. While he does not hold a formal position in Obama's economic team, he occupies the position of co-Chairman of the Board of the powerful Council on Foreign Relations (CFR), which sets the economic and financial agenda of the U.S. administration.

Paul Volcker was president of the Federal Reserve Bank of New York from 1975 to 1979. In 1979 he was appointed chairman of the Federal Reserve Board by President Jimmy Carter, a position which he held until 1987. Volcker played a central role in implementing the first stage of financial deregulation, which was conducive to mass bankruptcies, mergers and acquisitions, leading up to the 1987 financial crisis. In 2008, he was appointed by President Obama to chair the Economic Recovery Advisory Board.

Timothy Geithner, who was appointed Treasury Secretary by President Obama, was President and CEO of the Federal Reserve Bank of New York (FRBNY), which is the most powerful private financial institution in America. He was also a former Clinton administration Treasury official. He has worked for Kissinger Associates and has also held a senior position at the IMF. The FRBNY plays a behind the scenes role in shaping financial policy. Geithner acts on behalf of powerful financiers who are behind the FRBNY. He is also a member of the Council on Foreign Relations (CFR).

What is striking in the various appointments is the how these individuals are shuffled back and forth from Wall Street to the Treasury, to the World Bank and the IMF, to the Federal Reserve and the Council on Foreign Relations. These government appointments indelibly serve the interests of the financial elites.

PART III FROM BUSH TO OBAMA: AMERICA'S FISCAL COLLAPSE

"We will rebuild, we will recover, and the United States of America will emerge stronger."

–President Barack Obama, State of the Union Address 24 Feb 2009

"Those of us who manage the public's dollars will be held to account – to spend wisely, reform bad habits, and do our business in the light of day – because only then can we restore the vital trust between a people and their government."

–President Barack Obama, A New Era of Responsibility, the 2010 Budget

What has been implemented under Obama is strong economic medicine with a "human face". "Promise amid peril". The stated priorities of the Obama economic package are health, education, renewable energy, investment in infrastructure and transportation. "Quality education" is at the forefront. Obama has also promised to "make health care more affordable and accessible" for every American.

At first sight, the budget proposal had all the appearances of an expansionary program, a demand-oriented "Second New Deal" geared towards creating employment, rebuilding shattered social programs and reviving the real economy.

TEXT BOX 1.6
THE WALL STREET – WASHINGTON CONSENSUS

The term "Washington Consensus" was initially formulated by economist John Williamson. It described a set of accepted neoliberal economic propositions. It was subsequently understood as the consensus on macroeconomic issues underlying several Washington-based institutions, including the IMF, the World Bank, the U.S. Treasury and Washington think tanks, including the Brookings Institution.

Lawrence Summers, Timothy Geithner, Stanley Fischer, Phil Gramm, Paul Volcker, Ben Bernanke, Hank Paulson, Robert E. Rubin, not to mention former Fed Chairman Alan Greenspan, belong to the Washington Consensus. They have links to Wall Street, the Council on Foreign Relations and the Bilderberg Group. They act concurrently in accordance with the interests of Wall Street. They meet behind closed doors; they are on the same wavelength. They are Democrats and Republicans. We are looking at the broader Washington-Wall Street consensus, whereby the decisions taken by various governmental and intergovernmental bodies including the U.S. Treasury and the Bretton Woods institutions serve the interests of Wall Street.

TEXT BOX 1.7
THE HEDGE FUNDS

The hedge funds play a key role in this process of restructuring. These speculative transactions (the panoply of derivatives, options, futures, index funds, etc) often transacted through hedge funds overshadow the workings of stock market transactions, and their relationship to real economic activity.

The hedge funds are private investment funds, which manage the pooled funds of wealthy investors. While they are often linked to major financial institutions, they are totally unregulated. They operate with a large pool of money capital, which is used to undertake highly leveraged speculative transactions. The latter have the characteristic that profits can be reaped when the market goes up, but also when the market goes down.[4]

The realities are otherwise. Obama's promise is based on a mammoth austerity program. The entire fiscal structure is shattered, turned upside down. To reach these stated objectives, a significant hike in public spending on social programs (health, education, housing, social security) would be required, as well as the implementation of a large-scale public investment program. Major shifts in the composition of public expenditure would also be required, i.e. a move out of a war economy, requiring a shift out of military-related spending in favor of civilian programs.

In actuality, what we are dealing with is the most drastic curtailment in public spending in American history, leading to social havoc and the potential impoverishment of millions of people. The Obama promise largely serves the interests of Wall Street, the defense contractors, the oil conglomerates and Big Pharma. In turn, the Bush-Obama bank "bailouts" have led America into a spiraling public debt crisis. The economic and social dislocations are potentially devastating.

War and the Economic Crisis

The worldwide meltdown of financial markets occurs at the crossroads of a major military adventure. The global financial crisis is intimately related to the war. (For further analysis, see chapters 9-12). A spiraling defense budget backlashes on the civilian sectors of economic activity. The war economy has a direct bearing on fiscal and monetary policy. Defense appropriations are in excess of 700 billion dollars (for the 2010 fiscal year). An impending fiscal crisis is looming which threatens to undermine the entire structure of public spending.

"War is Good for Business": the powerful financial groups which routinely manipulate stock markets, currency and commodity markets, are also promoting the continuation and escalation of the Middle East war. The financial crisis is related to the structure of U.S. public investment in the war economy versus the funding, through tax dollars, of civilian social programs. "More broadly, this also raises the issue of the role of the US Treasury and the US monetary system, in relentlessly financing

---

TEXT BOX 1.8
BANK MERGERS: J.P. MORGAN CHASE VERSUS CITIGROUP

In 2000, J.P. Morgan merged with Chase Manhattan, leading to the integration of J.P. Morgan, Chase, Chemical and Manufacturers Hanover into a single financial entity. Bear Stearns was acquired in 2008 by J.P. Morgan Chase following its collapse. This banking empire controlled by the Rockefeller family has assets of more than 1.6 trillion dollars.

With assets of 1.7 trillion dollars, Citigroup's future remains undecided. It is facing serious financial difficulties which could lead it into bankruptcy. In 2008, Citigroup share prices collapsed alongside those of Fannie Mae. The Lehman debacle precipitated a further decline of Citigroup stock prices. Citigroup was the trustee "for unsecured creditors who are owed some $155 billion by Lehman Brothers," but according to Citigroup statements they "have little or no exposure to the failed investment bank." What this means is that the collapse of Lehman could lead to massive loan default in relation to the portfolios of Citigroup and NY Mellon clients, namely client banking institutions as well as individual investors.

Following the Bush administration's November 2008 bailout, Citigroup stock prices seem to have rebounded. In February 2009, Citigroup announced that the U.S. government "would be taking a 36% equity stake in the company by converting $25 billion in emergency aid into common shares."

the military industrial complex and the Middle East war at the expense of most sectors of civilian economic activity."[44]

The war is profit-driven, financed through the massive worldwide expansion of dollar denominated debt. War and globalization go hand in hand. Wall Street, the oil companies and the defense contractors have concurrent and overlapping interests. The oil companies were behind the 2008 speculative surge in crude oil prices on the London energy market, which preceded the collapse of the stock market in September-October of 2008. In turn, resulting from the military agenda, the U.S. civilian economy is in crisis as the nation's resources, including tax dollars, are diverted into funding a multibillion dollar Middle East war.

Defense Outlays for the Wars in Iraq and Afghanistan

This is a "war budget". The austerity measures hit all major federal spending programs with the exception of defense and the Middle East Central Asian War, the Wall Street bank bailout and interest payments on a staggering public debt. The nation's budget diverts tax revenues into financing the wars in Iraq and Afghanistan, not to mention the set-up of new military bases in Colombia. It legitimizes the fraudulent transfers of tax dollars to the financial elites under the bank bailouts.

The pattern of deficit spending is not expansionary. We are not dealing with a Keynesian-style deficit which stimulates investment and consumer demand, leading to an expansion of production and employment. The bank bailouts (involving several initiatives financed by tax dollars) constitute a component of government expenditure. Both the Bush and Obama bank bailouts were handouts to major financial institutions. They did not result in a positive spending injection into the real economy. In fact, the opposite is true. The bailouts have contributed to financing the restructuring of the banking system, leading to a massive concentration of wealth and centralization of banking power.

A large part of the bailout money granted by the U.S. government has already been transferred electronically to various affiliated accounts including the hedge funds. The largest banks in the U.S. are also using this windfall cash to buy out their weaker competitors, thereby consolidating their position. The tendency, therefore, is towards a new wave of corporate buyouts, mergers and acquisitions in the financial services industry.

In turn, the financial elites will use these large amounts of liquid assets (paper wealth), together with the hundreds of billions acquired through speculative trade, to buy out real economy corporations (airlines, the automobile industry, telecoms, media, etc.), whose quoted value on the stock markets has tumbled. In essence, a budget deficit (combined with massive cuts in social programs) was required to fund the handouts to the banks, as well as finance defense spending and the military surge in both Iraq and Afghanistan.

Obama's 2010 Budget

Obama's budget for the 2010 fiscal year was of the order of 3.94 trillion dollars, an increase of 32 percent. Total government revenues for the 2010 fiscal year, according to estimates by the Bureau of Budget, were quoted at 2.381 trillion dollars. This puts the predicted budget deficit at 1.75 trillion dollars, equaling almost twelve percent of the U.S. Gross Domestic Product.[45]

1. Defense spending of 534 billion dollars for 2010, a supplemental 130 billion dollars appropriation for fiscal 2010 for the wars in Afghanistan and Iraq, and a supplemental 75.5 billion dollars emergency war funding for the rest of the 2009 fiscal year. Defense spending and the Middle East war, with various supplemental budgets, was (officially) of the order of 739.5 billion dollars. Some estimates placed aggregate defense and military related spending at over one trillion dollars.

2. A bank bailout of 750 billion dollars announced by Obama, which was added on to the 700 billion dollars in bailout money already allocated by the outgoing Bush administration under the Troubled Assets Relief Program (TARP). The total of both programs is a staggering 1.45 trillion dollars, to be financed by the Treasury. (See Table 1.3 next page). It should be understood that the actual amount of cash financial "aid" to the banks is significantly larger than 1.45 trillion dollars.

3. Net interest on the outstanding public debt was estimated by the Bureau of the Budget at 164 billion dollars in 2010.[46]

The magnitude of these allocations is staggering. Under a "balanced budget" criterion – which has been a priority of government economic policy since the Reagan era – almost all the revenues of the federal government amounting to 2.381 trillion dollars would be used to finance the bank bailout (1.45 trillion), the war (739.5 billion) and interest payments on the public debt (164 billion). In other words, no money would be left over for other categories of public expenditure.

The Budget Deficit

Three categories of expenditure, namely defense, the bank bailout and interest on the public debt, had virtually swallowed up the entire 2010 federal government revenue of 2381.0 billion dollars.[47]

Moreover, as a basis of comparison, all the revenue accruing from individual federal income taxes (1.061 trillion dollars in fiscal 2010), that is, all the money households across America paid annually in the form of federal taxes, did not suffice to finance the handouts to the banks, which officially amounted to 1.45 trillion dollars. This amount includes the 700 billion dollars granted during fiscal year 2009 under the TARP, program plus the proposed 750 billion dollars granted by the Obama administration.

Bush's Troubled Assets Relief Program and Obama's 750 billion dollar bank bailout – although disbursed over more than one fiscal year – nonetheless represented almost half of total government expenditure (half of Obama's 3.94 trillion dollar budget for fiscal 2010), which was financed by regular sources of revenue (2381 billion dollars), plus a staggering 1.75 trillion dollar budget deficit, which ultimately required the issuing of Treasury Bills and government bonds. The feasibility of a large short-term expansion of the public debt at a time of crisis was yet another matter, particularly with interest rates at abysmally low levels.

The budget deficit was 1.58 trillion dollars according to official sources. Obama acknowledged a 1.3 trillion dollar budget deficit, inherited from the Bush administration. In actuality, the

---

TABLE 1.3 Budgetary allocations to Defense (Fiscal Years 2009 and 2010), the Bank Bailout and Net Interests on the Public Debt (Fiscal Year 2010) (billions of dollars)

Defense including Supplementary allocations; $534 billion (FY 2010), $130 billion supplemental (FY 2010), $75.5 billion emergency funding (FY2009)	**739.5**
Bank bailout (TARP plus Obama)*	1450.0
Net Interest	164.0
TOTAL	2353.5
Total Individual (Federal) Income Tax Revenues (FY 2010)	1061.0
Total Federal Government Revenue (FY 2010)	2381.0

Sources: Bureau of the Budget and official statements.
See *A New Era of Responsibility: The 2010 Budget*
See also *Office of Management and Budget*

* The officially announced bank bailouts to be financed from Treasury Funds. The timing of disbursements could take place over more than one fiscal year. The actual value of bank bailout cash injections is substantially higher.

---

budget deficit was much larger. The official figures tended to underestimate the seriousness of the budgetary predicament. The 1.58 trillion dollar budget deficit figure was questionable because the various amounts disbursed under TARP and other related bank bailouts including Obama's 750 billion dollar aid program to financial institutions were not acknowledged in the government's expenditure accounts.

The aid hasn't been requested formally, but appears in a line item "for potential additional financial stabilization efforts," according to the budget overview. The budget office calculated a $250 billion net cost to taxpayers this year, because it anticipates it would eventually recoup some, though not all, of the money expended to help financial companies.

The funds would come on top of the $700 billion rescue package approved last October by Congress. The White House budgets no money for fiscal 2010 and beyond for such aid.[48]

Fiscal Collapse

A major crisis of the federal fiscal structure was in the making. The multibillion dollar allocations to the war budget and to the Wall Street bank bailout program backlash on all other categories of public expenditure. In November 2008, the federal government's bank rescue program was estimated at a staggering 8.5 trillion dollars, an amount equivalent to more than sixty percent of the U.S. public debt estimated at fourteen trillion dollars (2007).[49] Meanwhile, under the Obama budget proposal, 634 billion dollars were allocated to a reserve fund to finance universal health care.

At first glance, it appears to be a large amount. But it is to be spent over a ten year period, i.e. a modest annual commitment of 63.4 billion. Thus public spending will be slashed with a view to curtailing a spiraling budget deficit. Health and education programs will not only remain heavily underfunded, they will be cut, revamped and privatized.

The likely outcome is the outright privatization of public services and the sale of state assets, including public infrastructure, urban services, highways and national parks. Fiscal collapse leads to the privatization of the state. The fiscal crisis is further exacerbated by the compression of tax revenues resulting from decline of the real economy. Unemployed workers do not pay taxes, nor do bankrupt firms. The process is cumulative. The solution to the fiscal crisis becomes the cause of further collapse.

The Structure of the Public Debt

This large-scale appropriation of liquid money assets under the bank bailouts by a handful of financial institutions serves to increase the public debt overnight. When the U.S. Treasury under the Bush administration allocates 700 billion dollars to the Troubled Assets Relief Program, it constitutes a budgetary outlay which inevitably must be financed from within the structure of government revenues and expenditures. A similar reasoning applies to the bank bailouts under the Obama presidency.

Unless all other categories of public expenditure including health, education and social services are slashed, the various outlays under the bank bailouts will require running a massive budget deficit, which in turn will increase the U.S. public debt. Bear

TABLE 1.4 **The U.S. (Federal Government) Gross Public Debt**

Year	Gross Debt in Billions	% of GDP
1940	43.0	52.4
1950	257.4	94.1
1960	290.5	56.1
1970	380.9	37.6
1980	909.0	33.3
1990	3,206.3	55.9
2000	5,628.7	58.0
2001	5,769.9	57.4
2002	6,198.4	59.7
2003	6,760.0	62.5
2004	7,354.7	64.0
2005	7,905.3	64.6
2006	8,451.4	64.9
2007	8,950.7	65.5
2008	9,985.8	70.2
2009 (est.)	12,867.5	90.4
2010 (est.)	14,456.3	98.1
2011 (est.)	15,673.9	101.1
2012 (est.)	16,565.7	100.6
2013 (est.)	17,440.2	99.7
2014 (est.)	18,350.0	99.9

Source: Office of the President. Historical Tables, Budget of the United States, Fiscal Year 2010. http://www.whitehouse.gov/omb/budget/fy2010/assets/hist.pdf

in mind, this budget deficit is not expansionary (in the Keynesian context). It does revive investment and consumer spending. It has no direct bearing on the real economy. It is a money transfer from U.S. tax payers into the coffers of a handful of financial institutions.

America is the most indebted country on earth. The United States (federal government) gross public debt is currently of the order of fourteen trillion dollars. This does not include mounting public debts at the state and municipal levels.

This U.S. dollar denominated (federal) debt is composed of outstanding treasury bills and government bonds. The public debt, also called "the national debt" is the amount of money owed by the federal government to holders of U.S. debt instruments. These are held by American residents (as part of their savings portfolios), companies and financial institutions, U.S. government agencies, foreign governments and individuals in foreign countries, but does not include intergovernmental debt obligations or debt held in the Social Security Trust Fund. Types of securities held by the public include, but are not limited to, Treasury Bills, Notes, Bonds, TIPS, United States Savings Bonds, and State and Local Government Series securities.

The proposed solution becomes the cause of the crisis. The 700 billion dollar bailout under the Troubled Asset Relief Program, combined with Obama's 750 billion dollar aid package to the financial services industry, is but the tip of the iceberg. A panoply of bailout allocations in addition to the 700 billion dollars have been decided upon. Moreover, an additional budgetary overrun was implemented under Obama's stimulus package of 787 billion dollars launched in February 2009 under The American Recovery and Reinvestment Act of 2009. The stimulus package, as distinct from Obama's bank bailout program, is in part directed towards the real economy.

Spiraling Public Debt Crisis

Is the Treasury in a position to finance this mounting budget deficit officially tagged at 1.58 trillion dollars through the emission of Treasury bills and government bonds?[50] The actual budget deficit is much higher.

We are facing the largest ever budget deficit coupled with the lowest interest rates in U.S. history. With the Fed's "near zero" percent discount rate, the markets for U.S. dollar denominated government bonds and Treasury bills are in a straightjacket. Moreover, the essential functions of savings (which are central to the functioning of a national economy) are in crisis.

Who wants to invest in U.S. government debt? What is the demand for Treasury bills at exceedingly low interest rates? The market for U.S. dollar denominated debt instruments is potentially at a standstill, which means that the Treasury lacks the ability to finance its mammoth budget deficit through public debt operations, leading the entire budgetary process into a quandary. The question is whether China and Japan will continue to purchase U.S. dollar denominated debt instruments. Washington is running a public relations campaign to lure Asian investors into buying T-bills and U.S. government bonds.

With the markets for U.S. dollar denominated debt (both domestically and internationally) in crisis, further pressure will be exerted on the Treasury to slash (civilian) public expenditure to the bone, exact user fees for public services and sell off public assets, including state infrastructure and institutions. In all likelihood, this crisis is leading us to the privatization of the state, where activities hitherto under government jurisdiction will be transferred into private hands.

Who will be buying state assets at rock bottom prices? The financial elites, who are also the recipients of the bank bailout.

Consolidation of the Banks

A massive amount of liquidity has been injected into the financial system, from the bailouts but also from pension funds, individual savings, etc. The stated objective of the bank bailout programs is to alleviate the banks' burden of bad debts and non-performing loans. In actuality what is happening is that these massive amounts of money are being used by a handful of institutions to consolidate their position in global banking. The exposure of the banks, largely the result of derivative trade, is estimated in the tens of trillions of dollars, to the extent that the amounts and guarantees granted by the Treasury and the Fed will not resolve the crisis. Nor are they intended to resolve the crisis.

The mainstream media suggests that the banks are being nationalized as a result of TARP. In fact, it is exactly the opposite: the state is being taken over by the banks, the state is being privatized. The establishment of a worldwide unipolar financial system is part of the broader project of the Wall Street financial elites to establish the contours of a world government.

In a bitter irony, the recipients of the bailout under TARP and Obama's proposed 750 billion dollar aid to financial institutions are the creditors of the federal government. The Wall Street banks are the brokers and underwriters of the U.S. public debt. Although they hold only a portion of the debt, they transact and trade in U.S. dollar denominated public debt instruments worldwide. They act as creditors of the U.S. State; they evaluate the creditworthiness of the U.S. government; they rank the public debt through Moody's and Standard and Poor; they control the U.S. Treasury, the Federal Reserve Board and the U.S. Congress; they oversee and dictate fiscal and monetary policy, ensuring that the state acts in their interest. The government hands money to assist the banks under the bank bailout. As a result, its credit rating established by Wall Street is affected.

The U.S. Government Finances its Own Indebtedness: Circular and Contradictory Relationship

Since the Reagan era, Wall Street dominates most areas of economic and social policy. It sets the budgetary agenda, ensuring the curtailment of social expenditures. Wall Street preaches balanced budgets but the practice has been to lobby for the elimination of corporate taxes, grant handouts to corporations and tax write-offs in mergers and acquisitions, all of which lead to a spiraling public debt. It oversees the U.S. public debt and the banks are involved in the sale of treasury bills and government bonds on financial markets in the U.S. and around the world. They also hold part of the public debt and are the creditors of the U.S. government.

In a bitter irony, the massive increase in the public debt (2009-2010) required to "rescue the banks" was financed and brokered by the financial institutions which were the direct beneficiaries of the Bush and Obama bank bailouts.

The Federal Reserve System is a privately owned central bank. While the Federal Reserve Board is a government body, the process of money creation is controlled by the twelve Federal Reserve banks, which are privately owned. The shareholders of the Federal Reserve banks (with the New York Federal Reserve Bank playing a dominant role) are among America's most powerful financial institutions.

The increase in the U.S. public debt in 2009-2010 was a direct result of the bailout monies transferred to the banks. To finance the bank bailouts, the Treasury was obliged to run up a massive budget deficit. While the Federal Reserve creates money out of thin air, the multibillion dollar outlays of the Treasury (including the Bush and Obama bank bailouts) required a massive emission of public debt in the form of Treasury Bills and government bonds. Only part of these T-Bills are held by the Fed.

We are dealing with a pernicious circular relationship. When the banks pressured the Treasury to assist them in the form of a major bank rescue operation, it was understood from the outset in September 2008 that the banks as creditors would in turn "assist" the Treasury in coping with a skyrocketing public debt.

Public opinion had been misled. A diabolical circular process had been set in motion. The U.S. government is in a sense financing its own indebtedness: the money granted to the banks is in part financed by borrowing from the banks. To finance the 1.45 trillion dollar bailout, the government needs to borrow, through the emission of public debt. Where does the government go? To the banks. In other words, with the money the banks lend to the government, the Treasury finances the bailout in favor of the banks.

In turn, the banks impose conditionalities on the management of the U.S. public debt. They dictate how the money should be spent. After having cashed in on their bailout money, they impose "fiscal responsibility" on the U.S. Treasury; they demand massive cuts in public spending, which eventually results in the collapse and/or privatization of public services; they impose the privatization of urban infrastructure, roads, sewer and water systems, public recreational areas – everything is up for privatization.

This public debt crisis triggered by Wall Street is all the more serious because the U.S. federal government does not control monetary policy. All public debt operations go through the Federal Reserve, which is in charge of monetary policy, acting on behalf of private financial interests. The government as such has no authority over money creation. This means that public debt operations essentially serve the interests of the banks.

Where is the Money Going?

The Obama economic stimulus program constitutes a continuation of the Bush administration's bank bailout packages. The proposed policy solution to the crisis becomes the cause, ultimately resulting in further real economy bankruptcies and a corresponding collapse of the standard of living of Americans. Both the Bush and Obama bank bailouts are intended to come to the rescue of troubled financial institutions, to ensure the payment of "inter-bank" debt operations. In practice, large amounts of money transit through the banking system, from the banks to the hedge funds, to offshore banking havens and back to the banks.

The government and the media tend to focus on the ambiguous notion of "inter-bank debts". The identity of the ultimate creditors is rarely mentioned. The legitimacy of the creditors is never questioned. Multibillion dollar transfers are conducted electronically from one financial entity to another. Where is the money going? Who is collecting these multibillion debts, which are in large part the consequence of financial manipulation and derivative trade?

There are indications that the financial institutions are transferring billions of dollars into their affiliated financial entities and hedge funds. From these hedge funds, money is also being used to acquire real economy assets. Through what circuitous financial mechanisms were these debts created? Where is the bailout money going? Who is cashing in on the multibillion dollar government bailout money? This process is contributing to an unprecedented concentration of private wealth.

Financial manipulation is an integral part of the New World Order. It constitutes a powerful means to accumulate wealth. It has contributed to destabilizing the U.S. fiscal structure. Under the present political arrangement, those responsible for monetary policy are quite deliberately serving the interests of the financiers, to the detriment of working people, leading to economic dislocation, unemployment and mass poverty.

More generally, this restructuring of global financial markets and institutions (alongside the pillage of national economies) has enabled the accumulation of vast amounts of private wealth, a large portion of which has been amassed as a result of strictly speculative transactions. This critical drain of billions of dollars of household savings and state tax revenues paralyzes the functions of government spending and spurs the accumulation of a public debt, which can no longer be financed through the emission of U.S. dollar denominated debt instruments.

What we are dealing with is the fraudulent confiscation of life-long savings and pension funds and the appropriation of tax revenues to finance the bank bailouts. To understand what has happened, follow the money trail of electronic transfers with a view to establishing where the money has gone. What is at stake is the outright criminalization of the financial system, financial theft on an unprecedented scale.

The monetary system, which is integrated into the state budgetary process, has been destabilized. The fundamental relationship between the monetary system and the real economy is in crisis. The creation of money "out of thin air" threatens the value of the U.S. dollar as an international currency. Similarly, the financing of a mammoth U.S. budget deficit through dollar denominated debt instruments is impaired as a result of exceedingly low interest rates. Moreover, the process of household savings is undermined with interest rates close to zero.

What we have dealt with in this chapter is one central aspect of an evolving process of global financial collapse. While the financial apparatus has not collapsed, the Great Depression of the 21st century is by no means over. We can expect a renewed wave of bank failures, mergers and acquisitions in the years to come.

Financial Disarmament

The complexity of this crisis is overwhelming. While specific *ad hoc* measures including the freeze of speculative trade can be envisaged, there are no ready solutions under the prevailing global financial architecture. What is at stake is the power configuration behind these measures. Economic policy quite deliberately serves the interests of the financial elites, who in turn control the political process. Meaningful policies cannot be achieved without radically reforming the workings of the international banking system.

What is required is an overhaul of the monetary system including the functions and ownership of the central bank, the arrest and prosecution of those involved in financial fraud both in the financial system and in governmental agencies, the freeze of all accounts where fraudulent transfers have been deposited and the cancellation of debts resulting from fraudulent trade and/or market manipulation.

People across the land, nationally and internationally, must mobilize. This struggle to democratize the financial and fiscal apparatus must be broad-based and democratic, encompassing all sectors of society at all levels, in all countries. What is ultimately required is to disarm the financial establishment:

- confiscate those assets which were obtained through fraud and financial manipulation
- restore the savings of households through reverse transfers
- restore home ownership to those who lost their homes through the process of foreclosures
- return the bailout money to the Treasury
- freeze the activities of the hedge funds
- freeze the gamut of speculative transactions including short-selling and derivative trade

◆

NOTES

1. Daniel R. Amerman, "AIG's Dangerous Collapse", *Financialsense*, http://www.financialsense.com/fsu/editorials/amerman/2008/0917.html, 17 September 2008.
2. Vikas Bajaj and Michael M. Grynbaum, "For Stocks, Worst Single-Day Drop in Two Decades", *New York Times*, http://www.nytimes.com/2008/09/30/business/30markets.html, 29 September 2008.
3. Eric Dash and Ben White, "Wells Fargo Swoops In", *New York Times*, http://www.nytimes.com/2008/10/04/business/04bank.html, 3 October 2008.
4. Michael M. Grynbaum, "Stocks Soar 11 Percent on Aid to Banks", *New York Times*, http://www.nytimes.com/2008/10/14/business/14markets.html, 13 October 2008.

5. The Financial Times, http://www.ft.com/home/us, 14 November 2008, emphasis added.

6. Eric Holme, Edward Klump and Linda Shen, "Buffett's Berkshire Boosts Stake in ConocoPhillips", *Bloomberg*, http://www.bloomberg.com/apps/news?pid=20601087&sid=aImc36VyXh0g, 14 November 2009.

7. The Financial Times, http://www.ft.com/home/us, 17 September 2008.

8. Wall Street Journal, http://online.wsj.com, 18 September 2008.

9. Paul Davidson, "Bernanke: Economy on verge of recovery, worst of crisis is over", *USA Today*, August 2009.

10. Gavin Jones and Ruth Pitchford, "Italy's Tremonti Says Worst of Crisis is Over", *Reuters*, May 2009.

11. *Asia Pacific Summit Statement*, November 2008.

12. Paul Krugman, "How Did Economists Get It So Wrong?", *New York Times*, 2 September 2009.

13. Laura Mandaro, "U.S. Economic Recovery Faces Possible 2010 Setback: Forecasters Raise U.S. Outlooks for This Year, Disagree Over Next", *MarketWatch*, 6 August 2009.

14. John Kenneth Galbraith, *The Great Crash*, Penguin, London, 1929.

15. Greg Burns, "Two Americans Share Nobel in Economics", *Chicago Tribune*, 15 October 1997.

16. Bikya Masr, "Tough Times for Suez Canal Continue", *Bikya Masr*, http://bikyamasre.com/?p=4728, 11 October 2009.

17. South China Morning Post, http://www.scmp.com/portal/site/SCMP, February 6, 2009; several reports in the Philippines media, February 2009.

18. Patrick O'Connor, "Warnings of Deep Recession as US Layoffs Spread Coast-to-Coast", *Global Research*, http://www.globalresearch.ca/index.php?context= va&aid=10743, 29 October 2009.

19. *Ibid*.

20. This section is in part based on the author's analysis in Chapter 28 of the *Globalization of Poverty and the New World Order* by Michel Chossudovsky, Global Research, Montreal, 2003.

21. *Ibid*.

22. *Ibid.*, p. 309-310.

23. Martin Khor, "Baring and the Search for a Rogue Culprit", *Third World Economics*, No. 108, 1-15, March 1995, p. 10.

24. *Bank for International Settlements Review*, No. 46, 1997.

25. Michel Chossudovsky, *The Globalization of Poverty and the New World Order, op. cit.*, Global Research, Montreal, 2003, Chapter 28.

26. New York Stock Exchange, www.nyse.com.

27. *Ibid.*
28. The Financial Times, "Five Years On, the Crash Still Echoes", *The Financial Times*, 19 October 1992.
29. Michel Chossudovsky, *The Globalization of Poverty and the New World Order, op. cit.*, Global Research, Montreal, 2003, Chapter 28.
30. Hong Kong Standard, "Broker Cleared of Manipulation", *Hong Kong Standard*, 1 November 1997.
31. Michel Chossudovsky, *The Globalization of Poverty and the New World Order*, Global Research, Montreal, 2003, *op. cit.*, p. 314.
32. Wall Street Journal, http://online.wsj.com, 8 November 2008.
33. Michel Chossudovsky, *The Globalization of Poverty and the New World Order*, Global Research, Montreal, 2003, *op. cit.*, Chapter 22.
34. *Ibid.*, Chapter 22.
35. *Ibid.*, Chapter 22.
36. Mark Drajem, "IMF, World Bank Reforms Leave Poor Behind, Bank Economist Finds", *Bloomberg*, 7 November 2000.
37. Michel Chossudovsky, *The Globalization of Poverty, op. cit.*, p. 314.
38. *Ibid,* p. 315.
39. Martin McLaughlin, "Clinton Republicans agree to Deregulation of US Banking System", *World Socialist Website*, http://www.wsws.org/index.shtml, http://www.wsws.org/articles/1999/nov1999/bank-n01.shtml, 1 November 1999.
40. *Ibid.*
41. *Ibid.*
42. The Financial Times, 9 November 1999, p. 21.
43. Michel Chossudovsky, unpublished notes on the 1999 Financial Services Modernization Act, *Legislation*, November 1999.
44. Michel Chossudovsky, "The Democrats Endorse the 'Global War on Terrorism': Obama 'goes after' Osama", *Global Research*, http://www.global research.ca/index.php?context=va&aid=9995, 29 August 2008.
45. *A New Era of Responsibility: The 2010 Budget*, See also Office of Management and Budget.
46. *Ibid.*
47. *Ibid.*
48. Bloomberg, http://www.bloomberg.com, 27 February 2010.
49. Kathleen Pender, "Government Bailout hits $8.5 Trillion", *San Francisco Chronicle*, 28 November 2009.
50. Detroit Free Press, "U.S. Budget Deficit to top $1.58 Trillion this Year", *Detroit Free Press*, http://www.freep.com, 26 August 2009.

CHAPTER 2

Death of the American Empire

Tanya Cariina Hsu

"I sincerely believe... that banking establishments are more dangerous than standing armies."

–U.S. President Thomas Jefferson; Letter to John Taylor, May 1816

America is dying. It is self-destructing and bringing the rest of the world down with it.

Often referred to as a sub-prime mortgage collapse, this obfuscates the real reason. By associating tangible useless failed mortgages, at least something 'real' can be blamed for the carnage.

The banking industry renamed insurance betting guarantees as "credit default swaps" and risky gambling wagers were called "derivatives".

Financial managers and banking executives were selling the ultimate con to the entire world, akin to the snake-oil salesmen from the 18th century but this time in suits and ties. And by October 2008, it was a quadrillion-dollar (that's 1 000 trillion dollar) industry that few could understand.[1]

Propped up by false hope, America is now falling like a house of cards.

The Beginning of the End

It all began in the early part of the 20th century. In 1907, J.P. Morgan, a private New York banker, published a rumor that a competing unnamed large bank was about to fail. It was a false charge but customers nonetheless raced to their banks to withdraw their money, in case it was their bank. As they pulled out their funds, the banks lost their cash deposits and were forced to call in their loans. People therefore had to pay back their mortgages to fill the banks with income, going bankrupt in the process. The 1907 panic resulted in a crash that prompted the creation of the Federal Reserve, a private banking cartel with the veneer of an independent government organization. Effectively, it was a coup by elite bankers in order to control the industry.

When signed into law in 1913, the Federal Reserve would loan and supply the nation's money, but with interest. The more money it was able to print, the more "income" it generated for itself. By its very nature, the Federal Reserve would forever keep producing debt to stay alive. It was able to print America's monetary supply at will, regulating its value. To control valuation, however, inflation had to be kept in check.

The Federal Reserve then doubled America's money supply within five years, and in 1920, it called in a mass percentage of loans. Over five thousand banks collapsed overnight. One year later, the Federal Reserve again increased the money supply by 62 percent, but in 1929, it again called the loans back in, *en masse*.[2] This time, the crash of 1929 caused over sixteen thousand banks to fail and an 89 percent plunge on the stock market.[3] The private and well-protected banks within the Federal Reserve system were able to snap up the failed banks at pennies on the dollar.

The nation fell into the Great Depression and in April 1933, President Roosevelt issued an executive order that confiscated all gold bullion from the public. Those who refused to turn in their gold would be imprisoned for ten years, and by the end of the year the gold standard was abolished.[4] What had been redeemable for gold became paper "legal tender", and gold could no longer be exchanged for cash as it had once been.

Later, in 1971, President Nixon removed the dollar from the gold standard altogether, therefore no longer trading at the internationally fixed price of 35 dollars. The U.S. dollar was now worth whatever the U.S. decided it was worth because it was "as good as gold". It had no standard of measure and became the universal currency. Treasury bills (short-term notes) and bonds (long-term notes) replaced gold as value, promissory notes of the U.S. government and paid for by the taxpayer. Additionally, gold could not be traced because it was exempt from currency reporting requirements, unlike the fiduciary (i.e. that based upon trust) monetary systems of the West. That was not in America's best interest.

After the Great Depression, private banks remained afraid to make home loans, so Roosevelt created Fannie Mae. A state-supported mortgage bank, it provided federal funding to finance home mortgages for affordable housing. In 1968, President Johnson privatized Fannie Mae, and in 1970, Freddie Mac was created to compete with Fannie Mae. Both of them bought mortgages from banks and other lenders and sold them on to new investors.

Flush With Cash

The post World War II boom had created an America flush with cash and assets. With its military industrial complex, war exponentially profited the U.S. and unlike any empire in history, it shot to superpower status. But it failed to remember that historically, whenever empires rose, they also fell in direct proportion.

Americans could afford all the modern conveniences, exporting their manufactured goods all over the world. After the Vietnam War, the U.S. went into an economic decline. But people were loath to give up their elevated standard of living despite the loss of jobs and production was increasingly sent overseas. A sense of delusion and entitlement kept Americans on the treadmill of consumer consumption.

In 1987 the U.S. stock market plunged by 22 percent in one day because of high-risk futures trading, called derivatives, and in 1989 the Savings & Loan crisis resulted in President George H. W. Bush using 142 billion dollars in taxpayer funds to rescue half of the S&Ls.[5] To do so, Freddie Mac was given the task of giving sub-prime (at or near prime-rate) mortgages to low-income families. In 2000, the "irrational exuberance" of the dot-com bubble burst, and fifty percent of high-tech firms went bankrupt, wiping five trillion dollars from their over-inflated market values.[6]

After this crisis, Federal Reserve Chairman Alan Greenspan kept interest rates so low they were less than the rate of inflation. Anyone saving his or her income actually lost money, and the savings rate soon fell into negative territory.

During the 1990s, advertisers went into overdrive, marketing an ever more luxurious lifestyle, all made available with cheap, easy credit. Second mortgages became commonplace, and home equity loans were used to pay credit card bills. The more Americans bought, the more they fell into debt. But as long as they had a house their false sense of security remained: their home was their equity, it would always go up in value, and they could always remortgage at lower rates if needed. The financial industry also believed that housing prices would forever climb, but should they ever fall the central bank would cut interest rates so that prices would jump back up. It was, everyone believed, a win-win situation.

Greenspan's rock-bottom interest rates let anyone afford a home. Minimum wage service workers with aspirations to buy a half million dollar house were able to secure one hundred percent loans, the mortgage lenders fully aware that they would not be able to keep up the payments. So many people received these sub-prime loans that the investment houses and lenders came up with a new scheme: bundle these virtually worthless home loans and sell them as solid U.S. investments to unsuspecting countries who would not know the difference. American lives of excess and consumer spending never suffered, and were being propped up by foreign nations none the wiser.

It has always been the case that a bank would lend out more than it actually had, because interest payments generated its income. The more the bank loaned, the more interest it collected even with no money in the vault. It was a lucrative industry of giving away money it never had in the first place. Mortgage banks and investment houses even borrowed money on international money markets to fund these one hundred percent plus sub-prime mortgages, and began lending more than ten times their underlying assets.

Post 9/11 Militarization: Financing the "Global War on Terrorism"

After 9/11, George Bush told the nation to spend, and during a time of war, that's what the nation did. It borrowed at unprecedented levels so as to pay not only for its war on terror in the Middle East (calculated to cost four trillion dollars) but also pay for tax cuts at the very time it should have increased taxes.[7] Bush removed the reserve requirements in Fannie Mae and Freddie

Mac, from ten percent to 2.5 percent. They were free to not only lend even more at bargain basement interest rates, but they only needed a fraction of reserves. Soon banks lent thirty times asset value. It was, as one economist put it, an "orgy of excess".[8]

It was flagrant overspending during a time of war. At no time in history has a nation gone into conflict without sacrifice, cutbacks, tax increases, and economic conservation. And there was a growing chance that, just like in 1929, investors would rush to claim their money all at once.

To guarantee, therefore, these high risk mortgages, the same financial houses that sold them then created "insurance policies" against the sub-prime investments they were selling, marketed as Credit Default Swaps (CDS). But the government must regulate insurance policies, so by calling them CDS they remained totally unregulated. Financial institutions were "hedging their bets" and selling premiums to protect the junk assets. In other words, the asset that should go up in value could also have a side-bet, just in case it might go down. By October 2008, CDS were trading at 62 trillion dollars, more than the stock markets of the whole world combined.[9]

These bets had absolutely no value whatsoever and were not investments. They were just financial instruments called derivatives – high stakes gambling, "nothing from nothing" – or as Warren Buffet referred to them, "Weapons of Financial Mass Destruction."[10] The derivatives trade was "worth" more than one quadrillion dollars, or larger than the economy of the entire world. (In September 2008, the global Gross Domestic Product was sixty trillion dollars).

Challenged as being illegal in the 1990s, Greenspan legalized the derivatives practice. Soon hedge funds became an entire industry, betting on the derivatives market and gambling as much as they wanted. It was easy because it was money they did not have in the first place. The industry had all the appearances of banks, but the hedge funds, equity funds, and derivatives brokers had no access to government loans in the event of a default. If the owners defaulted, the hedge funds had no money to pay "from nothing". Those who had hedged on an asset going up or down would not be able to collect on the winnings or losses.

The market had become the largest industry in the world, and all the financial giants were cashing in: Bear Stearns, Lehman

Brothers, Citigroup and AIG. But homeowners, long maxed out on their credit, were now beginning to default on their mortgages. Not only were they paying for their house but also all the debt amassed over the years for car, credit card and student loans, medical payments and home equity loans. They had borrowed to pay for groceries and skyrocketing health insurance premiums to keep up with their bigger houses and cars; they refinanced the debt they had for lower rates that soon ballooned. The average American owed 25 percent of their annual income to credit card debts alone.[11]

In 2008, housing prices began to slide precipitously downwards and mortgages were suddenly losing value. Manufacturing orders were down 4.5 percent by September, inventories began to pile up, unemployment was soaring and average house foreclosures had increased by 121 percent and up to 200 percent in California.[12]

The financial giants had to stop trading these mortgage-backed securities, as now their losses would have to be visibly accounted for. Investors began withdrawing their funds. Bear Stearns, heavily specialized in home loan portfolios, was the first to go in March.

The Wall Street Coup

Just as they had done in the 20th century, J.P. Morgan swooped in and picked up Bear Stearns for a pittance.[13] One year prior, Bear Stearns shares traded at 159 dollars but J.P. Morgan was able to buy in and take over at two dollars a share. In September 2008, Washington Mutual collapsed, the largest bank failure in history. J.P. Morgan again came in and paid 1.9 billion dollars for assets valued at 176 billion dollars.[14] It was a fire sale.

Relatively quietly over the summer Freddie Mac and Fannie Mae, the publicly traded companies responsible for eighty percent of the home mortgage loans, lost almost ninety percent of their value for the year. Together they were responsible for half the outstanding loan amounts but were now in debt eighty dollars to every one dollar in capital reserves.

To guarantee they would stay alive, the Federal Reserve stepped in and took over Freddie Mac and Fannie Mae. On September 7, 2008, they were put into "conservatorship", known as nationalization to the rest of the world, but Americans have difficulty with the idea of any government run industry that required tax-payer increases.

What the government was really doing was handing out an unlimited line of credit. Done by the Federal Reserve and not U.S. Treasury, it was able to bypass Congressional approval. The Treasury Department then auctioned off Treasury bills to raise money for the Federal Reserve's own use, but nonetheless the taxpayer would be funding the rescue. The bankers had bled tens of billions from the system by hedging and derivative gambling, and triggered the portfolio inter-bank lending freeze, which then seized up and crashed.

The takeover was presented as a government funded bailout of an arbitrary 700 billion dollars, which does nothing to solve the problem. No economists were asked to present their views to Congress, and the loan only perpetuates the myth that the bank-ing system is not really dead.

In reality, the damage will not be 700 billion dollars but closer to five trillion dollars, the value of Freddie Mac and Fannie Mae's mortgages. It was nothing less than a bailout of the quadrillion-dollar derivatives industry which otherwise faced payouts of over a trillion dollars on CDS mortgage-backed securities they had sold. It was necessary, said Treasury Secretary Henry Paulson, to save the country from a "housing correction". But, he added, the 700 billion dollar taxpayer funded takeover would not prevent other banks from collapsing, in turn causing a stock market crash.

In other words, Paulson was blackmailing Congress in order to lead a coup by the banking elite under the false guise of neces-sary legislation to stop the dyke from flooding. It merely shifted wealth from one class to another, as it had done almost a century prior. No sooner were the words were out of Paulson's mouth before other financial institutions began imploding and with them the disintegration of the global financial system – much modeled after the lauded system of American banking.

In September 2008 the Federal Reserve, its line of credit assured, then bought the world's largest insurance company, AIG, for 85 billion dollars for an eighty percent stake.[15] AIG was the largest seller of CDS, but now that it was in the position of having to pay out, from collateral it did not have, it was teetering on the edge of bankruptcy.

In October 2008, the entire country of Iceland went bankrupt, having bought American worthless sub-prime mortgages as investments.[16] European banks began exploding, all wanting to cash in concurrently on their inflated U.S. stocks to pay off the low interest rate debts before rates climbed higher. The year before the signs had been evident, when the largest U.S. mortgage lender Countrywide fell. Soon after, the largest lender in the U.K., Northern Rock, went under – London long having copied Wall Street creative financing. Japan and Korea's auto manufacturing nosedived by 37 percent, global economies contracting. Pakistan was on the edge of collapse too, with real reserves at three billion dollars – enough to only buy a month's supply of food and oil and attempting to stall payments to Saudi Arabia for the 100 000 barrels of oil per day it provides to the country.[17] Under President Musharraf, who left office in the nick of time, Pakistan's currency lost 25 percent of its value, its inflation running at 25 percent.

Meanwhile energy costs had soared, with oil reaching a peak of almost 150 dollars per barrel in the summer. The costs were immediately passed on to the already spent homeowner, in rising heating and fuel, transport and manufacturing costs. Yet, thirty percent of the cost of a barrel of oil was based upon Wall Street speculators, climbing to sixty percent as a speculative fear factor during the summer months. As soon as the financial crisis hit, suddenly oil prices slid down, slicing oil costs to 61 dollars from a high of 147 dollars in June and proving that the sixty percent speculation factor was far more accurate. This sudden decline also revealed OPEC's lack of control over spiraling prices during the past few years, almost lay squarely upon the shoulders of Saudi Arabia alone. When OPEC, in September 2008, sought to maintain higher prices by cutting production, it was Saudi Arabia who voted against such a move at the expense of its own revenue.

Europe then decided that no more would it be ruined by the excess of America. "Olde Europe" may have had enough of being dictated to by the U.S., who refused to compromise on loans lent to their own broken nations after WWII. On October 13, 2008, the once divided EU nations unilaterally agreed to an emergency rescue plan totaling 2.3 trillion dollars. It was more than three times greater than the U.S. package in payment for a catastrophe America alone had created.

By mid October 2008, the Dow, NASDAQ and S&P 500 had erased all the gains they made over the previous decade. Greenspan's pyramid scheme of easy money from nothing resulted in a massive overextension of credit, inflated housing prices and incredible stock valuations, achieved because investors would never withdraw their money all at once. But now it was crashing at breakneck speed and no solution in sight. President Bush said that people ought not to worry at all because "America is the most attractive destination for investors around the globe."[18]

◆

NOTES

1. Bank for International Settlements (BIS), *Triennial Central Bank Survey of Foreign Exchange and Derivatives Market Activity in 2007* – Final Results, 19 December 2007. Report available at http://www. bis.org/press/p071219.htm. The amounts actually exceeded one quadrillion dollars. According to the BIS report, outstanding derivatives worldwide had reached US $1.144 quadrillion, or US $1,144 trillion. This included Listed Credit Derivatives of $548 trillion, plus Over-The-Counter (OTC) notional (or face value) Derivatives of $596 trillion. The latter was comprised of Interest Rate Derivatives at or near $393+ trillion; Credit Default Swaps at or near $58+ trillion; Foreign Exchange Derivatives at or near $56+ trillion; Commodity Derivatives at or near $9 trillion; Equity Linked Derivatives at about $8.5 trillion; Unallocated Derivatives at about USD 71+ trillion. See also http://www.siliconvalleywatcher.com/ mt/archives/2008/10/the_size_of_der.php.
2. Murray N. Rothbard, *America's Great Depression*, Ludwig von Mises Institute, Auburn, 2000, p. 102.
3. Susan B. Carter, Scott Sigmund Gartner, Michael R. Haines, Alan L. Olmstead, Richard Sutch and Gavin Wright (Eds.), *Historical Statistics of the United States*, p. 235, 263, 1001, 1007.

4. *President Franklin D. Roosevelt Executive Order 6102*, 5 April 1933, requiring "all gold coin, gold bullion, and gold certificates" to be delivered to the Federal Reserve Bank by May 1st 1933 under a criminal penalty of a $10,000 fine, ten years' imprisonment, or both.

5. Dan Beighley, "Historical Perspectives", *Orange County Business Journal*, 13-19 October 2008. The FDIC places the total loss to the taxpayer even higher, at $153 billion; Timothy Curry and Lynn Shibut, "The Cost of the Savings and Loan Crisis: Truth and Consequences", *FDIC Banking Review*, July 2000.

6. NASDAQ Composite Index March 2000 – October 2002 (peak of 5048 to low of 1108).

7. David M. Herszenhorn, "Estimates of Iraq War Cost Were Not Close to Ballpark", *New York Times*, http://topics.nytimes.com/top/reference/times topics/people/h/david_m_herszenhorn/index.html?inline=nyt-per, 19 March 2008.

8. Speech by Richard W. Fisher to New York University, "Responding to Turbulence", *Federal Reserve Bank of Dallas*, 25 September 2008.

9. International Swaps and Derivatives Association, Inc. (ISDA), *Mid-Year 2008 Market Survey*.

10. BBC News, "Buffett Warns on Investment 'Time Bomb'", *BBC News*, http://news.bbc.co.uk/2/hi/2817995.stm, 4 March 2003.

11. Ben Woolsey and Matt Schulz, *Credit Card Statistics, Industry Facts, Debt Statistics*, Creditcards.com, 2008.

12. U.S. Census Bureau, *Manufacturers' Shipments, Inventories and Orders (M3)*, 2 July 2009; "Foreclosure Activity Up 14 Percent in Second Quarter: Activity Increases 121 Percent From Q2 2007", *Realty Trends*, August 2008, http://www.realtytrac.com/News-Trends/newsletter/2008/August.html; "California Foreclosures Up 200% From Last Year", *PRNewswire-USNewswire*, 6 September 2008.

13. Robin Sidel, Dennis K. Berman and Kate Kelly, "J.P. Morgan Buys Bear in Fire Sale, As Fed Widens Credit to Avert Crisis", *Wall Street Journal*, http://online.wsj.com/public/article_print/SB120569598608739825.html, 17 March 2008.

14. Robin Sidel, David Enrich and Dan Fitzpatrick, "WaMu Is Seized, Sold Off to J.P. Morgan, In Largest Failure in U.S. Banking History", *Wall Street Journal*, http://online.wsj.com/article/SB122238415586576687.html, 17 March 2008.

15. Matthew Karnitschnig, Deborah Solomon, Liam Pleven and Jon E. Hilsenrath, "U.S. to Take Over AIG in $85 Billion Bailout; Central Banks Inject Cash as Credit Dries Up", *Wall Street Journal*, http://

online.wsj.com/article/SB122156561931242905.html, 17 September 2008.

16. Ambrose Evans-Pritchard, "Financial Crisis: Countries at Risk of Bankruptcy from Pakistan to Baltics", *Telegraph*, http://www.telegraph.co.uk/finance/financetopics/financialcrisis/3174217/Financial-crisis-Countries-at-risk-of-bankruptcy-from-Pakistan-to-Baltics.html, 10 October 2008.

17. Isambard Wilkinson, "Pakistan Facing Bankruptcy", *Telegraph*, http://www.telegraph.co.uk/finance/financetopics/financialcrisis/3147266/Pakistan-facing-bankruptcy.html, 6 October 2008.

18. President George W. Bush, *Radio Address to the Nation*, 18 October 2008.

CHAPTER 3

Financial Implosion and Economic Stagnation

John Bellamy Foster and Fred Magdoff

> *But, you may ask, won't the powers that be step into the breach again and abort the crisis before it gets a chance to run its course? Yes, certainly. That, by now, is standard operating procedure, and it cannot be excluded that it will succeed in the same ambiguous sense that it did after the 1987 stock market crash. If so, we will have the whole process to go through again on a more elevated and more precarious level. But sooner or later, next time or further down the road, it will not succeed... We will then be in a new situation as unprecedented as the conditions from which it will have emerged.[1]*
>
> *–Harry Magdoff and Paul Sweezy (1988)*

Financial Crisis of a Magnitude Not Seen since the Great Depression

"The first rule of central banking," according to economist James K. Galbraith is that "when the ship starts to sink, central bankers must bail like hell."[2] In response to a financial crisis of a magnitude not seen since the Great Depression, the Federal Reserve and other central banks, backed by their treasury departments, have been "bailing like hell" for several years.

Beginning in July 2007 when the collapse of two Bear Stearns hedge funds that had speculated heavily in mortgage-backed securities signaled the onset of a major credit crunch, the Federal Reserve Board and the U.S. Treasury Department pulled out all the stops as finance imploded. They flooded the financial sector with hundreds of billions of dollars and promised to pour in trillions more if necessary – operating on a scale and with an array of tools that was unprecedented.

In an act of high drama, Federal Reserve Board Chairman Ben Bernanke and Secretary of the Treasury Henry Paulson appeared before Congress on the evening of September 18, 2008, during which the stunned lawmakers were told, in the words of Senator Christopher Dodd, "that we're literally days away from a complete meltdown of our financial system, with all the implications here at home and globally." This was immediately followed by Paulson's presentation of an emergency plan for a 700 billion dollar bailout of the financial structure, in which government funds would be used to buy up virtually worthless mortgage-backed securities (referred to as "toxic waste") held by financial institutions.[3]

The outburst of grassroots anger and dissent, following the Treasury secretary's proposal, led to an unexpected revolt in the U.S. House of Representatives, which voted down the bailout plan. Nevertheless, within a few days, Paulson's original plan (with some additions intended to provide political cover for representatives changing their votes) made its way through Congress. However, once the bailout plan passed, financial panic spread globally with stocks plummeting in every part of the world – as traders grasped the seriousness of the crisis. The Federal Reserve responded by literally deluging the economy with money, issuing a statement that it was ready to be the buyer of last resort for the entire commercial paper market (short-term debt issued by corporations), potentially to the tune of 1.3 trillion dollars.

Yet, despite the attempt to pour money into the system to effect the resumption of the most basic operations of credit, the economy found itself in liquidity trap territory, resulting in a hoarding of cash and a cessation of inter-bank loans as too risky for the banks compared to just holding money. A liquidity trap threatens when nominal interest rates fall close to zero. The usual monetary tool of lowering interest rates loses its effectiveness because of the inability to push interest rates below zero. In this situation the economy is beset by a sharp increase in what Keynes called the "propensity to hoard" cash or cash-like assets such as Treasury securities.

Fear for the future given what was happening in the deepening crisis meant that banks and other market participants sought the safety of cash, so whatever the Fed pumped in failed to stimulate lending. The drive to liquidity, partly reflected in purchases of Treasuries, pushed the interest rate on Treasuries down to a fraction of one percent, i.e., deeper into liquidity trap territory.[4]

Facing what *Business Week* called a "financial ice age", as lending ceased, the financial authorities in the United States and Britain, followed by the G-7 powers as a whole, announced that they would buy ownership shares in the major banks, in order to inject capital directly, recapitalizing the banks – a kind of partial nationalization. Meanwhile, they expanded deposit insurance. In the United States the government offered to guarantee 1.5 trillion dollars in new senior debt issued by banks. "All told," as the New York Times stated on October 15, 2008, only a month after the Lehman Brothers collapse that set off the banking crisis, "the potential cost to the government of the latest bailout package comes to $2.25 trillion, triple the size of the original $700 billion rescue package, which centered on buying distressed assets from banks."[5] But only a few days later the same paper ratcheted up its estimates of the potential costs of the bailouts overall, declaring:

> In theory, the funds committed for everything from the bailouts of Fannie Mae and Freddie Mac and those of Wall Street firm Bear Stearns and the insurer American International Group, to the financial rescue package approved by Congress, to providing guarantees to backstop selected financial markets [such as commercial paper] is a very big number indeed: an estimated $5.1 trillion.[6]

Despite all of this, the financial implosion has continued to widen and deepen, while sharp contractions in the "real economy" are everywhere to be seen. The major U.S. automakers are experiencing serious economic shortfalls, even after Washington agreed in September 2008 to provide the industry with 25 billion dollars in low interest loans. Single-family home construction has fallen to a 26 year low. Consumption is expected to experience record declines. Jobs are rapidly vanishing.[7] Given the severity of the financial and economic shock, there are now widespread fears among those at the center of corporate power that the financial implosion, even if stabilized enough to permit the orderly unwinding and settlement of the multiple insolvencies, will lead to a deep and lasting stagnation, such as hit Japan in the 1990s, or even a new Great Depression.[8]

The financial crisis, as the above suggests, was initially understood as a lack of money or liquidity (the degree to which assets can be traded quickly and readily converted into cash with relatively stable prices). The idea was that this liquidity problem could be solved by pouring more money into financial markets and by lowering interest rates. However, there are a lot of dollars out in the financial world, more now than before. The problem is that those who own the dollars are not willing to lend them to those who may not be able to pay them back, and that's just about everyone who needs the dollars these days. This then is better seen as a solvency crisis in which the balance sheet capital of the U.S. and U.K. financial institutions – and many others in their sphere of influence – has been wiped out by the declining value of the loans (and securitized loans) they own, their assets.

As an accounting matter, most major U.S. banks by the end of 2008 had become insolvent, resulting in a rash of fire-sale mergers, including J.P. Morgan Chase's purchase of Washington Mutual and Bear Stearns, Bank of America's absorption of Countrywide and Merrill Lynch, and Wells Fargo's acquiring of Wachovia. All of this is creating a more monopolistic banking sector with government support.[9] The direct injection of government capital into the banks in the form of the purchase of shares, together with bank consolidations, will at most buy the necessary time in which the vast mass of questionable loans can be liquidated in an orderly fashion, restoring solvency but at a far lower rate of economic activity – that of a serious recession or depression.

In this worsening crisis, no sooner is one hole patched than a number of others appear. The full extent of the loss in value of securitized mortgage, consumer and corporate debts, and the various instruments that attempted to combine such debts with forms of insurance against their default (such as the "synthetic collateralized debt obligations" which have credit-debt swaps "packaged in" with the CDOs), is still unknown. Key categories of such financial instruments were revalued down to ten to twenty percent in the course of the Lehman Brothers bankruptcy and the take-over of Merrill Lynch.[10] As sharp cuts in the value of such assets are applied across the board, the equity base of financial institutions vanishes along with trust in their solvency. Hence, banks are now doing what John Maynard Keynes said they would in such circumstances: hoarding cash.[11] Underlying all of this is the deteriorating economic condition of households at the base of the economy, impaired by decades of frozen real wages and growing consumer debt.

"It" and the Lender of Last Resort

To understand the full historical significance of these developments, it is necessary to look at what is known as the "lender of last resort" function of the U.S. and other capitalist governments. This has now taken the form of offering liquidity to the financial system in a crisis, followed by directly injecting capital into such institutions and finally, if needed, outright nationalizations. It is this commitment by the state to be the lender of last resort that over the years has ultimately imparted confidence in the system – despite the fact that the financial superstructure of the capitalist economy has far outgrown its base in what economists call the "real" economy of goods and services. Nothing therefore is more frightening to capital than the appearance of the Federal Reserve and other central banks doing everything they can to bail out the system and failing to prevent it from sinking further – something previously viewed as unthinkable. Although the Federal Reserve and the U.S. Treasury have been intervening massively, the full dimensions of the crisis still seem to elude them.

Some have called this a "Minsky moment". In 1982, economist Hyman Minsky, famous for his financial instability hypothesis, asked the critical question: "Can 'It' – a Great Depression – happen again?" There were, as he pointed out, no easy answers to this question. For Minsky the key issue was whether a financial meltdown could overwhelm a real economy already in trouble, as in the Great Depression. The inherently unstable financial system had grown in scale over the decades, but so had government and its capacity to serve as a lender of last resort. "The processes which make for financial instability," Minsky observed, "are an inescapable part of any decentralized capitalist economy – i.e. capitalism is inherently flawed – but financial instability need not lead to a great depression; 'It' need not happen."[12]

Implicit, in this, however, was the view that "It" could still happen again – if only because the possibility of financial explosion and growing instability could conceivably outgrow the government's capacity to respond – or to respond quickly and decisively enough.

Theoretically, the capitalist state, particularly that of the United States, which controls what amounts to a surrogate world currency, has the capacity to avert such a dangerous crisis. The chief worry is a massive "debt-deflation" (a phenomenon explained by economist Irving Fisher during the Great Depression) as exhibited not only by the experience of the 1930s but also Japan in the 1990s. In this situation, as Fisher wrote in 1933, "deflation caused by the debt reacts on the debt. Each dollar of debt still unpaid becomes a bigger dollar, and if the over-indebtedness with which we started was great enough, the liquidation of debt cannot keep up with the fall of prices which it causes." Put differently, prices fall as debtors sell assets to pay their debts, and as prices fall the remaining debts must be repaid in dollars more valuable than the ones borrowed, causing more defaults, leading to yet lower prices, and thus a deflationary spiral.[13]

The economy is still not in this dire situation, but the specter looms. As Paul Asworth, chief U.S. economist at Capital Economics, stated in mid-October 2008, "With the unemployment rate rising rapidly and capital markets in turmoil, pretty much everything points toward deflation. The only thing you can hope is that the prompt action from policy makers can maybe head this off first." *The Economist* warned in early October:

> The rich world's economies are already suffering from a mild case of this 'debt-deflation.' The combination of falling house prices and credit contraction is forcing debtors to cut spending and sell assets, which in turn pushes house prices and other asset markets down further... A general fall in consumer prices would make matters even worse.[14]

The very thought of such events recurring in the U.S. economy today was supposed to be blocked by the lender of last resort function, based on the view that the problem was primarily monetary and could always be solved by monetary means by flooding the economy with liquidity at the least hint of danger. Thus Federal Reserve Board Chairman Ben Bernanke gave a talk in 2002 (as a Federal Reserve governor) significantly entitled "Deflation: Making Sure 'It' Doesn't Happen Here". In it he contended that there were ample ways of ensuring that "It" would not happen today, despite increasing financial instability:

> The U.S. government has a technology, called a printing press (or, today, its electronic equivalent) that allows it to produce as many U.S. dollars as it wishes at essentially no cost. By increasing the number of U.S. dollars in circulation, or even by credibly threatening to do so, the U.S. government can also reduce the value of a dollar in terms of goods and services, which is equivalent to raising the prices in dollars of those goods and services. We conclude that, under a paper-money system, a determined government can always generate higher spending and hence positive inflation.

> Of course, the U.S. government is not going to print money and distribute it willy-nilly (although as we will see later, there are practical policies that approximate this behavior). Normally, money is injected into the economy through asset purchases by the Federal Reserve. To stimulate aggregate spending when short-term interest rates have reached zero, the Fed must expand the scale of its asset purchases or, possibly, expand the menu of assets that it buys. Alternatively, the Fed, could find other ways of injecting money into the system – for example, by making low-interest-rate loans to banks or cooperating with fiscal authorities.[15]

In the same talk, Bernanke suggested that "a money-financed tax cut," aimed at avoiding deflation in such circumstances, was "essentially equivalent to Milton Friedman's famous 'helicopter drop' of money" – a stance that earned him the nickname "Helicopter Ben".[16]

An academic economist, who made his reputation through studies of the Great Depression, Bernanke was a product of the view propounded most influentially by Milton Friedman and Anna Schwartz in their famous work, *A Monetary History of the United States, 1867-1960*, that the cause of the Great Depression was monetary and could have been combated almost exclusively in monetary terms. The failure to open the monetary floodgates at the outset, according to Friedman and Schwartz, was the principal reason that the economic downturn was so severe.[17] Bernanke strongly opposed earlier conceptions of the Depression that saw it as based in the structural weaknesses of the "real" economy and the underlying accumulation process. Speaking on the 75th anniversary of the 1929 stock market crash, he stated:

> During the Depression itself, and in several decades following, most economists argued that monetary factors were not an important cause of the Depression. For example, many observers pointed to the fact that nominal interest rates were close to zero during much of the Depression, concluding that monetary policy had been about as easy as possible yet had produced no tangible benefit to the economy. The attempt to use monetary policy to extricate an economy from a deep depression was often compared to "pushing on a string".

During the first decades after the Depression, most economists looked to developments on the real side of the economy for explanations, rather than to monetary factors. Some argued, for example, that overinvestment and overbuilding had taken place during the ebullient 1920s, leading to a crash when the returns on those investments proved to be less than expected. Another once-popular theory was that a chronic problem of "under-consumption" – the inability of households to purchase enough goods and services to utilize the economy's productive capacity – had precipitated the slump.[18]

Bernanke's answer to all of this was to reassert that monetary factors virtually alone precipitated (and explained) the Great Depression, and were the key, indeed almost the sole, means of fighting debt-deflation. The trends in the real economy, such as the emergence of excess capacity in industry, need hardly be addressed at all. At most it was a deflationary threat to be countered by reflation.[19] Nor, as he argued elsewhere, was it necessary to explore Minsky's contention that the financial system of the capitalist economy was inherently unstable, since this analysis depended on the economic irrationality associated with speculative manias, and thus departed from the formal "rational economic behavior" model of neoclassical economics.[20] Bernanke concluded a talk commemorating Friedman's ninetieth birthday in 2002 with the words: "I would like to say to Milton and Anna: Regarding the Great Depression. You're right, we did it. We're very sorry. But thanks to you, we won't do it again."[21] "It" of course was the Great Depression.

Following the 2000 stock market crash, a debate arose in central bank circles about whether "preemptive attacks" should be made against future asset bubbles to prevent such economic catastrophes. Bernanke, representing the reigning economic orthodoxy, led the way in arguing that this should not be attempted, since it was difficult to know whether a bubble was actually a bubble (that is, whether financial expansion was justified by economic fundamentals or new business models or not). In addition, to prick a bubble was to invite disaster, as in the attempts by the Federal Reserve Board to do this in the late 1920s, leading (according to the monetarist interpretation) to the bank failures and the Great Depression. He concluded:

> Monetary policy cannot be directed finely enough to guide asset prices without risking severe collateral damage to the economy... Although eliminating volatility from the economy and the financial markets will never be possible, we should be able to moderate it without sacrificing the enormous strengths of our free-market system.

In short, Bernanke argued, no doubt with some justification given the nature of the system, that the best the Federal Reserve Board could do in face of a major bubble was to restrict itself primarily to its lender of last resort function.[22]

At the very peak of the housing bubble, Bernanke, then chairman of Bush's Council of Economic Advisors, declared with eyes wide shut:

> House prices have risen by nearly 25 percent over the past two years. Although speculative activity has increased in some areas, at a national level these price increases largely reflect strong economic fundamentals, including robust growth in jobs and incomes, low mortgage rates, steady rates of household formation, and factors that limit the expansion of housing supply in some areas.[23]

Ironically, it was these views that led to the appointment of Bernanke as Federal Reserve Board chairman (replacing Alan Greenspan) in early 2006.

The housing bubble began to deflate in early 2006 at the same time that the Fed was raising interest rates in an attempt to contain inflation. The result was a collapse of the housing sector and mortgage-backed securities. Confronted with a major financial crisis beginning in 2007, Bernanke as Fed chairman put the printing press into full operation, flooding the nation and the world with dollars, and soon found to his dismay that he had been "pushing on a string". No amount of liquidity infusions were able to overcome the insolvency in which financial institutions were mired. Unable to make good on their current financial claims – were they compelled to do so – banks refused to renew loans as they came due and hoarded available cash rather than lending and leveraging the system back up. The financial crisis soon became so universal that the risks of lending money skyrocketed, given that many previously creditworthy borrowers were now quite possibly on the verge of insolvency. In a liquidity trap, as Keynes taught, running the printing presses simply adds to the hoarding of money but not to new loans and spending.

However, the real root of the financial bust, we shall see, went much deeper: the stagnation of production and investment.

From Financial Explosion to Financial Implosion

Our argument in a nutshell is that both the financial explosion in recent decades and the financial implosion now taking place are to be explained mainly in reference to stagnation tendencies within the underlying economy. A number of other explanations for the current crisis (most of them focusing on the proximate causes) have been given by economists and media pundits. These include the lessening of regulations on the financial system; the very low interest rates introduced by the Fed to counter the effects of the 2000 crash of the "New Economy" stock bubble, leading to the housing bubble; and the selling of large amounts of sub-prime mortgages to many people that could not afford to purchase a house and/or did not fully understand the terms of the mortgages.

Much attention has rightly been paid to the techniques whereby mortgages were packaged together and then sliced and diced and sold to institutional investors around the world. Outright fraud may also have been involved in some of the financial shenanigans. The falling home values following the bursting of the housing bubble and the inability of many sub-prime mortgage holders to continue to make their monthly payments, together with the resulting foreclosures, was certainly the straw that broke the camel's back, leading to this catastrophic system failure. And few would doubt today that it was all made worse by the deregulation fervor avidly promoted by the financial firms, which left them with fewer defenses when things went wrong.

Nevertheless, the root problem went much deeper, and was to be found in a real economy experiencing slower growth, giving rise to financial explosion as capital sought to "leverage" its way out of the problem by expanding debt and gaining speculative profits.

Already by the late 1980s the seriousness of the situation was becoming clear to those not wedded to established ways of thinking. Looking at this condition in 1988 on the anniversary of the 1987 stock market crash, *Monthly Review* editors Harry Magdoff and Paul Sweezy, contended that sooner or later – no one could predict when or exactly how – a major crisis of the financial system that overpowered the lender of last resort function was likely to occur. This was simply because the whole precarious financial superstructure would have by then grown to such a scale that the means of governmental authorities, though massive, would no longer be sufficient to keep back the avalanche, especially if they failed to act quickly and decisively enough. As they put it, the next time around it was quite possible that the rescue effort would "succeed in the same ambiguous sense that it did after the 1987 stock market crash. If so, we will have the whole process to go through again on a more elevated and precarious level. But sooner or later, next time or further down the road, it will not succeed," generating a severe crisis of the economy.

As an example of a financial avalanche waiting to happen, they pointed to the "high flying Tokyo stock market," as a possible prelude to a major financial implosion and a deep stagnation to follow – a reality that was to materialize soon after, resulting in Japan's financial crisis and "Great Stagnation" of the 1990s. Asset values (both in the stock market and real estate) fell by an amount equivalent to more than two years of GDP. As interest rates zeroed-out and debt-deflation took over, Japan was stuck in a classic liquidity trap with no ready way of restarting an economy already deeply mired in overcapacity in the productive economy.[24]

"In today's world ruled by finance," Magdoff and Sweezy had written in 1987 in the immediate aftermath of the U.S. stock market crash:

> The underlying growth of surplus value falls increasingly short of the rate of accumulation of money capital. In the absence of a base in surplus value, the money capital amassed becomes more and more nominal, indeed fictitious. It comes from the sale and purchase of paper assets, and is based on the assumption that asset values will be continuously inflated. What we have, in other words, is ongoing speculation grounded in the belief that, despite fluctuations in price, asset values will forever go only one way – upward! Against this background, the October [1987] stock market crash assumes a far-reaching significance. By demonstrating the fallacy of an unending upward movement in asset values, it exposes the irrational kernel of today's economy.[25]

These contradictions, associated with speculative bubbles, have of course to some extent been endemic to capitalism throughout its history. However, in the post-Second World War era, as Magdoff and Sweezy, in line with Minsky, argued, the debt overhang became larger and larger, pointing to the growth of a problem that was cumulative and increasingly dangerous. In *The End of Prosperity* Magdoff and Sweezy wrote: "In the absence of a severe depression during which debts are forcefully wiped out or drastically reduced, government rescue measures to prevent collapse of the financial system merely lay the groundwork for still more layers of debt and additional strains during the next economic advance." As Minsky put it, "Without a crisis and a debt-deflation process to offset beliefs in the success of speculative ventures, both an upward bias to prices and ever-higher financial layering are induced."[26]

To the extent that mainstream economists and business analysts themselves were momentarily drawn to such inconvenient questions, they were quickly cast aside. Although the spectacular growth of finance could not help but create jitters from time to time – for example, Alan Greenspan's famous reference to "irrational exuberance" – the prevailing assumption, promoted by Greenspan himself, was that the growth of debt and speculation represented a new era of financial market innovation, i.e., a sustainable structural change in the business model associated with revolutionary new risk management techniques. Greenspan was so enamored of the "New Economy" made possible by financialization that he noted in 2004: "Not only have individual financial institutions become less vulnerable to shocks from underlying risk factors, but also the financial system as a whole has become more resilient."[27]

It was only with the onset of the financial crisis in 2007 and its persistence into 2008, that we find financial analysts in surprising places openly taking on the contrary view. Thus as Manas Chakravarty, an economic columnist for India's investor website, Livemint.com (partnered with the Wall Street Journal), observed on September 17, 2008, in the context of the Wall Street meltdown:

> American economist Paul Sweezy pointed out long ago that stagnation and enormous financial speculation emerged as symbiotic aspects of the same deep-seated, irreversible economic impasse. He said the stagnation of the underlying economy meant that business was increasingly dependent on the growth of finance to preserve and enlarge its money capital and that the financial superstructure of the economy could not expand entirely independently of its base in the underlying productive economy. With remarkable prescience, Sweezy said the bursting of speculative bubbles would, therefore, be a recurring and growing problem.[28]

Of course, Paul Baran and Sweezy in *Monopoly Capital*, and later on Magdoff and Sweezy in *Monthly Review*, had pointed to other forms of absorption of surplus such as government spending (particularly military spending), the sales effort, the stimulus provided by new innovations, etc.[29] But all of these, although important, had proven insufficient to maintain the economy at anything like full employment, and by the 1970s the system was mired in deepening stagnation (or stagflation). It was financialization – and the growth of debt that it actively promoted – which was to emerge as the quantitatively most important stimulus to demand. But it pointed unavoidably to a day of financial reckoning and cascading defaults.

Back to the Real Economy: The Stagnation Problem

Paul Baran, Paul Sweezy and Harry Magdoff argued indefatigably from the 1960s to the 1990s (most notably in *Monopoly Capital*) that stagnation was the normal state of the monopoly-capitalist economy, barring special historical factors. The prosperity that characterized the economy in the 1950s and 1960s, they insisted, was attributable to such temporary historical factors as: (1) the build-up of consumer savings during the war; (2) a second great wave of automobilization in the United States (including the expansion of the glass, steel and rubber industries, the construction of the interstate highway system and the development of suburbia); (3) the rebuilding of the European and the Japanese economies devastated by the war; (4) the Cold War arms race (and two regional wars in Asia); (5) the growth of the sales effort marked by the rise of Madison Avenue; (6) the expansion of FIRE (finance, insurance and real estate); and (7) the pre-eminence of the dollar as the hegemonic currency. Once the extraordinary stimulus from these factors waned, the economy began to subside back into stagnation: slow growth and rising excess capacity and unemployment/underemployment. In the end,

TABLE 2.1 U.S. Domestic Debt and GDP (trillions of dollars)

	GDP	Total debt	Debt by sector			
			Household	Financial firms	Non-fianncial business	Government (local, state, & federal)
1970	1.0	1.5	0.5	0.1	0.5	0.4
1980	2.7	4.5	1.4	0.6	1.5	1.1
1990	5.8	13.5	3.6	2.6	3.7	3.5
2000	9.8	26.3	7.0	8.1	6.6	4.6
2007	13.8	47.7	13.8	16.0	10.6	7.3

* The federal part of local, state, and federal debt includes only that portion held by the public. The total debt in 2007 when the federal debt held by federal agencies is added is $51.5 trillion.

Sources: Flow of Funds Accounts of the United States, Table L.1 Credit Market Debt Outstanding, Federal Reserve and Table B-1, Gross domestic product, 1959-2007, Economic Report of the President, 2008.

it was military spending and the explosion of debt and speculation that constituted the main stimuli keeping the economy out of the doldrums. These were not sufficient, however, to prevent the reappearance of stagnation tendencies altogether, and the problem got worse with time.[31]

The reality of creeping stagnation can be seen in table 2.2, which shows the real growth rates of the economy decade by decade over the last eight decades. The low growth rate in the 1930s reflected the deep stagnation of the Great Depression. This was followed by the extraordinary rise of the U.S. economy in the 1940s under the impact of the Second World War. During the years 1950-69, now often referred to as an economic "Golden Age", the economy, propelled by the set of special historical factors referred to above, was able to achieve strong economic growth in a "peacetime" economy. This, however, proved to be all too temporary. The sharp drop off in growth rates in the 1970s and thereafter points to a persistent tendency toward slower expansion in the economy, as the main forces pushing up growth rates in the 1950s and 1960s waned, preventing the economy from returning to its former prosperity. In subsequent decades, rather than recovering its former trend-rate of growth, the economy slowly subsided.

TABLE 2.2 Growth in Real GDP 1930-2007 (U.S.)

	Average annual percent
1930s	1.3
1940s	5.9
1950s	4.1
1960s	4.4
1970s	3.3
1980s	3.1
1990s	3.1
2000-07	2.6

Source: National Income and Products Accounts Table 1.1.1. Percent Change from Preceding Period in Real Gross Domestic Product, Bureau of Economic Analysis.

It was the reality of economic stagnation beginning in the 1970s, as heterodox economists Riccardo Bellofiore and Joseph Halevi have recently emphasized, that led to the emergence of "the new financialized capitalist regime," a kind of "paradoxical financial Keynesianism" whereby demand in the economy was stimulated primarily "thanks to asset-bubbles." Moreover, it was the leading role of the United States in generating such bubbles – despite (and also because of) the weakening of capital accumulation proper – together with the dollar's reserve currency status, that made U.S. monopoly-finance capital the "catalyst of world effective demand," beginning in the 1980s.[32] But such a financialized growth pattern was unable to produce rapid economic advance for any length of time, and was unsustainable, leading to bigger bubbles that periodically burst, bringing stagnation more and more to the surface.

A key element in explaining this whole dynamic is to be found in the falling ratio of wages and salaries as a percentage of national income in the United States. Stagnation in the 1970s led capital to launch an accelerated class war against workers to raise profits by pushing labor costs down. The result was decades of increasing inequality.[33] Chart 2.1 shows a sharp decline in the share of wages and salaries in GDP between the late 1960s and the present. This reflected the fact that real wages of private non-agricultural workers in the United States (in 1982 dollars) peaked in 1972 at $8.99 per hour, and by 2006 had fallen to $8.24 (equivalent to the real hourly wage rate in 1967), despite the enormous growth in productivity and profits over the past few decades.[34]

This was part of a massive redistribution of income and wealth to the top. Over the years 1950 to 1970, for each additional dollar made by those in the bottom ninety percent of income earners, those in the top 0.01 percent received an additional 162 dollars. In contrast, from 1990 to 2002, for each added dollar made by those in the bottom ninety percent, those in the uppermost 0.01 percent (today around 14 000 households) made an additional 18 000 dollars. In the United States the top one percent of wealth holders in 2001 together owned more than twice as much as the bottom eighty percent of the population. If this were measured simply in terms of financial wealth, i.e., excluding equity in owner-occupied housing, the top one percent owned more than four times the bottom eighty percent. Between 1983 and 2001, the

CHART 2.1 Wage and Salary Disbursements as a Percentage of GDP (U.S.)

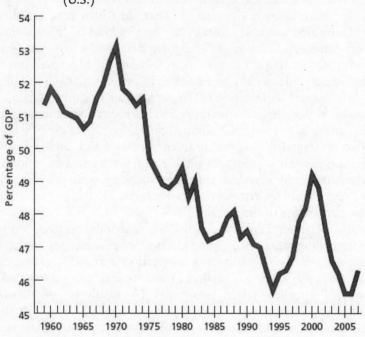

Sources: Economic Report of the President, 2008, Table B-1 (GDP), Table B-29—Sources of personal income, 1959-2007.

top one percent grabbed 28 percent of the rise in national income, 33 percent of the total gain in net worth, and 52 percent of the overall growth in financial worth.[35]

The truly remarkable fact under these circumstances was that household consumption continued to rise from a little over sixty percent of GDP in the early 1960s to around seventy percent in 2007. This was only possible because of more two-earner households (as women entered the labor force in greater numbers), people working longer hours and filling multiple jobs, and a constant ratcheting up of consumer debt. Household debt was spurred, particularly in the later stages of the housing bubble, by a dramatic rise in housing prices, allowing consumers to borrow more against their increased equity (the so-called housing "wealth effect") – a process that came to a sudden end when the bubble popped, and housing prices started to fall. Household debt increased from about forty percent of GDP in 1960 to one hundred percent of GDP in 2007, with an especially sharp increase starting in the late 1990s.[36]

This growth of consumption, based in the expansion of household debt, was to prove to be the Achilles heel of the economy. The housing bubble was based on a sharp increase in household mortgage-based debt, while real wages had been essentially frozen for decades. The resulting defaults among marginal new owners led to a fall in house prices. This led to an ever increasing number of owners owing more on their houses than they were worth, creating more defaults and a further fall in house prices. Banks seeking to bolster their balance sheets began to hold back on new extensions of credit card debt. Consumption fell, jobs were lost, capital spending was put off, and a downward spiral of unknown duration began.

During the last thirty or so years the economic surplus controlled by corporations, and in the hands of institutional investors, such as insurance companies and pension funds, has poured in an ever increasing flow into an exotic array of financial instruments. Little of the vast economic surplus was used to expand investment, which remained in a state of simple reproduction, geared to mere replacement (albeit with new, enhanced technology), as opposed to expanded reproduction. With corporations unable to find the demand for their output – a reality reflected in the long-run decline of capacity utilization in industry – and therefore confronted with a dearth of profitable investment opportunities, the process of net capital formation became more and more problematic.

Hence, profits were increasingly directed away from investment in the expansion of productive capacity and toward financial speculation, while the financial sector seemed to generate unlimited types of financial products designed to make use of this money capital. (The same phenomenon existed globally, causing Bernanke to refer in 2005 to a "global savings glut", with enormous amounts of investment-seeking capital circling the world and increasingly drawn to the United States because of its leading role in financialization.)[37]

Since financialization can be viewed as the response of capital to the stagnation tendency in the real economy, a crisis of financialization inevitably means a resurfacing of the underlying stagnation endemic to the advanced capitalist economy. The deleveraging of the enormous debt built up during recent decades is now contributing to a deep crisis. Moreover, with financialization arrested there is no other visible way out for monopoly-finance capital. The prognosis then is that the economy, even after the immediate devaluation crisis is stabilized, will at best be characterized for some time by minimal growth, and by high unemployment, underemployment, and excess capacity.

The fact that U.S. consumption (facilitated by the enormous U.S. current account deficit) has provided crucial effective demand for the production of other countries means that the slowdown in the United States is already having disastrous effects abroad, with financial liquidation now in high gear globally. "Emerging" and underdeveloped economies are caught in a bewildering set of problems. This includes falling exports, declining commodity prices, and the repercussions of high levels of financialization on top of an unstable and highly exploitative economic base – while being subjected to renewed imperial pressures from the center states.

The center states are themselves in trouble. Iceland, which has been compared to the canary in the coal mine, has experienced a complete financial meltdown, requiring rescue from outside, and possibly a massive raiding of the pension funds of the citizenry. For more than seventeen years Iceland has had a right-wing government led by the ultra-conservative Independence Party in coalition with the centrist social democratic parties. Under this leadership Iceland adopted neoliberal financialization and speculation to the hilt and saw an excessive growth of its banking and finance sectors with total assets of its banks growing from 96 percent of its GDP at the end of 2000 to nine times its GDP in 2006. Now Icelandic taxpayers, who were not responsible for these actions, are being asked to carry the burden of the overseas speculative debts of their banks, resulting in a drastic decline in the standard of living.[38]

A Political Economy

Economics in its classical stage, which encompassed the work of both possessive-individualists, like Adam Smith, David Ricardo, Thomas Malthus and John Stuart Mill, and socialist thinkers such as Karl Marx, was called political economy. The name was significant because it pointed to the class basis of the economy and the role of the state.[39] To be sure, Adam Smith introduced the notion of the "invisible hand" of the market in replacing the former visible hand of the monarch. But, the political-class context of economics was nevertheless omnipresent for Smith and all the other classical economists. In the 1820s, as Marx observed, there were "splendid tournaments" between political economists representing different classes (and class fractions) of society.

However, from the 1830s and 1840s on, as the working class arose as a force in society, and as the industrial bourgeoisie gained firm control of the state, displacing landed interests (most notably with the repeal of the Corn Laws), economics shifted from its previous questioning form to the "bad conscience and evil intent of the apologetics."[40] Increasingly the circular flow of economic life was reconceptualized as a process involving only individuals, consuming, producing and profiting on the margin. The concept of class thus disappeared in economics, but was embraced by the rising field of sociology (in ways increasingly abstracted from fundamental economic relationships). The state also was said to have nothing directly to do with economics and was taken up by the new field of political science.[41] Economics was thus "purified" of all class and political elements, and increasingly presented as a seemingly neutral science, addressing universal/transhistorical principles of capital and market relations.

Having lost any meaningful roots in society, orthodox neoclassical economics, which presented itself as a single paradigm, became a discipline dominated by largely meaningless abstractions, mechanical models, formal methodologies and mathematical language, divorced from historical developments. It was anything but a science of the real world; rather its chief importance lay in its role as a self-confirming ideology. Meanwhile, actual business proceeded along its own lines largely oblivious (sometimes intentionally so) of orthodox economic theories.

The failure of received economics to learn the lessons of the Great Depression, i.e., the inherent flaws of a system of class-based accumulation in its monopoly stage, included a tendency to ignore the fact that the real problem lay in the real economy, rather than in the monetary-financial economy.

Today nothing looks more myopic than Bernanke's quick dismissal of traditional theories of the Great Depression that traced the underlying causes to the buildup of overcapacity and weak demand – inviting a similar dismissal of such factors today. Like his mentor Milton Friedman, Bernanke has stood for the dominant, neoliberal economic view of the last few decades, with its insistence that by holding back "the rock that starts a landslide" it was possible to prevent a financial avalanche of "major proportions" indefinitely.[42] That the state of the ground above was shifting, and that this was due to real, time-related processes, was of no genuine concern. Ironically, Bernanke, the academic expert on the Great Depression, adopted what had been described by Ethan Harris, chief U.S. economist for Barclays Capital, as a "see no evil, hear no evil, speak no evil" policy with respect to asset bubbles.[43]

It is therefore to the contrary view, emphasizing the socioeconomic contradictions of the system, to which it is now necessary to turn. For a time in response to the Great Depression of the 1930s, in the work of John Maynard Keynes, and various other thinkers associated with the Keynesian, institutionalist and Marxist traditions – the most important of which was the Polish economist Michael Kalecki – there was something of a revival of political-economic perspectives. But following the Second World War Keynesianism was increasingly reabsorbed into the system. This occurred partly through what was called the "neoclassical-Keynesian synthesis" – which, as Joan Robinson, one of Keynes' younger colleagues claimed, had the effect of bastardizing Keynes – and partly through the closely related growth of military Keynesianism.[44] Eventually, monetarism emerged as the ruling response to the stagflation crisis of the 1970s, along with the rise of other conservative free-market ideologies, such as supply-side theory, rational expectations and the new classical economics (summed up as neoliberal orthodoxy). Economics lost its explicit political-economic cast, and the world was led back once again to the mythology of self-regulating, self-equilibrating markets free of issues of class and power. Anyone who questioned this, was characterized as political rather than economic, and thus largely excluded from the mainstream economic discussion.[45]

Needless to say, economics never ceased to be political; rather the politics that was promoted was so closely intertwined with the system of economic power as to be nearly invisible. Adam Smith's visible hand of the monarch had been transformed into the invisible hand, not of the market, but of the capitalist class, which was concealed behind the veil of the market and competition. Yet, with every major economic crisis that veil has been partly torn aside and the reality of class power exposed.

Treasury Secretary Paulson's request to Congress in September 2008, for 700 billion dollars with which to bail out the financial system may constitute a turning point in the popular recognition of, and outrage over, the economic problem, raising for the first time in many years the issue of a political economy. It immediately became apparent to the entire population that the critical question in the financial crisis and in the deep economic stagnation that was emerging was: Who will pay? The answer of the capitalist system, left to its own devices, was the same as always: the costs would be borne disproportionately by those at the bottom. The old game of privatization of profits and socialization of losses would be replayed for the umpteenth time. The population would be called upon to "tighten their belts" to foot "the bill" for the entire system. The capacity of the larger public to see through this deception in the months and years ahead will of course depend on an enormous amount of education by trade union and social movement activists, and the degree to which the empire of capital is stripped naked by the crisis.

There is no doubt that the present growing economic bankruptcy and political outrage have produced a fundamental break in the continuity of the historical process. How should progressive forces approach this crisis? First of all, it is important to discount any attempts to present the serious economic problems that now face us as a kind of "natural disaster". They have a cause, and it lies in the system itself. And although those at the top of the economy certainly did not welcome the crisis, they nonetheless have been the main beneficiaries of the system, shamelessly enriching themselves at the expense of the rest of the population, and should be held responsible for the main burdens now imposed on society. It is the well-to-do who should foot the bill – not only for reasons of elementary justice, but also because they collectively and their system constitute the reason that things are as bad as they are; and because the best way to help both the economy and those at the bottom is to address the needs of the latter directly. There should be no golden parachutes for the capitalist class paid for at taxpayer expense.

But capitalism takes advantage of social inertia, using its power to rob outright when it can't simply rely on "normal" exploitation. Without a revolt from below the burden will simply be imposed on those at the bottom. All of this requires a mass social and economic upsurge, such as in the latter half of the 1930s, including the revival of unions and mass social movements of all kinds, using the power for change granted to the people in the Constitution; even going so far as to threaten the current duopoly of the two-party system.

What should such a radical movement from below, if it were to emerge, seek to do under these circumstances? Here we hesitate to say, not because there is any lack of needed actions to take, but because a radicalized political movement determined to sweep away decades of exploitation, waste and irrationality will, if it surfaces, be like a raging storm, opening whole new vistas for change. Anything we suggest at this point runs the double risk of appearing far too radical now and far too timid later on.

Some liberal economists and commentators argue that, given the present economic crisis, nothing short of a major public works program aimed at promoting employment, a kind of new New Deal, will do. Robert Kuttner has argued in Obama's Challenge that "an economic recovery will require more like 700 billion dollars a year in new public outlay, or 600 billion dollars counting offsetting cuts in military spending. Why? Because there is no other plausible strategy for both achieving a general economic recovery and restoring balance to the economy."[46] This, however, will be more difficult than it sounds. There are reasons to believe that the dominant economic interests would block an increase in civilian government spending on such a scale, even in a crisis, as interfering with the private market. The truth is that civilian government purchases were at 13.3 percent of GNP in 1939 – what Baran and Sweezy in 1966 theorized as approximating their "outer limits" – and they have barely budged

since then, with civilian government consumption and investment expenditures from 1960 to the present averaging 13.7 percent of GNP (13.8 percent of GDP).[47] The class forces blocking a
major increase in nondefense governmental spending even in a
severe stagnation should therefore not be underestimated. Any
major advances in this direction will require a massive class
struggle.

Still, there can be no doubt that change should be directed
first and foremost to meeting the basic needs of people for food,
housing, employment, health, education, a sustainable environment, etc. Will the government assume the responsibility for providing useful work to all those who desire and need it? Will housing be made available (free from crushing mortgages) to everyone, extending as well to the homeless and the poorly housed?
Will a single-payer national health system be introduced to cover
the needs of the entire population, replacing the worst and most
expensive health care system in the advanced capitalist world?
Will military spending be cut back drastically, dispensing with
global imperial domination? Will the rich be heavily taxed and
income and wealth be redistributed? Will the environment, both
global and local, be protected? Will the right to organize be made
a reality?

If such elementary prerequisites of any decent future look
impossible under the present system, then the people should
take it into their own hands to create a new society that will deliv-
er these genuine goods. Above all it is necessary "to insist that
morality and economics alike support the intuitive sense of
the masses that society's human and natural resources can and
should be used for all the people and not for a privileged
minority."[48]

In the 1930s, Keynes decried the growing dominance of financial capital, which threatened to reduce the real economy to
"a bubble on a whirlpool of speculation" and recommended the
"euthanasia of the rentier." However, financialization is so essential to the monopoly-finance capital of today, that such a "euthanasia of the rentier" cannot be achieved – in contravention of
Keynes' dream of a more rational capitalism – without moving
beyond the system itself. In this sense we are clearly at a global
turning point, where the world will perhaps finally be ready
to take the step, as Keynes also envisioned, of repudiating an

alienated moral code of "fair is foul and foul is fair" – used to justify the greed and exploitation necessary for the accumulation of capital—turning it inside-out to create a more rational social order.[49] To do this, though, it is necessary for the population to seize control of their political economy, replacing the present system of capitalism with something amounting to a real political and economic democracy; what the present rulers of the world fear and decry most—as "socialism".[50]

◆

NOTES

1. Harry Magdoff and Paul M. Sweezy, *The Irreversible Crisis*, New York, Monthly Review Press, 1988, p. 76.

2. James K. Galbraith, *The Predator State*, New York, The Free Press, 2008, p. 48.

3. David M. Herszenhorn, "Congressional Leaders Were Stunned by Warnings", *New York Times*, http://www.nytimes.com/2008/09/20/washington/19cnd-cong.html, 19 September 2008.

4. Manas Chakravarty and Mobis Philipose, "Liquidity Trap: Fear of Failure", *Livemint.com*, http://www.livemint com/2008/10/110029 51/Liquidity-trap-fear-of-failur.html, 11 October 2008; John Maynard Keynes, *The General Theory of Employment, Interest and Money*, London, Macmillan, 1973, p. 174.

5. Mark Landler and Eric Dash, "Drama Behind a $250 Billion Banking Deal", *New York Times*, http://www.nytimes.com/2008/10/15/business/economy/15bailout.html, 15 October 2008.

6. Steve Lohr, "Government's Leap into Banking Has its Perils", *New York Times*, http://www.nytimes.com/2008/10/18/business/18 sys tem.html, 18 October 2008.

7. Bob Willis, "Single-Family Homes in U.S. Fall to a 26-Year Low", *Bloomberg*, http://www.bloomberg.com/apps/news?pid=20601087 &sid=agw6ytVK4KyM&refer=home, 17 October 2008; Sudeep Reddy, Jennifer Saranow, and Ann Zimmerman, "Economic Fears Reignite Market Slump", *Wall Street Journal*, http://online.wsj.com/article/SB122411376471138395.html, 16 October 2008.

8. David Smith, "Depression of 2008", *London Times*, http://business. time   sonline.co.uk/tol/business/economics/article4880829.ece,

5 October 2008. On the Japanese stagnation, see Paul Burkett and Martin Hart-Landsberg, "The Economic Crisis in Japan", *Critical Asian Studies 35*, no. 3, 2003, p. 339-72.

9. Mark Landler, "U.S. is Said to Be Urging New Mergers in Banking", *New York Times*, http://www.nytimes.com/2008/10/21/business/21 plan.html, 21 October 2008.

10. Neil Unmack, Abigail Moses and Shannon D. Harrington, "CDO Cuts Show $1 Trillion Corporate-Debt Bets Toxic", *Bloomberg*, http://www.bloomberg.com/apps/news?pid=20601087&sid=a5x0 jMKZf4yc, 22 October 2008.

11. Louise Story and Eric Dash, "Banks are Likely to Hold Tight to Bailout Money", *New York Times*, 17 October 2008.

12. Hyman Minsky, *Can "It" Happen Again?*, New York, M. E. Sharpe, 1982, p. vii-xxiv; Financial Times, "Hard Lessons to be Learnt from a Minsky Moment", *www.ft.com*, 18 September 2008; Riccardo Bellofiore and Joseph Halevi, "A Minsky Moment?: The Subprime Crisis and the New Capitalism", in C. Gnos and L. P. Rochon, *Credit, Money and Macroeconomic Policy: A Post-Keynesian Approach*, Cheltenham, Edward Elgar, forthcoming; For Magdoff and Sweezy's views on Minsky see *The End of Prosperity*, New York, Monthly Review Press, 1977, p. 133-36.

13. Irving Fisher, "The Debt-Deflation Theory of Great Depressions", *Econometrica*, no. 4, October 1933, p. 344; Paul Krugman, "The Power of Debt", *New York Times*, 8 September 2008.

14. Sudeep Reddy, "Amid Pressing Problems the Threat of Deflation Looms", *Wall Street Journal*, http://online.wsj.com/article/SB1224 28776277746551.html, 18 October 2008; The Economist, "A Monetary Malaise", *Economist.com*, http://www.economist.com/surveys/ displaystory.cfm?story_id=123736 82, 11-17 October 2008, p. 24.

15. Ben S. Bernanke, "Deflation: Making Sure 'It' Doesn't Happen Here", *National Economists Club*, Washington, D.C., http://www.fed-eralreserve.gov, 21 November 2002.

16. Ethan S. Harris, *Ben Bernanke's Fed*, Boston, Massachusetts, Harvard University Press, 2008, p. 2, 173; Milton Friedman, *The Optimum Quantity of Money and Other Essays*, Chicago, Aldine Publishing, 1969, p. 4-14.

17. Ben S. Bernanke, *Essays on the Great Depression*, Princeton, Princeton University Press, 2000, p. 5; Milton Friedman and Anna Schwartz, *A Monetary History of the United States, 1867-1960*, Princeton, Princeton University Press, 1963. For more realistic views of the Great Depression, taking into account the real economy, as well as monetary factors, and viewing it from the standpoint of the stagnation

of investment, which above all characterized the Depression see Michael A. Bernstein, *The Great Depression*, Cambridge, Cambridge University Press, 1987; and Richard B. DuBoff, *Accumulation and Power*, New York, M.E. Sharpe, 1989, p. 84-92. On classic theories of the Great Depression see William A. Stoneman, *A History of the Economic Analysis of the Great Depression in America*, New York, Garland Publishing, 1979.

18. Ben S. Bernanke, "Money, Gold, and the Great Depression", *H. Parker Willis Lecture in Economic Policy*, Washington and Lee University, Lexington, Virginia, http://www.federalreserve.gov, 2 March 2004.

19. Ben S. Bernanke, "Some Thoughts on Monetary Policy in Japan", *Japan Society of Monetary Economics*, Tokyo, http://www.federalreserve.gov, 31 May 2003.

20. Bernanke, Essays on the Great Depression, *op. cit.*, p. 43.

21. The Federal Reserve Board, "On Milton Friedman's Ninetieth Birthday", *Conference to Honor Milton Friedman*, University of Chicago, http://www.federalreserve.gov/BOARDDOCS/SPEE CHES/2002/20021108/default.htm, 8 November 2002. Ironically, Anna Schwartz, now 91, indicated in an interview for the Wall Street Journal that the Fed under Bernanke was fighting the last war, failing to perceive that the issue was uncertainty about solvency of the banks, not a question of liquidity as in the lead-up to the Great Depression; Brian M. Carney, "Bernanke is Fighting the Last War: Interview of Anna Schwartz", *Wall Street Journal*, http://online.wsj.com/article/SB1224 28279231046053.html, 18 October 2008.

22. Ben S. Bernanke, "Asset Prices and Monetary Policy", speech to the New York Chapter of the National Association for Business Economics, New York, N.Y., 15 October 2002, http://www.federalreserve.gov; Harris, *Ben Bernanke's Fed, op. cit.*, p. 147-58.

23. Ben S. Bernanke, "The Economic Outlook", 25 October 2005; quoted in Robert Shiller, *The Subprime Option*, Princeton, Princeton University Press, 2008, p. 40.

24. Harry Magdoff and Paul M. Sweezy, *The Irreversible Crisis*, p. 76; Burkett and Hart-Landsberg, "The Economic Crisis in Japan", p. 347, 354-56, 36-66; Paul Krugman, "Its Baaack: Japan's Slump and the Return of the Liquidity Trap", *Brookings Papers on Economic Activity*, no. 2, 1998, p. 141-42, 174-78; Michael M. Hutchinson and Frank Westermann (eds.), *Japan's Great Stagnation*, Cambridge, Massachusetts, MIT Press, 2006.

25. Harry Magdoff and Paul M. Sweezy, *The Irreversible Crisis*, *op. cit.*, p. 51.

26. Harry Magdoff and Paul M. Sweezy, *The End of Prosperity, op. cit.*, p. 136; Hyman Minsky, *John Maynard Keynes*, New York, Columbia University Press, 1975, p. 164.

27. Greenspan quoted, *New York Times*, 9 October 2008; See also John Bellamy Foster, Harry Magodff, and Robert W. McChesney, "The New Economy: Myth and Reality", *Monthly Review*, 52, no. 11, April 2001, p. 1-15.

28. Manas Chakravarty, "A Turning Point in the Global Economic System",*Livemint,*http://www.livemint.com/2008/09/17002644/A-turning-point-for- the-global.html, 17 September 2008.

29. See John Bellamy Foster, *Naked Imperialism*, New York, Monthly Review Press, 2006, p. 45-50.

30. Jim Reid, "A Trillion-Dollar Mean Reversion?", *Deutsche Bank*, 15 July 2008.

31. See Paul A. Baran and Paul M. Sweezy, *Monopoly Capital*, New York, Monthly Review Press, 1966; Harry Magdoff and Paul M. Sweezy, *The Dynamics of U.S. Capitalism*, New York, Monthly Review Press, 1972; *The Deepening Crisis of U.S. Capitalism*, New York, Monthly Review Press, 1981; and *Stagnation and the Financial Explosion*, New York, Monthly Review Press, 1987.

32. Bellofiore and Halevi, "A Minsky Moment?", *op. cit.*

33. Michael Yates, *Longer Hours, Fewer Jobs*, New York, Monthly Review Press, 1994; Michael Perelman, *The Confiscation of American Prosperity*, New York, Palgrave Macmillan, 2007.

34. Economic Report of the President, 2008, Table B-47, p. 282.

35. Correspondents of the New York Times, *Class Matters*, New York, Times Books, 2005, p. 186; Edward N. Wolff (ed.), *International Perspectives on Household Wealth*, Cheltenham, Edward Elgar, 2006, p. 112-15.

36. For a class breakdown of household debt see John Bellamy Foster, "The Household Debt Bubble", chapter 1 in John Bellamy Foster and Fred Magdoff, *The Great Financial Crisis: Causes and Consequences*, New York, Monthly Review Press, 2009.

37. Ben S. Bernanke, "The Global Savings Glut and the U.S. Current Account Deficit", *Sandridge Lecture*, Virginia Association of Economics, Richmond Virginia, 10 March 2005, http://www.federalreserve.gov.

38. Steingrímur J. Stigfússon, "On the Financial Crisis of Iceland", *MRzine.org*, http://mrzine.monthlyreview.org/2008/sigfusson2010 08.html, 20 October 2008; Eric Pfanner and Julia Werdigier, "Iceland in a Precarious Position", *New York Times*, http://www.nytimes.com/2008/10/08/business/worldbusi ness/08icebank.html, 8 Oc-

tober 2008; Charles Forelle, "Iceland Scrambles for Cash to Save Banks, Economy", http://online.wsj.com/article/SB1223 2460199 3405917.html, *Wall Street Journal*, 6 October 2008.

39. See Edward J. Nell, *Growth, Profits and Prosperity*, Cambridge, Cambridge University Press, 1980, p. 19-28.

40. Karl Marx, *Capital, vol. 1*, New York, Vintage, 1976, p. 96-98.

41. Crawford B. Macpherson, *Democratic Theory*, Oxford, Oxford University Press, 1973, p. 195-203.

42. Milton Friedman and Anna Jacobson Schwartz, *A Monetary History of the United States, op. cit.*, p. 419.

43. Ethan S. Harris, *Ben Bernanke's Fed, op. cit.*, p. 147-58.

44. John Bellamy Foster, Hannah Holleman, and Robert W. McChesney, "The U.S. Imperial Triangle and Military Spending", *Monthly Review Press*, 60, no. 5, October 2008, p. 1-19.

45. For a discussion of the simultaneous stagnation of the economy and of economics since the 1970s see Michael Perelman, *The Confiscation of American Prosperity*. See also E. Ray Canterbery, *A Brief History of Economics*, River Edge, NJ, World Scientific Publishing, 2001, p. 417-26.

46. Robert Kuttner, *Obama's Challenge*, White River Junction, Vermont, Chelsea Green, 2008, p. 27.

47. Paul A. Baran and Paul Sweezy, *Monopoly Capital, op. cit.*, p. 159, 161; *Economic Report of the President*, 2008, 224, 250.

48. Harry Magdoff and Paul M. Sweezy, "The Crisis and the Responsibility of the Left", *Monthly Review Press*, 39, no. 2, June 1987, p. 1-5.

49. Keynes, *The General Theory of Employment, Interest, and Money, op. cit.*, p. 376; *Essays in Persuasion*, New York, Harcourt Brace and Co., 1932, p. 372; Paul M. Sweezy, "The Triumph of Financial Capital", *Monthly Review Press*, 46, no. 2, June 1994, p. 1-11; John Bellamy Foster, "The End of Rational Capitalism", *Monthly Review Press*, 56, no. 10, March 2005, p. 1-13.

50. In this respect, it is necessary, we believe, to go beyond liberal economics, and to strive for a ruthless critique of everything existing. Even a relatively progressive liberal economist, such as Paul Krugman, recent winner of the Bank of Sweden's prize for economics in honor of Alfred Nobel, makes it clear that what makes him a mainstream thinker, and hence a member of the club at the top of society, is his strong commitment to capitalism and "free markets" and his disdain of socialism—proudly proclaiming that "just a few years ago...one magazine even devoted a cover story to an attack on me for my pro-capitalist views". Paul Krugman, *The Great Unraveling*,

New York, W. W. Norton, 2004, p. xxxvi. In this context, see Harry Magdoff, John Bellamy Foster, and Robert W. McChesney, "A Prizefighter for Capitalism: Paul Krugman vs. the Quebec Protestors", *Monthly Review Press*, 53, no. 2, June 2001, p. 1-5.

Editors' Note: We are much indebted to Monthly Review Press for granting permission to publish the above text by John Bellamy Foster and Fred Magdoff.

CHAPTER 4

Depression: The Crisis of Capitalism

James Petras

All the idols of capitalism over the past three decades crashed. The assumptions and presumptions, paradigm and prognosis of indefinite progress under liberal free market capitalism have been tested and have failed.

We are living the end of an entire epoch: experts everywhere witness the collapse of the U.S. and world financial system, the absence of credit for trade and the lack of financing for investment. A world depression, in which upward of a quarter of the world's labor force will be unemployed, is looming.

Crash of the U.S. Financial System

The biggest decline in trade in recent world history defines the future. The imminent bankruptcies of the biggest manufacturing companies in the capitalist world haunt Western political leaders.

The "market" as a mechanism for allocating resources and the government of the U.S. as the "leader" of the global economy have been discredited.[1]

All the assumptions about "self-stabilizing markets" are demonstrably false and outmoded. The rejection of public intervention in the market and the advocacy of supply-side economics have been discredited even in the eyes of their practitioners. Even official circles recognize that "inequality of income" contributed to the onset of the economic crash and should be corrected. Planning, public ownership and nationalization are on the agenda while socialist alternatives have become almost respectable.

With the onset of the depression, all the shibboleths of the past decade are discarded: as export-oriented growth strategies fail, import substitution policies emerge. As the world economy "de-globalizes" and capital is "repatriated" to save near bankrupt head offices – national ownership is proposed. As trillions of dollars/Euros/yen in assets are destroyed and devalued, massive layoffs extend unemployment everywhere. Fear, anxiety and uncertainty stalk the offices of state, financial directorships, the office suites, the factories and the streets...

We enter a time of upheaval, when the foundations of the world political and economic order are deeply fractured, to the point that no one can imagine any restoration of the political-economic order of the recent past. The future promises economic chaos, political upheavals and mass impoverishment. Once again, the specter of socialism hovers over the ruins of the former giants of finance. As free market capital collapses, its ideological advocates jump ship, abandon their line and verse of the virtues of the market and sing a new chorus: the State as Savior of the System – a dubious proposition, whose only outcome will be to prolong the pillage of the public treasury and postpone the death agony of capitalism as we have known it.

The crash of the U.S. financial system is symptomatic of a deeper and more profound collapse of the economic and financial system which has its roots in the dynamic development of capitalism in the previous three decades.

Contrary to the theorists who argue that finance and post-industrial capitalism have destroyed or de-industrialized the world economy and put in its place a kind of "casino" or speculative capital, in fact, we have witnessed the most spectacular long-term growth of industrial capital employing more industrial and salaried workers than ever in history. Driven by rising rates of profit, large scale and long-term investments have been the motor force for the penetration by industrial and related capital of the most remote underdeveloped regions of the world. New and old capitalist countries spawned enormous economic empires, breaking down political and cultural barriers to incorporating and exploiting billions of new and old workers in a relentless process. As competition from the newly industrialized countries intensified, and as the rising mass of profits exceeded the capacity to reinvest them most profitably in the older capitalist centers, masses of capital migrated to Asia, Latin America, Eastern Europe, and to a lesser degree, into the Middle East and Southern Africa.

Huge surplus profits spilled over into services, including finance, real estate, insurance, large-scale real estate and urban lands.

The dynamic growth of capitalism's technological innovations found expression in greater social and political power – dwarfing the organization of labor, limiting its bargaining power and multiplying its profits. With the growth of world markets, workers were seen merely as "costs of production", not as final consumers. Wages stagnated; social benefits were limited, curtailed or shifted onto workers. Under conditions of dynamic capitalist growth, the state and state policy became their absolute instrument: restrictions, controls, regulation were weakened. What was dubbed "neo-liberalism" opened new areas for investment of surplus profits; public enterprises, land, resources and banks were privatized.

As competition intensified, as new industrial powers emerged in Asia, U.S. capital increasingly invested in financial activity. Within the financial circuits it elaborated a whole series of financial instruments, which drew on the growing wealth and profits from the productive sectors.

U.S. capital did not "de-industrialize" – it relocated to China, Korea and other centers of growth, not because of "falling profits" but because of surplus profits and greater profits overseas.

Capital's opening in China provided hundreds of millions of workers with jobs subject to the most brutal exploitation at subsistence wages, no social benefits, little or no organized social power. A new class of Asian capitalist collaborators, nurtured and facilitated by Asian state capitalism, increased the enormous volume of profits. Rates of investment reached dizzying proportions, given the vast inequalities between income/property owning class and wageworkers. Huge surpluses accrued but internal demand was sharply constrained. Exports, export growth and overseas consumers became the driving force of the Asian economies. U.S. and European manufacturers invested in Asia to export back to their home markets – shifting the structure of internal capital toward commerce and finance. Diminished wages paid to the workers led to a vast expansion in credit. Financial activity grew in proportion to the entrance of commodities from the dynamic, newly industrialized countries. Industrial profits were re-invested in financial services. Profits and liquidity grew in proportion to the relative decline in real value generated by the shift from industrial to financial/commercial capital.

Super profits from world production, trade and the recycling of overseas earnings back to the U.S. (through both state and private financial circuits) created enormous liquidity. It was far beyond the historical capacity of the U.S. and European economies to absorb such profits in productive sectors.

The dynamic and voracious exploitation of the huge surplus labor forces in China, India, and elsewhere and the absolute pillage and transfer of hundreds of billions from ex-communist Russia and "neo-liberalized" Latin America filled the coffers of new and old financial institutions.

Over-exploitation of labor in Asia, and the over-accumulation of financial liquidity in the U.S. led to the magnification of the paper economy and what liberal economists later called "global disequilibrium" between savers/industrial investors/ exporters (in Asia) and consumers/financiers/importers (in the U.S.). Huge trade surpluses in the East were papered over by the purchase of U.S. T-notes. The U.S. economy was precariously backed by an increasingly inflated paper economy.

The expansion of the financial sector resulted from the high rates of return, taking advantage of the "liberalized" economy imposed by the power of diversified investment capital in previous decades. The internationalization of capital, its dynamic growth and the enormous growth of trade outran the stagnant wages, declining social payments, the huge surplus labor force. Temporarily, capital sought to bolster its profits via inflated real estate based on expanded credit, highly leveraged debt and outright massive fraudulent "financial instruments" (invisible assets without value). The collapse of the paper economy exposed the overdeveloped financial system and forced its demise. The loss of finance, credit and markets, reverberated to all the export-oriented industrial manufacturing powers. The lack of social consumption, the weakness of the internal market and the huge inequalities denied the industrial countries any compensatory markets to stabilize or limit their fall into recession and depression. The dynamic growth of the productive forces based on the over-exploitation of labor, led to the overdevelopment of the financial circuits, which set in motion the process of "feeding off" industry and subordinating and undermining the accumulation process to highly speculative capital.

Cheap labor, the source of profits, investment, trade and export growth on a world scale, could no longer sustain both the pillage by finance capital and provide a market for the dynamic industrial sector. What was erroneously dubbed a financial crisis or even more narrowly a mortgage or housing crisis, was merely the trigger for the collapse of the overdeveloped financial sector. The financial sector, which grew out of the dynamic expansion of "productive" capitalism, later "rebounded" against it. The historic links and global ties between industry and financial capital led inevitably to a systemic capitalist crisis, embedded in the contradiction between impoverished labor and concentrated capital. The current world depression is a product of the over-accumulation process of the capitalist system in which the crash of the financial system was the "detonator" but not the structural determinant. This is demonstrated by the fact that industrial Japan and Germany experienced a bigger fall in exports, investments and growth than "financial" U.S. and England.

The capitalist system in crisis destroys capital in order to purge itself of the least efficient, least competitive and most indebted enterprises and sectors, in order to re-concentrate capital and reconstruct the powers of accumulation – political conditions permitting. The re-composition of capital grows out of the pillage of state resources – so-called bailouts and other massive transfers from the public treasury (read "taxpayers"), which results from the savage reduction of social transfers (read "public services") and the cheapening of labor through firings, massive unemployment, wage, pension and health reductions and the general reduction of living standards in order to increase the rate of profit.

Worldwide Depression

Aggregate economic indicators are of limited value in understanding the causes, trajectory and impact of the world depression. At best, they describe the economic carnage; at worst, they obfuscate the leading (ruling) social classes, with their complex networks and transformations, which directed the expansion and economic collapse and the wage and salaried (working) classes, which then produced the wealth to fuel the expansive phase and now pay the cost of the economic collapse.

It is a well-known truism that those who caused the crisis are also the greatest beneficiaries of government largesse. The crude and simple everyday observations that the ruling class made the crisis and the working class pays the cost is, at a minimum, a recognition of the utility of class analyses in deciphering the social reality behind the aggregate economic data. Following the recession of the early 1970s, the Western industrial capitalist class secured financing to launch a period of extensive and deep growth covering the entire globe. German, Japanese and Southeast Asian capitalists flourished, competed and collaborated with their U.S. counterparts. Throughout this period the social power, organization and political influence of the working class witnessed a relative and absolute decline in their share of material income. Technological innovations, including the re-organization of work, compensated for wage increases by reducing the mass of workers and, in particular, their capacity to pressure the prerogatives of management. The capitalist strategic position in production was strengthened; they were able to exercise near absolute control over the location and movements of capital.

The established capitalist powers – especially in England and the U.S. – with large accumulations of capital and facing increasing competition from the fully recovered German and Japanese capitalists, sought to expand their rates of return by moving capital investments into finance and services. At first this move was linked and directed towards promoting the sale of their manufactured products by providing credit and financing toward the purchases of automobiles or "white goods". Less dynamic industrial capitalists relocated their assembly plants to low-wage regions and countries. The results were that industrial capitalists took on more the appearance of "financiers" in the U.S. even as they retained their industrial character in the operation of their overseas manufacturing subsidiaries and satellite suppliers. Both overseas manufacturing and local financial returns swelled the aggregate profits of the capitalist class. While capital accumulation expanded in the home country, domestic wages and social costs were under pressure as capitalists imposed the costs of competition on the backs of wage earners via the collaboration of the trade unions in the U.S. and social democratic political parties in Europe. Wage constraints, tying wages to productivity in an asymmetrical way and labor-capital pacts increased profits. U.S. workers were "compensated" by the cheap consumer imports produced by the low-wage labor force in the newly industrializing countries and access to easy credit at home.

The Western pillage of the former-USSR, with the collaboration of gangster-oligarchs, led to the massive flow of looted capital into Western banks throughout the 1990s. The Chinese transition to capitalism in the 1980s, which accelerated in the 1990s, expanded the accumulation of industrial profits via the intensive exploitation of tens of millions of wageworkers employed at subsistence levels. While the trillion dollar pillage of Russia and the entire former Soviet Union bloated the West European and U.S. financial sector, the massive growth of billions of dollars in illegal transfers and money laundering toward U.S. and U.K. banks added to the overdevelopment of the financial sector. The rise in oil prices and rents among "rentier" capitalists added a vast new source of financial profits and liquidity. Pillage, rents and contraband capital provided a vast accumulation of financial wealth disconnected from industrial production. On the other hand, the rapid industrialization of China and other Asian countries provided a vast market for German and Japanese high-end manufacturers: they supplied the high quality machines and technology to the Chinese and Vietnamese factories.

U.S. capitalists did not "de-industrialize" – the country did. By relocating production overseas and importing finished products and focusing on credit and financing, the U.S. capitalist class and its members became diversified and multi-sectoral. They multiplied their profits and intensified the accumulation of capital.

On the other hand, workers were subject to multiple forms of exploitation: wages stagnated, creditors squeezed interest and the conversion from high wage/high skill manufacturing jobs to lower-paid service jobs steadily reduced living standards.

The basic process leading up to the breakdown was clearly present: the dynamic growth of Western capitalist wealth was based, in part, on the brutal pillage of the USSR and Latin America, which profoundly lowered living standards throughout the 1990s. The intensified and savage exploitation of hundreds of millions of low-paid Chinese, Mexican, Indonesian and Indochinese workers, and the forced exodus of former peasants as migrant laborers to manufacturing centers led to high rates of accumulation. The relative decline of wages in the U.S. and Western Europe also added to the accumulation of capital. The German, Chinese, Japanese, Latin American and Eastern European emphasis on export-driven growth added to the mounting imbalance or contradiction between concentrated capitalist wealth and ownership and the growing mass of low-paid workers. Inequalities on a world scale grew geometrically. The dynamic accumulation process exceeded the capacity of the highly polarized capitalist system to absorb capital in productive activity at existing high rates of profit. This led to the large scale and multiform growth of speculator capital inflating prices and investing in real estate, commodities, hedge funds, securities, debt-financing, mergers and acquisitions – all divorced from real value-producing activity.

The industrial boom and the class constraints imposed on workers' wages undermined domestic demand and intensified competition in world markets. Speculator-financial activity with massive liquidity offered a "short-term solution": profits based on debt financing. Competition among lenders fueled the availability of cheap credit. Real estate speculation was extended into the working class, as wage and salaried workers, without personal savings or assets, took advantage of their access to easy loans to join the speculator-induced frenzy – based on an ideology of irreversible rising home values. The inevitable collapse reverberated throughout the system, detonated at the bottom of the speculative chain.

From the latest entrants to the real estate sub-prime mortgage holders, the crisis moved up the ladder affecting the biggest banks and corporations, who engaged in leveraged buyouts and acquisitions. All sectors, which had "diversified" from manufacturing to finance, trade and commodities speculation, were downgraded. The entire panoply of capitalists faced bankruptcy. German, Japanese and Chinese industrial exporters who exploited labor witnessed the collapse of their export markets.

The bursting financial bubble was the product of the over-accumulation of industrial capital and the pillage of wealth on a world scale. Over-accumulation is rooted in the most fundamental capitalist relation: the contradictions between private ownership and social production, the simultaneous concentration of capital and sharp decline of living standards.

Crisis of Conventional Economic Thought

Among almost all conventional economists, pundits, investment advisors and various and sundry experts and economic historians, there is a common faith that in the long-run, the stock market will recover, the recession will end and the government will withdraw from the economy. Fixed on notions of past cyclical patterns and historical trends, these analysts lose sight of the present realities which have no precedent: the world nature of the economic depression, the unprecedented speed of the fall, and the levels of debt incurred by governments to sustain insolvent banks and industries and the unprecedented public deficits, which will drain resources for many generations to come.

The academic prophets of long-term developments arbitrarily select trend markers from the past which were established on the basis of a political-economic context radically different from today. The idle chatter of "post crisis" economists overlooks the open-ended and constantly shifting parameters therefore missing the true trend markers of the current depression. As one analyst noted, "any starting conditions we select in the historical data cannot replicate the starting conditions at any other moment because the preceding events in the two cases are never identical."[2]

The current U.S. depression takes place in the context of a de-industrialized economy, an insolvent financial system, record fiscal deficits, record trade deficits, unprecedented public debt, multitrillion dollar foreign debt and well over 800 billion dollars committed in military expenditures for several ongoing wars and occupations. All of these variables defy the contexts in which previous depressions occurred. Nothing in previous contexts leading up to a crisis of capitalism resembles the present situation. The present configuration of economic, political and social structures of capitalism include astronomical levels of state pillage of the public treasury in order to prop up insolvent banks and factories, involving unprecedented transfers of income from wage and salaried taxpayers to non-productive "rent earners" and to failed industrial capitalists, dividend collectors and creditors. The rate and levels of appropriation and reduction of savings, pensions and health plans, all without any compensation, has led to the most rapid and widespread reduction of living standards and mass impoverishment in recent U.S. history.

Never in the history of capitalism has a deep economic crisis occurred without any alternative socialist movement, party or state present to pose an alternative. Never have states and regimes been under such absolute control by the capitalist class – especially in the allocation of public resources. Never in the history of an economic depression has so much of government expenditures been so one-sidedly directed towards compensating a failed capitalist class with so little going to wage and salaried workers.

Economic and Financial Management under Obama

The Obama regime's economic appointments and policies clearly reflect the total control by the capitalist class over state expenditures and economic planning. The programs put forth by the U.S. and West Europeans and other capitalist regions do not even begin to recognize the structural bases of the depression.

First, Obama is allocating one trillion dollars to buy worthless bank assets and over forty percent of his 787 billion dollar stimulus package to insolvent banks and tax breaks, rather than to the productive sector, in order to save stock and bond holders, while over 600 000 workers lose their jobs monthly.

Secondly, the Obama regime is channeling over 800 billion dollars to fund the wars in Iraq and Afghanistan to sustain military-driven empire building. This constitutes a massive transfer of public funds from the civilian economy to the military sector forcing tens of thousands of unemployed young people to enlist in the military.[3]

Thirdly, Obama's commission to oversee the "restructuring" of the U.S. auto industry has backed their plans to close scores of factories, eliminate company-financed health plans for retirees and force tens of thousands of workers to accept brutal reductions in employee health care and pensions. The entire burden for returning the privately owned auto industry to profits is placed on the shoulders of the wage, salaried and retired workers, and the U.S. taxpayers.

The entire economic strategy of the Obama regime is to save the bondholders by pouring endless trillions of dollars into insolvent corporations and buying the worthless debts and failed assets of financial enterprises. At the same time his regime avoids any direct state investments in publicly owned productive enterprises, which would provide employment for the ten million unemployed workers. While Obama's budget allocates over forty percent to military expenditures and debt payments, one out of every ten Americans have been evicted from their homes, the number of Americans without jobs is rising to double digits, and the number of Americans on food stamps to provide basic food needs is rising by the millions.

Obama's job creation scheme channels billions toward the privately owned telecommunication, construction, environmental and energy corporations, where the bulk of the government funds go to senior management and staff and provide profits to stock holders, while a lesser part will go to wage workers. Moreover, the bulk of the unemployed workers in the manufacturing and service areas are not remotely employable in the recipient sectors. Only a fraction of the "stimulus package" was allocated in 2009. Its purpose and impact is to sustain the income of the financial and industrial ruling class and to postpone their long-overdue demise. Its effect will be to heighten the socioeconomic inequalities between the ruling class and the wage and salaried workers. The tax increases on the rich are incremental, while the massive debts resulting from the fiscal deficits are imposed on present and future wage and salaried taxpayers.

Obama's wholehearted embrace and promotion of military-driven empire building even in the midst of record-breaking budget deficits, huge trade deficits and an advancing depression, defines a militarist without peer in modern history. Despite promises to the contrary, the military budget for 2009-2010 exceeds the Bush Administration by at least four percent. The numbers of U.S. military forces will increase by several hundred thousand. The number of U.S. troops in Iraq will remain close to its peak and increase by tens of thousands in Afghanistan, despite promises to the contrary. U.S.-based military air and ground attacks in Pakistan have multiplied geometrically.

In summary, the *highest priorities* of the Obama regime are evidenced by his allocation of financial and material resources, his appointments of top economic and foreign policy-makers and in terms of which classes benefit and which lose under his administration. Obama's policies demonstrate that his regime is totally committed to saving the capitalist class and the U.S. empire. To do so, he is willing to sacrifice the most basic immediate needs and future interests, as well as the living standards, of the vast majority of working and home-owning Americans who are most directly affected by the domestic economic depression. Obama has increased the scope of military-driven empire building and enhanced the power position of the warmongers in his administration. His "economic recovery" and military escalation strategies are financially and fiscally incompatible; the cost of one undermines the impact of the other and leaves a tremendous hole in any efforts to counteract the collapse of social services, rising home foreclosures, business bankruptcies and massive layoffs.

The horizontal transfers of public wealth from the Obama governing elite to the economic ruling class does not trickle down into jobs, credit and social services. Attempting to turn insolvent banks into credit-lending, profitable enterprises is an oxymoron. The central dilemma for Obama is how to create conditions to restore profitability to the failed sectors of the existing U.S. economy.

There are several fundamental problems with his strategy:

First, the U.S. economic structure, which once generated employment, profits and growth, no longer exists. It has been dismantled in the course of diverting capital overseas and into financial instruments and other non-productive economic sectors.

Secondly, the Obama "stimulus" policies reinforce the financial stranglehold over the economy by channeling great resources to that sector instead of rebalancing the economy toward the productive sector. Even within the productive sector, state resources are directed toward subsidizing capitalist elites who have demonstrated their incapacity to generate sustained employment, foster market competitiveness and innovate in line with consumer preferences and interests.

Thirdly, the Obama economic strategy of top-down recovery squanders most of its impact in subsidizing failed capitalists instead of raising working class income by doubling the minimum wage and unemployment benefits, which is the only real basis for increasing demand and stimulating economic recovery. Given the declining living standards resulting from domestic decay and the expansion of military-driven empire, both embedded in the institutional foundation of the state, there are no chances for the kind of structural transformation that can reverse the top-down, empire-absorbing policies promoted by the Obama regime.

Recovery from the deepening depression does not reside in running a multitrillion dollar printing operation, which only creates conditions for hyperinflation and the debasement of the dollar. The *root cause* is the over-accumulation of capital resulting from over-exploitation of labor, leading to rising rates of profit and the collapse of demand.

The vast disparity between capital expansion and decline of worker consumption set the stage for the financial bubble. The "rebalancing" of the economy means creating demand (not from an utterly prostrate private productive sector or an insolvent financial system) via direct state ownership and long-term, large-scale investment in the production of goods and social services. The entire speculative superstructure, which grew to enormous proportions by feeding off of the value created by labor, multiplied itself in a myriad of "paper instruments" divorced from any use value. The entire paper economy needs to be dismantled in order to free the productive forces from the shackles and constraints of unproductive capitalists and their entourage.

A vast re-training program needs to be established to convert stockbrokers into engineers and productive workers. The reconstruction of the domestic market and the invention and the application of innovations to raise productivity require the massive dismantling of the worldwide empire. Costly and unproductive military bases, the essential elements for military-driven empire building, should be closed and replaced by overseas trade networks, markets and economic transactions linked to producers operating out of their home markets. Reversing domestic decay requires the end of empire and the construction of a democratic socialist republic. Fundamental to the dismantling of empire is the end of political alliances with overseas militarist powers, in particular with the state of Israel and uprooting its entire domestic power configuration, which undermine efforts to create an open democratic society serving the interests of the American people.

◆

NOTES

1. Financial Times, *www.ft.com*, 9 March 2009.
2. Financial Times, *www.ft.com*, 26 February 2009, p. 24.
3. Boston Globe, *www.boston.com/bostonglobe*, 1 March 2009.

CHAPTER 5

Globalization and Neoliberalism: Is there an Alternative to Plundering the Earth?

Claudia von Werlhof

> *Is there an alternative to plundering the earth?*
>
> *Is there an alternative to making war?*
>
> *Is there an alternative to destroying the planet?*
>
> *No one asks these questions because they seem absurd. Yet, no one can escape them either.*
>
> *Until the onslaught of the global economic crisis, the motto of so-called "neoliberalism" was TINA: "There Is No Alternative!"*
>
> *No alternative to "neoliberal globalization"? No alternative to the unfettered "free market" economy?*

What Is "Neoliberal Globalization"?

Let us first clarify what globalization and neoliberalism are, where they come from, who they are directed by, what they claim, what they do, why their effects are so fatal, why they will fail and why people nonetheless cling to them. Then, let us look at the responses of those who are not - or will not - be able to live with the consequences they cause.

This is where the difficulties begin. For a good twenty years now we have been told that there is no alternative to neoliberal globalization, and that, in fact, no such alternative is needed either. Over and over again, we have been confronted with the TINA-concept: "There Is No Alternative!" The "iron lady", Margaret Thatcher, was one of those who reiterated this belief without end.

The TINA-concept prohibits all thought. It follows the rationale that there is no point in analyzing and discussing neoliberalism and so-called globalization because they are inevitable. Whether we condone what is happening or not does not matter, it is happening anyway. There is no point in trying to understand. Hence: Go with it! Kill or be killed!

Some go as far as suggesting that globalization – meaning, an economic system which developed under specific social and historical conditions – is nothing less but a law of nature. In turn, "human nature" is supposedly reflected by the character of the system's economic subjects: egotistical, ruthless, greedy and cold. This, we are told, works towards everyone's benefit.

The question remains: why has Adam Smith's "invisible hand" become a "visible fist"? While a tiny minority reaps enormous benefits from today's neoliberalism (none of which will remain, of course), the vast majority of the earth's population suffers hardship to the extent that their very survival is at stake. The damage done seems irreversible.

All over the world media outlets – especially television stations – avoid addressing the problem. A common excuse is that it cannot be explained.[1] The true reason is, of course, the media's corporate control.

What Is Neoliberalism

Neoliberalism as an economic policy agenda which began in Chile in 1973. Its inauguration consisted of a U.S.-organized coup against a democratically elected socialist president and the installment of a bloody military dictatorship notorious for systematic torture. This was the only way to turn the neoliberal model of the so-called "Chicago Boys" under the leadership of Milton Friedman – a student of Friedrich von Hayek – into reality.

The predecessor of the neoliberal model is the economic liberalism of the 18th and 19th centuries and its notion of "free trade". Goethe's assessment at the time was: "Free trade, piracy, war – an inseparable three!"[2]

At the center of both old and new economic liberalism lies: ·

Self-interest and individualism; segregation of ethical principles and economic affairs, in other words: a process of 'de-bedding' economy from society; economic rationality as a mere cost-benefit calculation and profit maximization; competition as the essential driving force for growth and progress; specialization and the replacement of a subsistence economy with profit-oriented foreign trade ('comparative cost advantage'); and the proscription of public (state) interference with market forces.[3]

Where the new economic liberalism outdoes the old is in its global claim. Today's economic liberalism functions as a model for each and everyone: all parts of the economy, all sectors of society, of life/nature itself. As a consequence, the once "de-bedded" economy now claims to "im-bed" everything, including political power. Furthermore, a new twisted "economic ethics" (and with it a certain idea of "human nature") emerges that mocks everything from so-called do-gooders to altruism to selfless help to care for others to a notion of responsibility.[4]

This goes as far as claiming that the common good depends entirely on the uncontrolled egoism of the individual and, especially, on the prosperity of transnational corporations. The allegedly necessary "freedom" of the economy – which, paradoxically, only means the freedom of corporations – hence consists of a freedom from responsibility and commitment to society.

The maximization of profit itself must occur within the shortest possible time; this means, preferably, through speculation and "shareholder value". It must meet as few obstacles as possible. Today, global economic interests outweigh not only extra-economic concerns but also national economic considerations since corporations today see themselves beyond both community and nation.[5] A "level playing field" is created that offers the global players the best possible conditions. This playing field knows of no legal, social, ecological, cultural or national "barriers".[6] As a result, economic competition plays out on a market that is free of all non-market, extra-economic or protectionist influences – unless they serve the interests of the big players (the corporations), of course. The corporations' interests – their maximal growth and progress – take on complete priority. This is rationalized by alleging that their well-being means the well-being of small enterprises and workshops as well.

The difference between the new and the old economic liberalism can first be articulated in quantitative terms: after capitalism went through a series of ruptures and challenges – caused by the "competing economic system", the crisis of capitalism, post-war "Keynesianism" with its social and welfare state tendencies, internal mass consumer demand (so-called Fordism), and the objective of full employment in the North. The liberal economic goals of the past are now not only euphorically resurrected but they are also "globalized". The main reason is indeed that the competition between alternative economic systems is gone. However, to conclude that this confirms the victory of capitalism and the "golden West" over "dark socialism" is only one possible interpretation. Another – opposing – interpretation is to see the "modern world system" (which contains both capitalism and socialism) as having hit a general crisis which causes total and merciless competition over global resources while leveling the way for investment opportunities, i.e. the valorization of capital.[7]

The ongoing globalization of neoliberalism demonstrates which interpretation is right. Not least, because the differences between the old and the new economic liberalism can not only be articulated in quantitative terms but in qualitative ones too. What we are witnessing are completely new phenomena: instead of a democratic "complete competition" between many small enterprises enjoying the freedom of the market, only the big corporations win. In turn, they create new market oligopolies and monopolies of previously unknown dimensions. The market hence only remains free for them, while it is rendered unfree for all others who are condemned to an existence of dependency (as enforced producers, workers and consumers) or excluded from the market altogether (if they have neither anything to sell or buy). About fifty percent of the world's population fall into this group today, and the percentage is rising.[8]

Anti-trust laws have lost all power since the transnational corporations set the norms. It is the corporations – not "the market" as an anonymous mechanism or "invisible hand" – that determine today's rules of trade, for example prices and legal regulations. This happens outside any political control. Speculation with an average twenty percent profit margin edges out honest producers who become "unprofitable".[9] Money becomes too precious for comparatively non-profitable, long-term projects, or projects that *only* – how audacious! – serve a good life. Money instead "travels upwards" and disappears. Financial capital determines more and more what the markets are and do.[10] By delinking the dollar from the price of gold, money creation no longer bears a direct relationship to production".[11] Moreover, these days most of us are – exactly like all governments – in debt. It is financial capital that has all the money – we have none.[12]

Small, medium, even some bigger enterprises are pushed out of the market, forced to fold or swallowed by transnational corporations because their performances are below average in comparison to speculation – rather: spookulation – wins. The public sector, which has historically been defined as a sector of not-for-profit economy and administration, is "slimmed" and its "profitable" parts ("gems") handed to corporations (privatized). As a consequence, social services that are necessary for our existence disappear. Small and medium private businesses – which, until recently, employed eighty percent of the workforce and provided normal working conditions – are affected by these developments as well. The alleged correlation between economic growth and secure employment is false. When economic growth is accompanied by the mergers of businesses, jobs are lost.[13]

If there are any new jobs, most are precarious, meaning that they are only available temporarily and badly paid. One job is usually not enough to make a living.[14] This means that the working conditions in the North become akin to those in the South, and the working conditions of men akin to those of women – a trend diametrically opposed to what we have always been told. Corporations now leave for the South (or East) to use cheap – and particularly female – labor without union affiliation. This has already been happening since the 1970s in the "Export Processing Zones" (EPZs, "world market factories" or "maquiladoras"), where most of the world's computer chips, sneakers, clothes and electronic goods are produced.[15] The EPZs lie in areas where century-old colonial-capitalist and authoritarian-patriarchal conditions guarantee the availability of cheap labor.[16] The recent shift of business opportunities from consumer goods to armaments is a particularly troubling development.[17]

It is not only commodity production that is "outsourced" and located in the EPZs, but service industries as well. This is a result of the so-called Third Industrial Revolution, meaning the development of new information and communication technologies. Many jobs have disappeared entirely due to computerization, also in administrative fields.[18] The combination of the principles of "high tech" and "low wage"/"no wage" (always denied by "progress" enthusiasts) guarantees a "comparative cost advantage" in foreign trade. This will eventually lead to "Chinese wages" in the West. A potential loss of Western consumers is not seen as a threat. A corporate economy does not care whether consumers are European, Chinese or Indian.

The means of production become concentrated in fewer and fewer hands, especially since finance capital – rendered precarious itself – controls asset values ever more aggressively. New forms of private property are created, not least through the "clearance" of public property and the transformation of formerly public and small-scale private services and industries to a corporate business sector. This concerns primarily fields that have long been (at least partly) excluded from the logic of profit – e.g. education, health, energy or water supply/disposal. New forms of so-called *enclosures* emerge from today's total commercialization of formerly small-scale private or public industries and services, of the "commons", and of natural resources like oceans, rain forests, regions of genetic diversity or geopolitical interest (e.g. potential pipeline routes), etc.[19] As far as the new virtual spaces and communication networks go, we are witnessing frantic efforts to bring these under private control as well.[20]

All these new forms of private property are essentially created by (more or less) predatory forms of appropriation. In this sense, they are a continuation of the history of so-called *original accumulation* which has expanded globally, in accordance with to the motto: "Growth through expropriation!"[21]

Most people have less and less access to the means of production, and so the dependence on scarce and underpaid work increases. The destruction of the welfare state also destroys the notion that individuals can rely on the community to provide for them in times of need. Our existence relies exclusively on private, i.e. expensive, services that are often of much worse quality and much less reliable than public services. (It is a myth that the private always outdoes the public.) What we are experiencing is undersupply formerly only known by the colonial South. The old claim that the South will eventually develop into the North is proven wrong. It is the North that increasingly develops into the South. We are witnessing the latest form of "development", namely, a world system of underdevelopment.[22] Development and underdevelopment go hand in hand.[23] This might even dawn on "development aid" workers soon.

It is usually women who are called upon to counterbalance underdevelopment through increased work ("service provisions") in the household. As a result, the workload and underpay of women takes on horrendous dimensions: they do unpaid work inside their homes and poorly paid "housewifized" work outside.[24] Yet, commercialization does not stop in front of the home's doors either. Even housework becomes commercially co-opted ("new maid question"), with hardly any financial benefits for the women who do the work.[25]

Not least because of this, women are increasingly coerced into prostitution, one of today's biggest global industries.[26] This illustrates two things: a) how little the "emancipation" of women actually leads to "equal terms" with men; and b) that "capitalist development" does not imply increased "freedom" in wage labor relations, as the Left has claimed for a long time.[27] If the latter were the case, then neoliberalism would mean the voluntary end of capitalism once it reaches its furthest extension. This, however, does not appear likely.

Today, hundreds of millions of quasi-slaves, more than ever before, exist in the "world system."[28] The authoritarian model of the "Export Processing Zones" is conquering the East and threatening the North. The redistribution of wealth runs ever more – and with ever accelerated speed – from the bottom to the top. The gap between the rich and the poor has never been wider. The middle classes disappear. This is the situation we are facing.

It becomes obvious that neoliberalism marks not the end of colonialism but, to the contrary, the colonization of the North. This new "colonization of the world"[29] points back to the beginnings of the "modern world system" in the "long 16th century", when the conquering of the Americas, their exploitation and colonial transformation allowed for the rise and "development" of Europe. [30] The so-called "children's diseases" of modernity keep on haunting it, even in old age. They are, in fact, the main feature of modernity's latest stage. They are expanding instead of disappearing.

Where there is no South, there is no North; where there is no periphery, there is no center; where there is no colony, there is no – in any case no "Western" – civilization.[31]

Austria is part of the world system too. It is increasingly becoming a corporate colony (particularly of German corporations). This, however, does not keep it from being an active colonizer itself, especially in the East.[32]

Social, cultural, traditional and ecological considerations are abandoned and give way to a mentality of plundering. All global resources that we still have – natural resources, forests, water, genetic pools – have turned into objects of utilization. Rapid ecological destruction through depletion is the consequence. If one makes more profit by cutting down trees than by planting them, then there is no reason not to cut them.[33] Neither the public nor the state interferes, despite global warming and the obvious fact that the clearing of the few remaining rain forests will irreversibly destroy the earth's climate – not to mention the many other negative effects of such actions.[34] Climate, animal, plants, human and general ecological rights are worth nothing compared to the interests of the corporations – no matter that the rain forest is not a renewable resource and that the entire earth's ecosystem depends on it. If greed, and the rationalism with which it is economically enforced, really was an inherent anthropological trait, we would have never even reached this day.

The commander of the Space Shuttle that circled the earth in 2005 remarked that "the center of Africa was burning". She meant the Congo, in which the last great rain forest of the continent is located. Without it there will be no more rain clouds above the sources of the Nile. However, it needs to disappear in order for corporations to gain free access to the Congo's natural resources that are the reason for the wars that plague the region today. After all, one needs diamonds and coltan for mobile phones.

Today, everything on earth is turned into commodities, i.e. everything becomes an object of "trade" and commercialization (which truly means liquidation, the transformation of all into liquid money). In its neoliberal stage it is not enough for capitalism to globally pursue less cost-intensive and preferably "wageless" commodity production. The objective is to transform everyone and everything into commodities, including life itself.

[35] We are racing blindly towards the violent and absolute conclusion of this "mode of production", namely total capitalization/liquidation by "monetarization".[36]

We are not only witnessing perpetual praise of the market – we are witnessing what can be described as "market fundamentalism". People believe in the market as if it was a god. There seems to be a sense that nothing could ever happen without it. Total global maximized accumulation of money/capital as abstract wealth becomes the sole purpose of economic activity. A "free" world market for everything has to be established – a world market that functions according to the interests of the corporations and capitalist money. The installment of such a market proceeds with dazzling speed. It creates new profit possibilities where they have not existed before, e.g. in Iraq, Eastern Europe or China.

One thing remains generally overlooked: the abstract wealth created for accumulation implies the destruction of nature as concrete wealth. The result is a "hole in the ground" and next to it a garbage dump with used commodities, outdated machinery and money without value.[37] However, once all concrete wealth (which today consists mainly of the last natural resources) will be gone, abstract wealth will disappear as well. It will, in Marx's words, "evaporate". The fact that abstract wealth is not real wealth will become obvious, and so will the answer to the question of which wealth modern economic activity has really created. In the end it is nothing but monetary wealth (and even this mainly exists virtually or on accounts) that constitutes a monoculture controlled by a tiny minority. Diversity is suffocated and millions of people are left wondering how to survive. And really: how do you survive with neither resources nor means of production nor money?

The nihilism of our economic system is evident. The whole world will be transformed into money – and then it will disappear. After all, money cannot be eaten. What no one seems to consider is the fact that it is impossible to re-transform commodities, money, capital and machinery into nature or concrete wealth. It seems that underlying all "economic development" is the assumption that "resources", the "sources of wealth",[38] are renewable and everlasting – just like the "growth" they create.[39]

The notion that capitalism and democracy are one is proven a myth by neoliberalism and its "monetary totalitarianism".[40]

The primacy of politics over economy has been lost. Politicians of all parties have abandoned it. It is the corporations that dictate politics. Where corporate interests are concerned, there is no place for democratic convention or community control. Public space disappears. The *res publica* turns into a *res privata*, or – as we could say today – a *res privata transnationale* (in its original Latin meaning, *privare* means "to deprive"). Only those in power still have rights. They give themselves the licenses they need, from the "license to plunder" to the "license to kill".[41] Those who get in their way or challenge their "rights" are vilified, criminalized and to an increasing degree defined as "terrorists" or, in the case of defiant governments, as "rogue states" – a label that usually implies threatened or actual military attack, as we can see in the cases of Yugoslavia, Afghanistan and Iraq, and maybe Syria and Iran in the near future. U.S. President Bush had even spoken of the possibility of "preemptive" nuclear strikes should the U.S. feel endangered by weapons of mass destruction.[42] The European Union did not object.[43]

Neoliberalism and war are two sides of the same coin.[44] Free trade, piracy and war are still "an inseparable three" – today maybe more so than ever. War is not only "good for the economy" but is indeed its driving force and can be understood as the "continuation of economy with other means".[45] War and economy have become almost indistinguishable.[46] Wars about resources – especially oil and water – have already begun.[47] The Gulf Wars are the most obvious examples. Militarism once again appears as the "executor of capital accumulation" – potentially everywhere and enduringly.[48]

Human rights and rights of sovereignty have been transferred from people, communities and governments to corporations.[49] The notion of the people as a sovereign body has practically been abolished. We have witnessed a coup of sorts. The political systems of the West and the nation state as guarantees for and expression of the international division of labor in the modern world system are increasingly dissolving.[50] Nation states are developing into "periphery states" according to the inferior role they play in the proto-despotic "New World Order".[51] Democracy appears outdated. After all, it "hinders business".[52]

The "New World Order" implies a new division of labor that does no longer distinguish between North and South, East and

West – today, everywhere is South. An according International Law is established which effectively functions from top to bottom ("top-down") and eliminates all local and regional communal rights. And not only that: many such rights are rendered invalid both retroactively and for the future.[53]

The logic of neoliberalism as a sort of totalitarian neo-mercantilism is that all resources, all markets, all money, all profits, all means of production, all "investment opportunities", all rights and all power belong to the corporations only. To paraphrase Richard Sennett: "Everything to the Corporations!"[54] One might add: "Now!"

The corporations are free to do whatever they please with what they get. Nobody is allowed to interfere. Ironically, we are expected to rely on them to find a way out of the crisis we are in. This puts the entire globe at risk since responsibility is something the corporations do not have or know. The times of social contracts are gone.[55] In fact, pointing out the crisis alone has become a crime and all critique will soon be defined as "terror" and persecuted as such.[56]

IMF Economic Medicine

Since the 1980s, it is mainly the Structural Adjustment Programs (SAPs) of the World Bank and the IMF that act as the enforcers of neoliberalism. These programs are levied against the countries of the South which can be extorted due to their debts. Meanwhile, numerous military interventions and wars help to take possession of the assets that still remain, secure resources, install neoliberalism as the global economic politics, crush resistance movements (which are cynically labeled as "IMF uprisings"), and facilitate the lucrative business of reconstruction.[57]

In the 1980s, Ronald Reagan and Margaret Thatcher introduced neoliberalism in Anglo-America. In 1989, the so-called "Washington Consensus" was formulated. It claimed to lead to global freedom, prosperity and economic growth through "deregulation, liberalization and privatization". This has become the credo and promise of all neoliberals. Today we know that the promise has come true for the corporations only – not for anybody else.

In the Middle East, the Western support for Saddam Hussein in the war between Iraq and Iran in the 1980s, and the Gulf War of the early 1990s, announced the permanent U.S. presence in the world's most contested oil region.

In continental Europe, neoliberalism began with the crisis in Yugoslavia caused by the Structural Adjustment Programs (SAPs) of the World Bank and the IMF. The country was heavily exploited, fell apart and finally beset by a civil war over its last remaining resources.[58] Since the NATO war in 1999, the Balkans are fragmented, occupied and geopolitically under neoliberal control.[59] The region is of main strategic interest for future oil and gas transport from the Caucasus to the West (for example the "Nabucco" gas pipeline that is supposed to start operating from the Caspian Sea through Turkey and the Balkans by 2011.[60] The reconstruction of the Balkans is exclusively in the hands of Western corporations.

All governments, whether left, right, liberal or green, accept this. There is no analysis of the connection between the politics of neoliberalism, its history, its background and its effects on Europe and other parts of the world. Likewise, there is no analysis of its connection to the new militarism.

The World Trade Organization (WTO): An Instrument of Economic Oppression

When the WTO was founded in 1995, the EU member states adapted all WTO agreements on neoliberal enforcement unanimously. These agreements included: the Multilateral Agreement on Investments (MAI), the General Agreement on Trade in Services (GATS), the Agreement on Trade-Related Aspects of Intellectual Property Rights (TRIPS) and the Agreement on Agriculture (AoA) which has meanwhile been supplemented by the Agreement on Non-Agricultural-Market Access (NAMA). All these agreements aim at a rapid global implementation of corporate rule.

Never before, not even in colonial times, have those in power so completely been "freed" from all responsibility for their actions. No wonder the MAI negotiations had been kept secret for years. However, the trade unions knew, since they were part of the negotiations through the Trade Union Advisory Committee

(TUAC) that took part at the OECD conferences in Paris when the MAI was discussed.

Information about the MAI was leaked to the public in 1997. Still, even then many political bodies simply tried to play it down and accuse its critics of "cowardice" (since they were supposedly afraid of "something new"), "xenophobia" (towards the multinationals!) and "conspiracy theories". No one ever spoke of "theories", though: the contents of the MAI – which truly transcend the wildest imaginations – are no theories but the praxis of neoliberalism. And no one spoke of "conspiracies" either – because there were none: governments were part of the agreement, certain NGOs were, of course corporations, and even trade unions. Then again, if all representatives of power can form their own conspiracy, then this truly was one. In any case, the people of this planet, who bear the agreement's weight, were not informed – leave alone invited to participate.

To a large degree, the contents of the MAI have become reality through bilateral treaties and the North American Free Trade Agreement, NAFTA, signed by the U.S., Canada and Mexico in 1994. The attempt to turn all of the Americas into a Free Trade Zone, the FTAA, has so far failed, due to the resistance of most Latin American governments – this, without doubt, provides hope.

Privatization

Negotiations of the GATS, the so-called General Agreement on Trade in Services, have also been kept secret since the late 1990s. The GATS stands for total corporate "privatization" and "commercialization" of life, and for the transformation of all of life's dimensions into "trade-related", meaning: "commercial", services or commodities.[61] The GATS can be understood as a global process of successive "liberalization" of services. Suggestions are collected from all WTO member countries and according demands directed back at them. It often enough proves impossible to gain insight into what these demands actually contain. "Sensitive" areas like education, health or water supply are reputedly excluded from the negotiations, which is a proven lie.

In the GATS, services are defined as "everything that cannot fall on your foot", as someone once remarked ironically. This means that they are no longer reduced to traditional services, but now extend to human thoughts, feelings and actions as well. Even the elements – air, water, earth, fire (energy) – are increasingly turned into commodities (in some places this process is already completed) in order to make profit from the fact that we have to breathe, drink, stand and move.[62]

In Nicaragua, there are water privatization plans that include fines of up to ten months' salary if one was to hand a bucket of water to a thirsty neighbor who cannot afford her own water connection.[63] If it were up to the water corporations – the biggest of which are French and German (Vivendi Universal, Suez, RWE), which means that the privatization of water is mainly a European business – then the neighbor was rather to die of thirst. After all, compassion only upsets business.

In India, whole rivers have been sold. Stories tell of women who came to the river banks with buffalos, children and their laundry, as they had done for generations, only to be called "water thieves" and chased away by the police. There are even plans to sell the "holy mother Ganges".[64]

Fresh water (just about two percent of the earth's water reserves) is as such neither renewable nor increasable and of such essential importance to local ecosystems that it seems utterly absurd to treat it is a commodity that can be traded away.[65] Nonetheless, this is already happening. The effects, of course, are horrendous. Coca-Cola has left parts of the southern Indian state of Kerala a virtual desert by exploiting their entire ground water reserves.

According to the intentionally "weak" corporate definition of the term, even "investments" can nowadays count as "services". There is, for example, much talk about "financial services" – which also means that the MAI has basically been incorporated into the GATS. The GATS is, so to speak, the MAI for the whole world.

The so-called "Bolkestein Directive" (named after the former EU Commissioner Bolkestein) can be seen as one of the GATS' latest versions.[66] It aims at a sort of privatization of wages within the EU. This means that migrant workers in the EU are paid according to the salaries of their countries of origin, irrespective of the wage standards of the countries they work in. Once this directive is in effect, all obstacles to "Chinese labor conditions" are gone, and European trade unions will basically be rendered obsolete. This makes the fact that they have shown so little resistance against neoliberalism ever more curious.

The GATS can be considered the most radical expression of militant neoliberalism so far because it formulates its ultimate ambition in a way it has not been formulated before; namely, that no social, cultural, public or natural sectors should remain outside of economic control and exploitation – without exception. The GATS has hence to be understood as the attempt to turn absolutely everything in this world into commodities or commercial services in order to extract profit. This applies to all of nature (animals and plants as much as natural elements and landscapes), the entire human being (including its skin, hair, etc.) and all aspects of human life: work and leisure, sexuality and pregnancy, birth and death, sickness and distress, peace and war, desire and will, spirit and soul.[67]

Intellectual Property Rights

The TRIPS overlaps with the GATS insofar as it tries to co-opt the thought and experience of thousand-year old cultures, meaning: their spiritual legacy. The goal, of course, is to get paid. Formerly persecuted cultures now become interesting as a source of corporate profit. Ironically, "trade-related" intellectual property rights are established not to protect these cultures' legacies but their corporate exploitation. And not only that: the same intellectual property rights are also used to force Western thought and experience onto others – if necessary, by violence. Patent rights are used to protect all related interests. So-called "patents for life" take on special meaning in this context as they go hand in hand with the rapid development of genetic engineering.[68] What happens is that once a genetic manipulation has occurred, something "new" has been invented that someone can lay a legal claim on. Sometimes, however, one does not even deem this necessary. The genes of plants, animals, even humans, are sometimes stolen, claimed as "discovered" and made one's own legal "property". This "bio piracy" exploits the profit potentials of all resources by charging others monopoly prices for using them.[69] There is now a patent on "Basmati" rice. A patent claim to the Indian *neem* tree almost passed.

The best known example for a company selling its "inventions" is the case of Monsanto. Monsanto tries to make all peasants and farmers of the planet dependent on its genetically modified seeds that are, intentionally, only fertile once ("terminator seeds"). This means that the farmers have to buy new seeds from the company every year. This is already happening in most parts of India where many thousands of peasants have been forced to give up farming which, in turn, led to a shocking number of suicides.[70] The Indian physician, ecologist and globalization critic Vandana Shiva calls this process "trading our lives away."[71] In Korea, "WTO kills farmers!" has become a popular slogan amongst many farming communities.

The transnational agro-industrial corporations now even discuss a general prohibition of traditional farming methods.[72] Iraqi farmers have already been forced to burn all their seeds since the U.S. invasion and use "terminator seeds" instead – this in Mesopotamia, the cradle of agriculture.[73] What these developments make clear is that genetic engineering is not about a better life but about installing global monopolies. This becomes most obvious in the current attempts to implement monopoly control on basic products and services which each human being's life depends on. Now we understand the meaning of the rally cries "Agrobusiness is the Biggest Business!" or "Wheat Becomes a Weapon!"[74]

Genetically Modified Organisms

Meanwhile, problems with genetically modified organisms (GMOs) are on the increase everywhere. Genetically modified seeds, for example, are expensive, vulnerable and of poor quality.[75] They constantly need more – instead of less – pesticides. They also "pollute", which means that they destroy the non-modified species (while not being able to reproduce themselves – or only partially).[76] It becomes harder and harder to deny that GMOs cause irreversible destruction of a still unknown part of flora and – depending on how they are used – fauna. A new infertility enters the world instead of a new creation. The consequence is an artificially created death – a death with no life to follow. No one seems to know how to prevent this.[77]

All this sounds like a nightmare. Unfortunately, it is reality. For example, there is no more natural rapeseed in Canada. In Argentina and China, millions of hectares are sown with GMO seeds. Emergency deliveries to regions affected by famine consist almost exclusively of such seeds. In Germany, cows that were fed with GMO feed died a horrible death after two-and-a-half years.[78] Even in Austria, where people take pride in being environmentally conscious, no GMO free animal feed remains on the market, and GMO rapeseed is being planted despite all negative experiences.[79]

It is hard to grasp what is happening. Food is produced that kills – yet people are forced to eat it. And not only that: they have to pay a lot of money for it too! A grosser distortion of life is hardly imaginable. Amongst the most ludicrous examples is the idea to distribute contraceptive GMO corn, developed by the Swiss company Syngenta, in regions that suffer from so-called "overpopulation".[80] This means genocide, murder and business, all in one!

Neoliberalism Justifies Robbery and Pillage

Neoliberalism is a conscious betrayal of the interests of 99 percent of the people on this planet. It justifies robbery and pillage. It is, both in intention and effect, a true "weapon of mass destruction" – even when no immediate wars are fought. How many lives are sacrificed to neoliberalism? Some estimate that the numbers already go into hundreds of millions.[81]

Paradoxically, the WTO and its agreements are anchored in international law while they rob and pillage the people whose rights are supposed to be protected by this law. Violations against the WTO agreements count hence as violations against a law that stands above all national and regional regulations. As a consequence, legal cases challenging the compatibility of WTO (or EU) law with national constitutions have repeatedly been rejected – in Austria as recently as in 2005.

The WTO and its agreements act effectively as a global oligarchic constitution. They are the first attempt at installing neo-totalitarian "global corporate governance" – or even a "global corporate government". It feels like despotism is establishing itself again, but this time globally. What we are witnessing might be dubbed a new kind of "AMP", the so-called former "Asiatic Mode of Production" – only that its origins are now American instead of Asiatic.

I think a more accurate name for the WTO would be WWO: "World War Order". Or, alternatively, W.K.O.: "World Knock Out". In any case, the organization sweeps across the globe like a tsunami, taking everything with it that promises profit.

Alternatives to Neoliberal Globalization

The real debate about alternatives to neoliberal globalization began on the 1st of January 1994 with the uprising of well organized Indios of the Southern Mexican jungle.[82] Men, women and children of the so-called "Zapatista National Liberation Army", named after the Mexican peasant and successful leader of the Mexican Revolution of 1910, Emiliano Zapata, occupied without force some central areas of the state of Chiapas. They declared to fight Mexico's integration into the neoliberal NAFTA, the North American Free Trade Agreement, alongside the U.S. and Canada. NAFTA was inaugurated the same day. One of the movement's speakers, the now world famous Subcommandante Marcos, declared that neoliberalism was a "world war waged by financial power against humanity" and an expression of the worldwide crisis of capitalism, not its success. The Indios had decided not to be part of this. They chose to resist. Their idea of an alternative life was clear and they practiced it despite the hostility they received from the government and the military.[83] Their resistance was based on an indigenous version of "good governance": direct democracy, egalitarianism and a non-exploitative subsistence economy entrenched in local independence and a respect for every individual's dignity – a concept derived from pre-colonial experience, from the so-called "deep Mexico", a cultural and spiritual heritage maintained throughout centuries.[84]

The Protest Movement

In the North, it was not before 1997-1998 that the social movement against neoliberalism gathered momentum with the struggle against the ratification of the MAI. The movement's first success was the failure of the MAI due to France's refusal to ratify it.

The movement then spread wide and fast across the globe and mobilized a total of up to fifteen million people for protests against the wars in Yugoslavia, Afghanistan and Iraq. In 2002 and 2003, the struggle focused on the "Stop GATS!" campaign, led by international groups like Attac. Support was widespread. Social Forums began to be organized and every year individuals, groups and organizations critical of neoliberal globalization met regionally, nationally, continentally and globally. The World Social Forums gathered up to 100 000 people and more from all over the world under the motto: "Another world is possible!"

Activists also came together regularly at the summits of the WTO, the WEF (World Economic Forum), the G8 or the World Bank. They managed to cause two WTO conferences, in Seattle and Cancún, to fail, which dealt a strong blow to the organization.[85]

Still, euphoria would be out of place. An alternative to neoliberalism is not created through analysis and protest alone. An alternative to neoliberalism has to be practiced. Opinions on how to do this differ. Some discuss "alternatives" that are none: a reform of the WTO; a "control" of globalization through NGOs; a return to Keynesianism; a restoration of the "social market economy"; or even a revival of socialism. Such ideas ignore reality and trivialize the problem. Much more is at stake – neoliberalism shows this every day.

Neoliberalism is an apocalypse, a "revelation". There is no way to deny this any longer. It is impossible for neoliberalism to justify itself by the reality it creates. No one can be fooled anymore by calling the corporations harmless "players" either. Things have become serious. There is no ambiguity. As a consequence, the perpetrators of neoliberal politics simply lie about what is happening.

In a way, we can say that the only good thing about neoliberalism is that it reveals the truth about "Western civilization" and "European values". This means that people now have the chance to draw the right conclusions about what is really needed.

What is really needed, of course, is nothing less than a different civilization. A different economy alone, or a different society or culture will not suffice. We need a civilization that is the exact opposite of neoliberalism and the patriarchal capitalist world system it is rooted in. The logic of our alternative must be one that completely undermines the logic of neoliberalism.[86]

Neoliberalism has turned everything that would ensure a good life for all beings on this planet upside down. Many people still have a hard time understanding that the horror we are experiencing is indeed a reality – a reality willingly produced, maintained and justified by "our" politicians. But even if the alternative got half-way on its feet – no more plundering, exploitation, destruction, violence, war, coercion, mercilessness, accumulation, greed, corruption – we would still be left with all the damage that the earth has already suffered.

The earth is not the paradise it was (at least in many places) five hundred years ago, two hundred years ago or even one hundred years ago. The devastation has been incredible: large parts of our drinking water are disappearing mainly due to the melting of the glaciers and polar caps; our climate has changed dramatically, causing turbulences and catastrophes; our atmosphere is no longer protected against ultraviolet radiation ("ozone layer problem"); many species of our fauna and flora are extinguished; most cultures and their knowledge are destroyed; most natural resources exhausted. And all this happened within what only comes to a nanosecond of the earth's history.

Establishing New Relationships within Society

We have to establish a new economy and a new technology; a new relationship with nature; a new relationship between men and women that will finally be defined by mutual respect; a new relationship between the generations that reaches even further than to the "seventh"; and a new political understanding based on egalitarianism and the acknowledgment of the dignity of each individual. But even once we have achieved all this, we will still need to establish an appropriate "spirituality" with regard to the earth.[87] The dominant religions cannot help us here. They have failed miserably.

We have to atone for at least some of the harm and violence that has been done against the earth. Nobody knows to what degree, and if at all, this is even possible. What is certain, however, is that if we want to have any chance to succeed, we need a completely new culture for this: a caring relationship with the earth based on emotional qualities that have been suppressed and destroyed in the name of commodity production and "progress". We need to regain the ability to feel, to endure pain, to lose fear and to love in ways that seem inconceivable today.[88] If this happens then a new life on and with our earth might really be possible. In any case, it is the only earth we have.

Fortunately, there are signs pointing in the right direction. In many regions in the South, indigenous movements have arisen following in the footsteps of the Zapatistas.[89] Especially the Indios in Latin America have returned (or, at the same time, "advanced") to ways of agriculture and subsistence that had been practiced for millions of years and produced a diversity of concrete wealth. Indios have also established mini-markets to trade products they themselves do not need. By doing this, they secure both the social and ecological survival of their immediate (and extended) environment.[90] The global peasants' movement *Via Campesina* defends the rights of small farmers all across the world. It counts millions of members today. The "localization" of politics and economy is on the rise everywhere.[91] New communities, as well as new "commons" and new cooperatives, are being formed. Local councils organize and network regionally. In India, this is called "living democracy" – a democracy that includes the earth and that we can hence call an "earth democracy" as well.[92]

In the North, thousands of local networks exist in which "free money" replaces money that comes with interest, accumulates value and serves as a means for speculation rather than trade.[93] A "solidarity economy" and a "green economy" expand globally and challenge the prevailing "profit economy".[94] In the North as well as in the South, people experiment with so-called "participatory budgets" in which the inhabitants of neighborhoods or whole towns decide on how to use tax money. Even the concept of an economy of gift-giving in a post-capitalist and post-patriarchal society is discussed.[95] In any case, fundamentally new communal experiences beyond egoism are sought. Communities are being created in which people support each other, allowing every individual to think, feel and act differently.

No alternatives have ever come from the top. Alternatives arise where people, alone or in groups, decide to take initiative in order to control their destiny.[96] From the bottom of society, a new feeling of life, a new energy and a new solidarity spread and strengthen each and every one involved.[97] As a result, people are able to free themselves from a notion of individuality that reduces them to "sentient commodities" or, even worse, "functioning machines".

The mentioned examples of resistance and alternatives do truly undermine neoliberalism and its globalization. People who are engaged in them reach a completely different way of thinking. They have lost faith in development and have seen through the game. To them, development has become an affront or an object of ridicule. Politicians are expected to "get lost", as we have recently seen in Argentina: *"Que se vayan todos!"* It has become clear that no one wants to have anything to do with conventional politics and politicians anymore. People have realized that politics as a "system" never serves but betrays and divides them. Some people have developed almost allergic reactions to conventional politics. They have experienced long enough that domination inevitably negates life.

Of course there are alternatives to plundering the earth, to making war and to destroying the planet. Once we realize this, something different already begins to take shape. It is mandatory to let it emerge before the hubris' boomerang finds us all.

◆

NOTES

1. Maria Mies and Claudia von Werlhof (Hg), *Lizenz zum Plündern. Das Multilaterale Abkommen über Investitionen MAI*. Globalisierung der Konzernherrschaft – und was wir dagegen tun können, Hamburg, EVA, 2003 (1998), p. 23, 36.

2. Johann Wolfgang von Goethe, *Faust: Part Two*, New York, Oxford University Press, 1999.

3. Maria Mies, *Krieg ohne Grenzen*. Die neue Kolonisierung der Welt, Köln, PapyRossa, 2005, p. 34.

4. Arno Gruen, *Der Verlust des Mitgefühls*. Über die Politik der Gleichgültigkeit, München, 1997, dtv.

5. Sassen Saskia, "Wohin führt die Globalisierung?," *Machtbeben*, 2000, Stuttgart-München, DVA.

6. Maria Mies and Claudia von Werlhof (Hg), *Lizenz zum Plündern. Das Multilaterale Abkommen über Investitionen MAI.* Globalisierung der Konzernherrschaft – und was wir dagegen tun können, Hamburg, EVA, 2003 (1998), p. 24.

7. Immanuel Wallerstein, Aufstieg und künftiger Niedergang des kapitalistischen Weltsystems, in Senghaas, *Dieter: Kapitalistische Weltökonomie.* Kontroversen über ihren Ursprung und ihre Entwicklungsdynamik, Frankfurt, 1979, Suhrkamp; Immanuel Wallerstein (Hg), *The Modern World-System in the Longue Durée*, Boulder/ London; Paradigm Publishers, 2004.

8. Susan George, im Vortrag, *Treffen von Gegnern und Befürwortern der Globalisierung im Rahmen der Tagung des WEF* (World Economic Forum), Salzburg, 2001.

9. Elmar Altvater, *Das Ende des Kapitalismus*, wie wir ihn kennen, Münster, Westfälisches Dampfboot, 2005.

10. Elmar Altvater and Birgit Mahnkopf, *Grenzen der Globalisierung.* Ökonomie, Ökologie und Politik in der Weltgesellschaft, Münster, Westfälisches Dampfboot, 1996.

11. Bernard Lietaer, *Jenseits von Gier und Knappheit*, Interview mit Sarah van Gelder, 2006, www.transaction.net/press/interviews/Lietaer 0497.html; Margrit Kennedy, *Geld ohne Zinsen und Inflation*, Steyerberg, Permakultur, 1990.

12. Helmut Creutz, *Das Geldsyndrom.* Wege zur krisenfreien Marktwirtschaft, Frankfurt, Ullstein, 1995.

13. Maria Mies and Claudia von Werlhof (Hg), *Lizenz zum Plündern. Das Multilaterale Abkommen über Investitionen MAI.* Globalisierung der Konzernherrschaft – und was wir dagegen tun können, Hamburg, EVA, 2003 (1998), p. 7.

14. Barbara Ehrenreich, *Arbeit poor.* Unterwegs in der Dienstleistungsgesellschaft, München, Kunstmann, 2001.

15. Folker Fröbel, Jürgen Heinrichs, and Otto Kreye, *Die neue internationale Arbeitsteilung.* Strukturelle Arbeitslosigkeit in den Industrieländern und die Industrialisierung der Entwicklungsländer, Reinbek, Rowohlt, 1977.

16. Veronika Bennholdt-Thomsen, Maria Mies, and Claudia von Werlhof, *Women, The Last Colony*, London/ New Delhi, Zed Books, 1988.

17. Michel Chossudovsky, *War and Globalization. The Truth Behind September 11th*, Oro, Ontario, Global Outlook, 2003.

18. Folker Fröbel, Jürgen Heinrichs, and Otto Kreye, *Die neue internationale Arbeitsteilung*. Strukturelle Arbeitslosigkeit in den Industrieländern und die Industrialisierung der Entwicklungsländer, Reinbek, Rowohlt, 1977.

19. Ana Isla, *The Tragedy of the Enclosures: An Eco-Feminist Perspective on Selling Oxygen and Prostitution in Costa Rica*, Man., Brock Univ., Sociology Dpt., St. Catherines, Ontario, Canada, 2005.

20. John Hepburn, *Die Rückeroberung von Allmenden – von alten und von neuen*, übers. Vortrag bei, Other Worlds Conference; Univ. of Pennsylvania; 28./29.4, 2005.

21. Claudia von Werlhof, *Was haben die Hühner mit dem Dollar zu tun?* Frauen und Ökonomie, München, Frauenoffensive, 1991; Claudia von Werlhof, *MAInopoly: Aus Spiel wird Ernst*, in Mies/Werlhof, 2003, p. 148-192.

22. Andre Gunder Frank, *Die Entwicklung der Unterentwicklung*, in ders. u.a., Kritik des bürgerlichen Antiimperialismus, Berlin, Wagenbach, 1969.

23. Maria Mies, *Krieg ohne Grenzen*, Die neue Kolonisierung der Welt, Köln, PapyRossa, 2005.

24. Veronika Bennholdt-Thomsen, Maria Mies, and Claudia von Werlhof, *Women, the Last Colony*, London/New Delhi, Zed Books, 1988.

25. Claudia von Werlhof, *Frauen und Ökonomie. Reden, Vorträge 2002-2004*, Themen GATS, Globalisierung, Mechernich, Gerda-Weiler-Stiftung, 2004.

26. Ana Isla, "Women and Biodiversity as Capital Accumulation: An Eco-Feminist View," *Socialist Bulletin*, Vol. 69, Winter, 2003, p. 21-34; Ana Isla, *The Tragedy of the Enclosures: An Eco-Feminist Perspective on Selling Oxygen and Prostitution in Costa Rica*, Man., Brock Univ., Sociology Department, St. Catherines, Ontario, Canada, 2005.

27. Immanuel Wallerstein, *Aufstieg und künftiger Niedergang des kapitalistischen Weltsystems*, in Senghaas, Dieter: Kapitalistische Weltökonomie. Kontroversen über ihren Ursprung und ihre Entwicklungsdynamik, Frankfurt, Suhrkamp, 1979.

28. Kevin Bales, *Die neue Sklaverei*, München, Kunstmann, 2001.

29. Maria Mies, *Krieg ohne Grenzen*, Die neue Kolonisierung der Welt, Köln, PapyRossa, 2005.

30. Immanuel Wallerstein, *Aufstieg und künftiger Niedergang des kapitalistischen Weltsystems*, in Senghaas, Dieter: Kapitalistische Weltökonomie. Kontroversen über ihren Ursprung und ihre Entwicklungsdynamik, Frankfurt, Suhrkamp, 1979; Andre Gunder Frank, *Orientierung im Weltsystem*, Von der Neuen Welt zum Reich der

Mitte, Wien, Promedia, 2005; Maria Mies, *Patriarchy and Accumulation on a World Scale, Women in the International Division of Labour*, London, Zed Books, 1986.

31. Claudia von Werlhof, "Questions to Ramona," in Corinne Kumar (Ed.), *Asking, We Walk. The South as New Political Imaginary*, Vol. 2, Bangalore, Streelekha, 2007, p. 214-268

32. Hannes Hofbauer, *Osterweiterung. Vom Drang nach Osten zur peripheren EU-Integration*, Wien, Promedia, 2003; Andrea Salzburger, *Zurück in die Zukunft des Kapitalismus*, Kommerz und Verelendung in Polen, Frankfurt – New York, Peter Lang Verlag, 2006.

33. Bernard Lietaer, *Jenseits von Gier und Knappheit*, Interview mit Sarah van Gelder, 2006, www.transaction.net/press/interviews/Lietaer 0497.html.

34. August Raggam, *Klimawandel, Biomasse als Chance gegen Klimakollaps und globale Erwärmung*, Graz, Gerhard Erker, 2004.

35. Immanuel Wallerstein, *Aufstieg und künftiger Niedergang des kapitalistischen Weltsystems*, in Senghaas, Dieter: Kapitalistische Weltökonomie. Kontroversen über ihren Ursprung und ihre Entwicklungsdynamik, Frankfurt, Suhrkamp, 1979.

36. Renate Genth, *Die Bedrohung der Demokratie durch die Ökonomisierung der Politik*, feature für den Saarländischen Rundfunk am 4.3., 2006.

37. Johan Galtung, *Eurotopia*, Die Zukunft eines Kontinents, Wien, Promedia, 1993.

38. Karl Marx, *Capital*, New York, Vintage, 1976.

39. Claudia von Werlhof, *Loosing Faith in Progress: Capitalist Patriarchy as an "Alchemical System,"* in Bennholdt-Thomsen et.al.(Eds.), *There is an Alternative*, 2001, p. 15-40.

40. Renate Genth, *Die Bedrohung der Demokratie durch die Ökonomisierung der Politik*, feature für den Saarländischen Rundfunk am 4.3., 2006.

41. Maria Mies and Claudia von Werlhof (Hg), *Lizenz zum Plündern. Das Multilaterale Abkommen über Investitionen MAI*. Globalisierung der Konzernherrschaft – und was wir dagegen tun können, Hamburg, EVA, 2003 (1998), p. 7; Maria Mies, *Krieg ohne Grenzen*, Die neue Kolonisierung der Welt, Köln, PapyRossa, 2005.

42. Michel Chossudovsky, *America's "War on Terrorism,"* Montreal, Global Research, 2005.

43. Michel Chossudovsky, "Nuclear War Against Iran," *Global Research*, Center for Research on Globalization, Ottawa 13.1, 2006.

44. Altvater, Chossudovsky, Roy, Serfati, *Globalisierung und Krieg*, Sand im Getriebe 17, Internationaler deutschsprachiger Rundbrief der ATTAC – Bewegung, Sonderausgabe zu den Anti-Kriegs-

Demonstrationen am 15.2., 2003; Maria Mies, *Krieg ohne Grenzen,* Die neue Kolonisierung der Welt, Köln, PapyRossa, 2005.

45. Hazel Hendersen, *Building a Win-Win World. Life Beyond Global Economic Warfare*, San Francisco, 1996.

46. Claudia von Werlhof, *Vom Wirtschaftskrieg zur Kriegswirtschaft.* Die Waffen der, Neuen-Welt-Ordnung, in Mies 2005, p. 40-48.

47. Michael T. Klare, *Resource Wars. The New Landscape of Global Conflict*, New York, Henry Holt and Company, 2001.

48. Rosa Luxemburg, *Die Akkumulation des Kapitals*, Frankfurt, 1970.

49. Tony Clarke, *Der Angriff auf demokratische Rechte und Freiheiten*, in Mies/Werlhof, 2003, p. 80-94.

50. Sassen Saskia, *Machtbeben. Wohin führt die Globalisierung?*, Stuttgart-München, DVA, 2000.

51. Michael Hardt and Antonio Negri, *Empire*, Cambridge, Harvard Univ. Press, 2001; Noam Chomsky, *Hybris. Die endgültige Sicherstellung der globalen – Vormachtstellung der USA*, Hamburg-Wien, Europaverlag, 2003.

52. Claudia von Werlhof, *Speed Kills!*, in Dimmel/Schmee, 2005, p. 284-292

53. See the "roll back" and "stand still" clauses in the WTO agreements in Maria Mies and Claudia von Werlhof (Hg), *Lizenz zum Plündern. Das Multilaterale Abkommen über Investitionen MAI.* Globalisierung der Konzernherrschaft – und was wir dagegen tun können, Hamburg, EVA, 2003.

54. Richard Sennett, zit. "In Einladung zu den Wiener Vorlesungen," 21.11.2005: *Alternativen zur neoliberalen Globalisierung*, 2005.

55. Claudia von Werlhof, *MAInopoly: Aus Spiel wird Ernst*, in Mies/Werlhof, 2003, p. 148-192.

56. Michel Chossudovsky, *America's "War on Terrorism,"* Montreal, Global Research, 2005.

57. Michel Chossudovsky, *Global Brutal. Der entfesselte Welthandel, die Armut, der Krieg*, Frankfurt, Zweitausendeins, 2002; Maria Mies, *Krieg ohne Grenzen. Die neue Kolonisierung der Welt*, Köln, PapyRossa, 2005; Bennholdt-Thomsen/Faraclas/Werlhof 2001.

58. Michel Chossudovsky, *Global Brutal. Der entfesselte Welthandel, die Armut, der Krieg*, Frankfurt, Zweitausendeins, 2002.

59. Wolfgang Richter, Elmar Schmähling, and Eckart Spoo (Hg), *Die Wahrheit über den NATO-Krieg gegen Jugoslawien*, Schkeuditz, Schkeuditzer Buchverlag, 2000; Wolfgang Richter, Elmar Schmähling, and Eckart Spoo (Hg), *Die deutsche Verantwortung für den NATO-Krieg gegen Jugoslawien*, Schkeuditz, Schkeuditzer Buchverlag, 2000.

60. Bernard Lietaer, *Jenseits von Gier und Knappheit*, Interview with Sarah van Gelder, 2006, www.transaction.net/press/interviews/Lietaer 0497.html.

61. Maria Mies and Claudia von Werlhof (Hg), *Lizenz zum Plündern. Das Multilaterale Abkommen über Investitionen MAI*. Globalisierung der Konzernherrschaft – und was wir dagegen tun können, Hamburg, EVA, 2003 (1998), p. 7.

62. Maude Barlow, "The Last Frontier", *The Ecologist*, February 2001; Ana Isla, "Women and Biodiversity as Capital Accumulation: An Eco-Feminist View," *Socialist Bulletin*, Vol. 69, Winter 2003, p. 21-34.

63. Südwind, *Nicaragua: Ausverkauf auf Kosten der Menschen*, Fliugblatt, November 12, 2003.

64. Vandana Shiva, *Der Kampf um das blaue Gold. Ursachen und Folgen der Wasserverknappung*, Zürich, Rotpunktverlag, 2003.

65. Maude Barlow and Tony Clarke, *Blaues Gold. Das globale Geschäft mit dem Wasser*, München, Kunstmann, 2003; Vandana Shiva, *Der Kampf um das blaue Gold. Ursachen und Folgen der Wasserverknappung*, Zürich, Rotpunktverlag, 2003.

66. Klaus Dräger, "Bolkesteins Hammer. Projekt Dienstleistungsbin-nenmarkt 2010", *Infobrief gegen Konzernherrschaft und neoliberale Politik*, 19: Täter EU – Raubzüge in Ost und West, Köln, 2005, p. 17-22.

67. Frauennetz Attac (Hg), *Dienste ohne Grenzen? GATS, Privatisierung und die Folgen für Frauen*, Dokumentation des Internationalen Kongresses, 9.-11.5.03 in Köln, Frankfurt, 2003.

68. Vandana Shiva, *Geraubte Ernte. Biodiversität und Ernährungspolitik*, Zürich, Rotpunktverlag, 2004.

69. Barbara Thaler, *Biopiraterie und indigener Widerstand*, Frankfurt, New York., Peter Lang Verlag, 2004.

70. Vandana Shiva, *Geraubte Ernte. Biodiversität und Ernährungspolitik*, Zürich, Rotpunktverlag, 2004.

71. Vandana Shiva, *Trading our Lives Away. An Ecological and Gender Analysis of "Free Trade" and the WTO*, New Delhi, Research Foundation for Science, Technology and Natural Resource Policy, 1995.

72. Sender Arte, *US-Firmen patentieren Nutzpflanzen und wollen tradition-ellen Anbau verbieten*, 15.11., 2005.

73. Junge Welt, *Die grüne Kriegsfront. USA verordnen dem von ihrem Militär besetzten Irak den Anbau von genmanipuliertem Getreide.* Millionen Kleinbauern droht der Ruin, 29.11., 2004.

74. Peter Krieg, *Septemberweizen*, Film, Freiburg, 1980.

75. Manfred Grössler (Hg), *Gefahr Gentechnik. Irrweg und Ausweg. Experten klären auf*, Graz; Concord, 2005.

76. Verhaag, *Leben außer Kontrolle* , München, Denkmalfilm, 2004.
77. Claudia von Werlhof, "The Utopia of a Motherless World. Patriarchy as ‹War-System›," Göttner-Abendroth, Hieide (Hg.): *Societies of Peace. Contributions to the 2nd World Congress of Matriarchal Studies*, Toronto, Inanna, 2006.
78. Gottfried Glöckner, *Der Genmais und das große Rindersterben*, Grössler, 2005, p. 25-37.
79. Jens Karg, *Trügerische Schönheit*, in Global News. Das Umweltmagazin von global 2000, 2005, p. 7.
80. Gerhard Reiter, *GEN OZID, Flugblatt der bioBauern Schärding*, ProLeben Oberösterreich, November, 2005.
81. Jean Ziegler, "Das tägliche Massaker des Hungers," *Widersrpuch* 47, 2004, p. 19-24; Widerspruch, "Beiträge zu sozialistischer Politik", *Agrobusiness – Hunger und Recht auf Nahrung*, Zürich, 47/ 2004.
82. Topitas (Hg), "Ya basta!", *Der Aufstand der Zapatistas*, Hamburg, Libertäre Assoziation, 1994.
83. Sergio Rodriguez, "Interviewt von Miguel Romero", *The Zapatista Approach to Politics*, in Viento Sur, Nr. 83, 2005, online: http://auto_sol.tao.ca/node/view/1649.
84. Claudia von Werlhof, "Questions to Ramona", Corinne Kumar (Ed.): *Asking, we walk. The south as new political imaginary*, Vol. 2, Bangalore, Streelekha, 2007, p.2149-268.
85. Vandana Shiva, *From Doha to Hong Kong via Cancún. Will WTO Shrink or Sink?, 2005,* web-mail2.uibk.ac.at/horde/imp/message.php?index=22627.
86. Claudia von Werlhof, "Capitalist Patriarchy and the Negation of Matriarchy: The Struggle for a "Deep" Alternative," in Genevieve Vaughan (Ed.), *Women and the Gift Economy, A Radically Different World View is Possible*, Toronto, Inanna, 2007, p. 139-153.
87. Claudia von Werlhof, "The Interconnectedness of All Being: A New Spirituality for a New Civilization," in Corinne Kumar (Ed.), *Asking, We Walk. The South as New Political Imaginary*, Vol.2, Bangalore, Streelekha, 2007, p. 379-386.
88. Günther Anders, *Die Antiquiertheit des Menschen, Bd.1: Über die Seele im Zeitalter der zweiten industriellen Revolution*, München, Beck, 1994; Genevieve Vaughan, *For- Giving. A Feminist Criticism of Exchange*, Austin, Anomaly Press, 1997.
89. Gustavo Esteva, *Mexico: Creating Your Own Path at the Grassroots*, in Bennholdt-Thomsen/ Faraclas/Werlhof, 2001, p. 155-166.
90. Veronika Bennholdt-Thomsen and Maria Mies, *The Subsistence Perspective. Beyond the Globalised Economy*, London, Zed Books, 1999; Veronika Bennholdt-Thomsen, Brigitte Holzer, and Christa Müller

(Hg), *Das Subsistenzhandbuch. Widerstandskulturen in Europa, Asien und Lateinamerika*, Wien, Promedia, 1999.

91. Helena Norberg-Hodge, *Local Lifeline: Rejecting Globalization – Embracing Localization*, in: Bennholdt-Thomsen/ Faraclas/Werlhof, 2001, p. 178-188.

92. Claudia von Werlhof, *Globale Kriegswirtschaft oder Earth Democracy?*, in Grüne Bildungswerkstatt (Hg.) Die Gewalt des Zusammenhangs. Neoliberalismus – Militarismus – Rechtsextremismus, Wien, Promedia, 2001, p. 125-142.

93. Bernard Lietaer, *Das Geld der Zukunft. Über die destruktive Wirkung des existierenden Geldsystems und die Entwicklung von Komplementärwährungen*, München, Riemann, 1999.

94. Brian Milani, *Designing the Green Economy. The Postindustrial Alternative to Corporate Globalization*, Lanham, Rowman & Littlefield, 2000.

95. Genevieve Vaughan (Hg), *The Gift, Il Donno, Athanor*, Anno XV, nuova serie, n. 8, 2004; Genevieve Vaughan (Hg), *A Radically Different World View is Posssible. The Gift Economy Inside and Outside Patriarchal Capitalism*, Inanna Press (Frühjahr), 2006.

96. David Korten, *When Corporations Rule the World*, San Francisco, Berret-Koehler, 1996.

97. Maria Mies, *Globalisierung von unten. Der Kampf gegen die Herrschaft der Konzerne*, Hamburg, Rotbuch, 2001.

CHAPTER 6

The Economy's Search for a "New Normal"

Shamus Cooke

> *When the reality of the economic crisis first emerged, many who re-*
> *alized what was happening dubbed it "the greatest crisis since the*
> *Great Depression". This description was more than bombast; it was*
> *a sober analysis of the immensity of the economic problems in the*
> *country – problems that had been building up for years.*

The Banks are Bankrupt

The mainstream media is now – for political reasons – in a constant clamor for the economy's elusive "rock bottom". This is so people will be more hopeful, less agitated, and more willing to let those who destroyed the economy continue running the country un-challenged. Every time a new economic indicator comes out that wasn't "as bad as expected", Wall Street cheers and politicians give their "we've turned the corner" speeches. Reality is thus turned on its head.

Regardless of what the media says, the reasons for calling this crisis the "worst since the Great Depression", still exist. Not only this, but new problems are being created that are compounding the old.

One of the original, major concerns of the economy was the fact that the banks were bankrupt. This problem still persists, even after trillions of dollars of taxpayer money was given away, not to mention a "stress test" where the banks in fact "negotiated" the terms of the test.[1] By pretending this problem doesn't exist, the Obama administration is continuing the Bush-era approach to the banks: don't ask, don't tell. Banks will thus continue to be bailed out when their problems are too explosive to be ignored; credit will continue to be restricted, and a general level of instability will taint the system itself.

Another major problem of the economy is that consumers are bankrupt. Unemployment continues to skyrocket, ensuring that every month hundreds of thousands of less people will be able to consume, driving more establishments out of business. The people who lose their jobs thus fail to pay their mortgages, credit cards, student loans, etc., all furthering the losses of the banks.

The issue of debt is fundamental to understanding the current crisis: households, corporations, banks and the government have all taken on massive levels of debt.

Getting rid of the debt is often referred to as "de-leveraging". On all levels of society a gigantic de-leveraging is taking place; and only after this process is done will the elusive "bottom of the recession" be found, amidst a society that looks far different than the one we are used to.

For example, households are rapidly getting rid of expenses they can no longer afford, due to either joblessness, low wages or lack of credit. They are thus saving more than they are spending. For an economy that depends on seventy percent consumer spending, this is a huge problem, not only for the U.S., but for the world as well, since many countries constructed their economies as export machines directed towards U.S. consumers.

Is this problem likely to go away anytime soon? Probably not. The recession is creating such dramatic effects on so many people that the consuming culture is being changed, much like what happened after the Great Depression. *The New York Times* noted:

> Forces that enabled and even egged on consumers to save less and spend more – easy credit and skyrocketing asset values – could be permanently altered [!] by the financial crisis that spun the economy into recession.[2]

If the U.S. consumer can no longer be the driving force of the economy, what will replace it? The elitist *Economist* magazine offered a cure: because consumer spending will be debilitated, "something else will have to grow more quickly. Ideally that would be exports and investment."[3]

There is in fact little else that can be done if one is playing by the strict rules of the market economy. Obama again gave his allegiance to this broken system by agreeing with the *Economist*, when he stated, "We must lay a new foundation for growth and prosperity, where we consume less at home and send more exports abroad."

The average person will be totally uninspired by this "solution". Nevertheless, Obama should have answered an important question: why isn't the U.S. an exporting economy now? And what would it take for it to be one in the future? The answers to these questions are intertwined with Obama's proposal that Americans "consume less."

In order for U.S. corporations to sell products (export) on the world marketplace, they must have competitive prices. Labor is a key ingredient in determining the price of a commodity, since the other ingredients have relatively stable prices. The price of labor in the U.S. was, in part, the result of a strong labor movement, which achieved a living wage. This not only drove down profits for corporations, but made them less competitive on the world market – they consequently defected to countries that pay slave wages.

How, then, does Obama plan to "send more exports abroad"? The answer is simple: by ensuring that Americans are able to "consume less". For example, Obama's Auto Task Force told Chrysler and GM workers that their incomes were too high, that they needed to make less so that their companies could "remain viable" (compete) on the global market. They were thus threatened with bankruptcy if they did not offer "significant concessions". The workers conceded, and bankruptcy happened anyway – a phenomenon that acted as a precedent for the much larger General Motors.

There is enormous significance in the GM bankruptcy and consequent restructuring: the UAW, an icon of American labor and still-powerful union, was brought to its knees. Decades of hard-fought victories over wages, benefits and work rules were shattered in moments.

This event was watched closely by financial tycoons everywhere and will be undoubtedly be copied. Corporations of all kinds are looking to "de-leverage" in the same way to successfully survive the recession. They need to balance the books, and workers' wages are one of the few options they have. Obama's Auto Task Force is overseeing the destruction of the UAW, and clearing the path for this restructuring to happen across the country.

In the battle between labor and the corporations, Obama has left no questions about where his allegiance lies.

But if Obama thinks that attacking unions to boost corporate profits is going to get the economy moving, he'd better think twice. Falling wages also have a negative, longer-term effect on the economy. As Nobel Prize winner Paul Krugman points out:

> Families are trying to work [their] debt down by saving more than they have in a decade – but as wages fall, they're chasing a moving target. And the rising burden of debt will put downward pressure on consumer spending, keeping the economy depressed.[4]

His conclusion is sobering: "The risk that America will turn into Japan – that we'll face years of deflation and stagnation – seems, if anything, to be rising."

Equally concerning for the economy is the amount of debt the U.S. government has taken in bailing out banks and fighting foreign wars. The New York Times notes, "[the national debt] has prompted warnings from the Treasury that the Congressionally mandated debt ceiling of $12.1 trillion will most likely be breached in the second half of this year."[5]

The debt is so high that those financing it are getting worried, and thus demanding a higher rate of interest in repayment (since they correctly think they'll be paid back in inflated dollars). Already the U.S. pays 176 billion dollars a year in simply paying the interest on the debt, a number that is expected to reach 806 billion dollars by 2019, according to the Congressional Budget Office.[6]

This debt is of course unsustainable. There are numerous signs that overseas' buyers are likely to reduce their investment, worried as they are about the U.S. money printing bonanza. In an effort to prevent this and bolster confidence in the dollar, Obama has plans to balance the budget by the end of his presidency. Again, a massive de-leveraging of debt will need to happen. Obama has made no secret of where this restructuring will come from: he has made repeated references to "reforming entitlement programs" (Social Security, Medicare, etc.).

It should be noted that the only other way Obama could balance the budget is if he taxed the super rich at a high rate while slashing military spending. Neither of these policies is likely to be implemented, based on Obama's staunch allegiances to both

Wall Street and the military. Nevertheless, these proposals must be central demands for the American worker, who is already under immense economic pressure, with more to come.

The recession is creating a "fight or die" environment for corporations and governments around the world. The super rich that currently control both entities are using their influence to ensure that workers carry the brunt of this burden. It doesn't have to be so.

The fight for jobs, a living wage, progressive taxation, social security and single payer healthcare are all issues capable of uniting the vast majority of U.S. citizens. If properly organized, and with the Labor Movement playing a leading role, such a coalition would have no problem overcoming the objections of those who oppose it – the tiny group of super rich benefiting from how things are currently.

◆

NOTES

1. David Cho, Tomoeh Murakami Tse and Brady Dennis, "Major Banks Negotiate, Spin, Chafe at Stress-test Results", *Washington Post*, http://www.washing tonpost.com/wp-dyn/content/article/2009/05/07/AR2009050704257.html?hpid=topnews, 8 May 2009.

2. Catherine Rampell, "Shift to Saving May Be Downturn's Lasting Impact", *The New York Times*, http://www.nytimes.com/2009/05/10/business/econo my/10saving.html, 9 May 2009.

3. The Economist, "American Consumer Spending may have hit Bottom, but the Climb back up will be slow and Painful", http://www.economist.com/world/unitedstates/displayStory.cfm?story_id=13605679, 6 May 2009.

4. Paul Krugman, "Falling Wage Syndrome", *The New York Times*, http://www.nytimes.com/2009/05/04/opinion/04krugman.html, 3 May 2009.

5. Graham Bowley and Jack Healy, "Worries Rise on the Size of US Debt", *The New York Times*, http://www.nytimes.com/2009/05/04/business/economy/ 04debt.html, 3 May 2009.

6. CBO, "Budget Projections", *Congressional Budget Office*, http://www.cbo.gov/budget/budproj.shtml.

PART II

Poverty and Unemployment

CHAPTER 7

Global Poverty and the Economic Crisis

Michel Chossudovsky

Humanity is undergoing in the post-Cold War era an economic and social crisis of unprecedented scale leading to the rapid impoverishment of large sectors of the world population. National economies are collapsing, unemployment is rampant. Local level famines have erupted in Sub-Saharan Africa, South Asia and parts of Latin America. This "globalization of poverty" – which has largely reversed the achievements of post-war decolonization – was initiated in the Third World coinciding with the debt crisis of the early 1980s and the imposition of the IMF's deadly economic reforms.

This worldwide crisis is more devastating than the Great Depression of the 1930s. It has far-reaching geo-political implications; economic dislocation has also been accompanied by the outbreak of regional wars, the fracturing of national societies and in some cases the destruction of entire countries. By far this is the most serious economic crisis in modern history.

–Michel Chossudovsky, The Globalization of Poverty,
First Edition, 1997

The Outbreak of Famine

The sugar-coated bullets of the "free market" are killing our children. The act to kill is instrumented in a detached fashion through computer program trading on the New York and Chicago mercantile exchanges, where the global prices of rice, wheat and corn are decided upon.

People in different countries are being impoverished simultaneously as a result of a global market mechanism. A small number of financial institutions and global corporations have the ability to determine the prices of basic food staples quoted on the commodity exchanges, thereby directly affecting the standard of living of millions of people around the world.

This process of global impoverishment has reached a major turning point, leading to the simultaneous outbreak of famines in all major regions of the developing world.

Famine is the result of a process of "free market" restructuring of the global economy which has its roots in the debt crisis of the early 1980s. It is not a recent phenomenon associated with the 2008-2009 economic crisis, as suggested by several Western analysts.

Poverty and chronic undernourishment are pre-existing conditions. The dramatic hikes in food and fuel prices which preceded the 2008-2009 financial crash contributed to exacerbating and aggravating the food crisis. These price hikes, which reached their peak in July 2008, have hit the market for basic food staples, including domestic retail prices, in all regions of the world.

Protest movements directed against the hikes in the prices of food and gasoline erupted simultaneously in different regions of the world. The conditions are particularly critical in Haiti, Nicaragua, Guatemala, India and Bangladesh:

Food prices in Haiti had risen on average by 40 percent in less than a year, with the cost of staples such as rice doubling... In Bangladesh [in late April 2008] some 20 000 textile workers took to the streets to denounce soaring food prices and demand higher wages. The price of rice in the country has doubled in the past year [2007-2008], threatening the workers, who earn a monthly salary of just $25, with hunger. In Egypt, protests by workers over food prices rocked the textile center of Mahalla al-Kobra, north of Cairo [April 2008], with two people shot dead by security forces. Hundreds were arrested, and the government sent plainclothes police into the factories to force workers to work. Food prices in Egypt have risen by 40 percent in the past year... [2007-2008] Earlier this month [April 2008] in the Ivory Coast, thousands marched on the home of President Laurent Gbagbo, chanting "we are hungry" and "life is too expensive, you are going to kill us."

Similar demonstrations, strikes and clashes have taken place in Bolivia, Peru, Mexico, Indonesia, the Philippines, Pakistan,

Uzbekistan, Thailand, Yemen, Ethiopia, and throughout most of sub-Saharan Africa.[1]

Spiraling food and fuel prices in Somalia in 2008 contributed to precipitating an entire country into a situation of mass starvation, coupled with severe water shortages. A similar and equally serious situation prevails in Ethiopia. But now with food costs spiraling out of reach and the livestock that people live off of dropping dead in the sand, villagers across this sun-blasted landscape say hundreds of people are dying of hunger and thirst:

> Many Somalis are trying to stave off starvation with a thin gruel made from mashed thorn-tree branches called *jerrin*. Some village elders said their children were chewing on their own lips and tongues because they had no food. The weather has been merciless – intensely hot days, followed by cruelly clear nights.[2]

> This is a catastrophe in the making; we have time to act before it becomes a reality. The cost of food [in Somalia and the Afar region of Ethiopia] has escalated by up to 500 percent in some places... People are increasingly becoming desperate... We fear that the worst could be yet to come as the crisis deteriorates across East Africa.[3]

Other countries which were affected by spiraling food prices in 2007-2008 include Indonesia, the Philippines, Liberia, Egypt, Sudan, Mozambique, Zimbabwe, Kenya and Eritrea, a long list of impoverished countries, not to mention those under foreign military occupation including Iraq, Afghanistan and Palestine.

While the price of food commodities declined markedly in the wake of the 2008 financial collapse, the underlying mechanisms of manipulation of world commodity prices by powerful corporate interests and institutional speculators has remained functionally intact. A new wave of speculative trade in food staples and fuel cannot be ruled out.

Food, Fuel and Water: A Precondition for Human Survival

The provision of food, fuel and water is a precondition for the survival of the human species. They constitute the economic and environmental foundations for development of civilized society. In recent years, both prior and leading up to the 2008-2009 financial meltdown, the prices of grain staples, including rice, corn and wheat, gasoline and water, increased dramatically at the global level with devastating economic and social consequences.

Unprecedented in the history of humanity, these three essential goods or commodities, which in a real sense determine the reproduction of economic and social life on planet Earth, are under the control of a small number of global corporations and financial institutions. The fate of millions of human beings is managed behind closed doors in the corporate boardrooms as part of a profit driven agenda.

Government and intergovernmental organizations are complicit in these developments. The state's economic and financial policies are controlled by private corporate interests. Speculative trade is not the object of regulatory policies, and in fact the opposite holds true: the framework of speculative trade in the commodity exchanges is protected by the state. Moreover, the provision of food, water and fuel are no longer the object of governmental or intergovernmental regulation or intervention with a view to alleviating poverty or averting the outbreak of famines.

Largely obfuscated by official and media reports, both the "food crisis" and the "oil crisis" are the result of the speculative manipulation of market values by powerful economic actors. And because these powerful economic actors operate through a seemingly neutral and "invisible" market mechanism, the devastating social impacts of engineered hikes in the prices of food, fuel and water are casually dismissed as the result of supply and demand considerations.

We are not dealing with distinct and separate food, fuel and water "crises" but with a global process of economic and social restructuring. The dramatic price hikes of these three essential commodities are not haphazard. All three variables, including the prices of basic food staples, water for production and consumption and fuel, are the object of a process of deliberate and simultaneous market manipulation.

At the heart of the 2005-2008 food crisis was a rising price of food staples, coupled with a dramatic increase in the price of fuel. Concurrently, the price of water, which is an essential input into agricultural and industrial production, social infrastructure, public sanitation and household consumption, has increased abruptly as a result of a worldwide movement to privatize water resources. We are dealing with a major economic and social upheaval and an unprecedented global crisis, characterized by the triangular relationship between water, food and fuel – three fundamental variables which together affect the very means of human survival.

In very concrete terms, these price hikes impoverish and destroy people's lives. Moreover, the worldwide collapse in living standards is occurring at a time of war. It is intimately related to the military agenda. The wars in the Middle East and Central Asia bear a direct relationship to the control over oil and water reserves. While water is not at present an internationally traded commodity in the same way as oil and food staples, it is also the object of market manipulation through the privatization of water. Water is a natural resource which is being appropriated and sold. The tendency is toward the commodification of water.

TEXT BOX 7.1

FOOD, FUEL AND WATER: THE ECONOMIC ACTORS OPERATING BEHIND CLOSED DOORS

- The major Wall Street banks and financial houses, including the institutional speculators which play a direct role in commodity markets including the oil and food markets.

- The Anglo-American oil giants, including British Petroleum (BP), ExxonMobil, Chevron-Texaco, Royal Dutch Shell.

- The biotech-agribusiness conglomerates, including Monsanto, Cargill and Archer Daniel Midlands (ADM) which own the intellectual property rights on seeds and farm inputs. The biotech companies are also major actors on the New York and Chicago mercantile exchanges.

- The water giants, including Suez, Veolia and Bechtel-United Utilities, involved in the extensive privatization of the world's water resources.

- The Anglo-American military-industrial complex, which includes the big five U.S. defense contractors (Lockheed Martin, Raytheon, Northrop Grunman, Boeing and General Dynamics) in alliance with British Aerospace Systems Corporation (BAES), constitutes a powerful overlapping force closely aligned with Wall Street, the oil giants and the biotech-agribusiness conglomerates.

Both the state as well as the gamut of international organizations – often referred to as the "international community" – serve the unfettered interests of global capitalism. The main intergovernmental bodies, including the United Nations, the Bretton Woods institutions and the World Trade Organization (WTO), have endorsed the New World Order on behalf of their corporate sponsors. Governments in both developed and developing countries have abandoned their historical role of regulating key economic variables as well as ensuring a minimum livelihood for their people.

The Speculative Surge in Grain Prices

The media has casually misled public opinion on the causes of the 2005-2008 price hikes, focusing almost exclusively on issues of costs of production, climate and other factors which result in reduced supply and which might contribute to boosting the price of food staples. While these factors may come into play, they are of limited relevance in explaining the impressive and dramatic surge in commodity prices.

Spiraling food prices are in large part the result of market manipulation. They are largely attributable to speculative trade on the commodity markets. Grain prices are boosted artificially by large scale speculative operations on the New York and Chicago mercantile exchanges. It is worth noting that in 2007, the Chicago Board of Trade (CBOT), merged with the Chicago Mercantile Exchange (CME), forming the largest worldwide entity dealing in commodity trade, including a wide range of speculative instruments (options, options on futures, index funds, etc).

Speculative trade in wheat, rice or corn can occur without the presence of real commodity transactions. The institutions speculating in the grain market are not necessarily involved in the actual selling or delivery of grain. The transactions may use commodity index funds which are bets on the general upward or downward movement of commodity prices. A "put option" is a bet that the price will go down, a "call option" is a bet that the price will go up. Through concerted manipulation, institutional traders and financial institutions make the price go up and then place their bets on an upward movement in the price of a particular commodity.

Speculation generates market volatility. In turn, the resulting instability encourages further speculative activity. Profits are made when the price goes up. Conversely, if the speculator is short-selling the market, money will be made when the price collapses.

The Role of Macroeconomic Reform

There are two interrelated dimensions to the ongoing global food crisis, which has spearheaded millions of people around the world into starvation and chronic deprivation, a situation in which entire population groups no longer have the means to purchase food.

First, there is a long-term historical process of macroeconomic policy reform and global economic restructuring which has contributed to depressing living standards worldwide in both the developing and developed countries.

Second, these pre-existing historical conditions of mass poverty have been exacerbated and aggravated by the 2005-2008 surge in quoted grain prices on international commodity exchanges, which have led in some cases to the doubling of the retail price of food staples. These price hikes are in large part the result of speculative trade in food staples.

With large sectors of the world population already well below the poverty line, the short-term hikes in the prices of food staples were devastating. Millions of people around the world are unable to purchase food for their survival.

According to the FAO, the price of grain staples increased by 88 percent from March 2007 to May 2008. The price of wheat increased by 181 percent over a three-year period.[4] The price of rice has tripled over a five-year period, from approximately six hundred dollars a ton in 2003 to more than 1 800 dollars a ton in May 2008.

The main actors in the grain market are Cargill and Archer Daniels Midland (ADM). These two corporate giants control a large share of the global grain market. They are also involved in speculative transactions in futures and options on the NYMEX and the Chicago Board of Trade (CBOT). In the U.S., "the world's largest grower of GM crops, Cargill, ADM and competitor Zen Noh, between them control 81 per cent of all maize exports and 65 per cent of all soyabean exports."[5]

"Eliminating the Poor"

These hikes in food prices are contributing in a very real sense to "eliminating the poor" through "starvation deaths":

> The most popular grade of Thailand rice sold for $198 a ton, five years ago and $323 a ton a year ago. In April 2008, the price hit $1,000. Increases are even greater on local markets – in Haiti, the market price of a 50 kilo bag of rice doubled in one week at the end of March 2008. These increases are catastrophic for the 2.6 billion people around the world who live on less than US$2 a day and spend 60% to 80% of their incomes on food. Hundreds of millions cannot afford to eat.[6]

This 2005-2008 surge in food prices was conducive to a world-wide process of famine formation on an unprecedented scale. These speculative operations do not purposely trigger famine. What triggers famine is the absence of regulatory procedures pertaining to speculative trade (options, options on futures, commodity index funds). In the present context, a freeze of speculative trade in food staples, taken as a political decision, would immediately contribute to lower food prices. Nothing prevents these transactions from being neutralized and defused through a set of carefully devised regulatory measures. Visibly, this is not what is being proposed by the World Bank and the International Monetary Fund.

The Role of the IMF and the World Bank

In 2008, the World Bank and the IMF put forth an emergency plan to boost agriculture in response to the food crisis. The causes of the food crisis, however, were not addressed. The World Bank's president Robert B. Zoellick described this initiative as a "new deal," an action plan "for a long-term boost to agricultural production," which consisted *inter alia* in a doubling of agricultural loans to African farmers. He stated, "We have to put our money where our mouth is now so that we can put food into hungry mouths."[7]

IMF-World Bank "economic medicine" is not the solution but in large part the cause of famine in developing countries. More IMF-World Bank lending "to boost agriculture" will serve to increase levels of indebtedness and exacerbate rather than alleviate poverty. World Bank policy-based loans are granted on condition that the countries abide by the neoliberal policy agenda which, since the early 1980s, has been conducive to the collapse of local level food agriculture. "Macroeconomic stabilization" and structural adjustment programs imposed by the IMF and the World Bank on developing countries (as a condition for the renegotiation of their external debt) have led to the impoverishment of hundreds of millions of people.

The harsh economic and social realities underlying IMF intervention are soaring food prices, local-level famines, massive lay-offs of urban workers and civil servants and the destruction of social programs. Internal purchasing power has collapsed, health clinics and schools have been closed down, and hundreds of millions of children have been denied the right to primary education.

Historically, spiraling food prices at the retail level have been triggered by currency devaluations, which have invariably resulted in a hyperinflationary situation. In Peru, in August 1990, for instance, fuel prices increased overnight by thirty times, on the orders of the IMF. The price of bread increased twelve times overnight.[8]

The Deregulation of Grain Markets

Since the 1980s, grain markets have been deregulated under the supervision of the World Bank, and US/EU grain surpluses are used systematically to destroy the peasantry and destabilize national food agriculture. In this regard, World Bank lending requires the lifting of trade barriers on imported agricultural staples, leading to the dumping of US/EU grain surpluses onto local markets. These and other measures have spearheaded local agricultural producers into bankruptcy.

A "free market" in grain – imposed by the IMF and the World Bank – destroys the peasant economy and undermines "food security". Malawi and Zimbabwe were once prosperous grain surplus countries; Rwanda was virtually self-sufficient in food until 1990 when the IMF ordered the dumping of EU and U.S. grain surpluses on the domestic market precipitating small farmers into bankruptcy. In 1991-1992, famine had hit Kenya, East Africa's most successful bread-basket economy. The Nairobi government had been previously placed on a black list for not having obeyed IMF prescriptions. The deregulation of the grain market had been demanded as one of the conditions for the rescheduling of Nairobi's external debt with the Paris Club of official creditors.

Throughout Africa, as well as in Southeast Asia and Latin America, the pattern of "sectoral adjustment" in agriculture under the custody of the Bretton Woods institutions has been unequivocally towards the destruction of food security. Dependency *vis-à-vis* the world market has been reinforced leading to a boost in commercial grain imports as well as an increase in the influx of "food aid". Agricultural producers were encouraged to abandon food farming and switch into "high value" export crops, often to the detriment of food self-sufficiency. The high value products as well as the cash crops for export were supported by World Bank loans.

Famines in the age of globalization are the result of policy. Famine is not the consequence of a scarcity of food but in fact quite the opposite: global food surpluses are used to destabilize agricultural production in developing countries. Tightly regulated and controlled by international agro-business, this oversupply is ultimately conducive to the stagnation of both production and consumption of essential food staples and the impoverishment of farmers throughout the world. Moreover, in the era of globalization, the IMF-World Bank structural adjustment program bears a direct relationship to the process of famine formation because it systematically undermines all categories of economic activity, whether urban or rural, which do not directly serve the interests of the global market system.

The earnings of farmers in rich and poor countries alike are squeezed by a handful of global agro-industrial enterprises which simultaneously control the markets for grain, farm inputs, seeds and processed foods. One giant firm, Cargill Inc. with more than 140 affiliates and subsidiaries around the world, controls a large share of the international trade in grain. Since the 1950s, Cargill became the main contractor of U.S. "food aid" funded under Public Law 480 (1954).

World agriculture has for the first time in history the capacity to satisfy the food requirements of the entire planet, yet the very nature of the global market system prevents this from occurring. The capacity to produce food is immense, yet the levels of food consumption remain exceedingly low because a large share of the world's population lives in conditions of abject poverty and deprivation. Moreover, the process of "modernization" of agriculture has led to the dispossession of the peasantry, increased landlessness and environmental degradation. In other words, the very forces which encourage global food production to expand are also conducive antithetically to a contraction in the standard of living and a decline in the demand for food.

Genetically Modified Seeds

Coinciding with the establishment the World Trade Organization (WTO) in 1995, another important historical change has occurred in the structure of global agriculture. Under the articles of agreement of the WTO, the food giants will have unrestricted freedom to enter the seeds markets of developing countries. The acquisition of exclusive "intellectual property rights" over plant varieties by international agro-industrial interests, also favors the destruction of bio-diversity.

Acting on behalf of a handful of biotech conglomerates, GMO seeds have been imposed on farmers, often in the context of "food aid programs". In Ethiopia, for instance, kits of GMO seeds were handed out to impoverished farmers with a view to rehabilitating agricultural production in the wake of a major drought.[10] The GMO seeds were planted, yielding a harvest. But then the farmer came to realize that the GMO seeds could not be replanted without paying royalties to Monsanto, Archer Daniels Midland, *et al*. Then the farmers discovered that the seeds would harvest only if they used the farm inputs including the fertilizer, insecticide and herbicide, produced and distributed by the biotech agribusiness companies. Entire peasant economies were locked into the grip of the agribusiness conglomerates.

Breaking the Agricultural Cycle

With the widespread adoption of GMO seeds, a major transition has occurred in the structure and history of settled agriculture since its inception ten thousand years ago.

The reproduction of seeds at the village level in local nurseries has been disrupted by the use of genetically modified seeds. The agricultural cycle, which enables farmers to store their organic seeds and plant them to reap the next harvest, has been broken. This destructive pattern – invariably resulting in famine – is replicated in country after country, leading to the worldwide demise of the peasant economy.

The FAO-World Bank Consensus

At the June 2008 FAO Rome Summit on the food crisis, politicians and economic analysts alike embraced the free market consensus: the outbreak of famines was presented as a result of the usual supply, demand and climatic considerations, beyond the control of policy-makers. "The solution": channel emergency relief to affected areas under the auspices of the World Food Program (WFP). Do not intervene with the interplay of market forces.

Ironically, these "expert opinions" are refuted by the data on global grain production: the FAO forecasts for world cereal production point to a record output in 2008. Contradicting their own textbook explanations, world prices are, according to the World Bank, expected to remain high, despite the forecasted increased supply of food staples. State regulation of the prices of food staples and gasoline is not considered an option in the corridors of the FAO and the World Bank. And of course that is what is taught in the economics departments of America's most prestigious universities. Meanwhile, local level farmgate prices barely cover production costs, spearheading the peasant economy into bankruptcy.

The Oil Price Bubble

The movement in global prices on the New York and Chicago mercantile exchanges bears no relationship to the costs of producing oil. The spiraling price of crude oil in 2006-2008 was not the result of a shortage of oil. It is estimated that the cost of a barrel of oil in the Middle East does not exceed fifteen dollars. The cost of a barrel of oil extracted from the tar sands of Alberta, Canada, is of the order of thirty dollars.[11] The price of crude oil in mid-2008 had reached 120 dollars a barrel. This market price was largely the result of the speculative onslaught.

Fuel enters·into the production of virtually all areas of manufacturing, agriculture and the services economy. The hikes in fuel prices contributed, in all major regions of the world, to precipitating tens of thousands of small and medium-sized businesses into bankruptcy as well as undermining and potentially paralyzing the channels of domestic and international trade.

The increased cost of gasoline at the retail level is leading to the demise of local level economies, increased industrial concentration and a massive centralization of economic power in the hands of a small number of global corporations. In turn, the hikes in fuel backlash on the urban transit system, schools and hospitals, the trucking industry, intercontinental shipping, airline transportation, tourism, recreation and most public services.

Fueling Inflation

The rise in fuel prices unleashes a broader inflationary process, which results in a compression of real purchasing power and a consequent worldwide decline in consumer demand. All major sectors of society, including the middle classes in the developed countries, are affected. These price movements are dictated by the commodity markets. They are the result of speculative trade in index funds, futures and options on major commodity markets including the London ICE, the New York and Chicago mercantile exchanges.

The dramatic price hikes are not the result of a shortage of fuel:

> At least 60% of the $128 per barrel price of crude oil comes from unregulated futures speculation by hedge funds, banks and financial groups using the London ICE Futures and New York NYMEX futures exchanges and uncontrolled inter-bank or Over-the-Counter trading to avoid scrutiny. US margin rules of the government's Commodity Futures Trading Commission

allow speculators to buy a crude oil futures contract on the Nymex, by having to pay only 6% of the value of the contract. At today's price of $128 per barrel, that means a futures trader only has to put up about $8 for every barrel. He borrows the other $120. This extreme "leverage" of 16 to 1 helps drive prices to wildly unrealistic levels and offset bank losses in sub-prime and other disasters at the expense of the overall population.[12]

Among the main players in the speculative market for crude oil are Goldman Sachs, Morgan Stanley, British Petroleum (BP), the French banking conglomerate Société Générale, Bank of America, the largest Bank in the U.S., and Switzerland's Mercuria.[13] British Petroleum controls the London-based International Petroleum Exchange (IPE), which is one of the world's largest energy futures and options exchanges. Among IPE's major shareholders are Goldman Sachs and Morgan Stanley. Morgan Stanley is one of the main institutional actors in the London-based speculative oil market (IPE). According to *Le Monde*, France's Société Générale, together with Bank of America and Deutsche Bank, were in 2008 involved in spreading rumors with a view to pushing up the price of crude oil.[14]

The Privatization of Water

According to UN sources, which vastly underestimate the seriousness of the water crisis, one billion people worldwide (fifteen percent of the world population) have no access to clean water "and 6,000 children die every day because of infections linked to unclean water."[15] A handful of global corporations including Suez, Veolia, Bechtel-United Utilities, Thames Water and Germany's RWE-AG are acquiring control and ownership over public water utilities and waste management. Suez and Veolia hold about seventy percent of the privatized water systems worldwide.

The privatization of water under World Bank auspices feeds on the collapse of the system of public distribution of safe tap drinking water: "The World Bank serves the interests of water companies both through its regular loan programs to governments, which often come with conditions that explicitly require the privatization of water provision."[16]

Furthermore:

The modus operandi [in India] is clear – neglect development of water resources [under World Bank budget austerity measures], claim a "resource crunch" and allow existing systems to deteriorate.[17]

Meanwhile, the markets for bottled water have been appropriated by a handful of corporations, including Coca-Cola, Danone, Nestlé and PepsiCo. These companies not only work hand in glove with the water utility companies, they are also linked up to the agribusiness-biotech companies involved in the food industry. Tap water is purchased by Coca-Cola from a municipal water facility and then resold on a retail basis. It is estimated that in the U.S., forty percent of bottled water is tap water.[18]

In India, Coca-Cola has contributed to the depletion of ground water to the detriment of local communities:

Communities across India living around Coca-Cola's bottling plants are experiencing severe water shortages, directly as a result of Coca-Cola's massive extraction of water from the common groundwater resource. The wells have run dry and the hand water pumps do not work any more. Studies, including one by the Central Ground Water Board in India, have confirmed the significant depletion of the water table.[19]

When the water is extracted from the common groundwater resource by digging deeper, the water smells and tastes strange. Coca-Cola has been indiscriminately discharging its wastewater into the fields around its plant and sometimes into rivers in the area, including the Ganges. The result has been that the groundwater has been polluted as well as the soil. Public health authorities have posted signs around wells and hand pumps advising the community that the water is unfit for human consumption.

Tests conducted by a variety of agencies, including the government of India, confirmed that Coca-Cola products contained high levels of pesticides, and as a result, the Parliament of India has banned the sale of Coca-Cola in its cafeteria. However, Coca-Cola not only continues to sell drinks laced with poisons in India (that could never be sold in the U.S. and EU), but it is also introducing new products in the Indian market. And as if selling drinks with DDT and other pesticides to Indians was not enough, one of Coca-Cola's latest bottling facilities to open in India, in

Ballia, is located in an area with a severe contamination of arsenic in its groundwater.[20]

In developing countries, the hikes in fuel prices have increased the costs of boiling tap water by households, which in turn favors the privatization of water resources. In the more advanced phase of water privatization, the actual ownership of lakes and rivers by private corporations is contemplated. Mesopotamia was not only invaded for its extensive oil resources, the Valley of the Two Rivers (Tigris and Euphrates) has extensive water reserves.

We are dealing with a complex and centralized constellation of economic power in which the instruments of market manipulation have a direct bearing on the lives of millions of people. The prices of food, water and fuel are determined at the global level, beyond the reach of national government policy. The price hikes of these three essential commodities constitute an instrument of "economic warfare", carried out through the "free market" on the futures and options exchanges.

The Commission on Population Growth and the American Future

But we are not dealing solely with market concepts. The outbreak of famines in different parts of the world, resulting from spiraling food and fuel prices, has broad strategic and geopolitical implications. In the words of Henry Kissinger:

> "Control oil and you control nations; control food and you control the people."

President Richard Nixon, at the outset of his term in office in 1969, asserted "his belief that overpopulation gravely threatens world peace and stability." Henry Kissinger, who at the time was Nixon's National Security adviser, directed various agencies of government to jointly undertake "a study of the impact of world population growth on U.S. security and overseas interests."[21]

In March 1970, the U.S. Congress set up a Commission on Population Growth and the American Future.[22] The Commission was no ordinary Task Force. It integrated representatives from USAID, the State Department and the Department of Agriculture with CIA and Pentagon officials. Its objective was not to assist developing countries but rather to curb world population with a view to serving U.S. strategic and national security interests. The Commission also viewed population control as a means to ensuring a stable and secure environment for U.S. investors as well as gaining control over developing countries' mineral and petroleum resources.

This Commission completed its work in December 1974 and circulated a classified document entitled *National Security Study Memorandum 200: Implications of Worldwide Population Growth for U.S. Security and Overseas Interests* to "designated Secretaries and Agency heads for their review and comments."[23] In November 1975, the report and its recommendations were endorsed by President Gerald Ford.

Kissinger had indeed intimated in the context of the National Security Study Memorandum 200 (NSSSM 200) that the recurrence of famines, disease and war could constitute a de facto instrument of population control. Although the NSSM 200 report did not assign, for obvious reasons, an explicit policy role to famine formation, it nonetheless intimated that the occurrence of famines could, under certain circumstances, provide a *de facto* solution to overpopulation:

> Accordingly, those countries where large-scale hunger and malnutrition are already present face the bleak prospect of little, if any, improvement in the food intake in the years ahead, barring a major foreign financial food aid program, more rapid expansion of domestic food production, reduced population growth or some combination of all three. Worse yet, a series of crop disasters could transform some of them into classic Malthusian cases with famines involving millions of people.

> While foreign assistance probably will continue to be forthcoming to meet short-term emergency situations like the threat of mass starvation, it is more questionable whether aid donor countries will be prepared to provide the sort of massive food aid called for by the import projections on a long-term continuing basis.

> Reduced population growth rates clearly could bring significant relief over the longer term... In the extreme cases where population pressures lead to endemic famine, food riots, and breakdown of social order, those conditions are scarcely conducive to systematic exploration for mineral deposits or the long-term

investments required for their exploitation. Short of famine, unless some minimum of popular aspirations for material improvement can be satisfied, and unless the terms of access and exploitation persuade governments and peoples that this aspect of the international economic order has "something in it for them," concessions to foreign companies are likely to be expropriated or subjected to arbitrary intervention. Whether through government action, labor conflicts, sabotage, or civil disturbance, the smooth flow of needed materials will be jeopardized. Although population pressure is obviously not the only factor involved, these types of frustrations are much less likely under conditions of slow or zero population growth.[24]

The report concludes with a couple of key questions pertaining to the role of food as "an instrument of national power", which could be used in the pursuit of U.S. strategic interests:

On what basis should such food resources then be provided? Would food be considered an instrument of national power? Will we be forced to make choices as to whom we can reasonably assist, and if so, should population efforts be a criterion for such assistance? Is the U.S. prepared to accept food rationing to help people who can't/won't control their population growth?

◆

NOTES

1. Bill Van Auken, "Amid Mounting Food Crisis, Governments fear Revolution of the Hungry", *Global Research*, http://www.global-research.ca/index.php?context=va&aid=8846, 30 April 2008.
2. Jeffrey Gettleman, "Famine Looms as Wars Rend Horn of Africa", *New York Times*, http://www.nytimes.com/2008/05/17/world/africa/17somalia.html, 17 May 2008.
3. Oxfam's Rob McNeil, quoted in Barry Mason, "Famine in East Africa: Catastrophe threatens as food prices rise", *World Socialist Website*, http://www.wsws.org/articles/2008/aug2008/east-a06.sh tml, 6 August 2008.

4. Ian Angus, "Food Crisis: 'The Greatest Demonstration of the Historical Failure of the Capitalist Model'", *Global Research*, http://www.globalresearch.ca/index.php?context=va&aid=8836, 28 April 2008.

5. Greg Muttitt, "Control Freaks, Cargill and ADM", *The Ecologist*, March 2001.

6. Ian Angus, "Food Crisis: 'The Greatest Demonstration of the Historical Failure of the Capitalist Model'", *Global Research*, http://www.globalresearch.ca/index.php?context=va&aid=8836, 28 April 2008.

7. Robert Zoellick, World Bank head, quoted by *BBC*, 2 May 2008.

8. Michel Chossudovsky, *The Globalization of Poverty and the New World Order*, Global Research, Montreal, 2003, p. 210.

9. Michel Chossudovsky, "Global Famine", *Global Research*, http://www.globalresearch.ca/index.php?context=va&aid=8877, 2 May 2008.

10. Michel Chossudovsky, *The Globalization of Poverty and the New World Order*, Global Research, Montreal, 2003, Chapter 9.

11. Interview with Canadian economist, Professor Antoine Ayoub, *Radio Canada*, May 2008.

12. Ed Wallace, "The Reason for High Oil Prices", *Business Week*, http://www.businessweek.com/lifestyle/content/may2008/bw20080513_720178.htm, May 13, 2008.

13. Miguel Angel Blanco, *La Clave*, Madrid, June 2008.

14. *Ibid.*

15. BBC News, "Free Water for all in Africa?", http://news.bbc.co.uk/2/hi/africa/ 4375409.stm, 24 March 2005.

16. Maude Barlow and Tony Clarke, "Water Privatization: The World Bank's Latest Market Fantasy", Polaris Institute, Ottawa, 2004.

17. Ann Ninan, "Private Water, Public Misery", India Resource Center, http://www.indiaresource.org/issues/water/2003/privatewater-publicmisery.html, 16 April 2003.

18. Jared Blumenfeld and Susan Leal, "The Real Cost of Bottled Water", *San Francisco Chronicle*, http://articles.sfgate.com/2007-02-18/opinion/17232292 _1_ bottled-drinking-water-container-recycling-institute, 18 February 2007.

19. Nagraj Adve, "Coca-Cola Crisis in India", *Indian Resource Center:* http://www.indiaresource.org/campaigns/coke/, 24 September, 2004.

20. *Ibid.*

21. Stephen D. Mumford, *National Security Study Memorandum 200: World Population Growth And U.S. Security*, *The Social Contract*, Vol. III,

No. 2, http://www.population-security.org/mumf-93-01.htm, Winter 1992-93.

22. The Center for Research on Population and Security, *Rockefeller Commission on Population and the American Future,* Introduction and Chapter 1, http://www.population-security.org/rockefeller/001_population_growth_and_the_american_future.htm , 18 July 1969.

23. United States National Security Council, *1974 National Security Study Memorandum 200: Implications of Worldwide Population Growth for U.S. Security and Overseas Interests*, November 1975.

24. *Ibid.*

25. *Ibid.*, emphasis added.

CHAPTER 8
Poverty and Social Inequality
Peter Phillips

A report from The World Bank admits that in 2005, three billion one hundred and forty million people lived on less than $2.50 a day, and about 44 percent of these people survive on less than $1.25. Complete and total wretchedness can be the only description for the circumstances faced by so many, especially those in urban areas. Simple items like phone calls, nutritious food, vacations, television, dental care and inoculations are beyond the possible for billions of people.

Globalization is accompanied by the increasing impacts of world hunger and starvation. Over 30 000 people a day (85 percent are children under the age of five) die of malnutrition, curable diseases and starvation. The numbers of unnecessary deaths has exceeded 300 million people over the past forty years.[1]

These are the people who David Rothkopf, in his book *Superclass*, calls *the unlucky*. "If you happen to be born in the wrong place, like sub-Saharan Africa... that is bad luck," Rothkopf writes.[2] Rothkopf goes on to describe how the top ten percent of the adults worldwide own 84 percent of the wealth and the bottom half owns barely one percent. Included in the top ten percent of wealth holders are the one thousand global billionaires. But is such a contrast of wealth inequality really the result of luck, or are there policies, supported by political elites, that protect the few at the expense of the many?

Farmers around the world grow more than enough food to feed the entire world adequately. Global grain production yielded a record 2.3 billion tons in 2007, up four percent from the year before, yet billions of people go hungry every day.

TEXT BOX 8.1
WHO ARE THE RICHEST MEN AND WOMEN IN AMERICA

Who's on and who's off; who's up and who's down on this year's list of America's richest?

According to *Forbes Magazine*:

> The rich haven't gotten richer – or poorer – this year. The price of admission to this, the 27th edition of The Forbes 400, is 1.3 billion dollars for the second year in a row. The assembled net worth of America's wealthiest rose by thirty billion dollars – only two percent – to 1.57 trillion dollars.

> Rising prices of oil and art paved the way for 31 new members and eight returnees, while volatile stock and housing markets forced 33 plutocrats from our rankings.

Source: Forbes.com, The Forbes 400, Richest People in America lists, http://www.forbes.com/2008/09/16/richest-american-billionaires-lists-400list08-cx_mm_dg_0917richintro.html

Among the richest Americans are Bill Gates, Warren Buffett, New York Mayor Michael Bloomberg and the Walton family, which owns the Walmart franchise. The Waltons are listed individually in the top ten richest people in America. The combined wealth of Christy, Alice, Robson and Jim Walton puts them ahead of Bill Gates and Warren Buffett.

The information tabulated by Forbes.com is based on declared wealth. It does not take into account the billions of dollars of undeclared wealth.

The Forbes 400 list notes that Mayor Mike Bloomberg:

> [Became] America's 8th-richest citizen after a transaction put a solid valuation on Bloomberg LP: he borrowed to buy a 20% stake in his company from Merrill Lynch in July for $4.5 billion. Today he owns 88% of the financial data and news outfit he founded in 1982. (*Ibid.*)

This transaction was completed by Mike Bloomberg prior to the collapse of Merrill Lynch two months later. On September 14, Merrill Lynch was sold off to Bank of America for a modest fifty billion dollars.

Michel Chossudovsky

Grain.org describes the core reasons for continuing hunger in an article entitled "Making a Killing from Hunger".[3] It turns out that while farmers grow enough food to feed the world, commodity speculators and huge grain traders like Cargill control the global food prices and distribution. Starvation is profitable for corporations when demands for food push the prices up. Cargill announced that profits for commodity trading for the first quarter of 2008 were 86 percent above 2007. World food prices grew 22 percent from June 2007 to June 2008 and a significant portion of the increase was propelled by the 175 billion dollars invested in commodity futures that speculate on price instead of seeking to feed the hungry. The result is wild food price spirals, both up and down, with food insecurity remaining widespread. (See Chapter 8).

Poverty in America

For a family on the bottom rung of poverty, a small price increase is the difference between life and death, yet the Obama administration has not declared a war on poverty and undernourishment.

Instead both parties talk about national security and the continuation of the war on terror as if this were the primary concern in the world. Given that ten times as many innocent people died on 9/11 than those in the World Trade centers, where is the Manhattan Project for global hunger? Where is the commitment to national security though unilateral starvation relief? Where is the outrage in the corporate media with pictures of dying children and an analysis of who benefits from hunger?

American people cringe at the thought of starving children, often thinking that there is little they can do about it, proclaiming, *I am glad I live in America.* However, in a globalized economy there are no safe enclaves, poverty and starvation elsewhere can become poverty and wretchedness here as well.

The Center for Budget and Policy Priorities, using Department of Commerce data, reported, "The share of national income going to wages and salaries in 2006 was at its lowest level on record, with data going back to 1929."[4]

Wages for American workers have been flat for thirty years and in decline for several. A family of three, for example, working full

TEXT BOX 8.2
POVERTY AND SOCIAL INEQUALITY IN AMERICA: OECD STUDY

According to a 2008 Study of the Organization for Economic Cooperation and Development (OECD), the levels of social inequality in
the United States are among the highest in the OECD countries.
OECD member countries consist, with the exception of Mexico of
the advanced developed countries. The data used for the OECD
study precedes the 2008 economic crisis, which has served to exacerbate prevailing conditions of social inequality:

- Rich households in America have been leaving both middle and
  poorer income groups behind. *This has happened in many countries,
  but nowhere has this trend been so stark as in the United States.* The average income of the richest ten percent is 93 000 U.S. dollars in
  purchasing power parities, the highest level in the OECD. However,
  the poorest ten percent of the U.S. citizens have an income of
  5 800 U.S. dollars per year – about twenty percent lower than the
  average for OECD countries.

- The distribution of earnings widened by twenty percent since the
  mid-1980s which is more than in most other OECD countries. This
  is the main reason for widening inequality in America.

- Redistribution of income by government plays a relatively minor
  role in the United States. Only in Korea is the effect smaller. This is
  partly because the level of spending on social benefits such as
  unemployment benefits and family benefits is low – equivalent to
  just nine percent of household incomes, while the OECD average
  is 22 percent. The effectiveness of taxes and transfers in reducing
  inequality has fallen still further in the past ten years.

- Child poverty – that is, children in a household with less than half
  the median income – has fallen since 1985, from 25 to 20 percent
  but poverty rates among the elderly increased from 20 to 23 percent. Both of these trends are in the opposite direction to those of
  the other countries in the OECD.

- Social mobility is lower in the United States than in other countries
  like Denmark, Sweden and Australia. Children of poor parents are
  less likely to become rich than children of rich parents.

- Wealth is distributed much more unequally than income: the top
  one percent control some 25 to 33 percent of total net worth and
  the top ten percent hold 71 percent. For comparison, the top ten
  percent have 28 percent of total income.

Source: Organization for Economic Cooperation and Development, *Growing Unequal?:
Income Distribution and Poverty in OECD Countries*, OECD, Paris 2008 (emphasis added).

TEXT BOX 8.3
MEASURING POVERTY IN AMERICA: THE U.S. CENSUS BUREAU

According to the 2008 U.S. Census Bureau on Poverty in America, the average household income fell between 2007 and 2008, "and the decline was widespread." The Census noted that the declines in income "coincide with the recession that started in December 2007."

Between 2007 and 2008:
The poverty rate increased
The number of uninsured increased
The average household income declined by 3.6 percent
Real per capita income declined by 3.1 percent for the total population
- per capita income declined by 2.9 percent for non-Hispanic Whites
- per capita income declined by 3.8 percent for Blacks
- per capita income declined by 3.3 percent for Hispanics

In 2008:
The official poverty rate was 13.2 percent (39.8 million), the highest poverty rate since 1997
- 12.5 percent in 2007
39.8 million people were in poverty
- 37.3 million in 2007
- this is the second consecutive annual increase in the number of people in poverty
The poverty rate increased for non-Hispanic Whites to 8.6 percent (17 million)
- 8.2 percent in 2007 (16 million)
- non-Hispanic Whites accounted for 42.7 percent of the people in poverty, while being 65.4 percent of the total population
The poverty rate increased for Asians to 11.8 percent (1.6 million)
- 10.2 percent in 2007 (1.3 million)
The poverty rate increased for Hispanics to 23.2 percent (11 million)
- 21.5 percent in 2007 (9.9 million)
The poverty rate was statistically unchanged between 2007 and 2008 for Blacks, at 24.7 percent, or 9.4 million
The poverty rate increased for children under 18 years old to 19 percent (18 percent in 2007)
The poverty rate increased for people 18-64 to 11.7 percent (10.9 percent in 2007)
Remained statistically unchanged for people 65 and over at 9.7 percent
Since 1960, the number of people below poverty has not exceeded the 2008 figure of 39.8 million people

Andrew Gavin Marshall

Source: U.S. Census Bureau, *Income, Poverty, and Health Insurance Coverage in the United States: 2008*. U.S. Department of Commerce: September 2009.

time at the new minimum wage of $7.25 an hour would only earn an annual income of 15 080 dollars – well below the poverty threshold. Costs for basic needs such as energy, housing and healthcare have soared while security in the form of living wage jobs, healthcare and retirement benefits are increasingly denied to American workers and their families.

As the world goes, so goes the American economy as well. Massive wealth inequality is the primary factor in starvation throughout the world and increasingly in the U.S. The average U.S. CEO makes over ten million dollars, and U.S. corporate tax collections at the federal level alone have fallen from 4.8 percent of the gross domestic product in the 1950s to only 1.6 percent in 2004 – a drop of two-thirds. There is more wealth now than ever in history, but it is sharply concentrated in the top ten percent of the people. Over ten trillion dollars from U.S. sources alone is hidden in offshore tax havens worldwide.

It is a moral imperative for us, as the richest nation in the world, to prioritize a political movement of human betterment and starvation relief for the billions in need both here and abroad. This is what Pope Benedict, in his recent *Charity in Truth* encyclical letter, called "distributive justice." Global hunger and massive wealth inequality are based on political policies and distributive mechanisms that can be changed. It is our task to democratically make these required changes. Our own individual security, wellbeing and freedom are in the balance.

◆

NOTES

1. Mark R. Elsis, "The Three Top Sins of the Universe", http://starvation.net/, 9 February 2002.
2. David Rothkopf, *Superclass: The Global Power Elite and the World They Are Making*, Penguin, Toronto, 2009.
3. GRAIN, "Making a Killing from Hunger", *Grain*, http://www.grain.org/articles/?id=39, April 2008.
4. Aviva Aron-Dine and Isaac Shapiro, "Share of National Income Going to Wages and Salaries at Record Low in 2006", *Center for Budget and Policy Priorities*, using Department of Commerce data, http://www.cbpp.org/cms/?fa=view&id=634, Revised 29 March 2007.

PART III

War, National Security and World Government

CHAPTER 9

War and the Economic Crisis

Michel Chossudovsky

Economic conquest is an integral part of America's military adventure. The U.S. military and intelligence apparatus consults with Wall Street and the Texas oil giants. Conversely, the IMF and the World Bank, which have a mandate to supervise macroeconomic reform in developing countries, are in liaison with the U.S. State Department and the Pentagon.

Economic warfare supports Washington's military roadmap. We are looking at an integrated process involving conquest through outright military operations and theater wars on the one hand, and the destabilization and conquest of sovereign countries through other means on the other.

Introduction

Economic warfare consists in destabilizing the economies of sovereign countries and impoverishing their respective populations. Since the early 1980s, this process has been marked by the deliberate fracture of national monetary institutions under the guidance of the International Monetary Fund (IMF), acting on behalf of Wall Street.

The manipulation of market forces through the imposition of strong "economic medicine" under the helm of the IMF supports U.S.-NATO strategic and geopolitical objectives. Similarly, the speculative attacks waged by powerful banking conglomerates in the currency, commodity and stock markets are acts of financial warfare. They seek to destabilize the monetary systems of nation states. With the onslaught of derivative trade, the gamut of speculative instruments has been used to appropriate and accumulate vast amounts of money wealth.

Destabilization of national institutions also occurs through "regime change", including the so-called "colored revolutions", often involving covert intelligence operations in support of "civil wars" with a view to fragmenting and ultimately destabilizing national societies and enforcing the outright privatization of state assets. The U.S.-led war and the global economic crisis are intimately related. The implications of the military "surge" on the U.S. economy are far-reaching. The increased levels of military spending are largely at the expense of social programs and employment creation in the civilian economy.

The extension of the Middle East Central Asian war into new frontiers is intimately related to the New Cold War and the veiled threats directed against Moscow and Beijing. Both Russia and China have significant oil and gas interests in Central Asia, including investments in strategic pipeline projects.

One of the main objectives of the U.S.-sponsored war is to exclude Russia and China. What is contemplated by the U.S.-NATO-Israel alliance is the militarization of a region extending from the tip of the Arabian peninsula to the Caspian Sea, and from the Eastern Mediterranean to the Chinese border. This region encompasses approximately sixty percent of the world's reserves of oil and natural gas. Competing oil companies from China and Russia are viewed as encroaching upon the interests of the dominant Anglo-American oil conglomerates.

The development and production of advanced weapons systems, the construction of military bases, the recruitment of troops to serve in the war theater and the outsourcing of contracts to mercenary companies are an integral part of the U.S. economy.

In America and the member states of the Atlantic Alliance, human and material resources are allocated to a "killing machine", which results in the loss of life and the outright destruction, through invasion and conquest, of the national economies of sovereign countries.

The financing of an oversized U.S. war economy triggers imbalances in the U.S. monetary system, destabilizes the U.S. fiscal structure and creates imbalances in the allocation of human and material resources. The financing of the war economy through tax revenues undermines public spending and creates a vacuum in the provision of essential social services.

Background

The 2008-2009 financial meltdown occurred at the crossroads of a major escalation in U.S.-NATO military operations. This escalation is not limited to the Middle East and Central Asia; it directly threatens Russia and China. It is also marked by a process of militarization of the Western Hemisphere, as well as an extension of America's sphere of influence into the African continent.

Under the Obama administration, the Pentagon has outlined the next phase of America's "Star Wars", initially launched under Ronald Reagan at the height of the Cold War era. It consists in deploying a "global missile defense shield", as well as establishing a permanent U.S. military presence in Eastern Europe and the Caucasus, within proximity of the Russian border. While the rhetoric of U.S. foreign policy under the Obama administration is more "courteous" and diplomatic compared to that of the Bush administration, both Russia and China have been the object of veiled U.S.-NATO military threats.

The world is at a dangerous crossroads: a New Cold War predicated on "pre-emptive warfare" has unfolded. The "global missile shield" is based on the notion of a "successful first strike" pre-emptive nuclear attack directed against Russia and China. It is viewed by U.S. strategic analysts as a means to coercing Moscow and Beijing into accepting U.S.-NATO hegemony in military affairs, as well as a subordinate role in the global capitalist world economy.

A confrontation with Russia in the Caucasus was triggered in August 2008, barely two months before the meltdown of financial markets. A full-scale regional war erupted between Georgia and Russia. The attacks had been carefully coordinated by the U.S. military and NATO. In mid-July 2008, Georgian and U.S. troops held a joint military exercise entitled "Immediate Response" in preparation of an attack on Russian forces in South Ossetia. Georgia's U.S.-NATO sponsored war on South Ossetia was not meant to be won. It was intended to destabilize the region while also triggering an atmosphere of U.S.-NATO confrontation with Russia.

From the Truman Doctrine to Obama

Historically, warfare has been an instrument of economic conquest. U.S. foreign policy and the Pentagon's war plans are intimately related to the process of economic globalization. The Pentagon is not only in liaison with the State Department, it also has informal ties with Wall Street, the Texas oil giants, not to mention the IMF and World Bank, which have played a key role in the process of destabilizing national economies.

High-level consultations are held between the Bretton Woods, the U.S. State Department, NATO and the Pentagon with a view to coordinating military operations with various forms of policy intervention including monetary reform and the outright privatization of entire national economies.

From the Truman Doctrine formulated in the late 1940s by George Kennan to the Bush Junior and Obama administrations, there has been a consistent thread: the neo-cons have described it as "The Long War", a military blueprint for global economic and political domination, a "war without borders".

George F. Kennan outlined in a 1948 State Department brief what was later described as the "Truman doctrine."[1] What this 1948 document conveys is continuity in U.S. foreign policy, from "Containment" to "Pre-emptive" Warfare. U.S. foreign policy, alongside the Pentagon's military doctrine, have evolved from containment of the "Communist threat" to "the Global War on Terrorism". In retrospect, a modicum of global security prevailed in the Cold War environment in comparison to the present era.

In U.S. foreign policy, a bipartisan consensus has prevailed throughout what is euphemistically called the "Post War Era", an era of continuous U.S. sponsored theater wars (e.g. Korea, Vietnam, Cambodia, Yugoslavia, Afghanistan, Iraq), *ad hoc* military interventions, U.S. supported "civil wars" (e.g. Rwanda, The Congo, Sudan), covert intelligence operations, coups d'états, regime change and "colored revolutions". U.S. foreign policy supports the expansion of U.S. corporate capital. Successive Democratic and Republican administrations, from Harry Truman to George W. Bush and Barack Obama, have contributed to carrying out this military agenda of global economic conquest.

Kennan's writing points to the formation of a dominant Anglo-American alliance, which currently characterizes the close relationship between Washington and London. It also points to the inclusion of Canada in the Anglo-American military axis. Kennan also underscored the importance of preventing the development of a continental European power (i.e. The Franco-German alliance) which might compete or challenge the U.S. This objective was largely achieved in the wake of the 2003 invasion of Iraq. From skepticism concerning Iraq's alleged weapons of mass destruction (WMD) to outright condemnation, in the months leading up to the March 2003 invasion, France and Germany have unreservedly accepted and endorsed U.S. hegemony in military affairs.

With regard to Asia, including China and India, Kennan hinted to the importance of articulating a military solution: "The day is not far off when we are going to have to deal in straight power concepts. The less we are then hampered by idealistic slogans, the better."[2] Moreover, from the outset of the Cold War era, Washington was also intent upon weakening the United Nations as a genuine international body, an objective which has in large part been accomplished under the Clinton, Bush and Obama administrations.

When viewed in a historical context, the wars in Palestine, Yugoslavia, Afghanistan and Iraq are part of the same post Cold War "military roadmap", responding to the same strategic and economic objectives. From a geopolitical standpoint, these wars are intimately related. Iran and Syria have already been identified, as part of the military roadmap, as the next targets of the U.S.-NATO-Israeli led war.

The military road map is a planned sequence of military operations. According to an unnamed Pentagon official quoted by General Wesley Clark (ret): "[The] five-year campaign plan [includes]... a total of seven countries, beginning with Iraq, then Syria, Lebanon, Libya, Iran, Somalia and Sudan."[3]

According to General Wesley Clark, the Pentagon, by late 2001, was planning to attack Lebanon. The Israeli-led war on Lebanon was carried out five years later in 2006:

As I went back through the Pentagon in November 2001, one of the senior military staff officers had time for a chat. Yes, we were still on track for going against Iraq, he said. But there was more. This was being discussed as part of a five-year campaign plan, he said, and there were a total of seven countries, beginning with Iraq, then Syria, Lebanon, Libya, Iran, Somalia and Sudan...

He said it with reproach – with disbelief, almost – at the breadth of the vision. I moved the conversation away, for this was not something I wanted to hear. And it was not something I wanted to see moving forward, either... I left the Pentagon that afternoon deeply concerned.[4]

The "Global War on Terrorism"

Going after "Islamic terrorists" and carrying out a worldwide pre-emptive war to "protect the Homeland" are used to justify both a military as well as an economic agenda. "The Global War on Terrorism" (GWOT), launched in the wake of the 9/11 attacks, is presented as a "clash of civilizations", a war between competing values and religions, when in reality it is an outright war of conquest, guided by strategic and economic objectives.

The GWOT has become, in the wake of the Cold War, the ideological backbone of the American Empire. It defines U.S. military doctrine, including the pre-emptive use of nuclear weapons against the "state sponsors" of terrorism. The pre-emptive "defensive war" doctrine and the "war on terrorism" against Al Qaeda constitute essential building blocks of America's National Security Strategy as formulated in early 2002. The objective was to present "pre-emptive military action", meaning war as an act of "self-defense" against two categories of enemies, "rogue States" and "Islamic terrorists", both of which are said to possess "weapons of mass destruction".

The logic of the "outside enemy" and the evildoer allegedly responsible for American civilian deaths prevails over common sense. In the inner consciousness of Americans, the attacks of September 11, 2001, justify acts of war, which are presented to public opinion as a humanitarian endeavor, as an international campaign against Al Qaeda:

As was demonstrated by the losses on September 11, 2001, mass civilian casualties is the specific objective of terrorists and these losses would be exponentially more severe if terrorists acquired and used weapons of mass destruction."[5]

The economic objectives are acknowledged but rarely highlighted as a justification for waging war. The "Global War on Terrorism" supports U.S. corporate and strategic interests. It builds a consensus that America is being attacked by terrorists. It obfuscates what is tantamount to a profit driven military agenda which directly serves the interests of Wall Street, the oil giants, and the U.S. military industrial complex.

Amply documented, the war in the Middle East and Central Asia seeks to establish strategic control over more than sixty percent of the world's reserves of oil and natural gas. It also serves to destabilize national currencies and take over the financial and banking institutions of conquered nations. Close to seventy percent of the world's reserves of oil and natural gas are located in Muslim countries. The demonization of Muslims, which underlies a global crusade against Islamic terrorists, serves to justify the U.S. sponsored "Battle for Oil".

The Post Cold War doctrine of pre-emptive warfare is supported by the development of an increasingly sophisticated and advanced military arsenal, not to mention the pre-emptive use of nuclear weapons as an instrument of "self defense". These U.S.-NATO nuclear warheads are now directed against competing capitalist nations, including Russia, China, Iran and Syria.

The Project for a New American Century

The Neo-Cons' Project for a New American Century (PNAC), formulated in 2000, was the culmination of a broad military and strategic design geared towards establishing U.S. military hegemony and global economic domination, as initially formulated under the "Truman Doctrine" at the outset of the Cold War.[6]

The PNAC is a neo-conservative think tank linked to the Defense-Intelligence establishment, the Republican Party and the powerful Council on Foreign Relations (CFR) which plays a behind-the-scenes role in the formulation of U.S. foreign policy. The PNAC document posits the need to wage major, simultaneous theater wars in different regions of the world, while also developing so-called "constabulary functions". It also posits a major overhaul of the U.S. military arsenal.

The PNAC's declared objectives are:

- Defend the American homeland
- Fight and decisively win multiple, simultaneous major theater wars
- Perform the "constabulary" duties associated with shaping the security environment in critical regions
- Transform U.S. forces to exploit the "revolution in military affairs"

G. W. Bush's Deputy Defense Secretary Paul Wolfowitz, his Defense Secretary Donald Rumsfeld and Vice President Dick Cheney had commissioned the PNAC blueprint prior to the 2000 presidential elections. The PNAC outlines a roadmap of conquest. Distinct from theater wars, the so-called "constabulary duties" imply a form of global military policing using various instruments of military intervention including punitive bombings and the sending in of U.S. Special Forces:

> The Pentagon must retain forces to preserve the current peace in ways that fall short of conduction [of] major theater campaigns... These duties are today's most frequent missions, requiring forces configured for combat but capable of long-term, independent constabulary operations.[7]

"The Revolution in Military Affairs"

The PNAC's "revolution in military affairs" (meaning the development of new weapons systems) consists of:

1. The Strategic Defense Initiative (SDS), which has been the mainstay of both the Bush Junior and Obama administrations

2. The concurrent weaponization of space

3. The development of a new generation of nuclear weapons

The Strategic Defense Initiative, or "Star Wars", not only includes the controversial "Missile Shield", but also a wide range of offensive laser-guided weapons with striking capabilities anywhere in the world. The SDS also includes the instruments of weather and climatic warfare under the High Frequency Active Auroral Research Program (HAARP).[8] Recent scientific evidence suggests that HAARP is fully operational and has the ability of potentially triggering floods, droughts, hurricanes and earthquakes. From a military standpoint, HAARP is a weapon of mass destruction. Potentially, it constitutes an instrument of conquest capable of selectively destabilizing agricultural and ecological systems of entire regions.

Also contemplated is the Pentagon's so-called FALCON program. FALCON is the ultimate New World Order weapons system, to be used for global economic and political domination. It can strike from the continental U.S. anywhere in the world. It is described as a "global reach" weapon to be used to "react promptly and decisively to destabilizing or threatening actions by hostile countries and terrorist organizations". This hypersonic cruise weapon system to be developed by Northrop Grumman:

> Would allow the U.S. to conduct effective, time-critical strike missions on a global basis without relying on overseas military bases. FALCON would allow the U.S. to strike, either in support of conventional forces engaged in a war theater or in punitive bombings directed against countries that do not comply with U.S. economic and political diktats.[9]

The budgetary implications of these new weapons systems are far-reaching, requiring massive hikes in the outlays of the U.S. Department of Defense.

In this regard, the "Global War on Terrorism" served, in the post 9/11 era, to justify a major shift in the structure of military expenditure. In a bitter irony, five days before the 9/11 terrorist attacks on the World Trade Centre and the Pentagon, President Bush stated almost prophetically, "I have repeatedly said the only time to use Social Security money is in times of war, times of recession, or times of severe emergency. And I mean that. I mean that."[10]

The "emergency", "homeland security" and "war on terrorism" buzzwords have since then been used to mould U.S. public opinion into accepting a massive redirection of the nation's resources towards the military industrial complex. In turn, in the wake of the 9/11 terrorist attacks, "love of country", "allegiance" and "patriotism" increasingly pervade the media as well day-today political discourse. The hidden agenda was to create a new legitimacy, opening the door for a "revitalization of the nation's defense" while also providing a justification for direct military actions by the U.S. in different parts of the world.

Meanwhile, the post 9/11 shift from civilian into military production has been pouring wealth into the hands of defense contractors at the expense of civilian needs. The backlash on employment and social programs is the inevitable by-product of both the U.S. and NATO military projects, which channel vast amounts of state financial resources towards the war economy, at the expense of the civilian sectors. It is an essential feature of the economic crisis.

The results are plant closures and bankruptcies in the civilian economy and a rising tide of poverty and unemployment throughout the Western world. Moreover, contrary to the 1930s, the dynamic development of the weapons industry creates very few jobs.

In the development of the Pentagon's Joint Striker Fighter (JSF) program, creating each job, in the context of the 2001 Department of Defense procurement submissions by Lockheed Martin, Boeing and Northrop Grunman, was estimated to cost U.S. taxpayers between 37 and 66 million dollars.[11] Had this money been allocated to civilian production, the impact on employment creation would have been far-reaching.

Meanwhile, as the Western war economy flourishes, the relocation of the production of civilian manufactured goods to Third World countries has increased at a dramatic pace. The global economy is characterized by a bipolar relationship. The rich Western countries produce advanced weapons systems, whereas poor countries produce manufactured consumer goods. In a twisted logic, the military capabilities of the U.S. and its NATO allies are used to threaten and/or wage war on the developing countries, which supply Western markets with large amounts of consumer goods produced in cheap labor assembly plants.

America, in particular, has relied on this cheap supply of consumer goods to close down a large share of its manufacturing sector, while at the same time redirecting resources away from the civilian economy into the production of advanced weapons systems. And the latter, in a bitter irony, are slated to be used against China, the country which supplies America with a large share of its consumer goods.

This new direction of the U.S. economy generates hundreds of billions of dollars of surplus profits, which line the pockets of a handful of large corporations. While contributing very marginally to the rehabilitation of the employment of specialized scientific, technical and professional workers laid off by the civilian economy, this profit bonanza has also been used by the U.S. corporate establishment to finance – in the form of so-called "foreign investment" – the expansion of the American Empire in different parts of the world.[12]

Establishing Military Hegemony

In 2005, the Pentagon released the summary of a top secret document, which sketched America's agenda for global military domination.[13] While the document followed in the footsteps of the administration's "preemptive" war doctrine as detailed by the neo-cons' Project of the New American Century (PNAC), it went much further in setting the contours of Washington's global military agenda, including the notion of military "surge" applied in later part of Bush administration and at the outset of the Obama presidency.

The classified document called for a more "proactive" approach to warfare, beyond the weaker notion of "preemptive" and defensive actions, where military operations are launched against a "declared enemy" with a view to "preserving the peace" and "defending America". It also outlined America's global military mandate, beyond regional war theaters. This mandate included military operations directed against countries, which are not hostile to America, but which are considered strategic from the point of view of U.S. interests.

From a broad military and foreign policy perspective, the March 2005 Pentagon document constitutes an imperial design, which supports U.S. corporate interests worldwide:

> At its heart, the document is driven by the belief that the U.S. is engaged in a continuous global struggle that extends far beyond specific battlegrounds, such as Iraq and Afghanistan. The vision is for a military that is far more proactive, focused on changing the world instead of just responding to conflicts such as a North

Korean attack on South Korea, and assuming greater promi-nence in countries in which the U.S. isn't at war.[14]

The document suggests that its objective also consists in "offensive" rather than run-of-the-mill "preemptive" operations. There is, in this regard, a subtle nuance in relation to earlier post-9/11 national security statements:

> [The document presents] 'four core' problems, none of them in-volving traditional military confrontations. The services are told to develop forces that can: build partnerships with failing states to defeat internal terrorist threats; defend the homeland, includ-ing offensive strikes against terrorist groups planning attacks; influence the choices of countries at a strategic crossroads, such as China and Russia; and prevent the acquisition of weapons of mass destruction by hostile states and terrorist groups.[15]

The emphasis is no longer solely on waging major theater wars as outlined in the PNAC's Rebuilding America's Defenses; the 2005 Pentagon blueprint points to the need for a global deploy-ment of U.S. forces in acts of worldwide military policing and intervention. The PNAC in its September 2000 Report had described these non-theater military operations as "constabulary functions".

Recruitment of Troops to Police the Empire

The underlying emphasis is on the development and recruitment of specialized military manpower required to control and pacify "indigenous forces" and factions in different regions of the world:

> The classified guidance urges the military to come up with less doctrinaire solutions that include sending in smaller teams of culturally savvy soldiers to train and mentor indigenous forces.[16]

U.S. military involvement is not limited to the Middle East and Central Asia. The sending in of special forces in military policing operations, under the disguise of peace-keeping and training, is contemplated in all major regions of the world. A large part of these activities, however, is slated to be carried out by private mercenary companies on contract to the Penta-gon, NATO or the United Nations. The military manpower requirements as well as the equipment are specialized. The policing will not be conducted by regular army units as in a theater war.

From the "Post Cold War" to the "New Cold War"

While the "global war on terrorism" and the containment of "rogue states" still constitute the official justification and driving force, China and Russia are explicitly identified in the classified 2005 Pentagon document as potential enemies:

> The U.S. military... is seeking to dissuade rising powers, such as China, from challenging U.S. military dominance. Although weapons systems designed to fight guerrillas tend to be fairly cheap and low-tech, the review makes clear that to dissuade those countries from trying to compete, the U.S. military must retain its dominance in key high-tech areas, such as stealth technology, precision weaponry and manned and unmanned surveillance systems.[17]

While the European Union is not mentioned, the stated objective is to shunt the development of all potential military rivals.

"Trying to Run with the Big Dog"

An important and critical element stands out in this 2005 Pentagon statement, which has devastating economic and social implications: how does Washington intend to reach its goal of global military hegemony? Essentially through the continued development of the U.S. weapons industry, requiring a massive shift out of the production of civilian goods and services. In other words, the ongoing increase in defense spending feeds this new undeclared arms race, with vast amounts of public money channeled to America's major weapons producers.

The stated objective is to make the process of developing advanced weapons systems "so expensive" that no other power on earth will able to compete or challenge "The Big Dog" without jeopardizing its civilian economy:

> At the core of this strategy is the belief that the US must maintain such a large lead in crucial technologies that growing powers will conclude that it is too expensive for these countries to even think about trying to run with the big dog. *They will realize*

that it is not worth sacrificing their economic growth, said one defense consultant who was hired to draft sections of the document.[18]

The term "Big Dog" is part of the Pentagon's military jargon.

Military Surge under the Obama Presidency

The Pentagon's 2005 doctrine had set the stage for the "military surge". A significant hike in military spending under the disguise of a global "peacekeeping" mission was under way in the latter part of the Bush administration. A new military command: U.S. African Command (USAFRICOM) was established in October 2007, with a mandate to intervene in the U.S. sponsored "civil wars" in sub-Saharan Africa, including the Sudan, the Congo, Somalia and Nigeria.

At the very outset of the Obama presidency, at the height of the financial crisis, U.S. military bases were set up in Colombia, directly threatening Venezuela and Ecuador. This renewed and enhanced process of militarization of Latin America is being implemented to obstruct the emergence of nationalist, populist or progressive alternatives, which might challenge America's imperial design in the region. This course of action also serves to sustain free market reforms, while enforcing ongoing privatization programs under the helm of the IMF and the World Bank.

Militarization is an integral part of an economic agenda. The objective is to secure the hegemony of U.S. corporate capital throughout the hemisphere as well as enforce the control of the Federal Reserve and Wall Street over money creation, signifying the dollarization of national currencies throughout Latin America and the Caribbean. In turn, a new wide-ranging mandate was granted to U.S. Southern Command (USSOUTHCOM) in "counterinsurgency" and drug eradication operations, resulting in the presence of U.S. troops in much larger numbers in Central America and the Andean region of South America.

Veiled threats of a U.S. sponsored war on Venezuela have also been made. The unspoken mission of USSOUTHCOM, with headquarters in Miami and U.S. military installations throughout Latin America, is to ensure the maintenance of subservient national regimes, namely U.S. proxy governments committed to the Washington Consensus and the neoliberal policy agenda.

Protecting the Global Narcotics Economy

The Pentagon's design in Latin America is similar to that in Central Asia: "The qualitative escalations of counterinsurgency wars in Afghanistan and Colombia are... integrally related."[19] They are part of a similar regional strategy: USSOUTHCOM is to the Andean cocaine market what USCENTCOM and NATO are to the Afghan-Pakistani heroin economy. Afghanistan produces 92 percent of the world's heroin.[20] The underlying military and intelligence objective is to protect the cocaine and heroin markets, which feed billions of narco-dollars into the Western banking system. Drug trafficking constitutes "the third biggest global commodity in cash terms after oil and the arms trade."[21] Afghanistan and Colombia are the largest drug producing economies in the world, which feed a flourishing criminal economy. These countries are heavily militarized. The drug trade is protected. Amply documented, the CIA has played a central role in the development of both the Latin American and Asian drug triangles.

There are powerful business and financial interests behind narcotics. From this standpoint, geopolitical and military control over the drug routes is as strategic as oil and oil pipelines. The bulk of the revenues associated with the global trade in narcotics are not appropriated by terrorist groups and warlords, as suggested by the Vienna-based UN Office on Drugs and Crime (UNODC). Intelligence agencies, powerful business, drug traders and organized crime are competing for the strategic control over the heroin routes.

A large share of these multibillion dollar revenues of narcotics are deposited in the Western banking system. Most of the large international banks together with their affiliates in the offshore banking havens launder large amounts of narco-dollars. In the context of the ongoing financial crisis, the money flow of narco-dollars into the nexus of international banking has played a significant role: "Inter-bank loans were funded by money that originated from the drugs trade and other illegal activities... There were signs that some banks were rescued that way."[22]

This trade can only prosper if the main actors involved in narcotics have "political friends in high places". As legal and illegal undertakings are increasingly intertwined, the dividing line between "businesspeople" and criminals is blurred. In turn, the relationship among criminals, politicians and members of the intelligence establishment has tainted the structures of the state and the role of its institutions, including the military.

Geographic Extension of the Middle East Central Asian War Theater

Under the Obama presidency, we are no longer dealing with three separate and distinct war theaters: Afghanistan, Iraq and Palestine. Military escalation is conducive to the *de facto* integration of these individual war theaters.

The geographic boundaries of the Middle East Central Asian war zone extends from the tip of the Arabian Peninsula and the Gulf of Yemen to the Caspian Sea Basin, and from the Eastern Mediterranean to the heartland of Central Asia and southern Asia. In turn, with the surge in troop deployments initiated at the outset of the Obama administration, the Afghan war has spilled over into Pakistan.

The Persian Gulf is the world's most militarized naval seaway, with U.S. Central Command (USCENTCOM) based in Qatar and several military facilities in the Gulf states and Saudi Arabia. The Persian Gulf leads into the Arabian Sea and the Indian Ocean, which hosts Diego Garcia, one of America's largest combined naval and air force base.

While U.S. naval forces are deployed in the Persian Gulf and the Arabian Sea, the 2006 Israeli invasion and bombing of Lebanon set the stage for the militarization of the Eastern Mediterranean, with the stationing of German warships off the Israeli-Lebanese coastline. In the wake of the 2006 war on Lebanon, U.S.-NATO-Israeli threats directed against Syria and Iran became increasingly pervasive. In the months following the Lebanon war, Tel Aviv announced (in September 2006) plans to wage a pre-emptive "full-scale war" against Iran and Syria, implying the deployment of both air and ground force. These war plans were at the top of the Israeli defense agenda:

> "The challenge from Iran and Syria is now top of the Israeli defense agenda, higher than the Palestinian one," said an Israeli defense source. Shortly before the war in Lebanon Major-General Eliezer Shkedi, the commander of the air force, was placed in

charge of the 'Iranian front', a new position in the Israeli Defense Forces. His job will be to command any future strikes on Iran and Syria...

"In the past we prepared for a possible military strike against Iran's nuclear facilities," said one insider, "but Iran's growing confidence after the war in Lebanon means we have to prepare for a full-scale war, in which Syria will be an important player."[23]

Turkey and the frontline Arab States, through the NATO sponsored "Mediterranean Dialogue", are partners in this process.

Military Alliances: The U.S.-NATO-Israel Military Axis

At the 2004 NATO summit in Istanbul, NATO "upgraded" the Mediterranean Dialogue. The so-called Istanbul Cooperation Initiative "laid the groundwork for military integration of the six members of the Gulf Cooperation Council: Bahrain, Kuwait, Oman, Qatar, Saudi Arabia and the United Arab Emirates."[24]

In early 2005, the U.S., Israel and Turkey held military exercises in the Eastern Mediterranean, off the coast of Syria. These exercises were followed by NATO exercises which included Israel and several Arab countries.

NATO's sphere of influence includes Morocco, Algeria, Mauritania, Tunisia, Egypt, Jordan, as well Israel, all of which are members of NATO's Mediterranean Initiative. "Through this mechanism, the Mediterranean Sea has virtually become a NATO lake, surrounded almost entirely by NATO members or de facto [associate] NATO members."[25]

Israel's relationship to NATO, however, goes far beyond the "associate membership" status under the Mediterranean Initiative. In March 2005, NATO's Secretary General was in Tel Aviv with (former) prime minister Ariel Sharon and Israel's top military brass. This *de facto* bilateral military cooperation agreement, formally reached under the Mediterranean Dialogue, is viewed by the Israeli military as a means to "enhance Israel's deterrence capability regarding potential enemies threatening it, mainly Iran and Syria."[26]

The Israel-NATO protocol would in a sense obligate NATO to support Israel in an attack directed against Iran, as an act of "self-defense" on the part of Israel. The premise underlying NATO-Israel military cooperation is that Israel is under attack and that NATO would come to Israel's rescue invoking the doctrine of Collective Security under Article Five of the Washington Treaty, even though Israel is not a full member of the Atlantic alliance:

> The more Israel's image is strengthened as a country facing enemies who attempt to attack it for no justified reason, the greater will be the possibility that aid will be extended to Israel by NATO. Furthermore, Iran and Syria will have to take into account the possibility that the increasing cooperation between Israel and NATO will strengthen Israel's links with Turkey, also a member of NATO. Given Turkey's impressive military potential and its geographic proximity to both Iran and Syria, Israel's operational options against them, if and when it sees the need, could gain considerable strength. [27]

Underlying these military agreements, a cohesive U.S.-NATO-Israel military axis had emerged. This powerful alliance is dominated by Washington. The Pentagon ultimately controls the overall process of military decision making to the extent that neither Israel nor a NATO member state can undertake a separate military without the Pentagon's green light. Moreover, since 2009, Israel's air defense system is integrated into that of the U.S. and NATO.

Turkey and Israel

Turkey and Israel have been close military allies since the mid-1990s, paving the way for the subsequent integration of Israel as *de facto* member of NATO. In this context, the 2005 Israeli-NATO defense protocol also builds upon the framework of the bilateral military cooperation agreement between Israel and Turkey. Turkey is a major player inside NATO and has the largest capabilities within NATO to deploy ground forces.

A 1994 Security and Secrecy Agreement (SSA) was signed between Turkey and Israel. Initiated in Turkey under the Çiller government, the SSA had set the stage for a close relationship between the Tel Aviv and Ankara in military and intelligence cooperation, joint military exercises, weapons production and training.

The SSA has far-reaching implications. It also requires the exchange of military intelligence in what is described as the "guaranteed secrecy in the exchange and sharing of information".[28] Turkey and Israel have been actively cooperating in gathering intelligence directed against Syria and Iran and Iraq (prior to the 2003 invasion).

NATO Enlargement

By far, the U.S.-NATO-Israel axis constitutes the most powerful military alliance in world history. America's allies are the NATO member states, NATO associate member States and partners under the Istanbul Initiative (including Israel), the Mediterranean Dialogue, the Partnership for Peace, and various other bilateral agreements (New Zealand, Australia, Colombia, Mongolia, Singapore). All in all, the U.S.-NATO-Israel military axis includes more than fifty countries.[29]

The U.S.-NATO sponsored military alliance includes three recognized nuclear powers: the U.S., Britain and France. Germany is a *de facto* nuclear power in that it produces nuclear warheads for the French navy.[30] While Israel is not recognized officially as a nuclear power, its nuclear arsenal is considered by some observers to be more advanced and sophisticated than that of the UK.

Military Escalation: The "Af-Pak War"

Already in early 2008, following the assassination of Benazhir Bhutto, U.S.-NATO military extended its operations into Pakistan under the disguise of the "Global War on Terrorism". A report by the U.S. National Intelligence Council and the CIA forecast a "Yugoslav-like fate" for Pakistan "in a decade with the country riven by civil war, bloodshed and inter-provincial rivalries, as seen recently in Balochistan."[31] According to the NIC-CIA, Pakistan was slated to become a "failed state" by 2015, "as it would be affected by civil war, complete Talibanization and struggle for control of its nuclear weapons".[32]

The assassination of Benazir Bhutto as well as the installation of a weak "democratic" (and duly elected) successor government in Islamabad created conditions which paved the way for the destabilization and fragmentation of Pakistan as a nation state. There are indications that the assassination of Benazir Bhutto was anticipated by U.S. officials:

> It has been known for months that the Bush-Cheney adminis-tration and its allies have been maneuvering to strengthen their political control of Pakistan, paving the way for the expansion and deepening of the "war on terrorism" across the region.

> Various American destabilization plans, known for months by officials and analysts, proposed the toppling of Pakistan's mili-tary...

> The assassination of Bhutto appears to have been anticipated. There were even reports of "chatter" among U.S. officials about the possible assassinations of either Pervez Musharraf or Benazir Bhutto, well before the actual attempts took place.[33]

Coincidentally, at the height of the financial meltdown on Wall Street, on September 21, 2008, "a bomb ripped through the Marriott Hotel in Islamabad killing scores of people" in an alleged terrorist attack. This tragic event was used to justify the sending in of U.S. marines into Pakistan.[34]

This U.S. agenda for Pakistan is similar to that applied throughout the broader Middle East Central Asian region. U.S. strategy, supported by covert intelligence operations, consists in triggering ethnic and religious strife, abetting and financing secessionist movements, while also weakening the institutions of the central government.

Since 2008, in violation of Pakistan's national sovereignty, the U.S. military has carried out drone attacks in the Northern tribal areas, resulting in countless civilian deaths. The operation has been casually categorized by the Obama administration as a "counter-terrorist operation", rather than an undeclared act of military aggression. The surge in the number of troops to Afghanistan in 2010 is intended to allow for the deployment of a significant number of U.S. forces inside Pakistan. The broader objective is to foment separatist movements, fracture the Nation State and redraw the borders of Pakistan.

Continuity, characterized by the dominant role of the Pakistani military and intelligence, is being scrapped by the U.S. administration in favor of political breakup and balkanization

TEXT BOX 9.1
PAKISTAN'S OIL AND GAS RESERVES

Pakistan's extensive oil and gas reserves, largely located in Balochistan province, as well as its pipeline corridors, are considered strategic by the Anglo-American alliance, requiring the concurrent militarization of Pakistani territory.

Balochistan comprises more than forty percent of Pakistan's land mass, possesses important reserves of oil and natural gas as well as extensive mineral resources. It also houses a deep sea port largely financed by China located at Gwadar, on the Arabian Sea, not far from the Straits of Hormuz, where thirty percent of the world's daily oil supply moves by ship or pipeline. (See AsiaNews.it, 29 December 2007).

Pakistan has an estimated 25.1 trillion cubic feet (Tcf) of proven gas reserves of which nineteen trillion are located in Balochistan. The Iran-India pipeline corridor is slated to transit through Balochistan. Among foreign oil and gas contractors in Balochistan are BP, Italy's ENI, Austria's OMV, and Australia's BHP. It is worth noting that Pakistan's State oil and gas companies, including PPL which has the largest stake in the Sui oil fields of Balochistan are up for privatization under IMF-World Bank supervision.

According to the Oil and Gas Journal (OGJ), Pakistan had proven oil reserves of 300 million barrels, most of which are located in Balochistan. Other estimates place Balochistan oil reserves at an estimated six trillion barrels of oil reserves both on-shore and off-shore. (See Environment News Service, 27 October 2006).

of Pakistan.[35] Destabilization is also being implemented through covert operations, including support to terrorist groups inside Pakistan.

Under the scenario outlined in 2005 by the National Intelligence Council (NIC) document, applied by the Obama administration in the context of the Af Pak war: "Pakistan will not recover easily from decades of political and economic mismanagement, divisive policies, lawlessness, corruption and ethnic friction."[36] The U.S. course consists in fomenting social, ethnic and factional divisions and political fragmentation, including the territorial break-up of Pakistan. This course of action is also dictated by U.S. war plans in relation to both Afghanistan and Iran.[37]

The Strategic Role of India

While both India and Pakistan are formally allies of the U.S., Washington's design consists in:

1) destabilizing and breaking up Pakistan as a Nation State
2) fomenting long-standing divisions between Pakistan and India which could result in a regional war
3) developing a military and strategic alliance with India, which would be directed against China

Concurrent with these endeavors, Israel and India have entered into bilateral agreements in the sphere of military and space technology.

The Structure of Military Alliances: The Shanghai Cooperation Organization (SCO)

The structure of military alliances is crucial in assessing the outcome of military confrontations. Iran, Syria, China, Russia and North Korea are the object of military threats by the U.S., NATO and Israel, including the pre-emptive use of nuclear weapons. The confrontation – in what is described by some observers as "The New Cold War" – is between the U.S.-NATO-Israel military axis and the Shanghai Cooperation Organization (SCO), which regroups Russia, China and several former Soviet republics.

Iran has an observer member status in the Shanghai Cooperation Organization (SCO). In turn, the SCO has ties to the Collective Security Treaty Organization (CSTO), an overlapping military cooperation agreement between Russia, Armenia, Belarus, Uzbekistan, Kazakhstan, the Kyrgyz Republic and Tajikistan. Both China and Russia have far-reaching bilateral military cooperation agreements with Iran.

In October 2007, the Collective Security Treaty Organization (CSTO) and the Shanghai Cooperation Organization (SCO) signed a Memorandum of Understanding, laying the foundations for military cooperation between the two organizations. This SCO-CSTO agreement, barely mentioned by the Western media, involves the creation of a full-fledged military alliance between China, Russia and the member states of SCO-CSTO. It is worth noting that the CSTO and the SCO held joint military exercises in 2006, which coincided with those conducted by Iran.[38]

In the context of U.S. war plans directed against Iran, the U.S. is also intent upon targeting or weakening Iran's allies, namely Russia and China. In the case of China, Washington is seeking to disrupt Beijing's bilateral ties with Tehran, as well as Iran's rapprochement with the SCO, which has its headquarters in Beijing.

We are at a dangerous crossroads: The New Cold War is inherently unstable. U.S. and NATO military installations have been established directly on the borders of Russia and China. If Iran were to be the object of a pre-emptive bomb attack by the U.S. led alliance or by Israel, the entire Middle East-Central Asian region would flare up.

The Overriding Military Strength of the U.S.-NATO-Israel Axis

While the SCO-CSTO constitutes a potentially powerful military force, it does not match the combined military capabilities of the U.S.-NATO-Israel military axis, not to mention those of U.S.-NATO partner countries including Australia, South Korea, Taiwan, Singapore and Indonesia. Moreover, the SCO military alliance is weakened because both Russia and China remain, from an economic standpoint, subordinate to Western capitalism.

China is the West's cheap labor industrial colony. Its banking system was revamped in 2001 under a bilateral agreement between Washington and Beijing. This agreement, which was conditional upon China's entry into the WTO, has allowed Western and Japanese banks to play a dominant role in China's banking system. Western banks have entered the domestic market of retail banking and credit in Renminbi.

Similarly, Russia's financial system is extremely fragile, following the destructive macroeconomic reforms initially adopted in 1992 under President Boris Yeltsin. In both countries, Wall Street financial institutions, together with the IMF and the World Bank, play a behind the scenes role in shaping the direction of macroeconomic reform, not to mention the revamping of the national banking and financial architecture.

In other words, neither Russia nor China have the clout, in terms of their national banking institutions, to establish an alternative currency system which could challenge the dominion of the dollar and the Euro on global currency markets.

While Iran has observer status in the SCO, the Tehran government has indicated its desire to become a full member of the SCO. In recent years, Iran has strengthened its bilateral ties in the field of energy and oil and gas pipelines with India as well as Pakistan. The extension of the U.S. led war into Pakistan as well as the reinforcement of U.S.-India bilateral ties has served to further isolate Iran as well as create divisions between India and China. What Tehran is seeking is:

> ...nothing less than a blueprint for a new correlation of nations in Eurasia, whose collaboration in developing continental infrastructure – nuclear energy, gas and oil pipelines, and transportation – should establish the economic, and therefore political, basis for true independence.[39]

History points to the importance of competing military alliances. In the present context, the U.S. and its NATO partners are seeking to undermine the formation of a cohesive Eurasian SCO-CSTO military alliance, which could effectively challenge and contain U.S.-NATO military expansionism in Eurasia, combining the military capabilities not only of Russia and China, but also those of several former Soviet republics including Belarus, Armenia, Kazakhstan, Tajikistan Uzbekistan and the Kyrgyz Republic.

War and Globalization

"The Long War" supports a process of worldwide economic domination. War and globalization are intimately related. The U.S.-NATO military alliance supports the hegemony of both the U.S. dollar and the Euro. These two dominant global currency systems are intricately related. They are controlled and regulated by overlapping financial interests. The U.S.-Euro monetary arrangement and its imposition as a global currency system are protected by the Atlantic Alliance, which constitutes the military arm of the Western corporate establishment.

Wall Street creditors exert a significant influence within the European Monetary system. Since the early 1980s, this hegemonic role of Western financial institutions has been accompanied by the destabilization of national currencies. Devaluations coupled with monetary reform have been imposed on indebted developing countries under the brunt of the IMF's "bitter economic medicine". Throughout the Third World, currency devaluations ordered by the IMF have triggered hyperinflation and the collapse of national monetary systems.

In the wake of the Cold War, the destabilization of national monetary institutions has extended its grip into Eastern Europe, the former Soviet Union and the Balkans. Sovereignty over monetary policy is foregone. Central banks are under the surveillance of their external creditors. National currencies in the developing countries and in the former Soviet Bloc countries have become *de facto* proxy currencies linked either to the U.S. dollar or the Euro.

At the outset of the European common currency system, Britain decided not to adopt the Euro. London's High Street was closely aligned with Wall Street. Britain and America also signed an Anglo-American defense production agreement in 1999, the so-called "Atlantic Bridge". Meanwhile British Petroleum (BP) had become an Anglo-American conglomerate through the acquisition by BP, of AMOCO and Atlantic Ritchfield.

In the wake of the 2003 invasion Iraq, the relationship between America and the European Union, both in financial and military affairs, changed markedly. The Franco-German alliance as a common front directed against Anglo-American interests in oil and military production was significantly weakened. The U.S.-NATO military alliance became increasingly cohesive.

In turn, the "Dollar/Euro divide", which characterizes the Western dominated global monetary architecture, has also evolved. While there are important divisions within the Western financial establishment, the Federal Reserve and the European Monetary System are increasingly intertwined. Wall Street is also a major creditor of Euro denominated debts.

The structure of the global monetary system hinges upon geopolitics. There are geographic areas of jurisdiction between the Euro and the dollar. The tendency is towards regional Euro and dollar demarcations, within the respective spheres of influence of the European Union and the United States. In other words, the alliance in military affairs, namely the U.S.-NATO partnership, bears a direct relationship to the global monetary architecture. It should be noted that Washington plays a dominant role in strategic decision making within the Atlantic Alliance. Historically, NATO has been subordinate to the Pentagon. Similarly, under a U.S. dominated Atlantic Alliance, the Euro will not be allowed to undermine the hegemony of the dollar.

Money creation in Europe and the U.S. is controlled by private financial interests. The Federal Reserve System is composed of twelve constituent Federal Reserve banks, which are privately owned. The Federal Reserve board is formally a public institution. The European Central Bank is formally a state institution controlled by a handful of private European banks.

Economic Warfare

The U.S. Treasury is bankrupt. The U.S. fiscal crisis has led to a spiraling public debt, heightened by the Bush and Obama multitrillion dollar "bank bailouts" and the escalation in military spending. The United States is by far the most indebted country on earth. The public debt has been monetized. Money has been "created out of thin air".

From this gloomy description of the U.S. financial architecture, one would normally conclude that the dollar is "weak" and that the hegemony of the greenback as a global currency is threatened. Wall Street analysts have concluded, in chorus, that a plummeting dollar on the forex markets is a symptom of the weakness of the U.S. financial system. Under these premises, the media points to the inevitable: the demise of the U.S. dollar as the world's foremost global currency, to be replaced eventually by a new international currency arrangement.

This line of reasoning fails to address the strategic and geopolitical dimensions. U.S. military might supports the worldwide hegemony of the U.S. dollar. The Pentagon's "long war" endorses America as a creditor nation. It fosters the imposition of the "weak" U.S. dollar as a world currency. America is the largest debtor nation, and at the same time it is the world's creditor. "Creating money out of thin air", while at the same time imposing the U.S. dollar as a global currency constitutes the ultimate instrument of conquest and imperial domination.

The U.S. monetary system is supported by the most powerful military power on earth. The dollar is backed by U.S. military might, which constitutes a means for displacing national curren-

TEXT BOX 9.2
DECLINE OF THE DOLLAR?

The 2009-2010 decline of the dollar is only partially the result of "weakness". It is in large part driven by large scale speculative trade in the currency markets (e.g. short selling) which pushes the dollar down and then, at an opportune time, once a turning point is reached, pushes the dollar up again. The "weakness" of the dollar and the U.S. financial system are used to spur a consensus, so that investors will sell off their dollars at the opportune moment.

Wall Street is speculating against the dollar, pushing it down, with a view to ultimately pushing it up again. The military agenda is supportive of this process, as the objective of war is to impose a colonial currency on a defeated nation or countries in the U.S. sphere of influence.

cies and imposing the U.S. dollar. In this regard, the Federal Reserve's overwhelming powers of money creation constitute an essential lever of an imperial monetary agenda. The apparent "weakness" of the U.S. dollar constitutes its ultimate "strength" as an instrument of economic conquest.

The Western banking system controls a worldwide electronic banking network. The control of money creation at a world level constitutes the ultimate instrument of economic and social domination. The creation of fiat money provides a command over the real economies of countries worldwide. The ultimate lever of the U.S.-NATO imperial design is to override and destroy national currencies. This objective cannot be achieved, however, solely through financial means.

Historically, the "weakness" of the dollar has been sustained by U.S. foreign policy. Economic interference in the internal affairs of sovereign states as well as the persistent threat of military intervention have played a crucial role in sustaining and imposing the U.S. dollar as the *de facto* international currency.

Washington's military agenda, which includes all out war as well as the latent threat of military intervention, constitutes a means to displacing and ultimately destroying the financial and banking institutions of sovereign countries.

Control over Money Creation

The dollarization of national economies is an essential instrument of economic conquest. The IMF, acting on behalf of Wall Street, calls the shots on the reform of national monetary systems. National currencies in Latin America, Africa, the Middle East and South East Asia are in large part controlled by Western financial institutions. Without the backing of the world's foremost military power, the U.S. dollar would not have been able to retain its hegemonic role as a global currency.

National currencies are replaced either by the dollar or the Euro or by a proxy currency. Meanwhile, under the brunt of IMF economic medicine, imposed on developing countries, national central banks are prevented from expanding the supply of money thereby shunting the process of credit creation. Once these measures are imposed, which literally dismantle the central bank as an institution, the only way to finance public and private investment is through dollar denominated foreign loans. What this signifies is that Wall Street and the U.S. Federal Reserve control the domestic credit market of developing countries, namely the expansion of credit in domestic currency.

A global "imperial currency", where all other national monetary systems are subordinate to the U.S. dollar, is the means to achieving worldwide economic hegemony. This objective is supported by a global military agenda, a war without borders using the most advanced weapons systems, not to mention an expansive U.S. intelligence apparatus.

The ultimate control over the world economy is achieved through command over money creation: through fiat money, by creating money from nothing. The "long war" is intended to instate the hegemony of the U.S.-EU financial system as well as the contours of "world government". Global geopolitics has a direct bearing on the evolution of currency arrangements and the global financial architecture.

The intricacies and complexity of this global crisis are carefully camouflaged by the corporate media: the lie becomes the truth; concepts are turned upside down; war is upheld as a peacemaking operation; "the economic recession is over".

A World War III scenario potentially looms at the onslaught of the most serious economic crisis in world history. Humanity is at the crossroads of the Great Depression of the 21st century. The dangers of military escalation and the potential social devastation caused by economic collapse are overwhelming.

◆

NOTES

1. George F. Kennan, "PPS/23: Review of Current Trends in U.S. Foreign Policy", *Foreign Relations of the United States*, Washington D.C., 1948, Volume I, p. 509-529.
2. *Ibid.*; See also Michel Chossudovsky, "War Crimes and the 'Just War' Theory", *Global Research*, http://www.globalresearch.ca/index.php?context=va&aid= 698, 17 July 2005.
3. Pentagon official quoted by General Wesley Clark, *Winning Modern Wars: Iraq, Terrorism, and the American Empire*, Perseus Books, Cambridge, MA, 2003, p. 130.
4. *Ibid.*, p. 130.
5. National Security Council, "National Security Strategy", *White House*, Washington DC, 2002.
6. The Project for a New American Century, *Rebuilding America's Defenses, Strategy, Forces and Resources for a New Century*, Washington D.C., p. 18, http://www.newamericancentury.org/Rebuilding AmericasDefenses.pdf, September 2000.
7. *Ibid.*
8. Michel Chossudovsky, "Weather Warfare: Beware the US military's experiments with climatic warfare", *The Ecologist*, December 2007.
9. Michel Chossudovsky, "The US Nuclear Option and the 'War on Terrorism'", *Global Research*, http://www.globalresearch.ca/articles/CHO405A.html, 14 May 2004.
10. Transcript of Remarks by President G. W. Bush and Mexican President Vicente Fox on Departure to Toledo, Ohio, *U.S. Newswire, Inc*, 6 September 2001.
11. Seattle Post-Intelligencer, http://www.seattlepi.com, 7 September 2001; Michel Chossudovsky, "War is Good for Business", *Global Research*, http://www.globalresearch.ca/articles/CHO109D.html, 16 September 2001.
12. Michel Chossudovsky, "War is Good for Business", *Global Research*, http://www.globalresearch.ca/articles/CHO109D.html, 16 September 2001.

13. The summary of this secret document was leaked to the Wall Street Journal, *Wall Street Journal*, 11 March 2005; See Michel Chossudovsky, "New Undeclared Arms Race", *Global Research*, http://www.global-research.ca/articles/CHO5 03A.html, 17 March 2005.

14. Wall Street Journal, http://online.wsj.com, 11 March 2005.

15. *Ibid.*

16. *Ibid.*

17. *Ibid.*

18. *Ibid*, emphasis added.

19. Rick Rozoff, "The Pentagon's 21st Century Counterinsurgency Wars: Latin America and South Asia", *Global Research*, http://www.globalresearch.ca/index.php?context=va&aid=14599, 1 August 2009.

20. Michel Chossudovsky, "Who benefits from the Afghan Opium Trade?", *Global Research*, http://www.globalresearch.ca/index.php?context=va&aid= 3294, 21 September 2006.

21. The Independent, http://www.independent.co.uk, 29 February 2004.

22. Rajeev Syal, "Drug Money Saved Banks in Global Crisis, Claims UN Advisor", *The Guardian*, http://www.guardian.co.uk/global/2009/dec/13/drug-money-banks-saved-un-cfief-claims, 14 December 2009.

23. Sunday Times, http://www.timesonline.co.uk/tol/news/, 3 September 2006.

24. Rick Rozoff, "Afghan War: NATO Builds History's First Global Army", *Global Research*, http://www.globalresearch.ca/index.php?context=va&aid=14707, 9 August 2009.

25. Mahdi Darius Nazemroaya, "Towards the Conquest of the Middle East and North Africa: The U.S., the E.U. and Israel join hands", *Global Research*, http://www.globalresearch.ca/index.php?context=va&aid=8063, 14 February 2008.

26. Michel Chossudovsky, "Planned US-Israeli Attack on Iran", *Global Research*, http://www.globalresearch.ca/articles/CHO505A.html, 1 May 2005.

27. Jaffa Center for Strategic Studies, http://www.tau.ac.il/jcss/sa/v7n4p4Sha lom.html.

28. Michel Chossudovsky, "Triple Alliance: The US, Turkey, Israel and the War on Lebanon", *Global Research*, http://www.globalresearch.ca/index.php?con text=va&aid=2906, 6 August 2006.

29. Rick Rozoff, "The Great Game: U.S., NATO War In Afghanistan", *Global Research*, http://www.globalresearch.ca/index.php?aid=16 422 &context=va, 5 December 2009.

30. Natural Resources Defense Council, "NRDC: U.S. Nuclear Weapons in Europe – Post-Cold War Policy, Force Levels, War Planning", *NRDC*, New York, February 2005; Michel Chossudovsky, "Is the Bush Administration Planning a Nuclear Holocaust?", *Global Research*, http://www.globalresearch.ca/index.php?context=viewArticle&code=20060222&articleId=2032, 22 February 2006.

31. Energy Compass, http://www.energyintel.com, 2 March 2005.

32. Quoted by former Pakistan High Commissioner to the UK, Wajid Shamsul Hasan, *Times of India*, 13 February 2005.

33. Larry Chin, "Anglo-American Ambitions behind the Assassination of Benazir Bhutto and the Destabilization of Pakistan", *Global Research*, http://www.globalresearch.ca/index.php?context=va&aid=7699, 29 December 2007.

34. Talha Mujaddidi, "The U.S. Invades and Occupies Pakistan", *Global Research*, http://www.globalresearch.ca/index.php?context=va&aid=14984, 31 August 2009.

35. Michel Chossudovsky, "The Destabilization of Pakistan", *Global Research*, http://www.globalresearch.ca/index.php?context=va&aid=7705, 30 December 2007.

36. Quoted by former Pakistan High Commissioner to the UK, Wajid Shamsul Hasan, *Times of India*, 13 February 2005.

37. National Intelligence Council, quoted in *Times of India, op. cit.*

38. For further details see: Michel Chossudovsky, "Russia and Central Asian Allies Conduct War Games in Response to US Threats", *Global Research*, http://www.globalresearch.ca/index.php?context=va&aid=3056, 24 August 2006.

39. Muriel Mirak Weissbach, "Iran Opens War Avoidance Flank", *Global Research*, http://www.globalresearch.ca/index.php?context=va&aid=8868, 1 May 2008.

CHAPTER 10

The "Dollar Glut" Finances America's Global Military Build-Up

Michael Hudson

Large amounts of surplus dollars are pouring into the rest of the world.

Central banks have recycled these dollar inflows towards the purchase of U.S. Treasury bonds, which serve to finance the federal U.S. budget deficit.

Underlying this process is the military character of the U.S. payments deficit and the domestic federal budget deficit. Strange as it may seem and irrational as it would be in a more logical system of world diplomacy, the "dollar glut" is what finances America's global military build-up. It forces foreign central banks to bear the costs of America's expanding military empire: effective "taxation without representation".

Keeping international reserves in "dollars" means recycling their dollar inflows to buy U.S. Treasury bills, namely, U.S. government debt issued largely to finance the military.

To date, countries have been as powerless to defend themselves against the fact that this compulsory financing of U.S. military spending is built into the global financial system. Neoliberal economists applaud this as "equilibrium", as if it is part of economic nature and "free markets" rather than bare-knuckle diplomacy wielded with increasing aggressiveness by U.S. officials. The mass media chime in, pretending that recycling the dollar glut to finance U.S. military spending is showing their faith in U.S. economic strength by sending "their" dollars here to "invest". It is as if a choice is involved, not financial and diplomatic compulsion to choose merely between "Yes" (from China, reluctantly), "Yes, please" (from Japan and the European Union) and "Yes, thank you" (from Britain, Georgia and Australia).

It is not "foreign faith in the U.S. economy" that leads foreigners to "put their money here". This is a silly anthropomorphic picture of a more sinister dynamic. The "foreigners" in question are not consumers buying U.S. exports, nor are they private-sector "investors" buying U.S. stocks and bonds. The largest and most important foreign entities putting "their money" here are central banks, and it is not "their money" at all. They are sending back the dollars that foreign exporters and other recipients turn over to their central banks for domestic currency.

When the U.S. payments deficit pumps dollars into foreign economies, these banks are being given little option except to buy U.S. Treasury bills and bonds which the Treasury spends on financing an enormous, hostile military build-up to encircle the major dollar-recyclers: China, Japan and Arab OPEC oil producers. Yet these governments are forced to recycle dollar inflows in a way that funds U.S. military policies in which they have no say in formulating, and which threaten them more and more belligerently. That is why China and Russia took the lead in forming the Shanghai Cooperation Organization (SCO) a few years ago.

In Europe there is a clear awareness that the U.S. payments deficit is much larger than just the trade deficit. The deficit does not stem merely from consumers buying more imports than the United States exports as the financial sector de-industrializes its economy. U.S. imports are now plunging as the economy shrinks and consumers are finding themselves obliged to pay down the debts they have taken on.

Congress has told foreign investors in the largest dollar holder, China, not to buy anything except perhaps used-car dealerships and maybe more packaged mortgages and Fannie Mae stock. This is the equivalent of Japanese investors being steered into spending one billion dollars for the Rockefeller Center, on which they subsequently took a one hundred percent loss, and Saudi investment in Citigroup. That's the kind of "international equilibrium" that U.S. officials love to see. "CNOOK go home" is the motto when it comes to serious attempts by foreign governments and their sovereign wealth funds (central bank departments trying to figure out what to do with their dollar glut) to make direct investments in American industry.

So we are left with the extent to which the U.S. payments deficit stems from military spending. The problem is not only the war in Iraq, now being extended to Afghanistan and Pakistan. It is the expensive build-up of U.S. military bases in Asian, European, post-Soviet and Third World countries. The Obama administration has promised to make the actual amount of this military spending more transparent. That presumably means publishing a revised set of balance of payments figures as well as domestic federal budget statistics.

The military overhead is much like a debt overhead, extracting revenue from the economy. In this case it is to pay the military-industrial complex, not merely Wall Street banks and other financial institutions. The domestic federal budget deficit does not stem only from "priming the pump" to give away enormous sums to create a new financial oligarchy; it contains an enormous and rapidly growing military component.

So Europeans and Asians see U.S. companies pumping more and more dollars into their economies, not only to buy their exports in excess of providing them with goods and services in return, and not only to buy their companies and "commanding heights" of privatized public enterprises without giving them reciprocal rights to buy important U.S. companies (remember the U.S. turn-down of China's attempt to buy into the U.S. oil distribution business), and not only to buy foreign stocks, bonds and real estate. The U.S. media somehow neglects to mention that the U.S. Government is spending hundreds of billions of dollars abroad, not only in the Near East for direct combat, but to build enormous military bases to encircle the rest of the world, to install radar systems, guided missile systems and other forms of military coercion, including the "color revolutions" that have been funded and are still being funded all around the former Soviet Union. Pallets of shrink-wrapped hundred-dollar bills, adding up to tens of millions of dollars at a time, have become familiar "visuals" on some TV broadcasts, but the link is not made with U.S. military and diplomatic spending and foreign central-bank dollar holdings, which are reported simply as "wonderful faith in the U.S. economic recovery" and presumably the "monetary magic" being worked by Wall Street's Tim

Geithner at Treasury and "Helicopter Ben" Bernanke at the Federal Reserve.

Here's the problem: the Coca-Cola Company recently tried to buy China's largest fruit-juice producer and distributor. China already holds nearly two trillion dollars in U.S. securities, way more than it needs or can use, inasmuch as the United States government refuses to let it buy meaningful U.S. companies. If the U.S. buyout would have been permitted to go through, this would have confronted China with a dilemma:

Choice #1 would be to let the sale go through and accept payment in dollars, reinvesting them in what the U.S. Treasury tells it to do. With U.S. Treasury bonds yielding about one percent, China would take a capital loss on these when U.S. interest rates rise or when the dollar declines, as the United States alone is pursuing expansionary Keynesian policies in an attempt to enable the U.S. economy to carry its debt overhead.

Choice #2 is not to recycle the dollar inflows. This would lead the Renminbi to rise against the dollar, thereby eroding China's export competitiveness in world markets.

So China chose a third way, which brought U.S. protests. It turned the sale of its tangible company for merely "paper" U.S. dollars, which went with the "choice" to fund further U.S. military encirclement of the SCO. The only people who seem not to be drawing this connection are the American mass media, and hence U.S. public opinion. I can assure you from personal experience, it is being drawn in Europe. (Here's a good diplomatic question to discuss: Which will be the first European country besides Russia to join the SCO?)

Academic textbooks have nothing to say about how "equilibrium" in foreign capital movements, speculative as well as for direct investment, is infinite as far as the U.S. economy is concerned. The U.S. economy can create dollars freely, now that they no longer are convertible into gold or even into purchases of U.S. companies, inasmuch as America remains the world's most protected economy. It alone is permitted to protect its agriculture by import quotas, having "grandfathered" these into world trade rules half a century ago. Congress refuses to let "sovereign wealth" funds invest in important U.S. sectors.

So we are confronted with the fact that the U.S. Treasury prefers foreign central banks to keep on funding its domestic budget deficit, which means financing the cost of America's war in the Near East and encirclement of foreign countries with rings of military bases. The more "capital outflows" U.S. investors spend to buy up foreign economies' most profitable sectors, where the new U.S. owners can extract the highest monopoly rents, the more funds end up in foreign central banks to support America's global military build-up. No textbook on political theory or international relations has suggested axioms to explain how nations act in a way so adverse to their own political, military and economic interests. Yet this is just what has been happening for the past generation.

So the ultimate question turns out to be what countries can do to counter this financial attack. A Basque labor union asked me whether I thought that controlling speculative capital movements would ensure that the financial system would act in the public interest, or is outright nationalization necessary to better develop the real economy? It is not simply a problem of "regulation" or "control of speculative capital movements". The question is how nations can act as real nations, in their own interest, rather than being roped into serving whatever U.S. diplomats decide is in America's interest. Any country trying to do what the United States has done for the past 150 years is accused of being "socialist", and this from the most anti-socialist economy in the world, except when it calls bailouts for its banks "socialism for the rich", a.k.a. financial oligarchy. This rhetorical inflation almost leaves no alternative but outright nationalization of credit as a basic public utility.

Of course, the word "nationalization" has become a synonym for bailing out the largest and most reckless banks from their bad loans, and bailing out hedge funds and non-bank counterparties for losses on "casino capitalism", gambling on derivatives that AIG and other insurers or players on the losing side of these gambles are unable to pay. Such bailouts are not nationalization in the traditional sense of the term, bringing credit creation and other basic financial functions back into the public domain. It is the opposite: it prints new government bonds to turn over, along with self-regulatory power, to the financial sector, blocking the citizenry from taking back these functions.

Framing the issue as a choice between democracy and oligarchy turns the question into one of who will control the government doing the regulation and "nationalizing". If it is done by a government whose central bank and major congressional committees dealing with finance are run by Wall Street, this will not help steer credit into productive uses. It will merely continue the Greenspan-Paulson-Geithner era of more and larger free lunches for their financial constituencies.

The financial oligarchy's idea of "regulation" is to make sure that deregulators are installed in key positions and given only a minimal skeleton staff and little funding. Despite Mr. Greenspan's announcement that he has come to see the light and realizes that self-regulation doesn't work, the Treasury is still run by a Wall Street official and the Fed is run by a lobbyist for Wall Street. To lobbyists, the real concern is not ideology as such, it is naked self-interest for their clients. They may seek out well-meaning fools, especially prestigious figures from academia. But these are only front men, headed as they are by the followers of Milton Friedman at the University of Chicago. Such individuals are put in place as "gate-keepers" of the major academic journals to keep out ideas that do not well serve the financial lobbyists.

This pretence for excluding government from meaningful regulation is that finance is so technical that only someone from the financial "industry" is capable of regulating it. To add insult to injury, the additional counter-intuitive claim is made that a hallmark of democracy is to make the central bank "independent" of elected government. In reality, of course, that is just the opposite of democracy. Finance is the crux of the economic system. If it is not regulated democratically in the public interest, then it is "free" to be captured by special interests. So this becomes the oligarchic definition of "market freedom."

The danger is that governments will let the financial sector determine how "regulation" will be applied. Special interests seek to make money from the economy, and the financial sector does this in an extractive way. That is its marketing plan. Finance today is acting in a way that de-industrializes economies, not builds them up. The "plan" is austerity for labor, industry and all sectors outside of finance, as in the IMF programs imposed on hapless Third World debtor countries. The experiences of Iceland, Latvia and other "financialized" economies should be examined as object lessons, if only because they top the World Bank's ranking of countries in terms of the "ease of doing business".

The only meaningful regulation can come from outside the financial sector. Otherwise, countries will suffer what the Japanese call "descent from heaven": regulators are selected from the ranks of bankers and their "useful idiots". Upon retiring from government they return to the financial sector to receive lucrative jobs, "speaking engagements" and kindred paybacks. Knowing this, they regulate in favor of financial special interests, not that of the public at large.

The problem of speculative capital movements goes beyond drawing up a set of specific regulations. It concerns the scope of national government power. The International Monetary Fund's Articles of Agreement prevent countries from restoring the "dual exchange rate" systems that many retained down through the 1950s and even into the 60s. It was widespread practice for countries to have one exchange rate for goods and services (sometimes various exchange rates for different import and export categories) and another for "capital movements". Under American pressure, the IMF enforced the pretence that there is an "equilibrium" rate that just happens to be the same for goods and services as it is for capital movements. Governments that did not buy into this ideology were excluded from membership in the IMF and World Bank or were overthrown.

The implication today is that the only way a nation can block capital movements is to withdraw from the IMF, the World Bank and the World Trade Organization (WTO). For the first time since the 1950s this looks like a real possibility, thanks to worldwide awareness of how the U.S. economy is glutting the global economy with surplus "paper" dollars, and U.S. intransigence at stopping its free ride. From the U.S. vantage point, this is nothing less than an attempt to curtail its international military program.

◆

CHAPTER 11

Martial Law, the Financial Bailout and War

Peter Dale Scott

The U.S. Treasury's Financial Bailout

The bailout measures of late 2008 may have consequences at least as grave for an open society as the response to 9/11 in 2001. Many members of Congress felt coerced at the time into voting against their inclinations, and the normal procedures for orderly consideration of a bill were dispensed with.

The excuse for bypassing normal legislative procedures was the existence of an emergency. But one of the most reprehensible features of the legislation, that allowed Treasury Secretary Henry Paulson to permit bailed-out institutions to use public money for exorbitant salaries and bonuses, was inserted by Paulson after the immediate crisis had passed.

According to Congressman Peter Welch (D-Vermont) the bailout bill originally called for a cap on executive salaries, but Paulson changed the requirement at the last minute. Welch and other members of Congress were enraged by "news that banks getting taxpayer-funded bailouts are still paying exorbitant salaries, bonuses, and other benefits."[1] In addition, as the Associated Press reported in October 2008, "Sen. Charles Schumer, D-N.Y. questioned allowing banks that accept bailout bucks to continue paying dividends on their common stock. 'There are far better uses of taxpayer dollars than continuing dividend payments to shareholders,' he said."[2]

Even more reprehensible is the fact that after the bailouts, Paulson and the Treasury Department refused to provide details of the Troubled Assets Relief Program (TARP) spending of hundreds of billions of dollars, while the New York Federal Reserve refused to provide information about its own bailout (using government-backed loans) that amounted to trillions. This lack of transparency was challenged by Fox TV in a FOIA suit against the Treasury Department, and a suit by Bloomberg News against the Fed.[3]

The financial bailout legislation of September 2008 was only passed after members of both Congressional houses were warned that failure to act would threaten civil unrest and the imposition of martial law.

U.S. Sen. James Inhofe, R-Okla., and U.S. Rep. Brad Sherman, D-Calif., both said U.S. Treasury Secretary Henry Paulson brought up a worst-case scenario as he pushed for the Wall Street bailout in September. Paulson, former Goldman Sachs CEO, said that might even require a declaration of martial law, the two noted.[4]

Here are the original remarks by Senator Inhofe:

Speaking on Tulsa Oklahoma's 1170 KFAQ, when asked who was behind threats of martial law and civil unrest if the bailout bill failed, Senator James Inhofe named Treasury Secretary Henry Paulson as the source. "Somebody in D.C. was feeding you guys quite a story prior to the bailout, a story that if we didn't do this we were going to see something on the scale of the depression, there were people talking about martial law being instituted, civil unrest... who was feeding you guys this stuff?," asked host Pat Campbell. "That's Henry Paulson," responded Inhofe. "We had a conference call early on, it was on a Friday I think – a week and half before the vote on Oct. 1. So it would have been the middle... what was it – the 19th of September, we had a conference call. In this conference call – and I guess there's no reason for me not to repeat what he said, but he said – he painted this picture you just described. He said, 'This is serious. This is the most serious thing that we faced.'"[5]

Rep. Brad Sherman (D-CA 27th District) reported the same threat on the Congressional floor:

The only way they can pass this bill is by creating a panic atmosphere... Many of us were told that the sky would fall... A few of us were even told that there would be martial law in America if we voted no. That's what I call fear-mongering, unjustified, proven wrong.[6]

So it is clear that threats of martial law were used to get this reprehensible bailout legislation passed. It also seems clear that Congress was told of a threat of martial law, not itself threatened. It is still entirely appropriate to link such talk to the Army's rapid moves at the time to redefine its role as one of controlling the American people, not just protecting them. In a constitutional polity based on balance of powers, we have seen the emergence of a radical new military power that is as yet completely unbalanced.

Continuity of Operations (COOP)

The Army's New Role in 2001: Not Protecting American Society, but Controlling It. This new role for the Army is not wholly unprecedented. The U.S. military had been training troops and police in "civil disturbance planning" for the last three decades. The master plan, Department of Defense Civil Disturbance Plan 55-2, or "Operation Garden Plot," was developed in 1968 in response to the major protests and disturbances of the 1960s.

But on January 19, 2001, on the last day of the Clinton administration, the U.S. Army promulgated a new and permanent Continuity of Operations (COOP) Program. It encapsulated its difference from the preceding, externally oriented Army Survival, Recovery, and Reconstitution System (ASRRS) as follows:

a. In 1985, the Chief of Staff of the Army established the Army Survival, Recovery, and Reconstitution System (ASRRS) to ensure the continuity of essential Army missions and functions.

ASRRS doctrine was focused primarily on a response to the worst case 1980's threat of a massive nuclear laydown on CONUS as a result of a confrontation with the Soviet Union.

b. The end of the Cold War and the breakup of the former Soviet Union significantly reduced the probability of a major nuclear attack on CONUS but the probability of other threats has increased. Army organizations must be prepared for any contingency with a potential for interruption of normal operations.

To emphasize that Army continuity of operations planning is now focused on the full all-hazards threat spectrum, the name "ASRRS" has been replaced by the more generic title "Continuity of Operations (COOP) Program.[7]

This document embodied the secret Continuity of Government (COG) planning conducted secretly by Rumsfeld, Cheney and others through the 1980s and 1990s.[8] This planning was initially for continuity measures in the event of a nuclear attack, but soon called for suspension of the Constitution, not just "after a nuclear war" but for any "national security emergency". This was defined in Reagan's Executive Order 12656 of November 18, 1988, as "any occurrence, including natural disaster, military attack, technological emergency, or other emergency, that seriously degrades or seriously threatens the national security of the United States." The effect was to impose on domestic civil society the extreme measures once planned for a response to a nuclear attack from abroad.[9] In like fashion, ARR 500-3 Regulation clarified that it was a plan for "the execution of mission-essential functions without unacceptable interruption during a national security or *domestic emergency*."

Donald Rumsfeld, who as a private citizen had helped author the COG planning, promptly signed and implemented the revised ARR 500-3. Eight months later, on 9/11, Cheney and Rumsfeld implemented COG, a significant event of which we still know next to nothing.[10] What we do know is that plans began almost immediately – as foreseen by COG planning the 1980s – to implement warrantless surveillance and detention of large numbers of civilians, and that in January 2002 the Pentagon submitted a proposal for deploying troops on American streets.[11]

Then in April 2002, Defense officials implemented a plan for domestic U.S. military operations by creating a new U.S. Northern Command (CINC-USNORTHCOM) for the continental United States.[12] In short, what were being implemented were the most prominent features of the COG planning which Oliver North had worked on in the 1980s.

"Deep Events" and Changes of Party in the White House

Like so many other significant steps since World War Two towards a military-industrial state, the Army's Regulation 500-3 surfaced in the last days of a departing administration (in this case the very last day). It is worth noticing that, ever since the 1950s, dubious events – of the unpublic variety I have called *deep events* – have marked the last months before a change of party in the White House. These deep events have tended to a) constrain the incoming president, if he is a Democrat or, alternatively, b) to pave the way for the incomer, if he is a Republican.

Consider, in the first category, the following (when a Republican was succeeded by a Democrat):

- In December 1960 the CIA secured approval for the Bay of Pigs invasion of Cuba, and escalated events in Laos into a crisis for which the Joint Chiefs proposed sending 60 000 troops. These events profoundly affected President Kennedy's posture towards Cuba and Indochina.

- In 1976 CIA Director George H.W. Bush installed an outside Team B intelligence unit to enlarge drastically estimates of the Soviet threat to the United States, eventually frustrating and reversing presidential candidate Jimmy Carter's campaign pledge to cut the U.S. defense budget.[13]

Equally important were events in the second category (when a Democrat was succeeded by a Republican):

- In late 1968 Kissinger, while advising the Johnson administration, gave secret information to the Nixon campaign that helped Nixon to obstruct the peace agreement in Vietnam that was about to be negotiated at the peace talks then taking place in Paris. (According to Seymour Hersh, "The Nixon campaign, alerted by Kissinger to the impending success of the peace talks, was able to get a series of messages to the Thieu government" in Saigon, making it clear that a Nixon presidency would offer a better deal. This was a major factor in securing the defeat of Democratic candidate Hubert Humphrey.[14] Kissinger was not the kind of person to have betrayed his president on his own personal initiative. At the time Nixon's campaign manager, John Mitchell (one of the very few in on the secret), told Hersh, "I thought Henry [Kissinger] was doing it because Nelson [Rockefeller] wanted him to. Nelson asked Henry to help and he did."[15]

– In 1980 the so-called October Surprise, with the help of people inside the CIA, helped ensure that the Americans held hostage in Iran would not be returned before the inauguration of Reagan. This was a major factor in securing the defeat of incumbent Jimmy Carter.[16] Once again, the influence of the Rockefellers can be discerned. A CIA officer later reported hearing Joseph V. Reed, an aide to David Rockefeller, comment in 1981 to William Casey, the newly installed CIA Director, about their joint success in disrupting Carter's plans to bring home the hostages.[17]

Both the financial bailout, extorted from Congress and the escalated preparations for martial law can be seen as transitional events of the first category. Whatever the explanations for their timing, they constrained Obama's freedom to make his own policies. Moreover they have the consequence of easing this country into unforeseen escalations of the Afghan war.

The Intensive Quiet Preparations for Martial Law

Let us deal first with the preparations for martial law. In late September 2008, at the height of the financial meltdown, *The Army Times* announced the redeployment of an active Brigade Army Team from Iraq to America, in a new mission that "may become a permanent part of the active Army":

The 3rd Infantry Division's 1st Brigade Combat Team has spent 35 of the last 60 months in Iraq patrolling in full battle rattle, helping restore essential services and escorting supply convoys.

Now they're training for the same mission – with a twist – at home.

Beginning Oct. 1 for 12 months, the 1st BCT will be under the day-to-day control of U.S. Army North, the Army service component of Northern Command, as an on-call federal response force for natural or manmade emergencies and disasters, including terrorist attacks... After 1st BCT finishes its dwell-time mission, expectations are that another, as yet unnamed, active-duty brigade will take over and that the mission will be a permanent one... They may be called upon to help with civil unrest and crowd control.[18]

This announcement followed by two weeks the talk of civil unrest and martial law that was used to panic the Congress into passing Paulson's bailout legislation. Not only that, the two unprecedented events mirror each other: the bailout debate anticipated civil unrest and martial law, while the announced positioning of an active Brigade Combat Team on U.S. soil anticipated civil unrest (such as might result from the bailout legislation).

Then on December 17, 2008, U.S. Northern Command chief General Renuart announced that "the US military plans to mobilize thousands of troops to protect Washington against potential terrorist attack during the inauguration of president-elect Barack Obama."[18]

The U.S. Army War College also raised the possibility of the U.S. Army being used to control civil unrest, according to the Phoenix Business Journal:

A new report by the U.S. Army War College talks about the possibility of Pentagon resources and troops being used should the economic crisis lead to civil unrest, such as protests against businesses and government or runs on beleaguered banks.

"Widespread civil violence inside the United States would force the defense establishment to reorient priorities in extremis to defend basic domestic order and human security," said the War College report.

The study says economic collapse, terrorism and loss of legal order are among possible domestic shocks that might require military action within the U.S.[20]

It is clear that there has been a sustained move in the direction of martial law preparations, a trend that has been as continuous as it has been unheralded. Senator Leahy was thus right to draw our attention to it on September 29, 2006, in his objections to the final form of the Fiscal Year 2007 National Defense Authorization Act, which gave the president increased power to call up the National Guard for law enforcement:

It... should concern us all that the Conference agreement includes language that subverts solid, longstanding Posse Comitatus statutes that limit the military's involvement in law enforcement, thereby making it easier for the President to declare martial law. There is good reason for the constructive friction in existing law when it comes to martial law declarations.[21]

This quiet agglomeration of military power has not "just growed", like Topsy, through inadvertence. It shows sustained intention, even if no one has made a public case for it.

The Bush Administration Protected Predatory Lending and Let the Financial Crisis Grow

Let us now consider the financial crisis and the panic bailout. No one should think that the crisis was unforeseen. Back in February 2008, Eliot Spitzer, in one of his last acts as governor of New York, warned about the impending crisis created by predatory lending, and revealed that the Bush Administration was blocking state efforts to deal with it. His extraordinary warning, in the *Washington Post*, is worth quoting at some length:

Several years ago, state attorneys general and others involved in consumer protection began to notice a marked increase in a range of predatory lending practices by mortgage lenders...

Even though predatory lending was becoming a national problem, the Bush administration looked the other way and did nothing to protect American homeowners. In fact, the government chose instead to align itself with the banks that were victimizing consumers... Several state legislatures, including New York's, enacted laws aimed at curbing such practices... Not only did the Bush administration do nothing to protect consumers, it embarked on an aggressive and unprecedented campaign to prevent states from protecting their residents from the very problems to which the federal government was turning a blind eye.

Let me explain: The administration accomplished this feat through an obscure federal [Treasury] agency called the Office of the Comptroller of the Currency (OCC). The OCC has been in existence since the Civil War. Its mission is to ensure the fiscal soundness of national banks. For 140 years, the OCC examined the books of national banks to make sure they were balanced, an important but uncontroversial function. But a few years ago, for the first time in its history, the OCC was used as a tool against consumers.

In 2003, during the height of the predatory lending crisis, the OCC invoked a clause from the 1863 National Bank Act to issue formal opinions preempting all state predatory lending laws, thereby rendering them inoperative. The OCC also promulgated new rules that prevented states from enforcing any of their own consumer protection laws against national banks. The federal government's actions were so egregious and so unprecedented that all 50 state attorneys general, and all 50 state banking superintendents, actively fought the new rules.

But the unanimous opposition of the 50 states did not deter, or even slow, the Bush administration in its goal of protecting the banks. In fact, when my office opened an investigation of possible discrimination in mortgage lending by a number of banks, the OCC filed a federal lawsuit to stop the investigation.[22]

New York Governor Eliot Spitzer submitted his Op Ed to the *Washington Post* on February 13, 2008. If it had an impact, it was not the one Spitzer had hoped for. On March 10 the *New York Times* broke the story of Spitzer's encounter with a prostitute. According to a later Times story, "on Feb. 13 [the day Spitzer's Op Ed went up on the Washington Post website] federal agents staked out his hotel in Washington."[23]

It is remarkable that the Mainstream Media found Spitzer's private life to be big news, but not his charges that Paulson's Treasury was prolonging the financial crisis, or the relation of these charges to Spitzer's exposure. As a weblog commented:

The US news media failed to draw the obvious connection between the bizarre federal law enforcement investigation and leak campaign about the private life of New York Governor Spitzer and Spitzer's all out attack on the Bush administration for its collusion with predatory lenders.

While the international credit system grinds to a halt because of a superabundance of bad mortgage loans made in the US, the news media failed to cover the details of Spitzer's public charges against the White House.

Yet when salacious details were leaked about alleged details of Spitzer's private life, they took that information and made it the front page news for days.[24]

After Spitzer's Op Ed was published, according to Greg Palast, the Federal Reserve, "for the first time in its history, loaned a selected coterie of banks one-fifth of a trillion dollars to guarantee these banks' mortgage-backed junk bonds. The deluge of public loot was an eye-popping windfall to the very banking predators who have brought two million families to the brink of foreclosure."[25]

What are we to make of Spitzer's charge that the Bush administration interfered to preempt state laws against predatory lending, and of the fact that the mainstream media did not report that? A petty motive for the OCC's behavior in 2003 might have been to allow the housing bubble to continue through 2003 and 2004, thus facilitating Bush's re-election. But the persistence of Treasury obstruction thereafter, despite the unanimous opposition of all fifty states, and the continuing silence of the media about this disagreement, suggests that some broader policy intention may have been at stake.

One is struck by the similarities with the Savings and Loan scandal which was allowed to continue through the Reagan 1980s, long after it became apparent that deliberate bankruptcy was being used by unscrupulous profiteers to amass illegal fortunes at what was ultimately public expense.[26]

In the same way, the long, drawn-out housing bubble of the Bush decade, and particularly the derivative bubble that was floated upon it, allowed the Bush administration to help offset the trillion-dollar-plus cost of its Iraq misadventure, by creating spurious securities that sold for hundreds of billions, not just in the United States, but through the rest of the world.[27]

In the long run, this was not a sustainable source of wealth for America's financial class, which is now suffering like everyone else from the consequent recession. But in the short run, the financial crisis and bailout made it possible for Bush to wage a costly war without experiencing the kind of debilitating inflation that was brought on by America's Vietnam War.

The trillion dollar meltdown, in other words, can be rationalized as having helped finance the Iraq War.[28] When we turn to the martial law preparations, however, they are being made in anticipation of civil unrest in the future. Why such intense preparation for this?

The obvious answer of course is memory of the rioting that occurred in San Francisco and elsewhere during the great depression of the 1930s. Indeed that thought might have been uppermost among those who arranged for the redeployment of a Brigade Combat Team from Iraq to America. But the planning for martial law in America dates back almost three decades, from the days when Reagan appointed Rumsfeld, Cheney and others to plan secretly for what was misleadingly called Continuity [i.e., Change] of Government (COG). Concern about the 2008 recession cannot have been on their minds then, or on those who introduced the Army's "Continuity of Operations (COOP) Program" on January 19, 2001. Instead the "full all-hazards threat spectrum" envisaged in that document was clearly ancillary to the doctrine of "full-spectrum dominance" that had been articulated in the Joint Chiefs of Staff blueprint, Joint Vision 2020, endorsed eight months earlier on May 30, 2000.[29]

The interest of Cheney and Rumsfeld in COG planning, including planning for martial law, also envisaged full spectrum dominance. This is made clear by their simultaneous engagement in the 1990s in the public Project for the New American Century (PNAC). PNAC's goals were stated very explicitly in their document Rebuilding America's Defenses: to increase defense spending so as to establish America's military presence throughout the world as an unchallengeable power. This would entail permanent U.S. forces in central as well as East Asia, even after the disappearance of Saddam Hussein.[30]

In short, PNAC's program was a blueprint for permanent overseas American empire, a project they recognized would not be easily accepted by an American democracy. Their call frankly acknowledged that it would be difficult to gain support for their projected increase in defense spending to "a minimum level of 3.5 to 3.8 percent of gross domestic product, adding $15 billion to $20 billion to total defense spending annually." The document admitted that "the process of transformation... is likely to be a long one, absent some catastrophic and catalyzing event – like a new Pearl Harbor."[31]

At first there was reason to hope that the disastrous era of Rumsfeld and Cheney would end with the election of Barack Obama. Obama while campaigning promised that he would pursue a foreign policy dedicated to diplomacy and multilateralism. In this spirit he declared his willingness to talk to Iran without preconditions.

But Obama's stated reason for disengagement from Iraq – "The scale of our deployments in Iraq continues to set back our ability to finish the fight in Afghanistan"[32] – was ominous. Few serious students of the Afghan scene believed that America could "finish the fight in Afghanistan," any more successfully than could the Russians or British before them. The U.S. position there was already deteriorating, while the U.S. strategy of cross-border attacks was having the effect of destabilizing Pakistan as well. The U.S.-backed Karzai regime had so little control over the countryside that Kabul itself was coming under rocket attack. Experts on the scene agreed that any effort to "finish" would be a long-term proposition requiring at a minimum a vastly escalated commitment of U.S. troops.[33]

One cannot predict the future, but one can examine the past. For thirty years I have been writing about the persistence in America of a war mentality that, time after time, trumps reasonable policies of negotiation and leads us further into armed conflict. This dominant mindset is not restricted to any single agency or cabal, but is rather the likely outcome of on-going tensions between hawks and doves in the internal politics of Washington.

If a container of rocks and gravel is shaken vigorously, the probability is that the gravel will gravitate towards the bottom, leaving the largest rocks at the top. There is an analogous probability that, in an on-going debate over engaging or withdrawing from a difficult military contest, the forces for engagement will come out on top, regardless of circumstances. Available military power tends to be used, and one of the most remarkable features of history since 1945 is that this tendency has not so far repeated itself with atomic weapons.

Let me explain this metaphor in more concrete detail. Progressive societies (in this era usually democracies) tend to expand their presence beyond their geographic boundaries. This expanded presence calls for new institutions, usually (like the CIA) free from democratic accountability. This accretion of unaccountable power, in what I have elsewhere called the deep state, disrupts the public state's system of checks and balances that is the underpinning of sane, deliberative policy.

We might expect of progressive democracies that they would evolve towards more and more rational foreign policies. But because of the dialectic just described, what we see is the exact opposite – evolution towards foolish and sometimes disastrous engagements. When Britain became more democratic in the late 19th century, it also initiated the Boer War, a war very suited to the private imperial needs of Cecil Rhodes, but irrelevant if not deleterious to the interests of the British people.[34] Hitler's dreams of a Third Reich, entailing a doomed repeat of Napoleon's venture into the heart of Russia, suited the needs of the German industrialists who had financed the Nazis; but from the outset sane heads of the German military staff could foresee the coming disaster.

For over a half century now, beginning with Vietnam, unaccountable forces have been maneuvering America into unsustainable adventures on the Asian mainland. We now know that Kennedy did not intend ever to commit U.S. combat troops to Vietnam.[35] But the fatal planning to expand the Vietnam War north of the 17th parallel was authorized in the last week of his aborted presidency, probably without his being aware.[36] When elected, Jimmy Carter was determined to reduce the size and frequency of CIA covert operations.[37] Yet his national security advisor, Zbigniew Brzezinski, initiated maneuvers in Afghanistan that led to the largest CIA covert operation (and in my view, one of the most deleterious) of all time.[38]

Our archival historians have not yet fully understood either paradox, or the forces behind them. And as the philosopher George Santayana famously observed, "Those who cannot remember the past are condemned to repeat it."[39]

The Future: Military Escalation Abroad and at Home?

Like both Kennedy and Carter, Barack Obama is a complex mix of hopeful and depressing qualities. Among the latter are his unqualified desire to "finish" (i.e. "win") the war in Afghanistan, and his support, along with his party's, for the final version of the Paulson bailout. In my view they go together.

Like the government negotiated resolution of the savings-and-loan-scandal of the 1980s, the financial bailout undisguisedly taxed the public wealth of the republic to protect and even enrich those who for some time had been undeservedly enriching themselves. Old-line leftists might see nothing unusual about this: it conforms to their analysis of how the capitalist state has always worked.

But it is only characteristic of the recent American state since the Reagan revolution of the 1980s. For a half century before that time governmental policies were more likely to be directed towards helping the poor; afterwards the ideology of free-market liberalism, even under Clinton, was invoked in numerous ways for the enriching of the rich.

The result of these government policies has been summarized by Prof. Edward Wolff:

> We have had a fairly sharp increase in wealth inequality dating back to 1975 or 1976. Prior to that, there was a protracted period when wealth inequality fell in this country, going back almost to 1929. So you have this fairly continuous downward trend from 1929, which of course was the peak of the stock market before it crashed, until just about the mid-1970s. Since then, things have really turned around, and the level of wealth inequality today is almost double what it was in the mid-1970s...

> Up until the early 1970s, the U.S. actually had lower wealth inequality than Great Britain, and even than a country like Sweden. But things have really turned around over the last 25 or 30 years. In fact, a lot of countries have experienced lessening wealth inequality over time. The U.S. is atypical in that inequality has risen so sharply over the last 25 or 30 years.[40]

Past excesses of American wealth, as in the Gilded Age and the 1920s, have been followed by political reforms, such as the income tax, to reduce wealth and income disparity. But as Kevin Phillips has warned, this type of reform must happen again soon, or it may not happen at all:

> As the twenty-first century gets underway, the imbalance of wealth and democracy in the United States is unsustainable... Either democracy must be renewed, with politics brought back

to life, or wealth is likely to cement a new and less democratic regime – plutocracy by some other name.[41]

Judged by this criterion, the Paulson bailout as passed was not just an opportunity missed; it was a radical leap in the wrong direction. It is not reassuring that the bailout was passed with the support of Obama and the Democratic Party. This is rather a sign that plutocracy will not be seriously challenged by either party in their present state.

Warren Buffett may have been correct in saying that the bailout was necessary. But it is not hard to think of reforms that should have accompanied it:

1) there should have been transparency, not secrecy;

2) public funds should not have been made available for bonuses or dividends (The richest ten percent of Americans own 85 percent of all stock).[42]

I am not making these obvious suggestions with any expectation that they will be passed or seriously debated. The plutocratic corruption of both our parties makes such a prospect almost unthinkable.

What I do want to contemplate is the serious prospect of war. America escaped from the depression of the 1890s with the Spanish-American War.[43] It only escaped the Great Depression of the 1930s with the Second World War. There was even a recession in the late 1940s from which America only escaped with the Korean War. As we face the risk of major depression again, I believe we inevitably face the danger of major war again.

In the meantime, some aspects of the financial meltdown, although they arose for many reasons and were not the result of some conspiratorial cabal, may be prolonged because of their utility to the war-minded. Consider that, from the perspective of maintaining America's imperial thrust into Afghanistan (and even Pakistan), the financial crisis had some desired consequences:

1) The dollar's value improved against other international currencies, notably the euro, thus easing America's balance of payments deficit and also offsetting the threat to

the dollar's important role as the primary unit of international trade.[44]

2) Thanks to the determined international marketing of overvalued derivatives based on predatory lending, the resulting financial crisis has been internationalized, with economies elsewhere suffering even greater shocks than the United States. This has relatively improved America's capacity to finance a major war effort overseas (which has always had a major impact on the U.S. balance of payments).

3) The price of oil has plummeted from $147 a barrel in July 2008 to $30 in December, thus weakening the economies of Russia, China, and especially Saudi Arabia, the country whose international foundations have been supporting Al Qaeda.[45]

The Afghan situation was grim when Obama was elected, but it was not hopeless. Two skilled observers, Barnett R. Rubin and Ahmed Rashid, had proposed a political solution for the entire region that would promise greater security for the entire area than Obama's ill-considered decision to send 30 000 more U.S. troops.[46] In Rashid's words,

> President-elect Obama and Western leaders have to adopt a comprehensive approach that sees the region [with Afghanistan's neighbors, including Pakistan, India, Russia, China, Iran and the former Soviet states] as a unit with interlocking development issues to be resolved such as poverty, illiteracy and weak governance. There has to be a more comprehensive but more subtle approach to democratizing the region and forcing powerful but negative stakeholders in local power structures – such as the drug mafias – either to change their thinking or be eliminated.[47]

That observers with such recognized status were offering a sensible political solution did not provide one with much optimism. For three decades now Barnett Rubin has been offering sound advice on Iran and Afghanistan to Washington, only to be ignored by those lobbying for covert operations and military solutions. This dialectic is reminiscent of the Vietnam War, where for over a decade reasonable proposals to demilitarize the conflict were similarly ignored.

I repeat that the future is unpredictable. But I fear that Obama's decision to escalate in Afghanistan will become more and more reminiscent of America in Vietnam, with predictable consequences of a wider war in both Afghanistan and Pakistan.[48] With this I also fear an increased use of the U.S. Army to control protests by the American people.

◆

NOTES

1. WCAX, Burlington, Vermont, http://www.wcax.com/Global/story.asp?S= 9567271, 22 December 2008; Cf. CNBC, http://www.cnbc.com/id/27423117, 30 October 2008: "'You can get paid $30 million under this program', says Michael Kesner, who heads Deloitte Consulting executive compensation practice, 'There's no limit on what you can get paid.'"

2. John Dunbar, *AP*, http://biz.yahoo.com/ap/081025/meltdown_evolving_bailout.html, 25 October 2007.

3. David Hirst, "Fox Joins Battle cry for Details of US Bail-out", *BusinessDay*, http://www.businessday.com.au/business/fox-joins-battle-cry-for-details-of-us-bailout-20081223-74eh.html?page=-1, 24 December 2008.

4. Mike Sunnucks, "Ariz. Police say they are Prepared as War College warns Military must prep for Unrest; IMF warns of Economic Riots", *Phoenix Business Journal*, http://phoenix.bizjournals.com/phoenix/stories/2008/12/15/daily34.html, 17 December 2008.

5. 1170 KFAQ, "Paulson Was Behind Bailout Martial Law Threat", *Blacklisted News*, http://www.blacklistednews.com/news-2367-0-13-13--.html, 23 November 2008.

6. Rep. Brad Sherman, in the House, 8:07 EST PM, http://www.youtube.com/watch?v=HaG9d_4zij8&NR=1, 2 October 2008; Rep. Sherman later issued the following clarification: "I have no reason to think that any of the leaders in Congress who were involved in negotiating with the Bush Administration regarding the bailout bill ever mentioned the possibility of martial law – again, that was just an example of extreme and deliberately hyperbolic comments

being passed around by members not directly involved in the negotiations." See Rep. Sherman, *Alex Jones Show*, http://www.youtube.com/watch?v=_bH1mO8qhCs.

7. Army Regulation 500-3, "Emergency Employment of Army and Other Resources", *Army Continuity Of Operations (COOP) Program*, http://www.wikileaks.org/leak/us-army-reg-500-3-continuity-2001.pdf, emphasis added; Tom Burghardt, "Militarizing the 'Homeland' in Response to the Economic and Political Crisis: NORTHCOM's Joint Task Force-Civil Support", *Global Research*, http://www.globalresearch.ca/index.php?context=va&aid=10534, 11 October 2008.

8. Peter Dale Scott, *The Road to 9/11: Wealth, Empire, and the Future of America*, Berkeley and Los Angeles, University of California Press, 2007, p. 183-87; James Mann, *The Rise of the Vulcans: The History of Bush's War Cabinet*, New York, Viking, 2004, p. 138-45.

9. Peter Dale Scott, *Road to 9/11*, op. cit., p. 183-87.

10. National Commission on Terrorist Attacks Upon the United States, *9/11 Commission Report*, p. 38, 326; 555, footnote 9; Peter Dale Scott, *Road to 9/11*, op. cit., p. 228-30.

11. Ritt Goldstein, "Foundations are in Place for Martial Law in the US", *Sydney Morning Herald*, http://www.smh.com.au/articles/2002/07/27/10274974183 39.html, 27 July 2002.

12. Peter Dale Scott, *Road to 9/11*, op. cit., p. 240-41.

13. *Ibid.*, p. 60-61.

14. Robert Parry, "Henry Kissinger, Eminence Noire", *ConsortiumNews*, http://www.consortiumnews.com/2008/122808.html, 28 December 2008: "Kissinger... – while serving as a peace-talk adviser to the Johnson administration – made obstruction of the peace talks possible by secretly contacting people working for Nixon, according to Seymour Hersh's 1983 book, *The Price of Power*", p. 21.

15. Seymour Hersh, *The Price of Power*, 1983, p. 18; Jim Hougan, *Spooks: The Haunting of America*, New York, William Morrow, 1978, p. 435: "Kissinger, married to a former Rockefeller aide, owner of a Georgetown mansion whose purchase was enabled only by Rockefeller gifts and loans, was always the protégé of his patron, Nelson R[ockefeller], even when he wasn't directly employed by him."

16. Peter Dale Scott, *Road to 9/11*, op. cit., p. 93-118.

17. *Ibid.* p. 82-87, 91, 104-05.

18. Gina Cavallaro, "Brigade Homeland Tours Start Oct. 1", *Army Times*, http://www.armytimes.com/news/2008/09/army_homeland_090708w/, 30 September 2008; Michel Chossudovsky, "Pre-

election Militarization of the North American Homeland, US Combat Troops in Iraq Repatriated to 'Help with Civil Unrest'", *Global Research*, http://www.globalresearch.ca/index.php? context= va&aid=10341, 26 September 2008.

19. AFP, *Agence France-Presse*, http://www.google.com/hostednews/ afp/article/ALeqM5iTBOy3JF8pVAthIthq8C1NrMf4Cg, 17 December 2008.

20. Mike Sunnucks, "Ariz. Police say they are Prepared as War College warns Military must prep for Unrest; IMF warns of Economic Riots", *Phoenix Business Journal*, http://phoenix.bizjournals.com/ phoenix/stories/2008/12/ 15/daily34.html, 17 December 2008.

21. Remarks Of Sen. Patrick Leahy, "National Defense Authorization Act For Fiscal Year 2007 Conference Report", *Congressional Record*, http://leahy.senate.gov/press/200609/092906b.html, 29 September 2006.

22. Eliot Spitzer, "Predatory Lenders' Partner in Crime: How the Bush Administration Stopped the States from Stepping In to Help Consumers", *Washington Post*, http://www.washingtonpost.com/ wp-dyn/content/article/2008/02/13/AR2008021302783.html? nav=hcmodule, 14 February 2008. Three months earlier, on November 8, 2007, Governor Spitzer and New York Attorney General Andrew Cuomo had published a joint letter to Congress, "calling for continued federal action to combat subprime lending practices" (http://www.state.ny.us/governor/press/1108071.html).

23. David Johnston and Philip Shenon, "U.S. Defends Tough Tactics on Spitzer", *New York Times*, 21 March 2008.

24. Brasscheck TV, "Why Eliot Spitzer was Assassinated: The Predatory Lending Industry had a Partner in the White House", http://bras-schecktv.com/page/291.html, March 2008.

25. Greg Palast, "Eliot's Mess: The $200 billion Bail-out for Predator Banks and Spitzer Charges are Intimately Linked", *Air America Radio's Clout*, http://www.gregpalast.com/elliot-spitzer-gets-nailed/, 14 March 2008.

26. Without suggesting that the scandal was in any way centrally orchestrated or directed, it can be argued that the scandal was permitted to drag on so long because it was allowing profits from the illegal drug traffic to recapitalize the American economy and strengthen the beleaguered U.S. dollar.

27. Joseph E. Stiglitz and Linda J. Bilmes, *The Three Trillion Dollar War: The True Cost of the Iraq Conflict*, New York, W.W. Norton, 2008; Joseph Stiglitz and Linda Bilmes, "The three trillion dollar war", *The Times*, London, http://www.timesonline.co.uk/tol/comment/

columnists/guest_contributors/article 3419840.ece, 23 February 2008: "On the eve of war, there were discussions of the likely costs. Larry Lindsey, President Bush's economic adviser and head of the National Economic Council, suggested that they might reach $200 billion. But this estimate was dismissed as "baloney" by the Defence Secretary, Donald Rumsfeld. His deputy, Paul Wolfowitz, suggested that postwar reconstruction could pay for itself through increased oil revenues. Mitch Daniels, the Office of Management and Budget director, and Secretary Rumsfeld estimated the costs in the range of $50 to $60 billion, a portion of which they believed would be financed by other countries. (Adjusting for inflation, in 2007 dollars, they were projecting costs of between $57 and $69 billion). The tone of the entire administration was cavalier, as if the sums involved were minimal."

28. Charles R. Morris, *The Trillion Dollar Meltdown: Easy Money, High Rollers, and the Great Credit Crash*, New York, PublicAffairs, 2008.

29. United States Department of Defense, *Joint Vision 2020*, http://www.dtic.mil/jointvision/jvpub2.htm, 30 May, 2000; Peter Dale Scott, *The Road to 9/11,op. cit.*, p. 20, 24. "Full spectrum dominance" repeated what had been outlined earlier in a predecessor document, Joint Vision 2010 of 2005, but with new emphasis on the statement that "the United States must maintain its overseas presence forces" (Joint Vision 2020, 6); Office of Primary Responsibility, *Joint Vision 2010*, p. 4, www.dtic.mil/jv2010/jvpub.htm: "We will remain largely a force that is based in the continental United States."

30. Project for the New American Century, *Rebuilding America's Defenses, op. cit.*, http://www.newamericancentury.orgRebuildingAmericas-Defenses.pdf; Peter Dale Scott, *The Road to 9/11, op. cit.*, p. 23-24, 191-93.

31. *Rebuilding America's Defenses, op. cit.*, p. 51, 75.

32. President Obama, "War in Iraq", *BarackObama.com*, http://www.barackobama.com/issues/iraq/.

33. See e.g. Andrew Bacevich, "The Things We Need to Do Now: Five Leading Foreign-Policy Experts Offer their Recommendations on Dealing with some of the World's Most Difficult and Pressing Challenges", *Newsweek*, http://www.newsweek.com/id/171254, 8 December 2008: "In Afghanistan today, the United States and its allies are using the wrong means to pursue the wrong mission. Sending more troops to the region, as incoming president Barack Obama and others have suggested we should, will only turn Operation Enduring Freedom into Operation Enduring

Obligation. Afghanistan will be a sinkhole, consuming resources neither the U.S. military nor the U.S. government can afford to waste"; PBS, "The War Briefing", *Frontline*, http://www.pbs.org/wgbh/pages/frontline/warbriefing/view/, 28 October 2008.

34. For the role of the Rhodes-promoted Jameson Raid in instigating the Boer War, see Elizabeth Longford, *Jameson's Raid: The Prelude to the Boer War*, London, Weidenfeld and Nicolson, 1982.

35. Gordon M. Goldstein, *Lessons in Disaster: McGeorge Bundy and the Path to War in Vietnam*, New York, Times Books/Henry Holt, 2008.

36. John Newman, *JFK and Vietnam: Deception, Intrigue, and the Struggle for Power*, New York, Warner Books, 1992, p. 375-77, 434-35, 447; Peter Dale Scott, *The War Conspiracy: JFK, 9/11, and the Deep Politics of War*, Ipswich, MA, Mary Ferrell Foundation Press, 2008, p. 25-26, 28.

37. Ofira Seliktar, *Failing the Crystal Ball Test: The Carter Administration and the Fundamentalist Revolution in Iran*, Westport, CN, Praeger, 2000, p. 52.

38. Brzezinski later boasted that his "secret operation was an excellent idea. It drew the Russians into the Afghan trap", "Les Révélations d'un ancien conseiller de Carter", interview with Zbigniew Brzezinski, *Le Nouvel Observateur*, http://www.globalresearch.ca/articles/BRZ110A.html, 15-21 January 1998; French version: http://www.confidentiel.net/breve.php3?id_breve=1862; quoted at length in Peter Dale Scott, *Drugs, Oil, and War: The United States in Afghanistan, Colombia, and Indochina*, Lanham, MD, Rowman & Littlefield, 2003, p. 35. For my negative assessment of what some have described as the CIA's most successful covert operation, see *The Road to 9/11, op. cit.*, p. 114-37.

39. George Santayana, *Life of Reason, Reason in Common Sense*, New York, Scribner's, 1905, p. 284.

40. Edward Wolff, "The Wealth Divide: The Growing Gap in the United States Between the Rich and the Rest", *Multinational Monitor*, http://www.thirdworldtraveler.com/America/Wealth_Divide.html, May 2003; Edward Wolff, *Top Heavy: The Increasing Inequality of Wealth in America and What Can Be Done About It*, New York, New Press, 2002.

41. Kevin Phillips, *Wealth and Democracy: A Political History of the American Rich*, New York, Broadway Books, 2002, p. 422; quoted in Scott, *The Road to 9/11, op. cit.*, p. 3.

42. Edward Wolff, "The Wealth Divide", *op. cit.*

43. For McKinley's mercantilist "large policy" as a response to depression, see Philip Sheldon Foner, *The Spanish-Cuban-American War and*

the Birth of American Imperialism, 1895-1902, New York, Monthly Review Press, 1972.

44. The Euro to US$ rate dropped from 1.58 in July 2008 to 1.42 a year later. In February 2009 it was 1.28.

45. In July 2009, oil was trading at $70 a barrel.

46. Barnett R. Rubin and Ahmed Rashid, "From Great Game to Grand Bargain: Ending Chaos in Afghanistan and Pakistan", *Foreign Affairs*, http://www.foreignaffairs.org/20081001faessay87603-p40/barnett-r-rubin-ahmed-rashid/from-great-game-to-grand-bargain.html, November/December 2008.

47. Ahmed Rashid, "Obama's huge South Asia Headache", *BBC*, http://news.bbc.co.uk/2/hi/south_asia/7788321.stm, 2 January 2009.

48. Zia Sarhadi, "America's 'Good War' turns into Quicksand", *Media-Monitors*, http://usa.mediamonitors.net/content/view/full/58114, 5 January 2009: "Obama's announcement to send 20,000 additional troops to the 'good war' in Afghanistan has been greeted by the Taliban with glee. They regard it as an opportunity to attack a 'bigger army, bigger target and more shiny new weapons to take from the toy soldiers'. American generals have talked in terms of 40,000 to 100,000 additional troops, levels that are simply not available. America's killing of hundreds of Afghan civilians in indiscriminate aerial attacks has been the most effective recruiting tool for the Taliban. Even those Afghans not keen on seeing the Taliban back in power are appalled by the level of brutality inflicted on civilians."

CHAPTER 12

Pentagon and Intelligence Black Budget Operations

Tom Burghardt

As the global economic crisis deepens, ongoing efforts by the defense and security establishment to shore-up the empire's crumbling edifice consumes an ever-greater proportion of America's national budget, as much as 36 percent according to some estimates.

For all the sound and fury and promises of "change", the Obama administration has been a boon for defense corporations. Defense appropriations for 2010 are of the order of 700 billion dollars.

Continuing along the dark path marked out by his predecessors in the Oval Office, President Barack Obama's Defense and Intelligence budget will greatly expand the reach of unaccountable agencies – and the corporate grifters whom they serve:

> The Pentagon's 'black' operations, including the intelligence budgets nested inside it, are roughly equal in magnitude to the entire defense budgets of the UK, France or Japan, and ten percent of the total.[1]

Yes, you read that correctly. The "black" or secret portions of the budget are almost as large as the entire expenditure of defense funds by America's allies, hardly slouches when it comes to feeding their own militarist beasts. The U.S. Air Force alone intends to spend approximately twelve billion dollars on "black" programs in 2010 or 36 percent of its entire research and development budget. *Aviation Week* revealed:

Black-world procurement remains dominated by the single line item that used to be called 'Selected Activities,' resident in the USAF's 'other procurement' section. In 2010 this amounted to more than $16 billion. In inflation-adjusted terms, that's 240 percent more than it was ten years ago.

On the operations side, secret spending has risen 8 per cent over last year, to just over $15 billion – equivalent to more than a third of Air Force operating costs.

What does it all go for? In simple terms, we don't know. It is apparent that much if not all of the intelligence community is funded through the black budget: for example, an $850 million USAF line item is clearly linked to reconnaissance satellites. But even so, the numbers are startling – and get more so year by year.[2]

While the American government refuses to disclose the CIA or NSA's budget "both the Agency and other non-military spooks do get money of their own. Some of this is spent on military or quasi-military activities."[3]

Toss in the world-wide deployment of CIA and U.S. Special Operations Command (USSOCOM) paramilitary operatives hidden among a welter of Special Access Programs (SAPs) classified above top secret and pretty soon we're talking real money!

Hiding the State's Dirty Laundry

One such program may have been Dick Cheney's "executive assassination ring" disclosed by investigative journalist Seymour Hersh during a "Great Conversations" event in March at the University of Minnesota.[4]

Indeed the latest scandal to rock Washington arrived shortly before Congress' summer break. It was revealed that the CIA in fact had stood up a world-wide assassination program, and then concealed its existence from the U.S. Congress and the American people for eight years, the result of a *ukase* issued by the former Vice President, Richard Cheney.

The Wall Street Journal reported that "a secret Central Intelligence Agency initiative terminated by Director Leon Panetta was an attempt to carry out a 2001 presidential authorization to capture or kill al Qaeda operatives, according to former intelligence officials familiar with the matter." National security journalist

Siobhan Gorman wrote, "The precise nature of the highly classi-fied effort isn't clear, and the CIA won't comment on its substance."[5]

The Washington Post however, revealed that the assassination plan was sanctioned at the highest levels of the U.S. government. Unnamed "intelligence officials" told the newspaper that "a secret document known as a 'presidential finding' was signed by President George W. Bush that same month, granting the agency broad authority to use deadly force against bin Laden as well as other senior members of al-Qaeda and other terrorist groups."[6]

According to *Post* reporter Joby Warrick, Bush's finding "imposed no geographical limitations on the agency's actions" and that the CIA was "not obliged to notify Congress of each operation envisaged under the directive."[7] This implies of course, that targets could be hit anywhere, including on the soil of a NATO ally or *inside the United States itself.*

One can assume that secret, off-the-books "black" funds sus-tained the agency's operation. Should pesky investigators from the Government Accountability Office (GAO) have the temerity to probe said "executive assassination ring" or other DoD "black" programs well, their Inspector Generals had better think again!

According to the whistleblowing security and intelligence web site Cryptome, a May 8, 2009 letter from Susan Ragland, GAO Director of Financial Management and Assurance to Diane Watson (D-CA), Chairwoman of the House Committee on Government Management, Organization and Procurement, lays down the law in no uncertain terms. Ms. Ragland wrote:

> The IG Act authorizes the heads of six agencies to prohibit their respective IGs from carrying out or completing an audit or inves-tigation, or from issuing any subpoena if the head determines that such prohibition is necessary to prevent either the disclo-sure of certain sensitive information or significant harm to cer-tain national interests."[8]

Under statutory authority granted the Executive Branch by congressional grifters, Congress amended the IG Act "to estab-lish the Department of Defense (DOD) IG and placed the IG under the authority, direction, and control of the Secretary of Defense with respect to audits or investigations or the issuance of subpoenas that require access to certain information." What information may be withheld from public scrutiny? Ms. Ragland informs us:

> Specifically, the Secretary of Defense may prohibit the DOD IG from initiating, carrying out, or completing such audits or investigations or from issuing a subpoena *if the Secretary determines that the prohibition is necessary to preserve the national security interests of the United States.*[9]

This makes a mockery of effective oversight, indeed *any* oversight since an investigation can be quashed at the starting line by the department being investigated.

The same restrictions that apply to the Defense Department are similarly operative for the Departments of the Treasury, Homeland Security, Justice, the U.S. Postal Service, the Federal Reserve Board, and the Central Intelligence Agency. Talk about veritable mountains of dirty laundry – and "black" programs – that can be hidden here.

Superficially at least, some members of Congress are mounting a challenge to the Pentagon and the intelligence agencies' penchant for secrecy. The Federation of American Scientists reported that "the Senate version of the FY2010 intelligence authorization bill would require the President to disclose the aggregate amount requested for intelligence each year when the coming year's budget request is submitted to Congress."[10] According to *Secrecy News*, "currently, only the total appropriation for the National Intelligence Program is disclosed – not the request – and not before the end of the fiscal year in question."[11]

Under a new proposal that would update Executive Order 12958, the Obama administration plans to create a National Declassification Center within the National Archives and Records Administration for declassifying records. It is unclear whether the executive order would apply to various "black" budget items though it's doubtful.

The Washington Times reported in July the executive order "calls for limiting the government's ultra-secret Special Access Programs (SAPs).[12] In the future according to the report, these above top secret programs "can be created only by the secretaries of State, Defense, Energy and Homeland Security, and the Director of National Intelligence, or their main deputies, who must 'keep the number of these programs at an absolute minimum' and only to counter an 'exceptional' vulnerability or threat to specific information."[13]

But as with other congressional moves towards greater oversight, their implementation, even with presidential support, are slim to none. Both initiatives are opposed by the CIA and the Pentagon. A list of comments submitted by the Pentagon states that the Department of Defense "'is adamantly opposed to any changes that would significantly increase costs without associated gains and impair our wartime mission.' The Pentagon also said it cannot meet the requirement to 'immediately' set up the declassification center because of personnel issues."[14]

One would think that with plans afoot to expand the U.S. Army by some 22 000 soldiers as DoD Secretary Robert Gates announced in July 2009, such "personnel issues" would have been addressed. Apparently not.

Under the proposed "reform", information subject to classification includes:

> Military plans, weapons systems, or operations; foreign government information; intelligence activities, intelligence sources or methods, or cryptology; foreign relations or foreign activities of the United States, including confidential sources; scientific, technological, or economic matters relating to the national security; U.S. government programs for safeguarding nuclear materials or facilities; vulnerabilities or capabilities of systems, installations, infrastructures, projects, plans, or protection services relating to the national security, which includes defense against transnational terrorism; or the development, production, or use of weapons of mass destruction.[15]

But with gaping holes large enough to accommodate a B-1 bomber, the new era of transparency promised by the administration is several orders of magnitude less than what meets the eye.

Space-Based Spies

Among the items nestled within the dark arms of Pentagon war planners is a program called "Imagery Satellite Way Ahead," a joint effort between "the Office of the Director of National Intelligence and the Department of Defense designed to revamp the nation's constellation of spy satellites," *Congressional Quarterly* reported.[16]

America's fleet of military spy satellites flown by the secretive National Reconnaissance Office (NRO) are among the most opaque programs run by the Defense Department.[17]

According to the agency's own description:

> The NRO is a joint organization engaged in the research and development, acquisition, launch and operation of overhead reconnaissance systems necessary to meet the needs of the Intelligence Community and of the Department of Defense. The NRO conducts other activities as directed by the Secretary of Defense and/or the Director of National Intelligence.[18]

In other words, the agency engages in clandestine satellite reconnaissance and its assets are amongst the most technologically sophisticated in the entire U.S. arsenal. Unsurprisingly, it is also one of the more expensive Pentagon satrapies to operate, one that benefits equally opaque defense and security corporations.

As investigative journalist Tim Shorrock revealed in his essential book *Spies for Hire*, some 95 percent of NRO employees are contractors working for defense and security firms. Indeed as Shorrock disclosed, "with an estimated $8 billion annual budget, the largest in the IC, contractors control about $7 billion worth of business at the NRO, giving the spy satellite industry the distinction of being the most privatized part of the Intelligence Community."[19]

While the Office's website may be short on information, some of the "other activities" alluded to by NRO spooks included the (apparently) now-defunct National Applications Office (NAO) under the nominal administrative control of the Department of Homeland Security.

The NAO would have coordinated how domestic law enforcement and "disaster relief" agencies such as FEMA exploit the imagery intelligence (IMINT) generated by spy satellites. Based on the available evidence, hard to come by since these programs are classified above top secret, for sheer technological power these military assets are truly terrifying – and toxic – for a democracy.

Indeed, NAO's intrusiveness was so severe that even Rep. Jane Harman (D-CA), the author of the despicable "Violent Radicalization and Homegrown Terrorism Prevention Act of 2007" (H.R. 1955) vowed to pull the plug. Chairwoman of the Homeland Security Committee's Intelligence, Information Sharing and Terrorism Risk Assessment subcommittee, Harman introduced legislation in June that would shut down NAO immediately while prohibiting the agency from spending money on it or similar programs. When her bill was announced, Harman told *Federal Computer Week*:

> Imagine, for a moment, what it would be like if one of these satellites were directed on your neighborhood or home, a school or place of worship – and without an adequate legal framework or operating procedures in place for regulating their use. I daresay the reaction might be that Big Brother has finally arrived and the black helicopters can't be far behind. Yet this is precisely what the Department of Homeland Security has done in standing up the benign-sounding National Applications Office, or NAO.[21]

DHS described the National Applications Office as "the executive agent to facilitate the use of intelligence community technological assets for civil, homeland security and law enforcement purposes."[22] But as *Congressional Quarterly* revealed, the "classified plan" at DHS's disposal "would include new, redesigned 'electro-optical' satellites, which collect data from across the electromagnetic spectrum, as well as the expanded use of commercial satellite imagery. Although the cost is secret, most estimates place it in the multibillion dollar range."[23]

How NRO's redesigned assets will be deployed has not been announced. The more pertinent question here however, is whether or not DHS, reputedly a civilian agency but one that answers to the militarized Office of the Director of National Intelligence (ODNI), would have positioned these assets to illegally spy on Americans. The available evidence suggests this is precisely what they would have done.

DHS averred that "homeland security and law enforcement will also benefit from access to Intelligence Community capabilities."[24] But what those alleged benefits were and what their impact on privacy would have been was never spelled out by the department. After all, if satellite assets are to be deployed during a major disaster such as a flood, hurricane or earthquake, an office with statutory authority to perform such missions already exists, the Civil Applications Office (CAC) administered by the Interior Department's U.S. Geological Survey.

Unlike the civilian-administered CAC however, NAO would have been subject to the ODNI's more stringent requirements for secrecy and all that entails. With Pentagon "black" programs already costing taxpayers tens of billions of dollars the question remains: if NAO were designated as the "principal interface" between American spooks, DHS securocrats and law enforcement, who would have overseen the office's "more robust access to needed remote sensing information"?[25] Certainly not Congress.

Writing in *The Wall Street Journal*, investigative journalist Siobhan Gorman documented that despite a highly-critical June 2008 study by the Congressional Research Service (CRS), Congress partially-funded the program "in a little debated $634 billion spending measure."[26]

Indeed, a fully-operational NAO would have provided federal, state and local officials "with extensive access to spy-satellite imagery... to assist with emergency response and other domestic-security needs, such as identifying where ports or border areas are vulnerable to terrorism."[27] In other words, NAO would have folded the CAC's already existing disaster support operations into a secretive and opaque intelligence bureaucracy. As CRS investigators wrote:

> Members of Congress and outside groups have raised concerns that using satellites for law enforcement purposes may infringe on the privacy and Fourth Amendment rights of U.S. persons. Other commentators have questioned whether the proposed surveillance will violate the Posse Comitatus Act or other restrictions on military involvement in civilian law enforcement, or would otherwise exceed the statutory mandates of the agencies involved.[28]

While it appears that DHS Secretary Janet Napolitano had killed that particular program, it is a near certainty it has been off-loaded to the Pentagon or more likely, outsourced to private contractors who will do some interfacing of their own, directly marketing new surveillance systems to local authorities. It now appears this is precisely what has happened. The giant defense and security firm Raytheon has stood-up a new surveillance platform with a redesigned old technology, the blimp or airship, transforming it into an ubiquitous and silent sentinel, one that links commerce and repression.[29]

Newsweek revealed that "like most airships, it acted as an advertising vehicle."[30] But what set this airship apart as it hovered above the crowd on Memorial Day weekend at this year's Indy 500 race was that "hidden inside the 55-foot-long white balloon was a powerful surveillance camera adapted from the technology Raytheon provides the U.S. military."[31]

Commented Lee Silvestre, Raytheon's vice president for mission innovation at the firm's Integrated Defense division: "The airship is great because it doesn't have that Big Brother feel, or create feelings of invasiveness. But it's still a really powerful security tool."[32]

Known as RAID (Rapid Aerostat Initial Deployment) the system is kitted-out with "electro-optic infrared, radar, flash and acoustic detectors."[33] According to the firm, some 300 have been deployed in Iraq and Afghanistan. As *Newsweek* reported and Raytheon confirmed, the same military version "demonstrated to officials concerned with security and spectator safety its value by providing situational awareness in what is billed as one of the largest sporting events of the year."[34]

Along with a suite of sensors and high resolution video cameras, RAID's digitized mapping tools are similar to those developed for the National Geospatial-Intelligence Agency (NGA). In tandem with a preprogrammed mapping grid of the target location, the system can scan a wide area and relay video clips to a centralized command center.

Captured data known as GEOINT, or geospatial intelligence, is "tailored for customer-specific solutions" according to NGA.[35] That agency along with its "sister" organization, the National Reconnaissance Office (NRO), the super-secret agency that develops and flies America's fleet of spy satellites, are also among the most heavily-outsourced departments in the so-called Intelligence Community.

Nathan Kennedy, Raytheon's project manager for the spy blimp told *Newsweek* "large municipalities could find many uses for this [technology] once we figure out how to get it in their hands."[36]

While the company refused to divulge what the intrusive system might actually cost cash-strapped localities drastically cutting social services for their citizens as America morphs into a failed state, cities "without a Pentagon-size police budget" could look at the airship's "potential to display ads [that] may assist with financing." The firm claims that local authorities fearful of succumbing to what I'd call a dreaded *surveillance airship gap*, could install "a built-in LED screen to attract sponsors, generate revenue and defer operating costs."[37]

Raytheon's slimmed-down spy blimp is a spin-off however, from a much larger and highly-secretive Pentagon project. Among other high-tech, privacy-killing tools currently under development is the Defense Advanced Research Project Agency's (DARPA) Integrated Sensor Is Structure (ISIS) program. As conceived by the agency, ISIS will be a high-altitude autonomous airship built for the U.S. Air Force that can operate at seventy thousand feet and stay aloft for a decade.

Washington Technology reported that Lockheed Martin won a 400 million dollar deal to design the system. "Under the contract" the publication revealed, "Lockheed Martin will provide systems integration services, and Raytheon Co. will furnish a high-energy, low-power density radar, Lockheed Martin officials said."[38] Operating six miles above the earth's surface, well out of range of surface-to-air missiles, the airship will be some 450 feet long, powered by hydrogen fuel cells and packed with electronic surveillance gear and radar currently being field-tested by Raytheon.

While serious civil liberties' issues inherent to such programs have been swept under the proverbial carpet, huge funding outlays by Congress for Pentagon's "black" budget operations demonstrate the hollowness of President Obama's "change" mantra. Like much else in Washington, administration rhetoric is (if you'll pardon the pun) so much hot-air meant to placate the rubes.

Driven by a Corporatist Agenda

Wholesale spying by the American government on its citizens as numerous investigators have uncovered, is aided and abetted by a host of well-heeled corporate grifters in the defense, intelligence and security industries. These powerful, and influential, private players in the Military-Industrial-Security Complex are largely unaccountable; it can be said that America's intelligence and security needs are driven by firms that directly benefit from the Pentagon's penchant for secrecy.

Federal Computer Week reported that the program to revamp America's spy satellites "has the backing of the Obama administration, and the program is expected to win congressional approval, according to a senior intelligence official."[38] The same anonymous "senior official" told the publication "given the backing of the Defense Department, ODNI and the Obama administration, lawmakers are expected to approve the plan."[39] And as with other "black" programs, the cost is classified but is expected to run into the billions, a veritable windfall for enterprising defense corporations.

The top secret "electro-optical satellite modernization program" we're informed, "involves building new satellites that the National Reconnaissance Office (NRO) would operate and expanding the use of imagery from commercial providers."[40] According to a statement by the Office of the Director of National Intelligence, "the National Geospatial-Intelligence Agency would continue to integrate imagery products for government customers."[41]

While no decision has been reached on the "acquisition approach for the program," ODNI and NRO "would oversee the acquisition strategy for the new government-built satellites and a contract would likely be awarded within months."[42]

In a toss-off statement to justify the enormous outlay of taxpayer dollars for the new initiative, Obama's Director of National Intelligence Dennis Blair said, "When it comes to supporting our military forces and the safety of Americans, we cannot afford any gaps in collection."[43] Or perhaps "any gaps in collection" *on* Americans. As Tim Shorrock revealed:

The plans to increase domestic spying are estimated to be worth billions of dollars in new business for the intelligence contractors. The market potential was on display in October at GEOINT 2007, the annual conference sponsored by the U.S. Geospatial Intelligence Foundation (USGIF), a non-profit organization funded by the largest contractors for the NGA. During the conference, which took place in October at the spacious Henry B. Gonzalez Convention Center in downtown San Antonio, many companies were displaying spying and surveillance tools that had been used in Afghanistan and Iraq and were now being re-branded for potential domestic use.[44]

Indeed, according to Shorrock when the NAO was first conceived in 2005, former ODNI director Michael McConnell:

Turned to Booz Allen Hamilton of McLean, Virginia--one of the largest contractors in the spy business. The company was tasked with studying how intelligence from spy satellites and photoreconnaissance planes could be better used domestically to track potential threats to security within the U.S.[45]

Tellingly, McConnell was a senior vice president with the spooky firm for a decade. Booz Allen Hamilton was acquired by the private equity firm The Carlyle Group in a 2008 deal reportedly worth 2.54 billion dollars.[46] In addition to Booz Allen Hamilton, other giant defense and security corporations involved in running the now-defunct National Applications Office included the scandal-tainted British firm BAE Systems, ManTech, Boeing and L-3 Communications.

Among the firms in the running to land ODNI/NRO new spy satellite contracts are BAE, Boeing, Lockheed Martin and Northrop Grumman. All of these corporations according to the Project on Government Oversight's (POGO) Federal Contractor Mismanagement Database (FCMD) have "histories of misconduct such as contract fraud and environmental, ethics, and labor violations."[47]

Unsurprisingly, Lockheed Martin, Boeing, BAE and Northrop Grumman lead the pack in "total instances of misconduct" as well as fines levied by the federal government for abusive practices and outright fraud. Not that any of this mattered however, when it comes to the bottom line.

The Wall Street Journal reported that business for Northrop Grunman and Raytheon "was robust" and that both firms "have been able to escape largely unscathed" despite what are alleged to be Pentagon efforts "to shake up defense spending by cutting back on some high-profile weapons programs."[48]

Conclusion

Unaccountable federal agencies and corporations will continue the capitalist security grift, particularly when it comes to "black" programs run by the Department of Defense and the Office of the Director of National Intelligence. Despite a documented history of serious ethical and constitutional breaches, these programs will persist and expand well into the future. While the Obama administration has said it favors government transparency, it has continued to employ the opaque methods of its predecessors.

From the use of the state secrets privilege to conceal driftnet surveillance of Americans, to its refusal to launch an investigation – and prosecution – of Bush regime torture enablers and war criminals, the "change" administration instead, has delivered "more of the same".

◆

NOTES

1. Bill Sweetman, "Black Budget Blows by $50 Billion Mark", *Aviation Week*, 7 May 2009.
2. *Ibid.*
3. Lewis Page, "U.S. Forces ‹Black› Budget = 2nd Biggest Military on Earth", *The Register*, 8 May 2009.
4. Eric Black, "Investigative Reporter Seymour Hersh Describes 'Executive Assassination Ring'", *MinnPost.com*, 11 March 2009.
5. Siobhan Gorman, "CIA Had Secret Al Qaeda Plan", *The Wall Street Journal*, 13 July 2009.
6. Joby Warrick, "CIA Assassination Program Was Nearing New Phase", *The Washington Post*, 16 July 2009.
7. *Ibid.*

8. Susan Ragland, "Subject: Statutory Authorities to Prohibit Inspector General Activities", *United States Government Accountability Office*, http://cryptome.org/0001/gao-09-660r.htm, 8 May 2009.

9. *Ibid.*, emphasis added.

10. Steven Aftergood, "Senate Bill Would Disclose Intel Budget Request", *Secrecy News*, http://www.fas.org/blog/secrecy/2009/07/intel_budget_request.html, 23 July 2009.

11. *Ibid.*

12. Bill Gertz, "Inside the Ring", *The Washington Times*, http://www. washington times.com/news/2009/jul/23/inside-the-ring-786401 26/, 23 July 2009.

13. *Ibid.*

14. *Ibid.*

15. *Ibid.*

16. Tim Starks, "Obama Budget Fiscal 2010", *Congressional Quarterly*, 7 May 2009.

17. Tom Burghardt, "Homeland Security's Space-Based Spies", *Antifascist Calling*, 4 June 2008. See also Tom Burghardt, "Homeland Security's Space-Based Spying Goes Live", *Antifascist Calling*, 4 October 2008. Tom Burghardt, "Space-Based Domestic Spying: Kicking Civil Liberties to the Curb", *Antifascist Calling*, 9 November 2008. Tom Burghardt, "Look! Up in the Sky! It's a Bird... It's a Plane... It's a Raytheon Spy Blimp!", *Antifascist Calling*, 24 June 2009.

18. National Reconnaissance Office, "Welcome to the NRO", http://www.nro.gov/, no date.

19. Tim Shorrock, *Spies For Hire: The Secret World of Intelligence Outsourcing*, New York, Simon & Schuster, 2008, p. 16.

20. Tom Burghardt, "Homeland Security's Space-Based Spying Goes Live", *op. cit.*

21. Ben Bain, "Bills Would Kill DHS Satellite Surveillance Office", *Federal Computer Week*, http://fcw.com/articles/2009/06/05/web-nao-harman-legis lation.aspx, 5 June 2009.

22. U.S. Department of Homeland Security, "National Applications Office", 14 October 2008.

23. *Congressional Quarterly*, *op. cit.*

24. Department of Homeland Security, "Fact Sheet: National Applications Office", Department of Homeland Security, http://www.dhs.gov/xnews/releases/pr_1187188414685.shtm, 15 August 2007.

25. *Ibid.*

26. Siobhan Gorman, "Satellite-Surveillance Program to Begin Despite Privacy Concerns," *The Wall Street Journal*, 1 October 2008.

27. *Ibid.*
28. Richard A. Best and Jennifer K. Elsea, "Satellite Surveillance: Domestic Issues", *Congressional Research Service,* http://www.fas. org/sgp/crs/intel/RL34421.pdf, 27 June 2008.
29. Tom Burghardt, "Look! Up in the Sky! It's a Bird... It's a Plane... It's a Raytheon Spy Blimp!", 24 June 2009, *op. cit.*
30. Kurt Soller, "Are You Being Watched?", *Newsweek,* http://www. newsweek.com/id/201697, 11 June 2009.
31. *Ibid.*
32. *Ibid.*
33. Raytheon, "Raytheon's Lighter-Than-Air Systems Provide ISR", *Press Release,* 17 June 2009.
34. *Ibid.*
35. National Geospatial-Intelligence Agency, https://www1.nga.mil/ Pages/Default.aspx.
36. Kurt Soller, "Are You Being Watched?", *Newsweek,* http://www. newsweek.com/id/201697, 11 June 2009.
37. William Welsh, "Lockheed Team to Develop Surveillance Radar", *Washington Technology,* 29 April 2009.
38. *Ibid.*
39. Ben Bain, "Spy Satellite Tally Could Increase", *Federal Computer Week,* http://fcw.com/Articles/2009/04/08/spy-satellite-update. aspx, 8 April 2009.
40. *Ibid.*
41. *Ibid.*
41. *Ibid.*
43. Mike Musgrove, "U.S. Intelligence Plan Could Benefit Va. Satellite Imaging Firm", *The Washington Post,* http://www.washingtonpost. com/wp-dyn/content/article/2009/04/08/AR2009040804090. html, 9 April 2009.
44. Tim Shorrock, "Domestic Spying, Inc.", *CorpWatch,* http://www. corpwatch.org/article.php?id=14821, 27 November 2007.
45. *Ibid.*
46. Zachary A. Goldfarb, "Booz Allen Details Plans to Split Firm", *The Washington Post,* http://www.washingtonpost.com/wp-dyn/con- tent/article/2008/05/21 /AR2008052102775.html, 22 May 2008.
47. Project on Government Oversight, Washington, D.C., "Federal Contractor Mismanagement Database", http://www.contractor- misconduct.org/.
48. August Cole, "Defense Firms Call Business Solid", *The Wall Street Journal,* http://online.wsj.com/article/SB124838295838477029. html, 24 July 2009.

CHAPTER 13

The Economic Crisis
"Threatens National Security" in America

Bill Van Auken

In testimony before the Senate Committee on Intelligence, Obama's new Director of National Intelligence, Dennis Blair, warned that the deepening world capitalist crisis posed the paramount threat to U.S. national security and warned that its continuation could trigger a return to the "violent extremism" of the 1920s and 1930s.[1]

This frank assessment, contained in the unclassified version of the "annual threat assessment" presented by Blair on behalf of sixteen separate U.S. intelligence agencies, represented a striking departure from earlier years, in which a supposedly ubiquitous threat from Al Qaeda terrorism and the two wars launched under the Bush administration topped the list of concerns.

Clearly underlying his remarks are fears within the massive U.S. intelligence apparatus as well as among more conscious layers of the American ruling elite that a protracted economic crisis accompanied by rising unemployment and reduced social spending will trigger a global eruption of the class struggle and the threat of social revolution.

The presentation was not only the first for Blair, a former Navy admiral who took over as director of national intelligence only two weeks prior, but also marked the first detailed elaboration of the perspective of the U.S. intelligence apparatus since the inauguration of President Barack Obama.

Blair declared in his opening remarks:

The primary near-term security concern of the United States is the global economic crisis and its geopolitical implications... The crisis has been ongoing for over a year, and economists are divided over whether and when we could hit bottom. Some even fear that the recession could further deepen and reach the level of the Great Depression. Of course, all of us recall the dramatic political consequences wrought by the economic turmoil of the 1920s and 1930s in Europe, the instability, and high levels of violent extremism. *(Ibid.)*

Blair described the ongoing financial and economic meltdown as "the most serious one in decades, if not in centuries... Time is probably our greatest threat. The longer it takes for the recovery to begin, the greater the likelihood of serious damage to US strategic interests."

The intelligence chief noted that "roughly a quarter of the countries in the world have already experienced low-level instability such as government changes because of the current slowdown." He added that the "bulk of anti-state demonstrations" internationally have been seen in Europe and the former Soviet Union.

But Blair stressed that the threat that the crisis will produce revolutionary upheavals is global. The financial meltdown, he said, is "likely to produce a wave of economic crises in emerging market nations over the next year." He added that "much of Latin America, former Soviet Union states and sub-Saharan Africa lack sufficient cash reserves, access to international aid or credit, or other coping mechanism."

Noting that economic growth in these regions of the globe had fallen dramatically in preceding months, Blair stated, "When those growth rates go down, my gut tells me that there are going to be problems coming out of that, and we're looking for that." He cited "statistical modeling" showing that "economic crises increase the risk of regime-threatening instability if they persist over a one to two year period."

In another parallel to the 1930s, the U.S. intelligence director pointed to the implications of the crisis for world trade and relations between national capitalist economies.

The globally synchronized nature of this slowdown means that countries will not be able to export their way out of this recession... Indeed, policies designed to promote domestic export industries – so-called beggar-thy-neighbor policies such as competitive currency devaluations, import tariffs, and/or export subsidies – risk unleashing a wave of destructive protectionism.

It was precisely such policies pursued in the 1930s that set the stage for the eruption of the Second World War.

Blair also raised the damage that the crisis has done to the global credibility of American capitalism, declaring that the "widely held perception that excesses in U.S. financial markets and inadequate regulation were responsible has increased criticism about free market policies, which may make it difficult to achieve long-time U.S. objectives." The collapse of Wall Street, he added, "has increased questioning of U.S. stewardship of the global economy and the international financial structure."

The threat assessment also included evaluations of potential terrorist threats, the "arc of instability" stretching from the Middle East to South Asia, conditions in Latin America and Africa and strategic challenges from both China and Russia, centering in Eurasia. It likewise dealt with the war in Afghanistan, which the Obama administration is preparing to escalate, providing a scathing assessment of the Karzai regime in Kabul and the familiar demand for an escalation of the intervention in Pakistan. Nonetheless, the report's undeniable focus was on the danger that economic turmoil will ignite revolutionary challenges on a world scale.

Blair's emphasis on the global capitalist crisis as the overriding national security concern for American imperialism seemed to leave some of the Senate intelligence panel's members taken aback. They have been accustomed over the previous seven years to having all U.S. national security issues subsumed in the "global war on terrorism", a propaganda catch-all used to justify U.S. aggression abroad while papering over the immense contradictions underlying Washington's global position.

The committee's Republican vice chairman, Senator Christopher Bond of Missouri, expressed his concern that Blair was making the "conditions in the country" and the global economic crisis "the primary focus of the intelligence community."

Blair responded that he was "trying to act as your intelligence officer today, telling you what I thought the Senate ought to be caring about." It sounded like a rebuke and a warning to the senators that it is high time to ditch the ideological baggage of the past several years and confront the real and growing threat to capitalist rule posed by the crisis and the resulting radicalization of the masses in country after country.

It may have been lost on some of those sitting at the dais in the Senate hearing room, but when Blair referred to a return to the conditions of "violent extremism" of the 1920s and 1930s, he was warning that American and world capitalism once again faces the specter of a revolutionary challenge by the working class.

Extended Role of the U.S. Military in Civilian Politics

There is no doubt that behind the façade of Obama, the U.S. national security apparatus is making its counter-revolutionary preparations accordingly.

Including Blair, Obama has named several retired four-star military officers to serve in his cabinet. The other two are former Marine Gen. James Jones, his national security adviser, and former Army chief of staff Gen. Erik Shinseki, his Secretary of Veterans' Affairs. This unprecedented representation of the senior officer corps within the new Democratic administration is indicative of a growth in the political power of the U.S. military that poses a serious threat to basic democratic rights.

According to a November 2008 report of the U.S. Army War College, the Pentagon and the U.S. intelligence establishment are preparing for what they see as a historic crisis of the existing order that could require the use of armed force to quell social struggles at home.[2]

Preparing for "Violent, Strategic Dislocation inside the United States"

Entitled "Known Unknowns: Unconventional 'Strategic Shocks' in Defense Strategy Development," the monograph insists that one of the key contingencies for which the U.S. military must prepare is a "violent, strategic dislocation inside the United States," which could be provoked by "unforeseen economic collapse" or "loss of functioning political and legal order."[3]

The report states:

Widespread civil violence inside the United States would force the defense establishment to reorient priorities in extremis to defend basic domestic order... An American government and defense establishment lulled into complacency by a long-secure domestic order would be forced to rapidly divest some or most external security commitments in order to address rapidly expanding human insecurity at home.[4]

In other words, a sharp intensification of the unfolding capitalist crisis accompanied by an eruption of class struggle and the threat of social revolution in the U.S. itself could force the Pentagon to call back its expeditionary armies from Iraq and Afghanistan for use against American workers.

The document continues: "Under the most extreme circumstances, this might include use of military force against hostile groups inside the United States. Further, DoD [the Department of Defense] would be, by necessity, an essential enabling hub for the continuity of political authority in a multi-state or nationwide civil conflict or disturbance." The phrase – "an essential enabling hub for continuity of authority" – is a euphemism for military dictatorship.[5]

The working class must draw its own urgent conclusions from the rapid deepening of the present crisis, above all the necessity of building a mass independent political party based on a socialist and internationalist program and fighting to put an end to the capitalist profit system. This means, above all, joining and building the Socialist Equality Party.

◆

NOTES

1. Dennis C. Blair, Director of National Intelligence, "Annual Threat Assessment of the Intelligence Community for the Senate Select Committee on Intelligence", intelligence.senate.gov/090212/blair. pdf, 12 February 2009.

2. Nathan Freier, *Known Unknowns: Unconventional "Strategic Shocks" in Defense Strategy Development*, Strategic Studies Institute, United States Army War College, http://www.strategicstudiesinstitute. army.mil/pubs/display.cfm? pubID=890, November 2008.

3. *Ibid.*

4. *Ibid.*

5. *Ibid.*

CHAPTER 14

The Political Economy of World Government

Andrew Gavin Marshall

Capitalism has always changed and morphed; it has adapted to changes in the world and has forced the world to adapt to its changes. Capitalism has never, and never will be, entirely consistent in its structure and institutions.

The global economic crisis has sped up developments that have been underway for a long time, specifically within the last century. In the midst of a global crisis, these changes, which have been slow and evolutionary, are being rapidly sped up and accelerated.

Introduction

The global political economy is being transformed into a global government structure at the crossroads of a major financial crisis. However, far from the assumptions of many students of Capitalism and the global political economy, these changes are not natural and inevitable; these changes are planned, organized, socialized and institutionalized. The process towards creating a global government is not a new one; several institutions and organizations throughout the world have slowly been directing the world down this path.

This chapter examines the process of constructing a global government, with a particular focus on the major organizations that have and are currently shaping this transformation. What is being undertaken is the deconstruction of the global economy and national polity in order to rebuild the global political economy into a singular governance structure. Thus, destruction becomes a form of creation; the global economic crisis must be viewed in this context.

The Council on Foreign Relations

Nearing the end of the 19th century, American bankers and industrialists, specifically J.P. Morgan, were gaining close connections with major European banking interests. On the European side, specifically in Britain, the elite was largely involved in the Scramble for Africa at this time. Infamous among them was Cecil Rhodes, who made his fortune in diamond and gold mining in Africa, monopolizing the gold mines with financial help from Lord Rothschild.[1] Interestingly, "Rhodes could not have won his near-monopoly over South African diamond production without the assistance of his friends in the City of London: in particular, the Rothschild bank, at that time the biggest concentration of financial capital in the world."[2] As historian Niall Ferguson explained, "It is usually assumed that Rhodes owned De Beers, but this was not the case. Nathaniel de Rothschild was a bigger shareholder than Rhodes himself; indeed, by 1899 the Rothschilds' stake was twice that of Rhodes."[3]

Cecil Rhodes was also known for his radical views regarding America, particularly in that he would "talk with total seriousness of 'the ultimate recovery of the United States of America as an integral part of the British Empire'."[4] Rhodes saw himself not simply as a moneymaker, but even more so as an "empire builder." As historian Carroll Quigley explained, in 1891, three British elites met with the intent to create a secret society. The three men were Cecil Rhodes, William T. Stead, a prominent journalist of the day, and Reginald Baliol Brett, a "friend and confidant of Queen Victoria, and later to be the most influential adviser of King Edward VII and King George V." Within this secret society, "real power was to be exercised by the leader, and a 'Junta of Three.' The leader was to be Rhodes, and the Junta was to be Stead, Brett, and Alfred Milner."[5]

In 1901, Rhodes chose Milner as his successor within the society, of which the purpose was:

> The extension of British rule throughout the world, the perfecting of a system of emigration from the United Kingdom and of colonization by British subjects of all lands wherein the means of livelihood are attainable by energy, labor, and enterprise... [with] the ultimate recovery of the United States of America as an integral part of a British Empire, the consolidation of the

whole Empire, the inauguration of a system of Colonial Representation in the Imperial Parliament which may tend to weld together the disjointed members of the Empire, and finally the foundation of so great a power as to hereafter render wars impossible and promote the best interests of humanity.[6]

Essentially, it outlined a British-led cosmopolitical world order, one global system of governance under British hegemony. Among key players within this group were the Rothschilds and other leading banking interests.[7]

The creation of the Federal Reserve in the United States in 1913, cemented the connection between European and American banking interests, as the Fed created a very distinct alliance between New York and London bankers.[8]

In the midst of World War I, a group of American scholars were tasked with briefing "Woodrow Wilson about options for the postwar world once the Kaiser and imperial Germany fell to defeat." This group was called, "The Inquiry." The group advised Wilson mostly through his trusted aide, Col. Edward M. House, who was Wilson's "unofficial envoy to Europe during the period between the outbreak of World War I in 1914 and the intervention by the United States in 1917," and was the prime driving force in the Wilson administration behind the establishment of the Federal Reserve System.[9]

"The Inquiry" laid the foundations for the creation of the Council on Foreign Relations (CFR), the most powerful think tank in the U.S., and "the scholars of the Inquiry helped draw the borders of post World War I central Europe." On May 30, 1919, a group of scholars and diplomats from Britain and the U.S. met at the Hotel Majestic, where they "proposed a permanent Anglo-American Institute of International Affairs, with one branch in London, the other in New York." When the scholars returned from Paris, they were welcomed by New York lawyers and financiers, and together they formed the Council on Foreign Relations in 1921. The "British diplomats returning from Paris had made great headway in founding their Royal Institute of International Affairs." The Anglo-American Institute envisioned in Paris, with two branches and combined membership was not feasible, so both the British and American branches retained national membership, however, they would cooperate closely with one another.[10] They were referred to, and still are, as "Sister Institutes."[11]

The Milner Group, the secret society formed by Cecil Rhodes, "dominated the British delegation to the Peace Conference of 1919; it had a great deal to do with the formation and management of the League of Nations and of the system of mandates; it founded the Royal Institute of International Affairs in 1919 and still controls it."[12] There were other groups founded in many countries representing the same interests of the secret Milner Group, and they came to be known as the Round Table Groups, preeminent among them were the Royal Institute of International Affairs (Chatham House), the Council on Foreign Relations in the United States, and parallel groups in Canada, Australia, New Zealand, South Africa and India.[13] This had the effect of establishing a socializing institution for the elites of each nation, from which they would exert political, economic, academic and social influence.

The CFR, established less than ten years after the creation of the Federal Reserve, worked to promote an internationalist agenda on behalf of the international banking elite. It was to alter America's conceptualization of its place within the world from an isolationist industrial nation to an engine of empire working for international banking and corporate interests. Where the Fed took control of money and debt, the CFR took control of the ideological foundations of such an empire, encompassing the corporate, banking, political, foreign policy, military, media and academic elite of the nation into a generally cohesive overall world view. By altering one's ideology to that of promoting such an internationalist agenda, the big money that was behind it would ensure one's rise through government, industry, academia and media. The other major think tanks and policy institutions in the United States are also represented at the CFR.

Before America even entered World War II in late 1941, the Council began a "strictly confidential" project called the War and Peace Studies, in which top CFR members collaborated with the U.S. State Department in determining U.S. policy, and the project was entirely financed by the Rockefeller Foundation.[14] The post-War world was already being designed by members of the Council who would then go into government in order to make those designs into a reality.

The policy of "containment" towards the Soviet Union that would defined American foreign policy for nearly half a century was envisaged in a 1947 edition of *Foreign Affairs*, the academic journal of the Council on Foreign Relations. So too were the ideological foundations for the Marshall Plan and NATO envisaged at the Council on Foreign Relations, with members of the Council recruited to enact, implement and lead these institutions.[15] The Council also played a role in the establishment and promotion of the United Nations,[16] which was subsequently built on land bought from John D. Rockefeller, Jr.[17]

In 1944, representatives of the 44 Allied nations met for the Bretton Woods conference (the United Nations Monetary and Financial Conference) in New Hampshire, in an effort to reorganize and regulate the international financial and monetary order following the war. The UK was represented by John Maynard Keynes; the American contingent was represented by Harry Dexter White, an American economist and senior U.S. Treasury department official. It was out of this conference that the International Monetary Fund (IMF), the International Bank for Reconstruction and Development (IBRD), now part of the World Bank, and the General Agreement on Tariffs and Trade (GATT), now institutionalized in the World Trade Organization (WTO), originated. They were designed to be the institutionalized economic foundations of exerting American hegemony across the globe; they were, in essence, engines of economic empire.

In 1947, President Harry Truman signed the National Security Act, which created the position of Secretary of Defense overseeing the entire military establishment, and the Joint Chiefs of Staff; it created the CIA modeled on its war time incarnation of the Office of Strategic Services (OSS); the Act also created the National Security Council, headed by a National Security Adviser, designed to give the President further advice on foreign affairs issues separate from the State Department. Essentially, the Act created the basis for the national security state apparatus for empire building.

The founding of the CIA was urged by the War and Peace Studies Project of the Council on Foreign Relations in the early 1940s. The architects of the CIA, designing the shape and organization of the Agency, as well as its functions were all Wall Street lawyers, largely made up of members of the Council on Foreign

Relations. The Deputy Directors of the CIA for the first two decades were all "from the same New York legal and financial circles."[18]

The Bilderberg Group

In 1954, the Bilderberg Group was founded in the Netherlands, holding secretive meeting once a year, drawing roughly 130 of the political-financial-military-academic-media elites from North America and Western Europe as "an informal network of influential people who could consult each other privately and confidentially."[19] Regular participants included the CEOs of some of the largest corporations in the world, oil companies such as Royal Dutch Shell, British Petroleum, and Total SA, as well as various European monarchs, international bankers such as David Rockefeller, major politicians, presidents, prime ministers and central bankers of the world.[20]

Joseph Retinger, the founder of the Bilderberg Group, was also one of the original architects of the European Common Market and a leading intellectual champion of European integration. In 1946, he told the Royal Institute of International Affairs (the British counterpart and sister organization of the Council on Foreign Relations), that Europe needed to create a federal union and for European countries to "relinquish part of their sovereignty." Retinger was a founder of the European Movement (EM), a lobbying organization dedicated to creating a federal Europe. Retinger secured financial support for the European Movement from powerful U.S. financial interests such as the Council on Foreign Relations and the Rockefellers.[21] However, it is hard to distinguish between the CFR and the Rockefellers, as, especially following World War II, the CFR's main finances came from the Carnegie Corporation, Ford Foundation and most especially, the Rockefeller Foundation.[22]

The Bilderberg Group acts as a "secretive global think-tank," with an original intent to "to link governments and economies in Europe and North America amid the Cold War."[23] One of the Bilderberg Group's main goals was unifying Europe into a European Union. Apart from Retinger, the founder of the Bilderberg Group and the European Movement, another ideological founder of European integration was Jean Monnet, who founded the Action Committee for a United States of Europe, an organization dedicated to promoting European integration, and he was also the major promoter and first president of the European Coal and Steel Community (ECSC), the precursor to the European Common Market.[24]

Declassified documents (released in 2001) revealed that "the U.S. intelligence community ran a campaign in the Fifties and Sixties to build momentum for a united Europe. It funded and directed the European federalist movement."[25] Furthermore:

America was working aggressively behind the scenes to push Britain into a European state. One memorandum, dated July 26, 1950, gives instructions for a campaign to promote a fully-fledged European parliament. It is signed by Gen William J Donovan, head of the American wartime Office of Strategic Services, precursor of the CIA...

Washington's main tool for shaping the European agenda was the American Committee for a United Europe, created in 1948. The chairman was Donovan, ostensibly a private lawyer by then. The vice-chairman was Allen Dulles, the CIA director in the Fifties. The board included Walter Bedell Smith, the CIA's first director, and a roster of ex-OSS figures and officials who moved in and out of the CIA. The documents show that ACUE financed the European Movement, the most important federalist organisation in the post-war years...

The leaders of the European Movement - Retinger, the visionary Robert Schuman and the former Belgian prime minister Paul-Henri Spaak - were all treated as hired hands by their American sponsors. The US role was handled as a covert operation. ACUE's funding came from the Ford and Rockefeller foundations as well as business groups with close ties to the US government.[26]

The European Coal and Steel Community was formed in 1951, and signed by France, West Germany, Italy, Belgium, Luxembourg and the Netherlands. Newly released documents from the 1955 Bilderberg meeting show that a main topic of discussion was "European Unity":

The discussion affirmed complete support for the idea of integration and unification from the representatives of all the six nations of the Coal and Steel Community present at the conference...

A European speaker expressed concern about the need to achieve a common currency, and indicated that in his view this necessarily implied the creation of a central political authority...

A United States participant confirmed that the United States had not weakened in its enthusiastic support for the idea of integration, although there was considerable diffidence in America as to how this enthusiasm should be manifested. Another United States participant urged his European friends to go ahead with the unification of Europe with less emphasis upon ideological considerations and, above all, to be practical and work fast.[27]

Thus, at the 1955 Bilderberg Group meeting, they set as a primary agenda, the creation of a European common market.[28]

In 1957, two years later, the Treaty of Rome was signed, which created the European Economic Community (EEC), also known as the European Community. Over the decades, various other treaties were signed, and more countries joined the European Community. In 1992, the Maastricht Treaty was signed, which created the European Union and led to the creation of the Euro. The European Monetary Institute was created in 1994, the European Central Bank was founded in 1998, and the Euro was launched in 1999. Etienne Davignon, Chairman of the Bilderberg Group and former EU Commissioner, revealed in March of 2009 that the Euro was debated and planned at Bilderberg conferences.[29]

The Trilateral Commission

In the late 1960s, Western European economies (in particular West Germany) and Japan were rapidly developing and expanding. Their currencies rose against the U.S. dollar, which was pegged to the price of gold as a result of the Bretton Woods System, which, through the IMF, set up an international monetary system based upon the U.S. dollar. However, with the growth of West Germany and Japan, "by the late 1960s the system could no longer be expected to perform its previous function as a medium for international exchange, and as a surrogate for gold."

On top of this, to maintain its vast empire, the U.S. had developed a large balance-of-payments deficit.[30]

Richard Nixon took decisive, and what many referred to as "protectionist" measures, and in 1971, ended the dollar's link to gold, which "resulted in a devaluation of the dollar as it began to float against other currencies," and "was meant to restore the competitiveness of the U.S. economy,"[31] as with devaluation, "U.S.-made goods would cost less to foreigners and foreign-made goods would be less competitive on the U.S. market." The second major action taken by Nixon was when he "slapped a ten percent surcharge on most imports into the United States," which was to benefit U.S. manufacturing firms over foreign ones in competition for the U.S. market. The result was that less imports from Asia were coming into the U.S., more U.S. goods were sold in their markets at more competitive prices, forcing Japan and the EEC to relax their trade barriers to U.S. products.[32]

The Council on Foreign Relations referred to Nixon's New Economic Policy as "protectionist," encouraging a "disastrous isolationist trend,"[33] and that Nixon shattered "the linchpin of the entire international monetary system – on whose smooth functioning the world economy depends."[34] According to the CFR, the Atlanticist, or internationalist faction of the U.S. elite, were upset with Nixon's New Economic Policy:

> [They] agreed on the diagnosis: the relative balance of economic strengths had so changed that the United States could no longer play the role of economic leader. But they also argued that further American unilateralism would fuel a spiral of defensive reactions that would leave all the Western economies worse off. Their suggested remedy, instead, was much more far-reaching coordination among all the trilateral [North American, European and Japanese] governments.[35]

There was a consensus within the American ruling class that the Bretton Woods System was in need of a reform but there were divisions within the elites on how to carry out those reforms. The more powerful (and wealthy) international wing feared that U.S. policies may isolate and alienate Western Europe and Japan:

> The world economic roles of America must be reconciled with the growth to power of Europe and Japan. There must be

fundamental reform of the international monetary system. There must be renewed efforts to reduce world trade barriers. The underlying U.S. balance of payments has deteriorated.[36]

In 1970, David Rockefeller became Chairman of the Council on Foreign Relations, while also being Chairman and CEO of Chase Manhattan. In 1970, Zbigniew Brzezinski wrote *Between Two Ages: America's Role in the Technetronic Era*, in which he called for the formation of "A Community of the Developed Nations" consisting of Western Europe, the United States and Japan. He described how "the traditional sovereignty of nation states is becoming increasingly unglued as transnational forces such as multinational corporations, banks, and international organiza-tions play a larger and larger role in shaping global politics." David Rockefeller had taken note of Brzezinski's writings, and was "getting worried about the deteriorating relations between the U.S., Europe, and Japan," as a result of Nixon's economic shocks. In 1972, David Rockefeller and Brzezinski "presented the idea of a trilateral grouping at the annual Bilderberg meeting."[37]

In July of 1972, seventeen powerful people met at David Rockefeller's estate in New York to plan for the creation of the Commission. Also at the meeting were Brzezinski, McGeorge Bundy, the President of the Ford Foundation, (brother of William Bundy, editor of *Foreign Affairs*) and Bayless Manning, President of the Council on Foreign Relations. So, in 1973, the Trilateral Commission was formed to address these issues.

The CFR viewed,

Trilateralism as a linguistic expression – and the Trilateral Com-mission – arose in the early 1970s from the reaction of the more Atlanticist part of the American foreign policy community to the belligerent and defensive unilateralism that characterized the foreign economic policy of the Nixon Administration.[38]

The Commission's major concerns were to preserve for the "industrialized societies," in other words, seek mutual gain for the Trilateral nations, and to construct "a common approach to the needs and demands of the poorer nations." However, this should be read as, "constructing a common approach to [dealing with] poorer nations". As well as this, the Commission would undertake "the coordination of defense policies and of policies toward such highly politicized issues as nuclear proliferation, terrorism, and aerial hijacking, and such highly politicized geographic areas as the Middle East or Southern Africa."[39]

The end of the link of the dollar to gold meant that, "the U.S. was no longer subject to the discipline of having to try to maintain a fixed par value of the dollar against gold or anything else: it could let the dollar move as the U.S. Treasury [and ultimately, the Federal Reserve] wished and pointed towards the removal of gold from international monetary affairs." This created a dollar standard, as opposed to a gold standard, which "places the direction of the world monetary policy in the hands of a single country," which was "not acceptable to Western Europe or Japan."[40] The issue of the dollar standard was intricately related to the creation of the Trilateral Commission.

The New World Order Emerges

A key figure in the debate on a New World Order was Richard N. Gardner, a former U.S. ambassador to the United Nations, as well as a member of the Trilateral Commission, who wrote:

The quest for a world structure that secures peace, advances human rights and provides the conditions for economic progress – for what is loosely called world order – has never seemed more frustrating but at the same time strangely hopeful."[41]

Few people retain much confidence in the more ambitious strategies for world order that had wide backing a generation ago – 'world federalism,' 'charter review,' and 'world peace through world law'... The same considerations suggest the doubtful utility of bolding a [UN] Charter review conference.[42]

If instant world government, Charter review, and a greatly strengthened International Court do not provide the answers, what hope for progress is there? The answer will not satisfy those who seek simple solutions to complex problems, but it comes down essentially to this: The hope for the foreseeable future lies, not in building up a few ambitious central institutions of universal membership and general jurisdiction as was envisaged at the end of the last war, but rather in the much more decentralized, disorderly and pragmatic process of inventing or adapting

TEXT BOX 14.1
WHO RUNS THE WTO?

The first Director-General of the WTO was Peter D. Sutherland, who was previously the director general of GATT, former Attorney General of Ireland, and currently is Chairman of British Petroleum and Goldman Sachs International, as well as being special representative of the United Nations Secretary-General in matters pertaining to migration. He is also a member of the board of the Royal Bank of Scotland Group, the Foundation Board of the World Economic Forum, goodwill ambassador to the United Nations Industrial Development Organization, is a member of the Bilderberg Group, and is European Chairman of the Trilateral Commission, and he was presented with the Robert Schuman Medal for his work on European Integration and the David Rockefeller Award of the Trilateral Commission. Clearly, the WTO was an organ of the western banking elite to be used as a tool in expanding and institutionalizing their control over world trade.

Source: Membership, Peter Sutherland. The Trilateral Commission: October 2007: http://www.trilateral.org/membship/bios/ps.htm

institutions of limited jurisdiction and selected membership to deal with specific problems on a case-by-case basis, as the necessity for cooperation is perceived by the relevant nations.

In short, the 'house of world order' will have to be built from the bottom up rather than from the top down. It will look like a great 'booming, buzzing confusion,' to use William James' famous description of reality, but *an end run around national s overeignty, eroding it piece by piece, will accomplish much more than the old-fashioned frontal assault.*[43]

The term *New World Order* emerged in the early 1990s. It described a more unipolar world, addressing the collapse of the Soviet Union and the newfound role of the United States as the sole and unchallenged global power. The New World Order was meant to represent a new phase in the global political economy in which world authority rested in one place, and for the time, that place was to be the United States.

This era saw the continual expansion and formation of regional blocs, with the formation of the European Union, the signing of the North American Free Trade Agreement (NAFTA) and the creation of the WTO. The World Trade Organization was officially formed in 1995, as the successor to the General Agreements on Tariffs and Trade (GATT), which was formed in 1944 at the Bretton Woods conference. The WTO manages the international liberal trading order.

Towards a Socially Constructed Global Government

Social Constructivism brings some very important concepts to the discussion and analysis of the global political economy. This theory argues that "the social and political world, including the world of international relations, is not a physical entity or material object that is outside human consciousness. Consequently, the study of international relations must focus on the ideas and beliefs that inform the actors on the international scene as well as the shared understandings between them." Expanding upon this idea:

> The international system is not something 'out there' like the solar system. It does not exist on its own. It exists only as an intersubjective awareness among people; in that sense the system is constituted by ideas, not by material forces. It is a human invention or creation not of a physical or material kind but of a purely intellectual and ideational kind. It is a set of ideas, a body of thought, a system of norms, which has been arranged by certain people at a particular time and place.

Examples of socially constructed structures within the global political economy are national borders, as they have no physical lines, but are rather formed by a shared understanding between various actors as to where the border is. The nation itself is a social construct, as it has no physical, over-arching form, but is made up of a litany of shared values, ideas, concepts, institutions, beliefs and symbols. Thus:

> If the thoughts and ideas that enter into the existence of international relations change, then the system itself will change as well, because the system consists in thoughts and ideas. That is the

insight behind the oft-repeated phrase by constructivist Alexander Wendt: 'anarchy is what states make of it.'[44]

...If 'anarchy is what states make of it' there is nothing inevitable or unchangeable about world politics... The existing system is a creation of states and if states change their conceptions of who they are, what their interests are, what they want, etc. then the situation will change accordingly... [States could decide] to reduce their sovereignty or even to give up their sovereignty. If that happened there would no longer be an international anarchy as we know it. Instead, *there would be a brave new, non-anarchical world – perhaps one in which states were subordinate to a world government.*[45]

Strobe Talbott, Deputy Secretary of State in the Clinton administration, is an influential figure in both the Council on Foreign Relations and the Trilateral Commission. He is currently President of the Brookings Institution. According to Talbott:

Nationhood as we know it will be obsolete; all states will recognize a single, global authority. A phrase briefly fashionable in the mid-20th century – "citizen of the world" – will have assumed real meaning by the end of the 21st. [46]

Talbott endorsed the social constructivist perspective of nation-states and elaborated on his thesis:

All countries are basically social arrangements, accommodations to changing circumstances. No matter how permanent and even sacred they may seem at any one time, in fact they are all artificial and temporary. Through the ages, there has been an overall trend toward larger units claiming sovereignty and, paradoxically, a gradual diminution of how much true sovereignty any one country actually has.

Perhaps national sovereignty wasn't such a great idea after all... It has taken the events in our own wondrous and terrible century to clinch the case for world government... The cold war also saw the European Community pioneer the kind of regional cohesion that may pave the way for globalism.

The free world formed multilateral financial institutions that depend on member states' willingness to give up a degree of sovereignty. The International Monetary Fund can virtually dictate fiscal policies, even including how much tax a government should levy on its citizens. The General Agreement on Tariffs and Trade regulates how much duty a nation can charge on imports. These organizations can be seen as the protoministries of trade, finance and development for a united world.

Globalization has also contributed to the spread of terrorism, drug trafficking, AIDS and environmental degradation. But because those threats are more than any one nation can cope with on its own, they constitute an incentive for international cooperation... The best mechanism for democracy, whether at the level of the multinational state or that of the planet as a whole, is not an all-powerful Leviathan or centralized superstate, but a federation, a union of separate states that allocate certain powers to a central government while retaining many others for themselves.[47]

In essence, he advocated for the formation of a world federation, where nation-states as we know them today, would be relegated to the status of a province.

The European Superstate

In 1992, the Maastricht Treaty was signed, which officially formed the European Union in 1993. In 1994, the European Monetary Institute (EMI) was formed, with the European Central Bank (ECB) being formed in 1998, and the single European currency, the Euro, debuting in 1999. In 2004, the European Constitution was set to be signed by all 25-member states of the EU, which was a treaty to establish a constitution for the entire European Union.

The Constitution was a move towards creating a European superstate, creating an EU foreign minister, and with it, a coordinated foreign policy. The creation of a European Justice system, with the EU defining "minimum standards in defining offences and setting sentences," and creating a common asylum and immigration policy. It would also hand over to the EU the power to "ensure co-ordination of economic and employment policies", and EU law would supercede all law of the member states, thus making the member nations relative to mere provinces within a centralized federal government system.[48]

The Constitution was largely written up by Valéry Giscard d'Estaing, former President of the French Republic from 1974 to

1981. Giscard d'Estaing also happens to be a member of the Bilderberg Group, the Trilateral Commission, and is also a close friend of Henry Kissinger's, having co-authored papers with him. In 2005, French and Dutch voters answered the referendums in their countries, in which they rejected the EU Constitution, which required total unanimity in order to pass.

In 2007, a move was undertaken to introduce what was called the Lisbon Treaty, to be approved by all member-states. Giscard d'Estaing wrote an article for the *Independent* in which he stated that, "The difference between the original Constitution and the present Lisbon Treaty is one of approach, rather than content." Giscard described the process of creating the Lisbon Treaty:

> It was the legal experts for the European Council who were charged with drafting the new text. They have not made any new suggestions. They have taken the original draft constitution, blown it apart into separate elements, and have then attached them, one by one, to existing treaties. The Treaty of Lisbon is thus a catalogue of amendments. It is unpenetrable for the public. [49]

The main difference was that the word "constitution" was removed and banished from the text. Though the Treaty dropped the word "constitution," it remained the same in "giving the EU the trappings of a global power and cutting national sovereignty." It contained plans to create an EU President:

> [who] will serve a two and half year term but unlike democratic heads of state he or she will be chosen by Europe's leaders not by voters [and] will take over key international negotiations from national heads of government. [The] Foreign Minister [becomes the] High Representative [who] will run a powerful EU diplomatic service and will be more important on the global and European stage than national foreign ministers. [And] Interior Ministry [will] centralize databases holding fingerprints and DNA [and] make EU legislation on new police and surveillance powers. [The ability for EU nations to use vetoes will end, and the Treaty] includes a clause hardwiring an EU "legal personality" and ascendancy over national courts.[50]

One country in Europe has it written into its constitution that it requires a referendum on treaties, and that country is Ireland.

In June of 2008, the Irish went to vote on the Treaty of Lisbon, after weeks and months of being badgered by EU politicians and Eurocrats explaining that the Irish "owe" Europe a "Yes" vote because of the benefits the EU had bestowed upon Ireland. History will show, however, that the Irish don't take kindly to being bossed around and patronized, so when they went to the polls, "No" was on their lips and on their ballots. The Irish thus rejected the Lisbon Treaty.

However, the European elites didn't accept this outcome. In September of 2009, they were forced to vote again, and voted "Yes" the second time around, thus passing the Lisbon Treaty. From the perspective of the European elite, "democracy" is good only when it produces the results they desire.

North American Integration

The Canada-U.S. Free Trade Agreement (FTA) of 1989 was signed by President George H. W. Bush and Canadian Prime Minister Brian Mulroney. The FTA had devastating consequences for the people of Canada and the United States, while enriching the corporate and political elite. For example, GDP growth decreased, while unemployment reached its highest level since the Great Depression,[51] and meanwhile Brian Mulroney entered the corporate world, of which he now sits as a board member of Barrick Gold Corporation, as well as sitting on the International Advisory Board of the Council on Foreign Relations,[52] of which David Rockefeller remains on as Honorary Chairman.

In 1990, the private sector lobbying groups and think tanks began the promotion of the North American Free Trade Agreement (NAFTA) to expand the Canada-U.S. Free Trade Agreement to include Mexico. NAFTA was signed by then Canadian Prime Minister Jean Chrétien, U.S. President George H.W. Bush and Mexican President Carlos Salinas, in 1993, and went into effect in 1994. It was negotiated during a time in which Mexico was undergoing liberal economic reforms, so NAFTA had the effect of cementing those reforms in an "economic constitution for North America."[53]

David Rockefeller played a role in the push for NAFTA. In 1965, he had founded the Council for Latin America (CLA), which, as he wrote in a 1966 article in *Foreign Affairs*, was to mobilize private enterprise throughout the hemisphere "to stimulate and support economic integration." The CLA, Rockefeller wrote, "provides an effective channel of cooperation between businessmen in the United States and their counterparts in the countries to the south. It also offers a means of continuing communication and consultation with the White House, the State Department and other agencies of our government."[54]

The CLA later changed its name to the Council of the Americas (CoA) and maintains a very close relationship with the Americas Society, founded at the same time as the CLA, of which David Rockefeller remains to this day as Chairman of both organizations. As David wrote in his autobiography, *Memoirs*, in the lead up to NAFTA, the Council of the Americas sponsored a Forum of the Americas, which was attended by President George H. W. Bush, which resulted in the call for a "Western Hemisphere free trade area."[55]

In 1993, David Rockefeller wrote an article for the *Wall Street Journal*, in the run up to NAFTA, in which he advocated for the signing of NAFTA as essential, describing it as a vital step on the road to fulfilling his lifelong work:

> Everything is in place – after 500 years – to build a true 'new world' in the Western Hemisphere... I truly don't think that 'criminal' would be too strong a word to describe an action on our part, such as rejecting Nafta, that would so seriously jeopardize all the good that has been done – and remains to be done.[56]

In 1994, Mexico entered into a financial crisis, often referred to as the Mexican peso crisis. The 1980s debt crisis, instigated by the Federal Reserve's interest rate hikes on international loans, caused Mexico to default on its loans. The IMF had to enter the scene with its newly created Structural Adjustment Programs (SAPs) and reform Mexico's economy along neoliberal economic policies.

In the late 1980s, "the United States accounted for 73 percent of Mexico's foreign trade,"[57] and when NAFTA came into effect in 1994, it "immediately opened U.S. and Canadian markets to 84 percent of Mexican exports."[58] Mexico even became a member of the World Trade Organization (WTO). The peso crisis, which began at the end of 1994, with the ascension of Mexican President Zedillo, went into 1995, and the U.S. organized a bailout worth

52 billion dollars.[59] The bailout did not help the Mexican economy, as it was simply funneled into paying back loans to banks, primarily American banks, and the "crisis in 1995 was declared [by the IMF to be] over as soon as the banks and international lenders started to get repaid; but five years after the crisis, workers were just getting back to where they were beforehand."[60]

In 2002, Robert Pastor, Director of the Center for North American Studies at the American University in Washington, D.C., prepared a report that he presented to the Trilateral Commission meeting of that same year. The report, entitled, *A North American Community: A Modest Proposal to the Trilateral Commission,* advocated a continuation of the policy of "deep integration" in North America, recommending, "a continental plan for infrastructure and transportation, a plan for harmonizing regulatory policies, a customs union, [and] a common currency."[61] The report advocated the formation of a North American Community and Pastor wrote that "a majority of the public in all three countries is prepared to join a larger North American country."[62]

In 2003, prior to Paul Martin becoming Prime Minister of Canada, the Canadian Council of Chief Executives (CCCE) published a press release on their website in which they, "urged Paul Martin to take the lead in forging a new vision for North America." Thomas d'Aquino, CEO of the Council, "urged that Mr. Martin champion the idea of a yearly summit of the leaders of Canada, Mexico and the United States in order to give common economic, social and security issues the priority they deserve in a continental, hemispheric and global context." Among the signatories to this statement were all the Vice Chairmen of the CCCE, including David Emerson, who would go on to join Martin's Cabinet.[63]

The CCCE then launched the North American Security and Prosperity Initiative, advocating "redefining borders, maximizing regulatory efficiencies, negotiation of a comprehensive resource security pact, reinvigorating the North American defense alliance, and creating a new institutional framework."[64]

The Independent Task Force on the Future of North America was then launched in 2005, composed of an alliance and joint project between the CCCE in Canada, the Council on Foreign Relations (CFR) in the United States, and the Mexican Council on Foreign Relations in Mexico. A press release was published on March 14, 2005, in which it said, "the chairs and vice-chairs of the Independent Task Force on the Future of North America today issued a statement calling for a North American economic and security community by 2010."[65]

On March 23, 2005, a mere nine days following the Task Force press release, the leaders of Canada, the U.S. and Mexico, (Paul Martin, George W. Bush and Vicente Fox, respectively), announced "the establishment of the Security and Prosperity Partnership of North America," which constituted a course of "action into a North American framework to confront security and economic challenges."[66]

Within two months, the Independent Task Force on the Future of North America released their final report, *Building a North American Community*, proposing the continuation of "deep integration" into the formation of a North American Community, that "applauds the announced 'Security and Prosperity Partnership of North America,' but proposes a more ambitious vision of a new community by 2010 and specific recommendations on how to achieve it."[67]

At the 2006 meeting of the SPP, the creation of a new group was announced, called the North American Competitiveness Council (NACC), made up of corporate leaders from all three countries who produce an annual report and advise the three governments on how to implement the SPP process of "deep integration". The Secretariat in Canada is the CCCE, and the Secretariat of the group in the U.S. is made up of the U.S. Chamber of Commerce and the Council of the Americas.[68] The Council of the Americas was founded by David Rockefeller, of which he is still Honorary Chairman, and other board members include individuals from J.P. Morgan, Merck, McDonald's, Ford, the Federal Reserve Bank of New York, General Electric, Chevron, Shell, IBM, ConocoPhillips, Citigroup, Microsoft, Pfizer, Wal-Mart, Exxon, General Motors, Merrill Lynch, Credit Suisse and the U.S. Department of Treasury.[69]

The process of integration is still underway, and the formation of a North American Community is not far off, only to be followed by a North American Union, modeled on the structure of the European Union, with talk of a North American currency being formed in the future,[70] which was even proposed by the former Governor of the Bank of Canada.[71]

Renewed Calls for a New World Order

In 2007, UK Prime Minister Gordon Brown called for a New World Order in reforming the UN, World Bank, IMF and G7.[72] When the bank Bear Stearns collapsed, due to its heavy participation in the mortgage securities market, the Federal Reserve purchased the bank for J.P. Morgan Chase, whose CEO sits on the board of the New York Federal Reserve Bank. Shortly after this action, a major financial firm released a report saying that banks face a "new world order" of "consolidation and acquisitions."[73]

In October of 2008, at the height of the financial crisis, Gordon Brown said:

> [We] must have a new Bretton Woods – building a new international financial architecture for the years ahead... We must now reform the international financial system around the agreed principles of transparency, integrity, responsibility, good house-keeping and co-operation across borders. [Gordon Brown wanted] to see the IMF reformed to become a 'global central bank' closely monitoring the international economy and financial s ystem.[74]

Gordon Brown wrote that the "new Bretton Woods" should build upon the concept of "global governance."[75] There were also calls for a "global economic policeman," perhaps in the form of the Bank for International Settlements (BIS).[76] In November of 2008, it was reported that Baron David de Rothschild "shares most people's view that there is a new world order. In his opinion, banks will deleverage and there will be a new form of global governance."[77]

Reconstructing Class Structure under a World Government

In terms of labor adjustments within the New World Order, there are some important and vital factors to take into account. Primary among these concerns is the notion of transnational classes.

In the past several decades, the reality of class structures has been undergoing drastic changes, and with this, the structure of labor has changed. A concurrent class restructuring has been taking place, in which the middle classes of the world descend into debt bondage while the upper classes have begun a process of transnationalizing. What we have witnessed is the transnationalization of class structures, and with that, labor forces. Agreements like NAFTA have allowed for multinational corporations to move their labor overseas to highly underpaid and exploited populations, primarily made up of women. This has, in effect, deconstructed the manufacturing base of the United States, and with that, eroded the middle classes.

As William I. Robinson and Jerry Harris write in *Science and Society Journal*:

> One process central to capitalist globalization is transnational class formation, which has proceeded in step with the internationalization of capital and the global integration of national productive structures. Given the transnational integration of national economies, the mobility of capital and the global fragmentation and decentralization of accumulation circuits, class formation is progressively less tied to territoriality.[78]

They argue that a Transnational Capitalist Class (TCC) has emerged, "and that this TCC is a global ruling class. It is a ruling class because it controls the levers of an emergent transnational state apparatus and of global decision making."[79] This class has no borders, and is composed of the technocratic, media, corporate, banking, social and political elite of the world.

In terms of reshaping labor and class structures, the economic crisis provides the ground on which a new global class structure will be built. A major problem for the Transnational Capitalist Class and the formation of a Transnational State, or world government, is the lack of continuity in class structures and labor markets throughout the world. A transnational ruling class, or "Superclass" as David Rothkopf referred to it in his book, has emerged. It has no borders, yet has built a general continuity and consensus of goals among its members, albeit there are differences and conflicts within the class, but they are based upon the means of achieving the stated ends, rather than on the ends itself. There is not dissent within the ruling class on the aims of achieving a world governing body; the dissent is in how to achieve this, and in terms of what kind of structure, theoretical, philosophical leanings and political orientation such a government would have.

To achieve these ends, however, all classes must be transnationalized, not simply the ruling class. The ruling class is the first class to be transnationalized, because transnationalization was the goal of the ruling classes based in the powerful Western European nations, (and later in the United States), that started the process of transnationalization or internationalization. Now that there is an established "Superclass" of a transnational composition, the other classes must follow suit. The middle class is targeted for elimination in this sense, because most of the world has no middle class, and to fully integrate and internationalize a middle class, this would require industrialization and development in places such as Africa, and certain places in Asia and Latin America, and would represent a massive threat to the Superclass, as it would be a valve through which much of their wealth and power would escape them. Their goal is not to lose their wealth and power to a transnational middle class, but rather to extinguish the notion of a middle class, and transnationalize a lower, uneducated, labor oriented class, through which they will secure ultimate wealth and power.

The economic crisis serves these ends, as whatever remaining wealth the middle class holds is in the process of being eliminated, and as the crisis progresses, or rather, regresses and accelerates, the middle classes of the world will suffer, while a great percentage of lower classes of the world, poverty-stricken even prior to the crisis, will suffer the greatest, most probably leading to a massive reduction in population levels, particularly in the "underdeveloped" or "Third World" states.

Building the Global State

As Robinson and Harris explain in their essay, with the rise of the Transnational Capitalist Class (TCC), there is also a rise in the apparatus of a Transnational State (TNS), which is "an emerging network that comprises transformed and externally integrated national states, together with the supranational economic and political forums; it has not yet acquired any centralized institutional form."[80] Among the economic apparatus of the TNS we see the IMF, World Bank, WTO and regional banks. On the political side we see the Group of 7, Group of 22, United Nations, OECD, and the European Union. This was further accelerated with the Trilateral Commission, "which brought together transnationalized fractions of the business, political, and intellectual elite in North America, Europe, and Japan." Further, the World Economic Forum has made up an important part of this class, and, I might add, the Bilderberg Group. Robinson and Harris point out that "studies on building a global economy and transnational management structures flowed out of think tanks, university centers, and policy planning institutes in core countries."[81] The TNS apparatus has been a vital principle of organization and socialization for the transnational class:

> As have world class universities, transnationally oriented think tanks, the leading bourgeois foundations, such as Harvard's School of International Business, the Ford [and Rockefeller] and the Carnegie Foundations, [and] policy planning groups such as the Council on Foreign Relations. [These] elite planning groups are important forums for integrating class groups, developing new initiatives, collective strategies, policies and projects of class rule, and forging consensus and a political culture around these projects.[82]

Robinson and Harris identify the World Economic Forum as "the most comprehensive transnational planning body of the TCC and the quintessential example of a truly global network binding together the TCC in a transnational civil society."[83] I would take issue with this and instead point to the Bilderberg Group, of which they make no mention in their article, as *the* quintessential transnational planning body of the TCC, as it is composed of the elite of the elite, totally removed from public scrutiny, and acts as "a secretive global think-tank" of the world's 130 most powerful individuals.[84]

Many Bilderberg critics will claim that the group acts as a "secret world government" or as the organization "that makes all the key decisions for the world." However, this is not the case. Bilderberg is simply the most influential planning body, sitting atop a grand hierarchy of various planning bodies and institutions, and is itself a key part of the apparatus of the formation of a Transnational State, but is not, in and of itself, a "world government". It is a global think tank, which holds the concept of a "world government" in high regard and often works to achieve these ends, but it should not be confused with being the end it seeks.

The economic crisis is perhaps the greatest "opportunity" ever given to the TCC in re-shaping the world order according to their designs, ideals and goals. Through destruction, comes creation, and for these high-placed individuals within the TCC, destruction is itself a form of creation.

According to David Rothkopf, a scholar at the Carnegie Endowment for International Peace:

> In a world of global movements and threats that don't present their passports at national borders, it is no longer possible for a nation-state acting alone to fulfill its portion of the social contract... Progress will continue to be made, [however, and it will be challenging because it] undercuts many national and local power structures and cultural concepts that have foundations deep in the bedrock of human civilization, namely the notion of sovereignty... Mechanisms of global governance are more achievable in today's environment [and] are often creative with temporary solutions to urgent problems that cannot wait for the world to embrace a bigger and more controversial idea like real global government.[85]

According to Jacques Attali, former President of the European Bank for Reconstruction and Development and economic adviser to French President Nicolas Sarkozy, "either we're heading towards a world government or we're going to put national issues first." The interviewer stated that the idea of world government would frighten many people, to which Attali responded,

> Indeed, that's only to be expected, because it seems like a fantasy. But there is already global authority in many areas [and] even if it's hard to think of a European government at the moment, which is there, but very weak, Europe can at least press on its experience to the world. If they're not capable of creating an economic framework alongside a political framework, then they're never going to do it on a global scale. And then the world economic model will break up, and we'll be back to the Great Depression.[86]

In December of 2008, the *Financial Times* quoted former Bilderberg attendee Gideon Rachman:

> For the first time in my life, I think the formation of some sort of world government is plausible... A 'world government' would involve much more than co-operation between nations. It would be an entity with state-like characteristics, backed by a body of laws. The European Union has already set up a continental government for 27 countries, which could be a model. The EU has a supreme court, a currency, thousands of pages of law, a large civil service and the ability to deploy military force... It is increasingly clear that the most difficult issues facing national governments are international in nature: there is global warming, a global financial crisis and a 'global war on terror'.

Rachman suggested that the European model could "go global" and that a world government "could be done," because "[t]he financial crisis and climate change are pushing national governments towards global solutions, even in countries such as China and the U.S. that are traditionally fierce guardians of national sovereignty." He also quoted an adviser to French President Nicolas Sarkozy as saying, "Global governance is just a euphemism for global government," and that the "core of the international financial crisis is that we have global financial markets and no global rule of law."

Rachman nonetheless warned that any push towards a global government "will be a painful, slow process." He then stated that a key problem in this push could be explained with an example from the EU:

> ...which has suffered a series of humiliating defeats in referendums, when plans for 'ever closer union' have been referred to the voters. In general, the Union has progressed fastest when far-reaching deals have been agreed by technocrats and politicians – and then pushed through without direct reference to the voters. *International governance tends to be effective, only when it is anti-democratic.*[87]

In November of 2008, the United States National Intelligence Council (NIC) released a report that it produced in collaboration with numerous think tanks, consulting firms, academic institutions and hundreds of other experts.[88]

Outlining the global trends that the world will be going through up to the year 2025, the report stated that the financial crisis "will require long-term efforts to establish a new international system." It suggested that as the "China-model" for development becomes increasingly attractive, there may be a "decline in democratization" for emerging economies, authoritarian regimes, and "weak democracies frustrated by years of economic underperformance." Further, the dollar will cease to be the global reserve currency, as there would likely be a "move away from the dollar."[89]

The dollar will become "something of a first among equals in a basket of currencies by 2025. This could occur suddenly in the wake of a crisis, or gradually with global rebalancing."[90] The report elaborates on the construction of a new international system:

> By 2025, nation-states will no longer be the only – and often not the most important – actors on the world stage and the 'international system' will have morphed to accommodate the new reality. But the transformation will be incomplete and uneven. [It would be] unlikely to see an overarching, comprehensive, unitary approach to global governance. *Current trends suggest that global governance in 2025 will be a patchwork of overlapping, often ad hoc and fragmented efforts,* with shifting coalitions of member nations, international organizations, social movements, NGOs, philanthropic foundations, and companies... Most of the pressing transnational problems – including climate change, regulation of globalized financial markets, migration, failing states, crime networks, etc. – are unlikely to be effectively resolved by the actions of individual nation-states. *The need for effective global governance will increase faster than existing mechanisms can respond.*[91]

The report discussed regionalism, and stated that, "Asian regionalism would have global implications, possibly sparking or reinforcing a trend toward three trade and financial clusters that could become quasi-blocs (North America, Europe, and East Asia)." These blocs "would have implications for the ability to achieve future global World Trade Organization agreements and regional clusters could compete in the setting of trans-regional product standards for IT, biotech, nanotech, intellectual property rights, and other 'new economy' products."[92]

The Nature of the Global State

In discussing democracy and democratization, the trends report released by the National Intelligence Council stated that, "advances are likely to slow and globalization will subject many recently democratized countries to increasing social and economic pressures that could undermine liberal institutions." This is largely because:

> The better economic performance of many authoritarian governments could sow doubts among some about democracy as the best form of government. The surveys we consulted indicated that many East Asians put greater emphasis on good management, including increasing standards of livings, than democracy...

> Even in many well-established democracies, surveys show growing frustration with the current workings of democratic government and questioning among elites over the ability of democratic governments to take the bold actions necessary to deal rapidly and effectively with the growing number of transnational challenges.[93]

In other words, "well established democracies," such as those in Western Europe and North America, will, through successive crises (climate, finance, war), erode and replace their democratic systems of government with totalitarian structures that are able to "take the bold actions necessary" to deal with "transnational challenges." As the French scholar, Daniel Guerin, explained, "the bourgeoisie resorts to fascism less in response to disturbances in the street than in response to disturbances in their own economic system."[94]

The National Intelligence Council report stated that many governments will be "expanding domestic security forces, surveillance capabilities, and the employment of special operations-type forces." Counterterrorism measures will increasingly "involve urban operations as a result of greater urbanization," and governments "may increasingly erect barricades and fences around their territories to inhibit access. Gated communities will continue to spring up within many societies as elites seek to insulate themselves from domestic threats."[95] Ultimately what we are seeing is an increased trend toward totalitarianism.

The nature of totalitarianism is such that it is, "by nature (or rather by definition), a global project that cannot be fully accomplished in just one community or one country. Being fuelled by the need to suppress any alternative orders and ideas, it has no natural limits and is bound to aim at totally dominating everything and everyone." David Lyon explained in *Theorizing Surveillance*:

> The ultimate feature of the totalitarian domination is the absence of exit, which can be achieved temporarily by closing borders, but permanently only by a truly global reach that would render the very notion of exit meaningless. This in itself justifies questions about the totalitarian potential of globalization... Is abolition of borders intrinsically (morally) good, because they symbolize barriers that needlessly separate and exclude people, or are they potential lines of resistance, refuge and difference that may save us from the totalitarian abyss?... If globalization undermines the tested, state-based models of democracy, the world may be vulnerable to a global totalitarian etatization.[96]

In 2007, the British Defense Ministry released a report focusing on future global trends as well as the resulting changes in the social structure:

> The middle classes could become a revolutionary class, taking the role envisaged for the proletariat by Marx... The thesis is based on a growing gap between the middle classes and the super-rich on one hand and an urban under-class threatening social order: 'The world's middle classes might unite, using access to knowledge, resources and skills to shape transnational processes in their own class interest'. Marxism could also be revived, it says, because of global inequality. An increased trend towards moral relativism and pragmatic values will encourage people to seek the 'sanctuary provided by more rigid belief systems, including religious orthodoxy and doctrinaire political ideologies, such as popularism and Marxism'... Globalisation may lead to levels of international integration that effectively brings interstate warfare to an end. But it may lead to "inter-communal conflict" – communities with shared interests transcending national boundaries and resorting to the use of violence."[97]

According to economist Ronald Wintrobe, political scientists and economists are largely concerned with methods of organizing society in having people cooperate with each other. He argued that this way of thinking is based around the notion that "it is possible to organize society in such a way that individuals will cooperate, even when that cooperation is inconsistent with their self-interest narrowly conceived. The basic problem of social science is to discover how to do this." He continued in explaining that the problem is that "the most likely form of social organization which makes this cooperation possible is some kind of authoritarianism."[98]

Corporatism is an important concept which sheds light on how the world is being restructured. Corporatism revolves around the notion that the State acts as an organic body, in which each group within society acts as a necessary organ, playing its part for society, or the body, to function properly. The body's actions are thus dictated by the brain, or in other words, the state. The hand cannot dictate to the brain what to think and do.

A central tenet of Mussolini's Italian corporatism was "that the government's interventions in the economy should not be conducted on an *ad hoc* basis, but should be 'coordinated' by some kind of central planning board," and that Fascism would "introduce order in the economic field." A further principle of Italian corporatism, and economic fascism in general, "is that private property and business ownership are permitted, but are in reality controlled by government through a business-government 'partnership'." In fascist Italy, businesses were organized into "syndicates" controlled by the government.

Another major tenet of Italian economic fascism is that of mercantilism and protectionism. One Italian social critic wrote, during Mussolini's reign, that in a corporatist system, "it is the state, i.e., the taxpayer, who has become responsible to private enterprise. In Fascist Italy the state pays for the blunders of private enterprise," and that, "profit remained to private initiative," however, in times of economic crisis, "the government added the loss to the taxpayer's burden. Profit is private and individual. Loss is public and social."[99]

As economics professor Thomas J. DiLorenzo explained in his essay, *Economic Fascism*, "Corporatism, in other words, was a massive system of corporate welfare." As a result of the "collaboration" between government and big business, there was "a continual interchange of personnel between the... civil service and private business." As DiLorenzo argued, "From an economic perspective, fascism meant (and means) an interventionist industrial policy, mercantilism, protectionism, and an ideology that makes the individual subservient to the state."[100]

In the book, *Fascism and Big Business*, French scholar Daniel Guerin analyzed the role of big business in fascist systems of governance. He critically analyzed the notion that fascist governments in Italy and Germany arose out of intent to smash a proletarian revolution, explaining that it is an over-simplified explanation. He explained that, "Neither in Italy nor in Germany was revolution in the offing at the moment fascism took state power. The bourgeoisie resorts to fascism less in response to disturbances in the street than in response to disturbances in their own economic system."[101]

During a great economic crisis, the state "rescues business enterprises on the brink of bankruptcy, forcing the masses to foot the bill. Such enterprises are kept alive with subsidies, tax exemptions, orders for public works and armaments. In short, the state thrusts itself into the breach left by the vanishing private customers." However, Guerin elaborates, "such maneuvers are difficult under a democratic regime," because the masses still "have some means of defense" and are "still capable of setting some limit to the insatiable demands of the money power." Thus, "in certain countries and under certain conditions, the bourgeoisie throws its traditional democracy overboard."[102]

What we must understand is that the world is currently in the "conditions" in which the bourgeoisie is throwing democracy overboard. However, because the elite class is now transnationalized, democracy is being removed, albeit incrementally, from the global political economy as a whole. Government rescue packages around the world are corporatist in their very nature, as they save the capitalists at the expense of the people. At the same time, moves are being undertaken to establish a "new order" in the form of global governance. These issues are not separate, and are, in fact, directly related.

Conclusion

The world is moving towards establishing, within decades, a global government structure. Moving the utopian rhetoric of such an undertaking aside, we must analyze how such a structure is being built. Given the global economic crisis, the governments of the world are restructuring their economies, and the global economy as a whole, into a corporatist structure. Thus, this new international economic system being constructed is one representative of economic fascism. The governments now work directly for the banks, democracy is in decline everywhere, and the militarization of domestic society into creating "Homeland Security states" is underway and accelerating.

George Orwell wrote: "Power is not a means, it is an end. One does not establish a dictatorship in order to safeguard a revolution; one makes the revolution in order to establish the dictatorship. The object of persecution is persecution. The object of torture is torture. The object of power is power."

We may very well be entering into the most oppressive and destructive order the world has yet seen, but from its ruins and ashes, which are as inevitable as the tides and as sure as the sun rises, we may see the rise of a truly peaceful world order, in which we see the triumphs of individualism merge with the interests of the majority; a people's world order of peace for all. We must maintain, as Antonio Gramsci once wrote, *"Pessimism of the intellect, optimism of the will."*

◆

NOTES

1. Carroll Quigley, *Tragedy and Hope: A History of the World in Our Time*, New York, The Macmillan Company, 1966, p. 130.
2. Niall Ferguson, *Empire: The Rise and Demise of the British World Order and the Lessons for Global Power*, New York, Basic Books, 2004, p. 186.
3. *Ibid.*, p. 186-187.
4. *Ibid.*, p. 190

5. Carroll Quigley, *The Anglo-American Establishment*, GSG & Associates, 1981, p. 3.

6. *Ibid.*, p. 33.

7. *Ibid.*, p. 34.

8. William Engdahl, *A Century of War: Anglo-American Oil Politics and the New World Order*, London, Pluto Press, 2004, p. 51.

9. H.W. Brands, "He Is My Independent Self", *The Washington Post*, http://www.washingtonpost.com/wp-dyn/content/article/2006/06/08/AR2006060801 104.html, 11 June 2006.

10. CFR, "Continuing the Inquiry", *History of CFR*, http://www.cfr.org/about/history/cfr/inquiry.html.

11. Chatham House, "Chatham House (The Royal Institute of International Affairs)", *Background. Chatham House History*, http://www.chathamhouse.org.uk/about/history/.

12. Carroll Quigley, *The Anglo-American Establishment, op. cit.*, p. 5.

13. Carroll Quigley, *Tragedy and Hope: A History of the World in Our Time, op. cit.*, p. 132-133.

14. CFR, "War and Peace", *CFR History*, http://www.cfr.org/about/history/cfr/war_peace.html.

15. William P. Bundy, "The History of Foreign Affairs", *The Council on Foreign Relations*, http://www.cfr.org/about/history/foreign_affairs.html, 1994.

16. CFR, "War and Peace", *CFR History*, http://www.cfr.org/about/history/cfr/war_peace.html.

17. UN, "1945-1949", *Sixty Years: A Pictorial History of the United Nations*, http://www.un.org/issues/gallery/history/1940s.htm.

18. Peter Dale Scott, *The Road to 9/11: Wealth, Empire, and the Future of America*, Berkeley, University of California Press, 2007, p. 12.

19. CBC, "Informal Forum or Global Conspiracy?", *CBC News Online*, http://www.cbc.ca/news/background/bilderberg-group/, 13 June 2006.

20. Holly Sklar (ed.), *Trilateralism: The Trilateral Commission and Elite Planning for World Management*, South End Press, 1980, p. 161-171.

21. *Ibid.*, p. 161-162.

22. CFR, "The First Transformation", *CFR History*, http://www.cfr.org/about/history/cfr/first_transformation.html.

23. Glen McGregor, "Secretive Power Brokers Meeting Coming to Ottawa?", *Ottawa Citizen*, http://www.canada.com/topics/news/world/story.html?id=ff614eb8-02cc-41a3-a42d-30642def1421&k=62840, 24 May 2006.

24. William F. Jasper, "Rogues' Gallery of EU Founders", *The New American*, http://findarticles.com/p/articles/mi_m0JZS/is_14_20/ai_n25093084/pg_1?tag=artBody;col1, 12 July 2004.
25. Ambrose Evans-Pritchard, "Euro-Federalists Financed by US Spy Chiefs", *The Telegraph*, http://www.telegraph.co.uk/news/world-news/europe/1356047/Euro-federalists-financed-by-US-spy-chiefs.html, 19 June 2001.
26. *Ibid.*
27. Bilderberg Group, "Garmisch-Partenkirchen Conference", *The Bilderberg Group*, p. 7, http://wikileaks.org/leak/bilderberg-meetings-report-1955.pdf, 23-25 September 1955.
28. The Sunday Herald, "Who are These Bilderbergers and What Do They Do?", *The Sunday Herald*, http://findarticles.com/p/articles/mi_qn4156/is_19990 530/ai_n13939252, 30 May 1999.
29. Andrew Rettman, "'Jury's out' on Future of Europe, EU Doyen says", *EUobserver*, http://euobserver.com/9/27778, 16 March 2009.
30. Holly Sklar (ed.), *Trilateralism: The Trilateral Commission and Elite Planning for World Management*, *op. cit.*, p. 65.
31. Robert O'Brien and Marc Williams, *Global Political Economy: Evolution and Dynamics*, 2nd ed., Palgrave Macmillan, 2007, p. 215.
32. Holly Sklar, *op. cit.*, p. 66-67.
33. *Ibid.*, p. 67.
34. C. Fred Bergsten, "The New Economics and US Foreign Policy", *Foreign Affairs*, January 1972, p. 199.
35. Richard H. Ullman, "Trilateralism: 'Partnership' For What?", *Foreign Affairs*, October 1976, p. 3-4.
36. *Ibid.*
37. Holly Sklar, *op. cit.*, p. 76-78.
38. Richard H. Ullman, *op. cit.*, p. 3.
39. *Ibid.*, p. 5.
40. Peter Gowan, *The Globalization Gamble: The Dollar-Wall Street Regime and its Consequences*, p. 19-20.
41. Richard N. Gardner, "The Hard Road to World Order", *Foreign Affairs*, April 1974, p. 556.
42. *Ibid.*, p. 557.
43. *Ibid.*, p. 558, emphasis added.
44. Robert Jackson and Georg Sørensen, *Introduction to International Relations: Theories and Approaches*, Third Edition, OUP, 2006, p. 162.
45. *Ibid.*, p. 258, emphasis added.
46. Strobe Talbott, "America Abroad", *Time Magazine*, http://www.time.com/time/magazine/article/0,9171,976015,00.html, 20 July 1992.

47. The Daily Mail, "EU Constitution - The Main Points", *The Daily Mail*, http://www.dailymail.co.uk/news/article-307249/EU-Constitution-main-points.html, 19 June 2004.

48. Valéry Giscard d'Estaing, "Valéry Giscard d'Estaing: The EU Treaty is the same as the Constitution", *The Independent*, http://www.independent.co.uk/opinion/commentators/valeacutery-giscard-destaing-the-eu-treaty-is-the-same-as-the-constitution-398286.html, 30 October 2007.

49. Bruno Waterfield, "Lisbon Treaty Resurrects the Defeated EU Constitution", *The Telegraph*, http://www.telegraph.co.uk/news/newstopics/eureferendum/ 2123045/EU-Treaty-Lisbon-Treaty-resurrected-defeated-EU-Constitution.html, 13 June 2008.

50. Mel Hurtig, *The Vanishing Country: Is It Too Late to Save Canada?*, McClelland & Stewart Ltd., 2002, p. 365.

51. CFR, "Brian Mulroney", *About US, Leadership and Staff: International Advisory Board*, http://www.cfr.org/bios/9841/brian_mulroney.html.

52. Robert O'Brien and Marc Williams, *Global Political Economy: Evolution and Dynamics*, 2nd ed., Palgrave Macmillan, 2007, p. 226.

53. David Rockefeller, "What Private Enterprise Means to Latin America", *Foreign Affairs*, Vol. 44, No. 3, April 1966, p. 411.

54. David Rockefeller, *Memoirs*, New York, Random House, 2002, p. 436-437.

55. David Rockefeller, "A Hemisphere in the Balance", *The Wall Street Journal*, 1 October 1993.

56. Alexander Dawson, *First World Dreams: Mexico Since 1989*, Fernwood Books, 2006, p. 8-9.

57. *Ibid.*, p. 29.

58. *Ibid.*, p. 120.

59. Joseph Stiglitz, *Globalization and its Discontents*, W.W. Norton & Co., 2003, p. 121.

60. Robert Pastor, "A North American Community: A Modest Proposal to the Trilateral Commission", *The Trilateral Commission*, Toronto, Ontario, p. 4, www.american.edu/internationalaffairs/cnas/PastorTrilateral.pdf, 1-2 November 2002.

61. *Ibid.*, p. 6.

62. News and Information, "Paul Martin Urged to Take the Lead in Forging a New Vision for North American Cooperation", *CCCE*, http://www.ceocouncil.ca/en/view/?document_id=38&type_id=1, 5 November 2003.

63. CCCE, *North American Security and Prosperity*, http://www.ceocouncil.ca/en/north/north.php.

64. News and Information, "Trinational Call for a North American Economic and Security Community by 2010", *CCCE*, http://www.ceocouncil.ca/en/view/?document_id=395, 14 March 2005.

65. Office of the Press Secretary, "Joint Statement by President Bush, President Fox, and Prime Minister Martin", *The White House*, http://www.whitehouse.gov/news/releases/2005/03/20050323-2.html, 23 March 2005.

66. CFR, *Building a North American Community. Independent Task Force on the Future of North America*, http://www.cfr.org/publication/8102/building_a_north_american_community.html, May 2005.

67. Issues Center, "North American Competitiveness Council (NACC)", *US Chamber of Commerce*, http://www.uschamber.com/issues/index/internatio nal/nacc.htm.

68. COA, "Board of Directors", *The Council of the Americas*, http://coa.counciloft heamericas.org/page.php?k=bod.

69. Herbert Grubel, "Fix the Loonie", *The Financial Post*, http://www.nationalpost.com/opinion/story.html?id=245165, 18 January 2008; Herbert Grubel, "The Case for the Amero", *The Fraser Institute*, http://www.fraserinstitute.org/Commerce.Web/publication_details.aspx?pubID=2512, 1 September 1999; Thomas Courchene and Richard Harris, "From Fixing to Monetary Union: Options for North American Currency Integration", *C.D. Howe Institute*, http://www.cdhowe.org/display.cfm?page=research-fiscal&year=1999, June 1999; "Consider a Continental Currency, Jarislowsky Says", *The Globe and Mail*, http://www.theglobeandmail.com/servlet/story/LAC.20071123.RDOL LAR23/TPStory/?query=%22Steven%2BChase%22b, 23 November 2007.

70. Barrie McKenna, "Dodge Says Single Currency ‹Possible›", *The Globe and Mail*, 21 May 2007.

71. Larry Elliott, "Brown Calls for Overhaul of UN, World Bank and IMF", *The Guardian*, http://www.guardian.co.uk/business/2007/jan/17/globalisation.internationalaidanddevelopment, 17 January 2007.

72. Andrea Ricci, "Banks Face 'New World Order' Consolidation Report", *Reuters*, http://www.reuters.com/article/innovation News/idUSN174354172 0080317, 17 March 2008.

73. Robert Winnett, "Financial Crisis: Gordon Brown Calls for 'New Bretton Woods'", *The Telegraph*, http://www.telegraph.co.uk/finance/financetopics/financialcrisis/3189517/Financial-Crisis-Gordon-Brown-calls-for-new-Bret ton-Woods.html, 13 October 2008.

74. Gordon Brown, "Out of the Ashes", *The Washington Post*, http://www.washingtonpost.com/wp-dyn/content/article/2008/10/16/AR2008101603 179.html, 17 October 2008.

75. Gordon Rayner, "Global Financial Crisis: Does the World Need a New Banking 'Policeman'?", *The Telegraph*, http://www.telegraph.co.uk/finance/financetopics/financialcrisis/3155563/Global-financial-crisis-does-the-world-need-a-new-banking-policeman.html, 8 October 2008.

76. Rupert Wright, "The First Barons of Banking" *The National*, http://www.thenational.ae/article/20081106/BUSINESS/167536298/1005, 6 November 2008.

77. William I. Robinson and Jerry Harris, "Towards a Global Ruling Class? Globalization and the Transnational Capitalist Class", *Science & Society*, Vol. 64, No. 1, Spring 2000, p. 11-12.

78. *Ibid.*, p. 12.

79. *Ibid.*, p. 27.

80. *Ibid.*, p. 28.

81. *Ibid.*, p. 29.

82. *Ibid.*, p. 30.

83. Glen McGregor, "Secretive Power Brokers Meeting Coming to Ottawa?", *Ottawa Citizen*, http://www.canada.com/topics/news/world/story.html?id=ff614eb8-02cc-41a3-a42d-30642def1421&k=62840, 24 May 2006.

84. David Rothkopf, *Superclass: The Global Power Elite and the World They are Making*, Toronto, Penguin Books, 2008, p. 315-316.

85. EuroNews, "Jacques Attali: The Euronews Interview", *Euronews*, http://www.euronews.net/2009/06/04/jacques-attali-the-euronews-interview/, 6 April 2009.

86. Gideon Rachman, "And Now for a World Government", *The Financial Times*, http://www.ft.com/cms/s/0/7a03e5b6-c541-11dd-b516-000077b07658.html, emphasis added, 8 December 2008.

87. NIC, *Global Trends 2025: A Transformed World. The National Intelligence Council's 2025 Project*, Acknowledgements: http://www.dni.gov/nic/NIC_2025_project.html, November 2008.

88. *Ibid.*, p. 11-12.

89. *Ibid.*, p. 94.

90. *Ibid.*, p. 81, emphasis added.

91. *Ibid.*, p. 83.

92. *Ibid.*, p. 87.

93. Daniel Guerin, *Fascism and Big Business*, Monad Press, 1973, p. 22.

94. NIC, *Global Trends 2025: A Transformed World. The National Intelligence Council's 2025 Project*, p. 70-72, http://www.dni.gov/nic/NIC_2025_project.html, November 2008.

95. David Lyon, *Theorizing Surveillance: The Panopticon and Beyond*, Willan Publishing, 2006, p. 71.

96. Richard Norton-Taylor, "Revolution, Flashmobs, and Brain Chips. A Grim Vision of the Future", *The Guardian*, http://www.guardian.co.uk/science/ 2007/apr/09/frontpagenews.news, 9 April 2007.

97. Ronald Wintrobe, *The Political Economy of Dictatorship*, Cambridge University Press, 2000, p. 130.

98. Thomas J. DiLorenzo, "Economic Fascism", *The Freeman*, http://www.aapsonline.org/brochures/fascism.htm, June 1994.

99. *Ibid.*

100. Daniel Guerin, *op. cit.*, p. 22.

101. *Ibid.*, p. 23

PART IV

The Global Monetary System

CHAPTER 15

Central Banks in the Global Political Economy

Andrew Gavin Marshall

Introduction

To understand the historical context of the current crisis, it is pivotal to address the nature of the most vital and powerful force within the capitalist global political economy: the central banking system. One of the least understood, most widely ignored, and mysteries of capitalism, the central banking system, is also the source of the greatest wealth and power, essentially managing capitalism – controlling the credit and debt of both government and industry.

Any notion of a "free market" must be dispelled in its true meaning, for as long as the central banking system has been dominant, central bankers have managed and controlled capitalism for the benefit of the few and at the expense of the many. Comprehending the nature of central banking is necessary in order to understand the nature of the current economic crisis.

The Origins of Central Banking

Central banking has its origins in the development of bank-issued money, which falls under three categories: (1) Deposit money subject to written check or oral transfer; (2) Bank-issued paper money (bank notes); and (3) Bank-issued legal tender paper money. In 1609, the Bank of Amsterdam was founded "as a bank of deposit slipping secretly into the practice of monetary issue towards the middle of the 17th century." At the same time, "the goldsmiths of England are generally supposed to have introduced both deposit money and the earliest English unofficial bank note." And importantly, "In Sweden we find what are widely regarded as the first true bank notes in Europe being issued in 1661 by a private bank founded by Johan Palmstruch."[1]

As early as 1656, "the Bank of Amsterdam violated the one-hundred per cent reserve principle and, thus, created money," while "the goldsmiths in England became active as lenders in 1640." Further, the State Bank of Sweden "was founded November 30, 1656, and to Palmstruch, its founder, is attributed the first use of bank bills as credit money, not fully covered by the coin reserve."[2]

As economist John Kenneth Galbraith explained in *Money*, "The process by which banks create money is so simple that the mind is repelled. Where something so important is involved, a deeper mystery seems only decent. The deposits of the Bank of Amsterdam just mentioned were, according to the instruction of the owner, subject to transfer to others in settlement of accounts," and thus "the coin on deposit served less as money by being in a bank and being subject to transfer by the stroke of a primitive pen." Further, "another stroke of the pen would give a borrower from the bank, as distinct from a creditor of the original depositor, a loan from the original and idle deposit." Galbraith elaborated:

> The original deposit still stood to the credit of the original depositor. But there was now also a new deposit from the proceeds of the loan. Both deposits could be used to make payments, be used as money. Money had thus been created. The discovery that banks could so create money came very early in the development of banking. There was that interest to be earned.[3]

Expanding on this notion of money-creation, economist Rupert J. Ederer explained, in regards to the Bank of Amsterdam, that both the depositor "and a borrower could affect a purchase with the same money at the same time, [thus] we had here some increase in the quantity of money." However, "the more serious infractions followed when the Bank began to lend money to the government of Amsterdam and eventually succumbed to the temptations offered by the [Dutch] East India Company." As Ederer articulated, "What this bank did surreptitiously was soon to be institutionalized and to form the essence of a new monetary technique." Thus, this bank established a "new monetary era":

A marvelous new power probably equal to the potentialities of the discovery of coinage had evolved. The Bank had created money literally for over a hundred years without being discovered. Even after it was discovered, the Bank could have continued in operation in this new way except for public prejudice. The public was not yet ready to accept a money with no guarantee save the word of public authorities. It had been too seriously and too frequently misled in the past, and, paradoxically enough, it had fled to the banks for a more efficient money. Out of this flight grew the private money creation which is the essence of modern commercial banking.[4]

The Bank of England

As John Kenneth Galbraith explained in regards to the Bank of England, "Of all institutions concerned with economics none has for so long enjoyed such prestige," as "most of the art as well as much of the mystery associated with the management of money originated there. The pride of other central banks has been either in their faithful imitation of the Bank of England or in the small variations from its method."[5] As economist Rupert J. Ederer explained, it was with the founding of the Bank of England "which constituted the first complete official approval of money issue by private interests. In other words, private money-issue became a socially and legally sanctioned institution during the 17th century."[6]

Ederer analyzed the history leading up to the creation of the Bank of England in his book, *Evolution of Money*. He explained that the slippage of the process of money creation from public to private hands "was but another manifestation of the intense struggle of king vs. parliament going on there at the time." Ederer elaborated:

It had been customary in 17th century England for the wealthy classes to deposit their surplus metallic money in the London Tower for safe-keeping. Here, they felt confident, it was safe. This confidence was dealt a rude blow when King Charles I in need of money to conduct a civil war which he had precipitated with Scotland confiscated the hoards. As it was, Charles refused to release these funds until the merchants agreed to make him a loan. He did not repay the loan except after a long delay marked by sharp and bitter protests. The depositors had learned their lesson and would look for another safe-deposit bank. Most suited to the task, it seemed, were the vaults of the goldsmiths.[7]

The goldsmiths, being savvy businessmen, "served notice to their depositors that they would accept money on deposit only on the condition that they could lend it out." The goldsmiths developed a cunning method of managing the money, as the smith would issue a "warehouse receipt" to depositors wishing to withdraw money, which was "a document showing that a certain quantity of metallic money was left on deposit by 'X' and could be claimed by him upon presentation of the receipt." Ederer explained:

> These receipts were at first scrupulously honored thus establishing confidence that the money would always be available. As a result, the clientele whose original intention was to get away from using the sensitive and impractical coins, simply began circulating the receipts.[8]

The main obstacle to this development of money-creation was the state, as "Kings had insisted on the sole right to issue the monetary media ever since coinage began. Surrender of that right was fraught with dangers for the public welfare and for the very existence of the states involved." So the question was, as Ederer postulated, "How could these monarchs be induced to surrender or, at least, to share this power with private interests? The answer lay in the financially exposed position in which many monarchs found themselves during the 17th and 18th centuries because of constant wars and uprisings. They needed money desperately."[9]

In England, King Charles II "borrowed what money the smiths were able and willing to lend at 12 percent. The repayment was to come in the form of taxes which were to be paid directly to the goldsmiths." However, businessmen and other powerful interests did not want a return to coinage, having grown accustomed to the use of receipts, which had allowed their businesses to flourish. Naturally, there was a growing desire for banks to emerge, following on the heels of the example in Amsterdam. However, all that was needed "was a king who was especially in need of funds for some royal venture. When this monarch appeared, certain alert interests would be able to foist upon the public a system of private money issue."[10]

This opportunity emerged with King William and Queen Mary following the long war with Louis XIV, at a time in which the mercantile interests "had money that they were willing to lend on their own terms, and they were also aware of how lucrative banking in the new style could be, that is, when it involved the right to create money."[11] William was born a Dutch prince, whose mother was sister to King Charles II of England. He came to power in England in 1689 following the Glorious Revolution, in which King James II was forced to flee, which involved an invading Dutch army and resulted in the establishment of a constitutional monarchy and the English Bill of Rights, marking an end to the absolute monarchist era and the beginning of an era in which power was shared between monarch and the parliament.

Now, the monarch, desperate for funds, had to look to private interests, and the answer came from a Scotsman named William Patterson:

> Speaking for the wealthy London businessmen he offered to lend money amounting to 1,200,000 pounds at 8% interest, provided that the lenders be granted a charter to establish a bank of issue. On their behalf he demanded the right to issue notes in an amount equal roughly to the amount of the debt, which would circulate as money."[12]

These notes "would go out as loans to worthy private borrowers. Interest would be earned both on these loans and on the loans to the government. Again the wonder of banking."[13] The plan initially being put through Parliament in 1691 met opposition from the King and goldsmiths. However, it was eventually passed in 1694, and thus, the Bank of England was created.[14]

In 1833, Parliament passed legislation that made the Bank of England have the only legal notes of tender, granting it a partial monopoly, as other banks still had notes in circulation. With the Bank Act of 1844, "the issues of all the other banks were limited to the amounts in circulation at that time." Confidence grew in the bank, acting as the government's banker and agent, "and when the widespread establishment of joint-stock banks in England began in 1826, the Bank of England had already come to be regarded as the custodian of the cash reserves of the private banks, and thus of the country's gold reserves." Eventually, the bank entered into the role of being the "lender of last resort" and had the responsibility to "maintain not only the currency but also the credit system of the country."[15]

The Bank of France

In 1788, the French Monarchy was bankrupt, and as tensions grew between the increasingly desperate people of France and the aristocratic and particularly monarchic establishment, European bankers decided to pre-empt and co-opt the revolution. In 1788, prominent French bankers refused "to extend necessary short-term credit to the government,"[16] and they arranged to have shipments of grain and food to Paris "delayed" which triggered the hunger riots of the Parisians.[17] This sparked the Revolution, in which a new ruling class emerged, driven by violent oppression and political and actual terrorism. However, its violence grew, and with that, so too did discontentment with the Revolutionary Regime, and its stability and sustainability was in question. Thus, the bankers threw their weight behind a general in the Revolutionary Army named Napoleon, whom they entrusted to restore order.

Napoleon then gave the bankers his support, and in 1800, created the Bank of France, the privately owned central bank of France, and gave the bankers authority over the Bank. The bankers owned its shares, and even Napoleon himself bought shares in the bank.[18] In 1803, Napoleon granted the Bank of France the exclusive right of issue, abolishing competition, "and so the Bank of France assumed the role of the central bank." However, "the Bank's independence was scarcely altered. At the time when it assumed the role as the country's central bank, representatives of the 200 principal shareholders were still free to make policy themselves."[19]

The bankers thus sought to control commerce and government and restore order to their newly acquired and privately owned and operated empire. However, Napoleon continued with his war policies beyond the patience of the bankers, which had a negative impact upon commercial activities,[20] and Napoleon himself was interfering in the operations of the Bank of France and even declared that the Bank "belongs more to the Emperor than to the shareholders."[21] With that, the bankers again shifted their influence, and remained through regime change, while Napoleon did not.[22]

The Rothschilds ascended to the throne of international banking with the Battle of Waterloo. After having established banking houses in London, Paris, Frankfurt, Vienna and Naples, they profited off all sides in the Napoleonic wars.[23] The British patriarch, Nathan Rothschild, was known for being the first with news in London, ahead of even the monarchy and the Parliament, and so everyone watched his moves on the stock exchange during the Battle of Waterloo. Following the battle, Nathan got the news that the British won over 24 hours before the government itself had news, and he quietly went into the London Stock Exchange and sold everything he had, implying to those watching that the British lost.

A panic selling ensued, in which everyone sold stock, stock prices crumbled, and the market crashed. What resulted was that Rothschild then bought up the near-entire British stock market for pennies on the dollar, as when news arrived of the British victory at Waterloo, Rothschild's newly acquired stocks soared in value, as did his fortune, and his rise as the pre-eminent economic figure in Britain.[24]

As Georgetown University History professor, Carroll Quigley wrote in his monumental *Tragedy and Hope*, "the merchant bankers of London had already at hand in 1810-1850 the Stock Exchange, the Bank of England, and the London money market," and that:

> In time they brought into their financial network the provincial banking centers, organized as commercial banks and savings banks, as well as insurance companies, to form all of these into a single financial system on an international scale which manipulated the quantity and flow of money so that they were able to influence, if not control, governments on one side and industries on the other.[25]

Creating a Central Bank of the United States: The Federal Reserve

The history of the United States from its founding through the 19th century to the early 20th century was marked by a continual political battle revolving around the creation of a central bank of the United States. Mercantilists such as Alexander Hamilton, who was the first Treasury Secretary, were in favor of such a bank, and his advice won over George Washington, much to the dismay of Thomas Jefferson, who was a strong opponent to central banking. However, "[Alexander] Hamilton, believing that government must ally itself with the richest elements of society to make itself strong, proposed to Congress a series of laws, which it enacted, expressing this philosophy," and that, "A Bank of the United States was set up as a partnership between the government and certain banking interests,"[26] which lasted until the charter expired in 1811.

Again, during the tenure of Andrew Jackson (1829-1837), the primary political struggle was with the entrenched financial interests both domestic and from abroad (namely Western Europe), on the issue of creating a central bank of the U.S. Andrew Jackson stood in firm opposition to such a bank, saying that, "the bank threatened the emerging order, hoarding too much economic power in too few hands," and referred to it as "The Monster."[27] Congress passed the bill allowing for the creation of a Second Bank of the United States, however Andrew Jackson vetoed the bill, much to the dismay of the banking interests.

It was in the latter half of the 1800s that "European financiers were in favor of an American Civil War that would return the United States to its colonial status, they admitted privately that they were not necessarily interested in preserving slavery," as it had become unprofitable.[28] The Civil War was not based upon the liberation of slaves, it was, as Howard Zinn described it, a clash "of elites," with the northern elite wanting "economic expansion – free land, free labor, a free market, a high protective tariff for manufacturers, [and] a bank of the United States. [Whereas] the slave interests opposed all that."[29] The Civil War, which lasted from 1861 until 1865, resulted in hundreds of thousands of deaths, during which, "Congress also set up a national bank, putting the government into partnership with the banking interests, guaranteeing their profits."[30]

As Lincoln himself stated:

The money powers prey on the nation in times of peace and conspire against it in times of adversity. The banking powers are more despotic than monarchy, more insolent than autocracy, more selfish than bureaucracy. They denounce as public enemies all who question their methods or throw light upon their crimes.

I have two great enemies, the Southern Army in front of me, and the bankers in the rear. Of the two, the one at my rear is my greatest foe. As a most undesirable consequence of the war, corporations have been enthroned, and an era of corruption in high places will follow. The money power will endeavor to prolong its reign by working upon the prejudices of the people until the wealth is aggregated in the hands of a few, and the Republic is destroyed.[31]

Throughout much of the 1800s and into the 1900s, the United States suffered several economic crises, one of the most significant of which was the Great Depression of 1873. As Howard Zinn explained:

The crisis was built into a system which was chaotic in its nature, in which only the very rich were secure. It was a system of periodic crises – 1837, 1857, 1873 (and later: 1893, 1907, 1919, 1929) – that wiped out small businesses and brought cold, hunger, and death to working people while the fortunes of the Astors, Vanderbilts, Rockefellers, Morgans, kept growing through war and peace, crisis and recovery. During the 1873 crisis, Carnegie was capturing the steel market, Rockefeller was wiping out his competitors in oil.[32]

Massive industrial consolidation by a few oligarchic elites was the rule of the day, as J.P. Morgan expanded total control over railroad and banking interests, and John D. Rockefeller took control of the oil market, and expanded into banking. Zinn explained:

The imperial leader of the new oligarchy was the House of Morgan. In its operations it was ably assisted by the First National Bank of New York (directed by George F. Baker) and the National City Bank of New York (presided over by James Stillman, agent of the Rockefeller interests). Among them, these three men and their financial associates occupied 341 directorships in 112 corporations. The total resources of these corporations in 1912 was $22,245,000,000, more than the assessed value of all property in the twenty-two states and territories west of the Mississippi River.[33]

In the early 20th century, European and American banking interests achieved what they had desired for over a century within America, the creation of a privately owned central bank. It was created through collaboration of American and European bankers, primarily the Morgans, Rockefellers, Kuhn, Loebs and Warburgs.[34]

After the 1907 banking panic in the U.S., instigated by J.P. Morgan, pressure was placed upon the American political establishment to create a "stable" banking system. In 1910, a secret meeting of financiers was held on Jekyll Island, where they planned for the "creation of a National Reserve Association with fifteen major regions, controlled by a board of commercial bankers but empowered by the federal government to act like a central bank – creating money and lending reserves to private banks."[35]

It was largely Paul M. Warburg, a Wall Street investment banker, who "had come up with a design for a single central bank [in 1910]. He called it the United Reserve Bank. From this and his later service on the first Federal Reserve Board, Warburg has, with some justice, been called the father of the System."[36]

Senator Nelson W. Aldrich, "in the early years of the century, was by common calculation the most influential man in the Senate." He "had an unabashed commitment to high tariffs, sound money, [and] the untrammeled operations of big bankers and to all other measures which would, with reasonable certainty, enhance the wealth or power of the already rich, a community that very definitely included Aldrich himself." Further, his daughter married John D. Rockefeller, Jr.[37]

In 1912, Aldrich "introduced legislation to establish a National Reserve Association along with fifteen regional associations. These would hold the reserves – the deposits – of the participating banks. To them the banks would turn for loans, including rescue in a time of emergency. All would be solidly under the control of the bankers whom they comprised." Although, when the System was finally created, "the ultimate legislation was the work not of Aldrich and his fellow Republicans but of the Democrats."[38]

President Woodrow Wilson followed the plan almost exactly as outlined by the Wall Street financiers, and added to it the creation of a Federal Reserve Board in Washington, which the President would appoint.[39] It was two days before Christmas in 1913 that "Woodrow Wilson signed the Federal Reserve Act into law. It provided not for a central bank but for as many as twelve – the number later chosen. Washington guidance was to be by a Federal Reserve Board of seven, of which the Secretary of the Treasury and the Comptroller of the Currency were to be ex officio members. The powers of the board were slight. The regional idea had, in fact, triumphed, and the real authority lay with the twelve banks."[40] The regional banks:

> ...were each to be governed by a board of nine directors, six of whom were to be selected by the participating or member banks, although only three of these could be bankers. The remaining three were to be appointed by Washington.[41]

The Federal Reserve, or Fed, "raised its own revenue, drafted its own operating budget and submitted neither to Congress," while "the seven governors shared power with the presidents of the twelve Reserve Banks, each serving the private banks in its region," and "the commercial banks held stock shares in each of the twelve Federal Reserve Banks."[42]

The Great Depression

> *The modern banking system manufactures money out of nothing. The process is perhaps the most astounding piece of sleight of hand that was ever invented. Banking was conceived in inequity and born in sin... Bankers own the earth. Take it away from them but leave them the power to create money, and, with a flick of a pen, they will create enough money to buy it back again... Take this great power away from them, and all great fortunes like mine will disappear, for then this would be a better and happier world to live in... But, if you want to continue to be the slaves of bankers and pay the cost of your own slavery, then let bankers continue to create money and control credit.*[43]
>
> −Sir Josiah Stamp, Director of the Bank of England, 1927

Benjamin Strong, Governor of the Federal Reserve Bank of New York, and Montagu Norman, Governor of the Bank of England, who worked closely together throughout the 1920s, decided to "use the financial power of Britain and the United States to force all the major countries of the world to go on the gold standard and to operate it through central banks free from all political control, with all questions of international finance to be settled by agreements by such central banks without interference from governments." These men were not working for the governments and nations of whom they purportedly represented, but "were the technicians and agents of the dominant investment bankers of their own countries, who had raised them up and were perfectly capable of throwing them down."[44]

In the 1920s, the United States experienced a stock market boom, which was a result of the commercial banks providing "funds for the purchase of stock and took the latter as collateral," creating a massive wave of underwriting and purchasing of securities. The stock market speculation that followed was the result of the banks "borrowing substantially from the Federal Reserve. Thus the Federal Reserve System was helping to finance the great stock market boom."[45]

In 1927, a meeting took place in New York City between Montagu Norman of the Bank of England, Hjalmar Schacht, President of the Reichsbank, the German central bank of the Weimar Republic; Charles Rist, Deputy Governor of the Bank of France and Benjamin Strong of the New York Fed. The topic of the meeting was the "persistently weak reserve position of the Bank of England. This, the bankers thought, could be helped if the Federal Reserve System would ease interest rates to encourage lending. Holders of gold would then seek the higher returns from keeping their metal in London." The Fed obliged.[46]

The Bank of England had a weak reserve position because of Britain's position as champion of the gold standard. Foreign central banks, including the Bank of France, were transferring their exchange holdings into gold, of which the Bank of England did not have enough to supply. So the Fed lowered its discount rate, and began buying securities to equal French gold purchases. Money in the U.S., then, "was going increasingly into stock-market speculation rather than into production of real wealth."[47]

In early 1929, the Federal Reserve board of governors "called upon the member banks to reduce their loans on stock-exchange collateral," and took other actions with the publicly pronounced aim of reducing "the amount of credit available for speculation." Yet, it had the reverse effect, as "the available credit went more and more to speculation and decreasingly to productive business." On September 26, 1929, London was hit with a financial panic, and the Bank of England raised its bank rate, causing British money to leave Wall Street, "and the over inflated market commenced to sag," leading to a panic by mid-October.[48]

The longest-serving Federal Reserve Chairman, Alan Greenspan (1987 to 2006), wrote that the Fed triggered the speculative boom by pumping excess credit into the economy and eventually this resulted in the American and British economies collapsing due to the massive imbalances produced. Britain then "abandoned the gold standard completely in 1931, tearing asunder what remained of the fabric of confidence and inducing a world-wide series of bank failures. The world economies plunged into the Great Depression of the 1930's."[49]

The Bank for International Settlements

In 1929, the Young Committee was formed to create a program for the settlement of German reparations payments that emerged out of the Versailles Treaty, written at the Paris Peace talks in 1919. The Committee was headed by Owen D. Young, founder of Radio Corporation of America (RCA), a subsidiary of General Electric. He was also President and CEO of GE from 1922 until 1939, co-author of the 1924 Dawes Plan, was appointed to the Board of Trustees of the Rockefeller Foundation in 1928, and was also, in 1929, deputy chairman of the New York Federal Reserve Bank. When Young was sent to Europe in 1929 to form the program for German reparations payments, he was accompanied by J.P Morgan, Jr.[50]

What emerged from the Committee was the creation of the Young Plan, which "was assertedly a device to occupy Germany with American capital and pledge German real assets for a gigantic mortgage held in the United States." Further, the Young Plan "increased unemployment more and more," allowing Hitler to say he would "do away with unemployment," which, "really was the reason of the enormous success Hitler had in the election."[51]

The Plan went into effect in 1930, following the stock market crash. Part of the Plan entailed the creation of an international settlement organization, which was formed in 1930, and known as the Bank for International Settlements (BIS). (For further details on the BIS, see Chapter 16). It was purportedly designed to facilitate and coordinate the reparations payments of Weimar Germany to the Allied powers. However, its secondary function, which is much more secretive, and much more important, was to act as "a coordinator of the operations of central banks around the world." Described as "a bank for central banks," the BIS "is a private institution with shareholders but it does operations for public agencies. Such operations are kept strictly confidential so that the public is usually unaware of most of the BIS operations."[52]

The BIS was established "to remedy the decline of London as the world's financial center by providing a mechanism by which a world with three chief financial centers in London, New York, and Paris could still operate as one."[53] As Carroll Quigley explained:

> The powers of financial capitalism had another far-reaching aim, nothing less than to create a world system of financial control in private hands able to dominate the political system of each country and the economy of the world as a whole. This system was to be controlled in a feudalist fashion by the central banks of the world acting in concert, by secret agreements arrived at in frequent private meetings and conferences. The apex of the system was to be the Bank for International Settlements in Basel, Switzerland, a private bank owned and controlled by the world's central banks which were themselves private corporations.[54]

The BIS was founded by "the central banks of Belgium, France, Germany, Italy, the Netherlands, Japan, and the United Kingdom along with three leading commercial banks from the United States, including J.P. Morgan & Company, First National Bank of New York, and First National Bank of Chicago. Each central bank subscribed to 16,000 shares and the three U.S. banks also subscribed to this same number of shares." However, "Only central banks have voting power."[55]

Originally, "the major shareholders in the BIS were central banks. After its initial objective of facilitation of the German reparations settlements after World War I, its activities have focused on central banks and their major constituents, commercial banks around the world." Among the functions the BIS does for central banks, referred to as "facilities" are:

> Taking deposits and making loans, swaps of currency for gold, credits advanced against a pledge of gold or marketable short-term securities, foreign exchange operations [...and the BIS] also carries out foreign exchange and gold transactions within the market.[56]

Central bank members have bi-monthly meetings at the BIS where they discuss a variety of issues. It should be noted that most "of the transactions carried out by the BIS on behalf of central banks require the utmost secrecy,"[57] which is likely why most people have not even heard of it. The BIS can offer central banks "confidentiality and secrecy which is higher than a triple-A rated bank."[58]

In a letter dated November 21, 1933, President Franklin Roosevelt told Edward M. House, "The real truth is, as you and I know, that a financial element in the larger centers has owned the Government ever since the days of Andrew Jackson – and I am not wholly excepting the administration of W[oodrow] W[ilson]. The country is going through a repetition of Jackson's fight with the Bank of the United States – only on a far bigger and broader basis."[59]

The American Empire and the Federal Reserve

Following World War II, the Allied powers set up the Bretton-Woods System, in which the World Bank and IMF emerged, as well as the General Agreement on Tariffs and Trade (GATT), which later became the World Trade Organization (WTO). This system was set up under the hegemony of the United States.

Thus, the Federal Reserve became one of the most powerful institutions in the world, and the "Chairman of the Federal Reserve Board is generally one of the most powerful men in the United States, if not the most powerful," as the Fed has oversight responsibility over "Federal Reserve member banks, U.S. banking operations in foreign countries, and foreign banks operating in the United States."[60]

In 1971, Nixon abandoned the dollar's link with gold, which meant that the value of the world reserve currency, the U.S. dollar, was then determined by the U.S. Federal Reserve. The oil crisis of 1973 generated a massive surplus of oil money, called petrodollars, which were sold in U.S. dollars, in the major oil producing nations. They then invested this money into western, primarily American banks, which in turn, lent it to less developed nations, recently freed from the shackles of colonialism, which were trying to industrialize.

In 1979, there was another oil shock. In August of 1979, "on the advice of David Rockefeller and other influential voices of the Wall Street banking establishment, President Carter appointed Paul A. Volcker, the man who, back in August 1971, had been a key architect of the policy of taking the dollar off the gold standard, to head the Federal Reserve."[61]

Volcker got his start as a staff economist at the New York Federal Reserve Bank in the early 50s. After five years there, "David Rockefeller's Chase Bank lured him away."[62] So in 1957, Volcker went to work at Chase, where Rockefeller "recruited him as his special assistant on a congressional commission on money and credit in America and for help, later, on an advisory commission to the Treasury Department."[63] In the early 60s, Volcker went to work in the Treasury Department, and returned to Chase in 1965 "as an aide to Rockefeller, this time as vice president dealing with international business." With Nixon entering the White House, Volcker got the third highest job in the Treasury Department. This put him at the center of the decision making process behind the dissolution of the Bretton Woods agreement.[64] In 1973, Volcker became a member of Rockefeller's Trilateral Commission. In 1975, he got the job as President of the New York Federal Reserve Bank, the most powerful of the twelve branches of the Fed.

In 1979, Carter gave the job of Treasury Secretary to Arthur Miller, who had been Chairman of the Fed. This left an opening at the Fed, which was initially offered by Carter to David Rockefeller, who declined, and then to A. W. Clausen, Chairman of Bank of America, who also declined. Carter repeatedly tried to get Rockefeller to accept, and ultimately Rockefeller recommended Volcker for the job.[65] Volcker became Chairman of the

Federal Reserve System, and immediately took drastic action to fight inflation by radically increasing interest rates.

The world was taken by shock. This was not a policy that would only be felt in the U.S. with a recession, but was to send shock waves around the world, devastating the Third World debtor nations. This was the ultimate result of the 1970s oil shocks and the 1979 Federal Reserve shock therapy. With the raising of interest rates, the cost of international money also rose. Thus, the interest rates on international loans made throughout the 1970s rose from two percent in the 1970s to eighteen percent in the 1980s, dramatically increasing the interest charges on loans to developing countries.[66]

In the developing world, states that had to import oil faced enormous bills to cover their debts, and even oil producing countries, such as Mexico, faced huge problems as they had borrowed heavily in order to industrialize, and then suffered when oil prices fell again as the recession occurring in the developed states reduced demand. Thus, in 1982, Mexico declared that it could no longer pay its debt, meaning that, "they could no longer cover the cost of interest payments, much less hope to repay the debt." The result was the bursting of the debt bubble. Banks then halted their loans to Mexico, and "before long it was evident that states such as Brazil, Venezuela, Argentina, and many sub-Saharan African countries were in equally difficult financial positions."[67]

The IMF and World Bank entered the scene newly refurnished with a whole new outlook and policy program designed just in time for the arrival of the debt crisis. The IMF:

> ...negotiated standby loans with debtors offering temporary assistance to states in need. In return for the loans states agreed to undertake Structural Adjustment Programs (SAPs). These programs entailed the liberalization of economies to trade and foreign investment as well as the reduction of state subsidies and bureaucracies to balance national budgets.[68]

Thus, we saw the emergence of the Neoliberal era. Neoliberalism is "a particular organization of capitalism, which has evolved to protect capital(ism) and to reduce the power of labor. This is achieved by means of social, economic and political transformations imposed by internal forces as well as external pressure," and it entails the "shameless use of foreign aid, debt relief and balance of payments support to promote the neoliberal program, and diplomatic pressure, political unrest and military intervention when necessary."[69] Further, "neoliberalism is part of a hegemonic project concentrating power and wealth in elite groups around the world, benefiting especially the financial interests within each country, and U.S. capital internationally. Therefore, globalization and imperialism cannot be analyzed separately from neoliberalism."[70.]

Neoliberal economic policies were pushed on the less developed nations of the world through the Structural Adjustment Programs. The nature of SAPs is such that the conditions imposed upon countries that sign onto these agreements include: lowering budget deficits, devaluing the currency, limiting government borrowing from the central bank, liberalizing foreign trade, reducing public sector wages, price liberalization, deregulation and altering interest rates.[71] For reducing budget deficits, "precise 'ceilings' are placed on all categories of expenditure; the state is no longer permitted to mobilize its own resources for the building of public infrastructure, roads, or hospitals, etc."[72]

Joseph Stiglitz, former Chief Economist at the World Bank, wrote that, "the IMF staff monitored progress, not just on the relevant indicators for sound macromanagement – inflation, growth, and unemployment – but on intermediate variables, such as the money supply," and that "In some cases the agreements stipulated what laws the country's Parliament would have to pass to meet IMF requirements or 'targets' – and by when."[73] Further, "the conditions went beyond economics into areas that properly belong in the realm of politics," and that "the way conditionality was imposed made the conditions politically unsustainable; when a new government came into power, they would be abandoned. Such conditions were seen as the intrusion by the new colonial power on the country's own sovereignty."[74]

So thus, through the Fed's actions of raising interest rates, the West, and in particular, the United States and the powerful economic institutions that control it, we able to recapture the "developing world" in a neocolonial era of economic imperialism.

The BIS and the Global Economic Crisis

In 2007, it was reported that "the Bank for International Settlements, the world's most prestigious financial body, had warned that years of loose monetary policy has fuelled a dangerous credit bubble, leaving the global economy more vulnerable to another 1930s-style slump than generally understood." Further:

> The BIS, the ultimate bank of central bankers, pointed to a confluence a worrying signs, citing mass issuance of new-fangled credit instruments, soaring levels of household debt, extreme appetite for risk shown by investors, and entrenched imbalances in the world currency system...

> In a thinly-veiled rebuke to the US Federal Reserve, the BIS said central banks were starting to doubt the wisdom of letting asset bubbles build up on the assumption that they could safely be "cleaned up" afterwards – which was more or less the strategy pursued by former Fed chief Alan Greenspan after the dotcom bust.[75]

In 2008, the BIS again warned of the potential of another Great Depression, as "complex credit instruments, a strong appetite for risk, rising levels of household debt and long-term imbalances in the world currency system, all form part of the loose monetarist policy that could result in another Great Depression."[76]

In 2008, the BIS also said that, "the current market turmoil is without precedent in the postwar period. With a significant risk of recession in the U.S., compounded by sharply rising inflation in many countries, fears are building that the global economy might be at some kind of tipping point," and that all central banks have done "has been to put off the day of reckoning."[77]

In late June of 2009, the BIS reported that as a result of stimulus packages, it had only seen "limited progress" and that, "the prospects for growth are at risk," and further "stimulus measures won't be able to gain traction, and may only lead to a temporary pickup in growth." Ultimately, "A fleeting recovery could well make matters worse."[78] The same report of June of 2009 stated that, "fiscal stimulus packages may provide no more than a temporary boost to growth, and be followed by an extended period of economic stagnation."

The BIS, "the only international body to correctly predict the financial crisis... has warned the biggest risk is that governments might be forced by world bond investors to abandon their stimulus packages, and instead slash spending while lifting taxes and interest rates," as the annual report of the BIS "has for the past three years been warning of the dangers of a repeat of the depression." Further, "its latest annual report warned that countries such as Australia faced the possibility of a run on the currency, which would force interest rates to rise." The BIS warned that "a temporary respite may make it more difficult for authorities to take the actions that are necessary, if unpopular, to restore the health of the financial system, and may thus ultimately prolong the period of slow growth."

The BIS further warned that "at the same time, government guarantees and asset insurance have exposed taxpayers to potentially large losses," and explaining how fiscal packages posed significant risks, it said that "there is a danger that fiscal policymakers will exhaust their debt capacity before finishing the costly job of repairing the financial system," and that "there is the definite possibility that stimulus programs will drive up real interest rates and inflation expectations." Inflation "would intensify as the downturn abated," and the BIS "expressed doubt about the bank rescue package adopted in the US."[79]

The BIS and a Global Currency

As a result of the financial crisis, the Governor of the Bank of China, China's central bank, gave a speech advocating for the creation of a global currency to replace the U.S. dollar as the world reserve currency.[80] The Russian President also endorsed this plan to create a new global currency.[81] The UN has also endorsed the move to create a world currency, replacing the U.S. dollar.[82] In April of 2009, the G20 meeting set into motion a plan to construct a global reserve currency.[83]

In 2006, the BIS released its annual report in which it recommended "ditching many national currencies in favor of a small number of formal currency blocks based on the dollar, euro and renminbi or yen," and also "suggested ditching the current system of floating currencies and replacing it with 'a small number of more formally-based currency blocks'."[84]

While the new global reserve currency being created is tentatively under the authority of the IMF, in October of 2008, a former Governor of the Bank of England said that the solution to finding a global banking 'policeman' "might already be staring us in the face, in the form of the Bank for International Settlements" and that "the BIS has been spot on throughout this," he said. "The problem is that it has no teeth. The IMF tends to couch its warnings about economic problems in very diplomatic language, but the BIS is more independent and much better placed to deal with this if it is given the power to do so."[85]

While issues of the global currency are framed in terms of China and Russia being the primary supporters, it ignores the fact that they are within the sphere of influence of western financial capitalism, in particular, with the BIS. Following China's initial call for a global currency, Timothy Geithner, the U.S. Treasury Secretary and former CEO of the Federal Reserve Bank of New York said, at the Council on Foreign Relations, that the U.S. was "open" to the idea.[86]

There is more to this connection. In November of 2008, *China Stakes* published an article on the connection between Geithner and the Governor of the People's Bank of China, Zhou Xiaochuan, in which it reported that Zhou's relationship "with the Group of Thirty may hold important insights into China's rising role in international monetary affairs." Further:

> The Group of Thirty is an influential association of international financiers, economists and central bankers. They meet privately twice a year to discuss foreign exchange, central banks, international capital markets, international financial institutions and economic-supervisory issues. At the initiative of the Rockefeller Foundation, the group started in 1978 by Geoffrey Bell, one time assistant to Lord Richardson of Duntisbourne and Governor of the Bank of England.

Both Zhou and Geithner were members of the Group of 30 at the same time, while Geithner was President of the New York Fed. The article analyzed how Zhou is in step with the perspectives of the Group of 30 in reforming the international monetary system, and so China will be granted a larger voice in the global economy.[87] The Chairman of the Group of 30 is Paul Volcker, former Governor of the Board of Directors of the Federal Reserve System, who is also Chairman of the Economic Recovery Advisory Board under President Barack Obama.

All these central bankers have also become quite close through their bi-monthly meetings at the BIS, which they continually and increasingly turned to as a global monetary authority and coordinator. Zhou, Geithner, and Ben Bernanke, the current Fed Chairman, and Mervyn King, Governor of the Bank of England, would be seen having breakfast together, running in the same social and professional circles.[88] This has essentially fostered a cohesive class of central bankers, outside the purview of national boundaries, and within the confines of the BIS in Basel, Switzerland.

As Geithner himself said, "principal tables [at the BIS] now have twenty-six countries around them. China is always there." David Rothkopf, former Deputy Undersecretary of Commerce for International Trade during the administration of Bill Clinton, former Managing Director of Kissinger and Associates, and current Visiting Scholar at the Carnegie Endowment and member of the Council on Foreign Relations, wrote a book outlining the world's "*Superclass*," which is the title of the book, examining the role of the international elite in shaping world affairs.

Rothkopf stated that the Bank for International Settlement "meetings are themselves part of the world's semiformal structure, which is evolving out of an agreement among the most powerful countries on how they would like to see the management of the planet's financial affairs handled." Rothkopf interviewed Geithner, who explained that, "this community of actors has become very interconnected and that he [as President of the New York Fed] in fact probably speaks more often to them [at the BIS] than to all but one or two key players in the U.S. Fed system." Geithner was quoted as saying, "I spend a lot of time with these central bankers and they have world-class educations and experience. They share similar training and perspectives; we speak a similar language."[89]

Conclusion

The central banking system has been the most powerful network of institutions in the world; it reigns supreme over the capitalist world order, almost since its inception. Central banks are the perfect merger of private interests and public power. They have played key roles in every major development and drastic change in the capitalist world economy, and continue to do so. Central bank policies caused the Great Depression and played an enormous role in creating the Global Economic Crisis of 2008 onwards.

As the "solutions" to the economic crisis are being implemented, it would appear that those that created the crisis are being rewarded. The central banking system is becoming more globalized, more centralized and more powerful. This is why it is of immense importance to understand the history of the central banking system, in order to understand how we got to this place, and to be critical and more comprehensive in understanding where we are going in the future.

Central banks are kings without people; generals without armies; captains without crews and leaders without followers. They work behind the scenes; their weapons are the financial instruments they create and employ. With the stroke of a pen, they can destroy a nation and bankrupt a people. Their methods are covert, yet their powers are monumental. Never should such authority be granted to so few hands.

◆

NOTES

1. Rupert J. Ederer, *The Evolution of Money*, Public Affairs Press, 1964, p. 102.
2. *Ibid.*, p. 103.
3. John Kenneth Galbraith, *Money: Whence it Came, Where it Went*, Houghton Mifflin Company, Boston, 1975, p. 18-19.
4. Rupert J. Ederer, *op. cit.*, p. 118-119.
5. John Kenneth Galbraith, *op. cit.*, p. 30.
6. Rupert J. Ederer, *op. cit.*, p. 103.

7. *Ibid.*, p. 119-120.

8. *Ibid.*, p. 120-121.

9. *Ibid.*, p. 121-122.

10. *Ibid.*, p. 122.

11. *Ibid.*, p. 122.

12. *Ibid.*, p. 123.

13. John Kenneth Galbraith, *op. cit.*, p. 31.

14. Rupert J. Ederer, *op. cit.*, p. 123.

15. M.H. De Kock, *Central Banking*, 3rd edition, Staples Press, London, 1969, p. 12.

16. Donald Kagan, *et. al.*, *The Western Heritage. Volume C: Since 1789*, Ninth edition, Pearson Prentice Hall, 2007, p. 596.

17. Curtis B. Dall, *F.D.R: My Exploited Father-in-Law*, Institute for Historical Review, 1982, p. 172.

18. Carroll Quigley, *Tragedy and Hope: A History of the World in Our Time*, New York, Macmillan Company, 1966, p. 515; Robert Elgie and Helen Thompson (eds.), *The Politics of Central Banks*, New York, Routledge, 1998, p. 97-98.

19. Robert Elgie and Helen Thompson (eds.), *The Politics of Central Banks*, New York, Routledge, 1998, p. 98.

20. Carroll Quigley, *op. cit.*, p. 516.

21. Robert Elgie and Helen Thompson, ed., *op. cit.*, p. 98-99.

22. Carroll Quigley, *op. cit.*, p. 516.

23. Sylvia Nasar, "Masters of the Universe", *The New York Times*, http://query.nytimes.com/gst/fullpage.html?res=9C04E3D6123AF930A 15752C0A9669C8B63, 23 January 2000; BBC News, "The Family That Bankrolled Europe", http://news.bbc.co.uk/1/hi/uk/389053.stm, 9 July 1999.

24. New Scientist, "Waterloo Windfall", *New Scientist Magazine*, Issue 2091, http://www.newscientist.com/article/mg15520913.300-waterloo-windfall.html, 19 July 1997; BBC News, "The Making of a Dynasty: The Rothschilds", http://news.bbc.co.uk/2/hi/uk_news/50997.stm, 28 January 1998.

25. Carroll Quigley, *op. cit.*, p. 51.

26. Howard Zinn, *A People's History of the United States*, Harper Perennial, New York, 2003, p. 101.

27. Michael Waldman, *My Fellow Americans: The Most Important Speeches of America's Presidents, from George Washington to George W. Bush*, Longman Publishing Group, 2004, p. 25.

28. Dr. Ellen Brown, "Today We're All Irish: Debt Serfdom Comes to America", *Global Research*, http://www.globalresearch.ca/index.php

?context=viewArticle&code=BRO20080315&articleId=8349, 15 March 2008.

29. Howard Zinn, *op. cit.*, p. 189.

30. *Ibid.*, p. 238.

31. Steve Bachman, "Unheralded Warnings from the Founding Fathers to You", *Gather*, http://www.gather.com/viewArticle.jsp?articleId= 281474977031677, 19 June 2007.

32. Howard Zinn, *op. cit.*, p. 242.

33. *Ibid.*, p. 323.

34. Murray N. Rothbard, "Wall Street, Banks, and American Foreign Policy", *World Market Perspective*, http://www.lewrockwell.com/ rothbard/rothbard66.html, 1984.

35. William Greider, *Secrets of the Temple: How the Federal Reserve Runs the Country*, New York, Simon and Schuster, 1987, p. 276.

36. John Kenneth Galbraith, *op. cit.*, p. 121-122.

37. *Ibid.*, p. 120-121.

38. *Ibid.*, p. 122.

39. William Greider, *op. cit.*, p. 277.

40. John Kenneth Galbraith, *op. cit.*, p. 123-124.

41. *Ibid.*, p. 124.

42. William Greider, *op. cit.*, p. 50.

43. Ellen Hodgson Brown, *Web of Debt*, Third Millennium Press, 2007, p. 2.

44. Carroll Quigley, *op. cit.*, p. 326-327.

45. John Kenneth Galbraith, *op. cit.*, p. 173.

46. *Ibid.*, p. 174-175.

47. Carroll Quigley, *op. cit.*, p. 342.

48. *Ibid.*, p. 344.

49. Alan Greenspan, "Gold and Economic Freedom", in Ayn Rand (ed.), *Capitalism: The Unknown Ideal*, New York, Signet, 1967, p. 99-100.

50. Time Magazine, "HEROES: Man-of-the-Year", http://www.time. com/time/magazine/article/0,9171,738364-1,00.html, 6 January 1930.

51. Antony C. Sutton, *Wall Street and the Rise of Hitler*, G S G & Associates Pub, 1976, p. 15-16.

52. James Calvin Baker, *The Bank for International Settlements: Evolution and Evaluation*, Greenwood Publishing Group, 2002, p. 2.

53. Carroll Quigley, *op. cit.*, p. 324-325.

54. *Ibid.*, p. 324.

55. James Calvin Baker, *op. cit.*, p. 6.

56. *Ibid.*, p. 139.

57. *Ibid.*, p. 148.

58. *Ibid.*, p. 149.

59. Melvin Urofsky and Paul Finkelman, *A March of Liberty: A Constitutional History of the United States Volume II From 1877 to the Present*, 2nd Edition, Oxford University Press, 2002, p. 674.

60. James Calvin Baker, *op. cit.*, p. 149.

61. F. William Engdahl, *A Century of War: Anglo-American Oil Politics and the New World Order*, London, Pluto Press, 2004, p. 174.

62. Joseph B. Treaster, *Paul Volcker: The Making of a Financial Legend*, John Wiley and Sons, 2004, p. 36.

63. *Ibid.*, p. 37.

64. *Ibid.*, p. 38.

65. *Ibid.*, p. 57-60.

66. Robert O'Brien and Marc Williams, *Global Political Economy: Evolution and Dynamics*, 2nd ed., Palgrave Macmillan, 2007, p. 223.

67. *Ibid.*, p. 224.

68. *Ibid.*, p. 224.

69. A. Paloni and M. Zonardi (eds.), *Neoliberalism: A Critical Introduction*, London, Pluto, 2005, p. 3.

70. *Ibid.* p. 1.

71. Marc Williams, *International Economic Organizations and the Third World*, Hemel Hempstead, Harvester Wheatsheaf, 1994, p. 85.

72. Michel Chossudovsky, *The Globalization of Poverty and the New World Order*, 2nd ed., Quebec, Global Research, 2003, p. 52.

73. Joseph Stiglitz, *Globalization and its Discontents*, New York, Norton, 2003, p. 43-44.

74. *Ibid.*, p. 44-46.

75. Ambrose Evans-Pritchard, "BIS Warns of Great Depression Dangers from Credit Spree", *The Telegraph*, http://www.telegraph.co.uk/finance/economics/2811081/BIS-warns-of-Great-Depression-dangers- from-credit-spree.html, 27 June 2009.

76. Gill Montia, "Central bank body warns of Great Depression", *Banking Times*, http://www.bankingtimes.co.uk/09062008-central-bank-body-warns-of-great-depression/, 9 June 2008.

77. Ambrose Evans-Pritchard, "BIS Slams Central Banks, Warns of Worse Crunch to Come", *The Telegraph*, http://www.telegraph.co.uk/finance/markets/ 27924 50/BIS-slams-central-banks-warns-of-worse-crunch-to-come.html, 30 June 2008.

78. Heather Scoffield, "Financial Repairs Must Continue: Central Banks", *The Globe and Mail*, http://v1.theglobeandmail.com/servlet/story/RTGAM.20090629.wcentralbanks0629/BNStory/HEATHER+SCOFFIELD/,29 June 2009.

79. David Uren, "Bank for International Settlements Warning over Stimulus Benefits", *The Australian*, http://www.theaustralian.news.com.au/story/ 0,,25710566-601,00.html, 30 June 2009.

80. Zhou Xiaochuan, "Reform the International Monetary System", *The People's Bank of China*, http://www.pbc.gov.cn/english/detail.asp?col=6500&id=178, 23 March 2009.

81. China View, "Russian President Calls for Creating New Int'l Currency System", *Xinhua*, http://news.xinhuanet.com/english/2009-04/01/content_ 11109506.htm, 1 April 2009.

82. Edmund Conway, "UN Wants New Global Currency to Replace Dollar", *The Telegraph*, http://www.telegraph.co.uk/finance/currency/6152204/UN-wants-new-global-currency-to-replace-dollar.html, 7 September 2009.

83. Ambrose Evans-Pritchard, "The G20 Moves the World a Step Closer to a Global Currency", *The Telegraph*, http://www.telegraph.co.uk/finance/com ment/ambroseevans_pritchard/5096524/The-G20-moves-the-world-a-step-closer-to-a-global-currency.html, 3 April 2009.

84. Edmund Conway, "UK Policy Blamed for Soaring Debt Levels", *The Telegraph*, http://www.telegraph.co.uk/finance/2932605/UK-policy-blamed-for-soaring-debt-levels.html, 20 February 2006.

85. Gordon Rayner, "Global Financial Crisis: Does the World Need a New Banking 'Policeman'?", *The Telegraph*, http://www.telegraph.co.uk/finance/financetopics/financialcrisis/3155563/Global-financial-crisis-does-the-world-need-a-new-banking-policeman.html, 8 October 2008.

86. Ambrose Evans-Pritchard, "A World Currency Moves Nearer After Tim Geithner's Slip", *The Telegraph*, http://www.telegraph.co.uk/finance/econo mics/5051075/ A-world-currency-moves-nearer-after-Tim-Geithners-slip.html, 26 March 2009.

87. Thomas Wilkins, "The Zhou-Geithner Connection", *China Stakes*, http://www.chinastakes.com/2008/11/the-zhou-geithner-connection.html, 23 November 2008.

88. John Fraher, "Bernanke, Trichet Turn to BIS as Markets Ignore Risk", *Bloomberg*, http://www.bloomberg.com/apps/news?pid=20601109&refer=home&sid=a1cW8RYVARJM, 19 June 2007.

89. David Rothkopf, *The Superclass: The Global Power Elite and the World They are Making*, Penguin Group, 2008, p. 174.

CHAPTER 16

The Tower of Basel: Secretive Plan to Create a Global Central Bank

Ellen Brown

> *By acting together to fulfill these pledges we will bring the world economy out of recession and prevent a crisis like this from recurring in the future.*
>
> *We are committed to take all necessary actions to restore the normal flow of credit through the financial system and ensure the soundness of systemically important institutions, implementing our policies in line with the agreed G20 framework for restoring lending and repairing the financial sector.*
>
> *We have agreed to support a general SDR allocation which will inject $250bn into the world economy and increase global liquidity.*
>
> *– G20 Communiqué, London, April 2, 2009*

Towards a New Global Currency?

Is the Group of Twenty Countries (G20) envisaging the creation of a Global Central bank? Who or what would serve as this global central bank, cloaked with the power to issue the global currency and police monetary policy for all humanity?

When the world's central bankers met in Washington in September 2008 at the height of the financial meltdown, they discussed what body might be in a position to serve in that awesome and fearful role. A former governor of the Bank of England stated:

> The answer might already be staring us in the face, in the form of the Bank for International Settlements (BIS)... The IMF tends to couch its warnings about economic problems in very diplomatic

language, but the BIS is more independent and much better placed to deal with this if it is given the power to do so.[1]

And if the vision of a global currency outside government control was not enough to set off conspiracy theorists, putting the BIS in charge of it surely would be. The BIS has been scandal-ridden ever since it was branded with pro-Nazi leanings in the 1930s. Founded in Basel, Switzerland, in 1930, the BIS has been called "the most exclusive, secretive, and powerful supranational club in the world." Charles Higham wrote in his book *Trading with the Enemy* that by the late 1930s, the BIS had assumed an openly pro-Nazi bias, a theme that was expanded on in a BBC Timewatch film titled "Banking with Hitler" broadcast in 1998.[2] In 1944, the American government backed a resolution at the Bretton Woods Conference calling for the liquidation of the BIS, following Czech accusations that it was laundering gold stolen by the Nazis from occupied Europe; but the central bankers succeeded in quietly snuffing out the American resolution.[3]

In *Tragedy and Hope: A History of the World in Our Time* (1966), Dr. Carroll Quigley revealed the key role played in global finance by the BIS behind the scenes. Dr. Quigley was Professor of History at Georgetown University, where he was President Bill Clinton's mentor. He was also an insider, groomed by the powerful clique he called "the international bankers." His credibility is heightened by the fact that he actually espoused their goals. Quigley wrote:

> I know of the operations of this network because I have studied it for twenty years and was permitted for two years, in the early 1960's, to examine its papers and secret records. I have no aversion to it or to most of its aims and have, for much of my life, been close to it and to many of its instruments... In general my chief difference of opinion is that it wishes to remain unknown, and I believe its role in history is significant enough to be known...

> The powers of financial capitalism had another far-reaching aim, nothing less than to create a world system of financial control in private hands able to dominate the political system of each country and the economy of the world as a whole. This system was to be controlled in a feudalist fashion by the central banks of the world acting in concert, by secret agreements ar-

rived at in frequent private meetings and conferences. The apex of the system was to be the Bank for International Settlements in Basel, Switzerland, a private bank owned and controlled by the world's central banks which were themselves private corporations.[4]

The key to their success, said Quigley, was that the international bankers would control and manipulate the money system of a nation while letting it appear to be controlled by the government. The statement echoed one made in the 18th century by the patriarch of what became the most powerful banking dynasty in the world. Mayer Amschel Bauer Rothschild is quoted as saying in 1791: "Allow me to issue and control a nation's currency, and I care not who makes its laws."

Mayer's five sons were sent to the major capitals of Europe – London, Paris, Vienna, Berlin and Naples – with the mission of establishing a banking system that would be outside government control. The economic and political systems of nations would be controlled not by citizens but by bankers, for the benefit of bankers. Eventually, a privately-owned "central bank" was established in nearly every country. This central banking system has now gained control over the economies of the world. Central banks have the authority to print money in their respective countries, and it is from these banks that governments must borrow money to pay their debts and fund their operations. The result is a global economy in which not only industry but government itself runs on "credit" (or debt) created by a banking monopoly headed by a network of private central banks. At the top of this network is the BIS, the "central bank of central banks" in Basel.

Behind the Curtain

For many years the BIS kept a very low profile, operating behind the scenes in an abandoned hotel. It was here that decisions were reached to devalue or defend currencies, fix the price of gold, regulate offshore banking, and raise or lower short-term interest rates. In 1977, however, the BIS gave up its anonymity in exchange for more efficient headquarters. The new building has been described as "an eighteen story-high circular skyscraper that rises above the medieval city like some misplaced nuclear reactor." It quickly became known as the "Tower of Basel." Today the BIS has governmental immunity, pays no taxes, and has its own private police force.[5] It is, as Mayer Rothschild envisioned, above the law.

The BIS is now composed of 55 member nations, but the club that meets regularly in Basel is a much smaller group; and even within it, there is a hierarchy. In a 1983 article in *Harper's Magazine* called "Ruling the World of Money," Edward Jay Epstein wrote that where the real business gets done is in "a sort of inner club made up of the half dozen or so powerful central bankers who find themselves more or less in the same monetary boat" – those from Germany, the United States, Switzerland, Italy, Japan and England. Epstein said:

> The prime value, which also seems to demarcate the inner club from the rest of the BIS members, is the firm belief that central banks should act independently of their home governments... A second and closely related belief of the inner club is that politicians should not be trusted to decide the fate of the international monetary system.[6]

In 1974, the Basel Committee on Banking Supervision was created by the central bank Governors of the Group of 10 nations (now expanded to twenty). The BIS provides the twelve-member Secretariat for the Committee. The Committee, in turn, sets the rules for banking globally, including capital requirements and reserve controls. In a 2003 article titled "The Bank for International Settlements Calls for Global Currency," Joan Veon wrote:

> The BIS is where all of the world's central banks meet to analyze the global economy and determine what course of action they will take next to put more money in their pockets, since they control the amount of money in circulation and how much interest they are going to charge governments and banks for borrowing from them...

> When you understand that the BIS pulls the strings of the world's monetary system, you then understand that they have the ability to create a financial boom or bust in a country. If that country is not doing what the money lenders want, then all they have to do is sell its currency.[7]

The Controversial Basel Accords

The power of the BIS to make or break economies was demonstrated in 1988, when it issued a Basel Accord raising bank capital requirements from six percent to eight percent. By then, Japan
had emerged as the world's largest creditor; but Japan's banks
were less well capitalized than other major international banks.
Raising the capital requirement forced them to cut back on lending, creating a recession in Japan like that suffered in the U.S.
today. Property prices fell and loans went into default as the
security for them shriveled up. A downward spiral followed, ending with the total bankruptcy of the banks. The banks had to be
nationalized, although that word was not used in order to avoid
criticism.[8]

Among other "collateral damage" produced by the Basel
Accords was a spate of suicides among Indian farmers unable to
get loans. The BIS capital adequacy standards required loans to
private borrowers to be "risk-weighted," with the degree of risk
determined by private rating agencies; farmers and small business owners could not afford the agencies' fees. Banks therefore
assigned one hundred percent risk to the loans, and then resisted
extending credit to these "high-risk" borrowers because more
capital was required to cover the loans. When the conscience of
the nation was aroused by the Indian suicides, the government,
lamenting the neglect of farmers by commercial banks, established a policy of ending the "financial exclusion" of the weak;
but this step had little real effect on lending practices, due largely
to the strictures imposed by the BIS from abroad.[9]

Economist Henry C K Liu has analyzed how the Basel Accords
have forced national banking systems "to march to the same
tune, designed to serve the needs of highly sophisticated global
financial markets, regardless of the developmental needs of their
national economies." He wrote:

> National banking systems are suddenly thrown into the rigid
> arms of the Basel Capital Accord sponsored by the Bank of Inter-
> national Settlement (BIS), or to face the penalty of usurious risk
> premium in securing international interbank loans... National
> policies suddenly are subjected to profit incentives of private
> financial institutions, all members of a hierarchical system
> controlled and directed from the money center banks in

New York. The result is to force national banking systems to privatize...

BIS regulations serve only the single purpose of strengthening the international private banking system, even at the peril of national economies... The IMF and the international banks regulated by the BIS are a team: the international banks lend recklessly to borrowers in emerging economies to create a foreign currency debt crisis, the IMF arrives as a carrier of monetary virus in the name of sound monetary policy, then the international banks come as vulture investors in the name of financial rescue to acquire national banks deemed capital inadequate and insolvent by the BIS.

Ironically, noted Liu, developing countries with their own natural resources did not actually need the foreign investment that trapped them in debt to outsiders:

Applying the State Theory of Money [which assumes that a sovereign nation has the power to issue its own money], any government can fund with its own currency all its domestic developmental needs to maintain full employment without inflation.[10]

When governments fall into the trap of accepting loans in foreign currencies, however, they become "debtor nations" subject to IMF and BIS regulation. They are forced to divert their production to exports, just to earn the foreign currency necessary to pay the interest on their loans. National banks deemed "capital inadequate" have to deal with strictures comparable to the "conditionalities" imposed by the IMF on debtor nations: "escalating capital requirement, loan write-offs and liquidation, and restructuring through selloffs, layoffs, downsizing, cost-cutting and freeze on capital spending." Liu wrote:

Reversing the logic that a sound banking system should lead to full employment and developmental growth, BIS regulations demand high unemployment and developmental degradation in national economies as the fair price for a sound global private banking system.[11]

The Last Domino to Fall

While banks in developing nations were being penalized for falling short of the BIS capital requirements, large international banks managed to skirt the rules, although they actually carried enormous risk because of their derivative exposure. The mega-banks took advantage of a loophole that allowed for lower charges against capital for "off-balance sheet activities." The banks got loans off their balance sheets by bundling them into securities and selling them off to investors, after separating the risk of default out from the loans and selling it off to yet other investors, using a form of derivative known as "credit default swaps."

It was evidently not in the game plan, however, that U.S. banks should escape the regulatory net indefinitely. Complaints about the loopholes in Basel I prompted a new set of rules called Basel II, which based capital requirements for market risk on a "Value-at-Risk" accounting standard. The new rules were established in 2004, but they were not levied on U.S. banks until November 2007, the month after the Dow passed 14 000 to reach its all-time high. On November 1, 2007, the Office of the Controller of the Currency "approved a final rule implementing advanced approaches of the Basel II Capital Accord."[12] On November 15, 2007, the Financial Accounting Standards Board or FASB, a private organization that sets U.S. accounting rules for the private sector, adopted FAS 157, the rule called "mark-to-market accounting."[13] The effect on U.S. banks was similar to that of Basel I on Japanese banks: they have been struggling to survive ever since.[14]

The mark-to-market rule requires banks to adjust the value of their marketable securities to the "market price" of the security.[15] The rule has theoretical merit, but the problem is timing: it was imposed *ex post facto*, after the banks already had the hard-to-market assets on their books. Lenders that had been considered sufficiently well capitalized to make new loans suddenly found they were insolvent; at least, they would have been if they had tried to sell their assets, an assumption required by the new rule. Financial analyst John Berlau complained in October 2008:

> Despite the credit crunch being described as the spread of the 'American flu,' the mark-to-market rules that are spreading it were hatched [as] part of the Basel II international rules for

financial institutions. It's just that the U.S. jumped into the really icy water last November when our Securities and Exchange Commission and bank regulators implemented FASB's Financial Accounting Standard 157, which makes healthy banks and financial firms take a 'loss' in the capital they can lend even if a loan on their books is still performing, even when the 'market price' [of] an illiquid asset is that of the last fire sale by a highly leveraged bank. Late last month, similar rules went into effect in the European Union, playing a similar role in accelerating financial failures...

The crisis is often called a 'market failure,' and the term 'mark-to-market' seems to reinforce that. But the mark-to-market rules are profoundly anti-market and hinder the free-market function of price discovery... In this case, the accounting rules fail to allow the market players to hold on to an asset if they don't like what the market is currently fetching, an important market action that affects price discovery in areas from agriculture to antiques.[16]

Imposing the mark-to-market rule on U.S. banks caused an instant credit freeze, which proceeded to take down the economies not only of the U.S. but of countries worldwide. In early April 2009, the mark-to-market rule was finally softened by the FASB; but critics said the modification did not go far enough, and it was done in response to pressure from politicians and bankers, not out of any fundamental change of heart or policies by the BIS or the FASB. Indeed, the BIS was warned as early as 2001 that its Basel II proposal was "procyclical," meaning that in a downturn it would only serve to make matters worse. In a formal response to a Request for Comments by the Basel Committee for Banking Supervision, a group of economists stated:

> Value-at-Risk can destabilize an economy and induce crashes when they would not otherwise occur... Perhaps our most serious concern is that these proposals, taken altogether, will enhance both the procyclicality of regulation and the susceptibility of the financial system to systemic crises, thus negating the central purpose of the whole exercise. Reconsider before it is too late.[17]

The BIS did not reconsider, however, even after seeing the dev-astation its regulations had caused; and that is where the con-spiracy theorists came in. Why did the BIS sit idly by, they asked, as the global economy came crashing down? Was the goal to cre-ate so much economic havoc that the world would rush with relief into the waiting arms of a global economic policeman with its privately-created global currency?

The Plot Thickens: The Shadowy Financial Stability Board

Alarm bells went off again when the leaders of the G20 nations agreed in April 2009 to expand the powers of an advisory group called the Financial Stability Forum (FSF) into a new group called the Financial Stability Board (FSB). The old FSF was chaired by the General Manager of the BIS and was set up in 1999 to serve in a merely advisory capacity for the G7 (a group of finance ministers formed from the seven major industrialized nations). The new FSB has been expanded to include all G20 members (nineteen nations plus the EU) and has real teeth, imposing "obligations" and "commitments" on its members. The secretariat is based at the BIS headquarters in Basel, Switzerland. What has particularly alarmed observers is a vague parenthetical reference in a press release titled "Financial Stability Forum Re-established as the Financial Stability Board," issued by the BIS on April 3, 2009. It states:

As obligations of membership, member countries and territories commit to... implement international financial standards (in-cluding the 12 key International Standards and Codes).[18]

This was not just friendly advice from an advisory board. It was a commitment to comply, so some detailed discussion would be expected concerning what those standards entailed. But a search of the major media revealed virtually nothing. The 12 key International Standards and Codes were left undefined and undiscussed. The FSB website listed them but was vague. The Standards and Codes cover broad areas that are apparently sub-ject to modification as the overseeing committees sees fit. They include:

- Monetary and financial policy transparency
- Fiscal policy transparency

- Data dissemination
- Insolvency
- Corporate governance
- Accounting
- Auditing
- Payment and settlement
- Market integrity
- Banking supervision
- Securities regulation
- Insurance supervision

Take "fiscal policy transparency" as an example. The "Code of Good Practices on Fiscal Transparency" was adopted by the IMF Interim Committee in 1998. The "synoptic description" says:

> The code contains transparency requirements to provide assurances to the public and to capital markets that a sufficiently complete picture of the structure and finances of government is available so as to allow the soundness of fiscal policy to be reliably assessed.[19]

We learn that members are required to provide a "picture of the structure and finances of government" that is complete enough for an assessment of its "soundness" – but an assessment by whom, and what if a government fails the test? Is an unelected private committee based in the BIS allowed to evaluate the "structure and function" of a particular national government and, if that government is determined to have fiscal policies that are not "sound," to require them to be brought in line with the committee's mandates?

Consider this scenario: the new Financial Stability Board (FSB) rules precipitate a global depression the likes of which have never before been seen. XYZ country wakes up to the fact that all of this is unnecessary – that it could be creating its own money, freeing itself from the debt trap, rather than borrowing from bankers who create money on computer screens and charge interest for the privilege of borrowing it. But this realization comes too late. The FSB has ruled that for a government to issue money is an impermissible "merging of the public and private sectors" and an "unsound banking practice" forbidden under the "12 Key International Standards and Codes". XYZ is forced into line. National sovereignty has been abdicated to a private committee, with no say by the voters.

A Bloodless Coup?

Wary observers might say that this is how you pull off a private global dictatorship:

(1) create a global crisis;

(2) appoint an "advisory body" to retain and maintain "stability"; then

(3) "formalize" the advisory body as global regulator.

By the time the people wake up to what has happened, it's too late. Marilyn Barnewall, who was called by *Forbes Magazine* the "dean of American private banking," wrote in an April 2009 article titled "What Happened to American Sovereignty at G-20?":

> It seems the world's bankers have executed a bloodless coup and now represent all of the people in the world... President Obama agreed at the G20 meeting in London to create an international board with authority to intervene in U.S. corporations by dictating executive compensation and approving or disapproving business management decisions. Under the new Financial Stability Board, the United States has only one vote. In other words, the group will be largely controlled by European central bankers. My guess is, they will represent themselves, not you and not me and certainly not America.[20]

Adoption of the FSB was never voted on by the U.S. public, either individually or through their legislators. The G20 Summit has been called "a New Bretton Woods," referring to agreements entered into in 1944 establishing new rules for international trade. But Bretton Woods was adopted in the United States by Congressional Executive Agreement, requiring a majority vote of the legislature. It probably should have been done by treaty, requiring a two-thirds vote of the Senate, since it was an international agreement binding on the nation. That sort of legislative vote should also be mandated before imposing the will of the

BIS-based Financial Stability Board on the United States, its banks and its businesses.

Even with a two-thirds Senate vote, before Congress gives its approval, legislation should be drafted ensuring that the checks and balances imposed by the U.S. Constitution are built into the agreement. Ideally, the legislatures of the member nations would be required to elect a representative body to provide oversight and take corrective measures as needed, with that body's representatives answerable to their national electorates. If we the people of the world are to avoid abdicating the sovereignty of our respective nations to a private foreign banking elite, we need to insist on compliance with the constitutional and legal mandates on which our nations were founded.

◆

NOTES

1. Andrew Gavin Marshall, "The Financial New World Order: Towards a Global Currency and World Government", *Global Research,* http://www.global research.ca/index.php?context=va&aid=13070, 6 April 2009. See also Chapter 17.
2. Alfred Mendez, "The Network", *The World Central Bank: The Bank for International Settlements*, http://copy_bilderberg.tripod.com/bis.htm.
3. HubPages, "BIS – Bank of International Settlement: The Mother of All Central Banks", *hubpages.com*, 2009.
4. Carroll Quigley, *Tragedy and Hope: A History of the World in Our Time*, 1966.
5. HubPages, "BIS – Bank of International Settlement: The Mother of All Central Banks", *hubpages.com*, 2009.
6. Edward Jay Epstein, "Ruling the World of Money", *Harper's Magazine*, November 1983.
7. Joan Veon, "The Bank for International Settlements Calls for Global Currency", *News with Views*, 26 August 2003.
8. Peter Myers, "The 1988 Basle Accord – Destroyer of Japan's Finance System", http://www.mailstar.net/basle.html, 9 September 2008.
9. Nirmal Chandra, "Is Inclusive Growth Feasible in Neoliberal India?", *networkideas.org*, September 2008.

10. Henry C. K. Liu, "The BIS vs National Banks", *Asia Times*, http://www.atimes.com/global-econ/DE14Dj01.html, 14 May 2002.
11. *Ibid.*
12. Comptroller of the Currency, "OCC Approves Basel II Capital Rule", *Comptroller of the Currency Release*, 1 November 2007.
13. Vinny Catalano, "FAS 157: Timing Is Everything", *vinnycatalano. blogspot.com*, 18 March 2008.
14. Bruce Wiseman, "The Financial Crisis: A look Behind the Wizard's Curtain", *Canada Free Press*, 19 March 2009.
15. Ellen Brown, "Credit Where Credit Is Due", webofdebt.com/articles/creditcrunch.php, 11 January 2009.
16. John Berlau, "The International Mark-to-Market Contagion", *OpenMarket.org*, 10 October 2008.
17. Jon Danielsson, *et al.*, "An Academic Response to Basel II", *LSE Financial Markets Group Special Paper Series*, May 2001.
18. Financial Stability Board, "Financial Stability Forum Re-established as the Financial Stability Board", issued by the *BIS*, www.financial-stabilityboard.org/press/pr_090402b.pdf, 3 April 2009.
19. Financial Stability Board, "12 Key Standards for Sound Financial Systems", http://www.financialstabilityboard.org/cos/key_standards.htm, 23 April 2008.
20. Marilyn Barnewall, "What Happened to American Sovereignty at G-20?", *NewsWithViews.com*, 18 April 2009.

CHAPTER 17

The Financial New World Order: Towards A Global Currency

Andrew Gavin Marshall

Introduction

Following the 2009 G20 summit, plans were announced for implementing the creation of a new global currency under the IMF's Special Drawing Rights (SDRs), to replace the U.S. dollar's role as the world's reserve currency. SDRs are "a synthetic paper currency issued by the International Monetary Fund":

> The G20 leaders have activated the IMF's power to create money and begin global "quantitative easing". In doing so, they are putting a *de facto* world currency into play. It is outside the control of any sovereign body. Conspiracy theorists will love it... There is now a world currency in waiting. In time, SDRs are likely to evolve into a parking place for the foreign holdings of central banks, led by the People's Bank of China... The creation of a Financial Stability Board looks like the first step towards a global financial regulator [global central bank].[1]

It is important to take a closer look at these "solutions" being proposed and implemented in the midst of the current global financial crisis. These are not new suggestions, as they have been in the plans of the global financial establishment for a long time. However, in the midst of the current financial crisis, the elite has fast-tracked its agenda of forging a New World Order in finance. It is important to address the background to these proposed and imposed "solutions" and what effects they will have on the International Monetary System (IMS) and the global political economy as a whole.

A New Bretton Woods

In October 2008, at the height of the 2008 financial meltdown, British Prime Minister Gordon Brown called for:

> A new Bretton Woods – building a new international financial architecture for the years ahead... We must now reform the international financial system [and that he would want] to see the IMF reformed to become a 'global central bank' closely monitoring the international economy and financial system.[2]

This "new Bretton-Woods," said Brown, should work towards "global governance... shared global standards for accounting and regulation [and] the renewal of our international institutions to make them effective early-warning systems for the world economy."[3]

As the world's central bankers gathered in Washington DC in early October 2008, under the auspices of the IMF and the World Bank, "the big question they [faced was] whether it [was] time to establish a global economic 'policeman' to ensure the crash of 2008 can never be repeated."

Further, "any organization with the power to police the global economy would have to include representatives of every major country – a United Nations of economic regulation." A former governor of the Bank of England suggested that, "the answer might already be staring us in the face, in the form of the Bank for International Settlements (BIS)", while underscoring that "[the BIS] has no teeth. The IMF tends to couch its warnings about economic problems in very diplomatic language, but the BIS is more independent and much better placed to deal with this if it is given the power to do so."[4]

Emergence of Regional Currencies

On January 1, 1999, the European Union established the Euro as its regional currency. The Euro has grown in prominence over the past several years. However, it is not to be the only regional currency in the world. There are moves and calls for other regional currencies throughout the world.

In a 2007 article entitled "The End of National Currency", *Foreign Affairs*, the mouthpiece of the powerful Council on

Foreign Relations, addressed the question of how to deal with successive currency crises, stating:

> The right course is not to return to a mythical past of monetary sovereignty, with governments controlling local interest and exchange rates in blissful ignorance of the rest of the world. Governments must let go of the fatal notion that nationhood requires them to make and control the money used in their territory. National currencies and global markets simply do not mix; together they make a deadly brew of currency crises and geopolitical tension and create ready pretexts for damaging protectionism. In order to globalize safely, countries should abandon monetary nationalism and abolish unwanted currencies, the source of much of today's instability...

> Monetary nationalism is simply incompatible with globalization. It has always been, even if this has only become apparent since the 1970s, when all the world's governments rendered their currencies intrinsically worthless... Since economic development outside the process of globalization is no longer possible, countries should abandon monetary nationalism. Governments should replace national currencies with the dollar or the euro or, in the case of Asia, collaborate to produce a new multinational currency over a comparably large and economically diversified area...[5]

> European Central Bank council member Ewald Nowotny said a "tri-polar" global currency system is developing between Asia, Europe and the U.S. and that he's skeptical the U.S. dollar's centrality can be revived.[6]

In South America, there are moves to create a regional currency and central bank under the Union of South American Nations, which was established in May 2008.[7] The Gulf Cooperation Council (GCC), a regional trade bloc of Arabic Gulf nations, has also been making moves towards creating a regional central bank and common currency for its member nations, following the example of Europe, and even being advised by the European Central Bank.[8] From the time of the East Asian financial crisis in the late 1990s, there have been calls for the creation of a regional currency for East Asia among the ten member nations of the ASEAN bloc, as well as China, Japan and South

Korea. In 2008, ASEAN central bank officials and financial ministers met to discuss monetary integration in the region.[9] Within Africa, there are already certain regional monetary unions, and within the framework of the African Union, there are moves being implemented to create an African currency under the control of an African Central Bank (ACB), to be located in Nigeria.[10] In North America, there are moves, coinciding with the deepening economic and political integration of the continent under NAFTA and the Security and Prosperity Partnership of North America (SPP), to create a regional currency for North America, aptly given the current designation as the Amero, and even the then-Governor of the Central Bank of Canada, David Dodge, in 2007, said that a regional currency was "possible."[11]

A Global Currency

The Phoenix

In 1988, *The Economist* ran a provocative article titled, "Get Ready for the Phoenix", advocating the formation of a new global currency:

> Thirty years from now, Americans, Japanese, Europeans, and people in many other rich countries and some relatively poor ones will probably be paying for their shopping with the same currency. Prices will be quoted not in dollars, yen or D-marks but in, let's say, the phoenix. The phoenix will be favored by companies and shoppers because it will be more convenient than to-day's national currencies, which by then will seem a quaint cause of much disruption to economic life in the late twentieth century...

> The market crash [of 1987] taught [governments] that the pretence of policy cooperation can be worse than nothing, and that until real co-operation is feasible (i.e. until governments surrender some economic sovereignty) further attempts to peg currencies will flounder... Several more big exchange-rate upsets, a few more stock market crashes and probably a slump or two will be needed before politicians are willing to face squarely up to that choice. This points to a muddled sequence of emergency followed by patch-up followed by emergency, stretching out far beyond 2018-except for two things. As time passes, the damage

caused by currency instability is gradually going to mount; and the very trends that will make it mount are making the utopia of monetary union feasible...

[The formation of a global central bank] means a big loss of economic sovereignty, but the trends that make the phoenix so appealing are taking that sovereignty away in any case...

The phoenix would probably start as a cocktail of national currencies, just as the Special Drawing Rights is today. In time, though, its value against national currencies would cease to matter, because people would choose it for its convenience and the stability of its purchasing power...

Pencil in the phoenix for around 2018, and welcome it when it comes.[12]

Recommendations for a Global Currency

In 1999, economist Judy Shelton told the U.S. House of Representatives Committee on Banking and Financial Services that regional currencies are the "next step in the evolution toward some kind of global monetary order." She also advocated the creation of a global reserve asset, which every nation should fix its exchange rate to.[13] Former Federal Reserve Governor Paul Volcker has said that "if we are to have a truly global economy, a single world currency makes sense." A European Central Bank executive stated that "we might one day have a single world currency," in "a step towards the ideal situation of a fully integrated world."[14]

The IMF held a conference in 2000 discussing how the world was segmenting into regional currency blocs and that a single world currency was possible, and that it would be, in fact, preferable.[15] Nobel Prize winning economist Robert Mundell has long advocated for the creation of a global currency, which "would restore a needed coherence to the international monetary system, give the International Monetary Fund a function that would help it to promote stability, and be a catalyst for international harmony."[16]

Renewed Calls for a Global Currency

In March of 2009, Russia suggested that the G20 should "consider the possibility of creating a supra-national reserve currency or a 'super-reserve currency'" based on the IMF's Special Drawing Rights (SDRs).[17] A week later, China's central bank governor proposed the creation of a global currency controlled by the IMF, replacing the U.S. dollar as the world reserve currency, also using the IMF's SDRs as the reserve currency basket against which all other currencies would be fixed.[18]

Days after this proposal (April 2009), the U.S. Treasury Secretary Timothy Geithner, in an address to the Council on Foreign Relations, confirmed Washington's tacit support of the Chinese proposal: "we're actually quite open to that suggestion. But you should think of it as rather evolutionary, building on the current architectures, than – rather than – rather than moving us to global monetary union."[19]

Meanwhile, a UN panel of economists had recommended the creation of a new global currency reserve that would replace the U.S. dollar, and that it would be an "independently administered reserve currency."[20]

Creating a World Central Bank

In 1998, the creation of a "Global Fed" was put forth by Jeffrey Garten, Undersecretary of Commerce for International Trade in the Clinton administration. Garten was an influential figure, who served on the White House Council on International Economic Policy under the Nixon administration and on the policy planning staffs of Secretaries of State Henry Kissinger and Cyrus Vance of the Ford and Carter administrations. He was a former Managing Director at Lehman Brothers and a member of the Council on Foreign Relations. He wrote:

> Over time the United States set up crucial central institutions – the Securities and Exchange Commission (1933), the Federal Deposit Insurance Corporation (1934) and, most important, the Federal Reserve (1913). In so doing, America became a managed national economy. These organizations were created to make capitalism work, to prevent destructive business cycles and to moderate the harsh, invisible hand of Adam Smith... This is what

now must occur on a global scale. The world needs an institution that has a hand on the economic rudder when the seas become stormy. It needs a global central bank.

One thing that would not be acceptable would be for the bank to be at the mercy of short-term-oriented legislatures [i.e. it is not to be accountable to the people of the world. So, he asks the question:] To whom would a global central bank be accountable? It would have too much power to be governed only by technocrats, although it must be led by the best of them. One possibility would be to link the new bank to an enlarged Group of Seven – perhaps a "G-15" [or in today's context, the G20] that would include the G-7 plus rotating members like Mexico, Brazil, South Africa, Poland, India, China and South Korea... There would have to be very close collaboration [between the global bank and the Fed].[21]

Ten years later, In September of 2008, at the height of the financial crisis, Jeffrey Garten called for the establishment of a "Global Monetary Authority":

Even if the US's massive financial rescue operation succeeds, it should be followed by something even more far-reaching – the establishment of a Global Monetary Authority to oversee markets that have become borderless... [The] need for a new Global Monetary Authority. It would set the tone for capital markets in a way that would not be viscerally opposed to a strong public oversight function with rules for intervention, and would return to capital formation the goal of economic growth and development rather than trading for its own sake.[22]

In October of 2008, Morgan Stanley CEO John Mack stated that, "it may take continued international coordination to fully unlock the credit markets and resolve the financial crisis, perhaps even by forming a new global body to oversee the process."[23]

Jeffrey Garten called upon world leaders to "begin laying the groundwork for establishing a global central bank", explaining that:

There was a time when the U.S. Federal Reserve played this role [as governing financial authority of the world], as the prime financial institution of the world's most powerful economy, overseeing the one global currency. But with the growth of capital markets, the rise of currencies like the euro and the emergence of powerful players such as China, the shift of wealth to Asia and the Persian Gulf and, of course, the deep-seated problems in the American economy itself, the Fed no longer has the capability to lead single-handedly. [24]

In January of 2009, Dr. William Overholt, senior research fellow at Harvard's Kennedy School, called for the "management of global liquidity":

To avoid another crisis, we need an ability to manage global liquidity. Theoretically that could be achieved through some kind of global central bank, or through the creation of a global currency, or through global acceptance of a set of rules with sanctions and a dispute settlement mechanism.[25]

In a related proposal, Guillermo Calvo, Professor of Economics at Columbia University, recommended:

[The] establishment of a lender of last resort (LOLR) that would radically soften the severity of financial crisis by providing timely credit lines. With that aim in mind, the 20th century saw the creation of national or regional central banks in charge of a subset of the capital market. It has now become apparent that the realm of existing central banks is very limited and the world has no institution that fulfills the necessary global role. The IMF is moving in that direction, but it is still too small and too limited to adequately do so.[26]

Conclusion

The future of the global political economy is one of increasing moves toward a global system of governance, or a world government, with a world central bank and global currency. Concurrently, these initiatives are likely to result in a decline in democracy around the world, as well as a rise in authoritarian forms of government. What we are witnessing is the creation of a New World Order, composed of a totalitarian global government structure. (For further details see Chapter 14.)

In fact, the very concept of a global currency and global central bank is authoritarian in its very nature, as it removes any vestiges of oversight and accountability away from the people of the world, toward a small, increasingly interconnected group of international elites.

Indeed, the policy "solutions" tend to benefit those who caused the financial crisis over those who are poised to suffer the most as a result of the crisis: the disappearing middle classes, the world's dispossessed, poor, indebted people. The proposed solutions to this crisis represent the manifestations and actualization of the ultimate generational goals of the global elite, and thus, represent the least favorable conditions for the vast majority of the world's people.

It is imperative that the world's people throw their weight against these "solutions" and usher in a new era of world order, one of the People's World Order; with the solution lying in local governance and local economies, so that the people have greater roles in determining the future and structure of their own political-economy, and thus, their own society. With this alternative of localized political economies, in conjunction with an unprecedented global population and international democratization of communication through the internet, we have the means and possibility before us to forge the most diverse manifestation of cultures and societies that humanity has ever known.

The answer lies in the individual's internalization of human power and destination, and a rejection of the externalization of power and human destiny to a global authority of which all but a select few people have access to. To internalize human power and destiny is to realize the gift of a human mind, which has the ability to engage in thought beyond the material, such as food and shelter, and venture into the realm of the conceptual. Each individual possesses – within themselves – the ability to think critically about themselves and their own life; now is the time to utilize this ability with the aim of internalizing the concepts and questions of human power and destiny: Why are we here? Where are we going? Where should we be going? How do we get there?

The supposed answers to these questions are offered to us by a tiny global elite who fear the repercussions of what would take place if the people of the world were to begin to answer these questions themselves. I do not know the answers to these questions, but I do know that the answers lie in the human mind and spirit, that which has overcome and will continue to overcome the greatest of challenges to humanity, and will, without doubt, triumph over the New World Order.

◆

NOTES

1. Ambrose Evans-Pritchard, "The G20 Moves the World a Step Closer to a Global Currency", *The Telegraph*, http://www.telegraph. co.uk/finance/com ment/ambroseevans_pritchard/5096524/The-G20-moves-the-world-a-step-closer-to-a-global-currency.html, 3 April 2009.

2. Robert Winnett, "Financial Crisis: Gordon Brown Calls for 'New Bretton Woods'", *The Telegraph*, http://www.telegraph.co.uk/finance/financetopics/financialcrisis/3189517/Financial-Crisis-Gordon-Brown-calls-for-new-Bretton-Woods.html, 13 October 2008.

3. Gordon Brown, "Out of the Ashes", *The Washington Post*, http://www.washingtonpost.com/wp-dyn/content/article/2008/10/16/AR20081016031 79.html, 17 October 2008.

4. Gordon Rayner, "Global Financial Crisis: Does the World Need a New Banking 'Policeman'?" *The Telegraph*, http://www.telegraph. co.uk/finance/financetopics/financialcrisis/3155563/Global-finan cial-crisis-does-the-world-need-a-new-banking-policeman.html, 8 October 2008.

5. Benn Steil, "The End of National Currency", *Foreign Affairs*, Vol. 86, Issue 3, May/June 2007, p. 83-96.

6. Jonathan Tirone, "ECB's Nowotny Sees Global 'Tri-Polar' Currency System Evolving", *Bloomberg*, http://www.bloomberg.com/apps/news?pid=20601087&sid=apjqJKKQvfDc&refer=home, 19 October 2008.

7. CNews, "South American Nations to Seek Common Currency", *China View*, http://news.xinhuanet.com/english/2008-05/27/content_8260847.htm, 26 May 2008.

8. Forbes, "TIMELINE – Gulf single currency deadline delayed beyond 2010", http://www.forbes.com/feeds/afx/2009/03/24/afx 6204462.html, 23 March 2009.

9. Barry Eichengreen, "International Monetary Arrangements: Is There a Monetary Union in Asia's Future?", *The Brookings Institution*,

http://www.brookings.edu/articles/1997/spring_globaleconomics_eichengreen.aspx, Spring 1997.

10. Eric Ombok, "African Union, Nigeria Plan Accord on Central Bank", *Bloomberg*, http://www.bloomberg.com/apps/news?pid=20601116&sid=afoY1vOnEMLA&refer=africa, 2 March 2009.
    Ministry of Foreign Affairs, "Africa in the Quest for a Common Currency", *Republic of Kenya*, http://www.mfa.go.ke/mfacms/index.php?option=com_content&task=view&id=346&Itemid=6, March 2009.

11. Barrie McKenna, "Dodge Says Single Currency 'Possible'", *The Globe and Mail*, 21 May 2007.

12. The Economist, "Get Ready for the Phoenix", Vol. 306, p. 9-10, http://www.economist.com, 9 January 1988.

13. Judy Shelton, "Testimony of Judy Shelton Before the United States House of Representatives Committee on Banking and Financial Services", *Hearing on Exchange Rate Stability in International Finance*, http://financialservices.house.gov/banking/52199she.htm, 21 May 1999.

14. ECB, "The Euro and the Dollar - New Imperatives for Policy Co-ordination", *Speeches and Interviews*, http://www.ecb.int/press/key/date/2000/html/sp 000918.en.html, 18 September 2000.

15. IMF, "One World, One Currency: Destination or Delusion?", *Economic Forums and International Seminars*, http://www.imf.org/external/np/exr/ecforums/ 110800.htm, 8 November 2000.

16. Robert A. Mundell, "World Currency", *The Works of Robert A. Mundell*, http://www.robertmundell.net/Menu/Main.asp?Type=5&Cat=09&ThemeName=World%20Currency.

17. Itar-Tass News Agency, "Russia Proposes Creation of Global Super-reserve Currency", http://www.itar-tass.com/eng/level2.html?NewsID=13682035& PageNum=0, 16 March 2009.

18. Jamil Anderlini, "China Calls for New Reserve Currency", *The Financial Times*, http://www.ft.com/cms/s/0/7851925a- 17a2-11de-8c9d-0000779fd2ac.html, 23 March 2009.

19. CFR, "A Conversation with Timothy F. Geithner", *Council on Foreign Relations Transcripts*, http://www.cfr.org/publication/18925/, 25 March 2009.

20. The Sunday Telegraph, "UN Backs New New Global Currency Reserve", http://www.news.com.au/business/story/0,27753,25255091-462,00.html, 29 March 2009.

21. Jeffrey E. Garten, "Needed: A Fed for the World", *The New York Times*, http://www.nytimes.com/1998/09/23/opinion/needed-a-fed-for-the-world.html, 23 September 1998.

22. Jeffrey Garten, "Global Authority can Fill Financial Vacuum", *The Financial Times*, http://www.ft.com/cms/s/0/7caf543e-8b13- 11dd-b634-0000779fd18 c.html?nclick_check=1, 25 September 2008.
23. CNBC, "Morgan's Mack: Firm Was Excessively Leveraged", *CNBC*, http://www.cnbc.com/id/27216678, 16 October 2008.
24. Jeffrey Garten, "We Need a Bank Of the World", *Newsweek*, http://www.newsweek.com/id/165772, 25 October 2008.
25. Sean Davidson, "'Global Central Bank Could Prevent Future Crisis'", *Business 24/7*, http://www.business24-7.ae/articles/2009/1/pages/01102009_350bc822e4ee4508b724e55b0f1393df.aspx, 10 January 2009.
26. Guillermo Calvo, "Lender of Last Resort: Put it on the Agenda!", *VOX*, http://www.voxeu.org/index.php?q=node/3327, 23 March 2009.
27. Walden Siew, "Banks Face 'New World Order,' Consolidation: Report", *Reuters*, http://www.reuters.com/article/innovationNews/idUSN1743541720 080317, 17 March 2008.
    James Politi and Gillian Tett, "NY Fed chief in push for global bank framework", *The Financial Times*, http://us.ft.com/ftgateway/superpage.ft?news_id=fto060820081850443845, 8 June 2008.
    Rupert Wright, "The First Barons of Banking", *The National*, http://www.thenational.ae/article/20081106/BUSINESS/167536298/1005, 6 November 2008.
    Michael Lafferty, "New World Order in Banking Necessary After Abject Failure of Present Model", *The Times Online*, http://business.timesonline.co.uk/tol/business/management/article5792585.ece, 24 February 2009.
    Richard Gwyn, "Change not Necessarily for the Better", *The Toronto Star*, http://www.thestar.com/comment/article/612822, 3 April 2009.
    The Financial Express, "Growth to Slow Down Hitting Hard the Poor Countries", http://www.thefinancialexpress-bd.com/search_index.php?page =detail_news&news_id=62661, 1 April 2009.
    David Rothkopf, *Superclass: The Global Power Elite and the World They are Making*, Toronto, Penguin Books, 2008, p. 315.
    Ibid., p. 315-316.
    Ibid., p. 316.

CHAPTER 18

The Democratization of the Monetary System

Richard C. Cook

Real economic democracy, defined as the unfettered opportunity for every person to achieve his/her productive potential and be fairly rewarded for doing so, does not exist on the earth today.

The economic life of the world today is based on predatory capitalism, where the people with the most money are the ones in charge.

The Debt-Based Monetary System as the Chief Means of Control

Instrumental in control of economics by the rich has been the debt-based monetary system, where credit is treated as the monopoly of private financial interests who in turn control governments, intelligence services and military establishments. Politicians are bought and sold, elected or removed, or even assassinated for this purpose. The global monetary system is tightly controlled and coordinated at the top by the leaders of the central banks who work for the world's richest people.

Currency manipulations are done through the floating exchange system instituted when the U.S. went off the international gold standard in 1971-2. The system allows the dominant institutional traders to keep Western currencies overvalued, take down the currencies of regions like Southeast Asia when they become too strong, and assure that no nation will ever be able to create its own indigenous currency for internal commerce.

The financial systems of all nations have been arranged so that money only comes into existence when it is lent into circulation by a bank. Banks are organized to be under the control of central banks which are controlled by the international financial oligarchs. Consequently, the division between the haves and the have-nots, both among nations and individuals, is synchronous with the division between creditors and debtors. An exception is the class of professionals whose knowledge and skills are essential in the operation of technology and whose independence is tolerated as long as they don't rock the economic or political boats.

It is the rich who are the creditors, because not only do they have the money to lend, they enjoy, under law, the privilege of creating more lending capacity through the fractional reserve banking system. The bankers are allowed by public charters to create money out of thin air, lend it, and collect interest and fees on that lending.

Monopoly control of the money supply by private financial interests is inherently unjust, anti-democratic, and a prime cause of exploitation and abuse. The abuses include the fact that financial profits benefit the monetary controllers to the detriment of people who actually do the work, mine the resources, sell the products, etc.

The financiers are able to create huge financial bubbles that inflate the costs of necessities such as housing, then profit from bankruptcies, foreclosures and public bailouts when the system crashes, as happened in the U.S. in 2008. This crash spread worldwide, but the crisis has nothing to do with any failure of the world's productive capacity. It was simply the result of financial system manipulations by the world's richest people.

Thus there is a constant tendency for the wealth of the world to pass more and more into the bankers' hands. This is why in every major city of the world the banks have replaced churches and temples as the central institutions and most prominent features of the urban landscape.

The bankers and their controllers rule towns, cities, nations and the world. The armies and domestic police forces are used by the rich to keep the debtors under control. That's simply the way it is and the way those with money are determined to keep it. With their profits, they are able to buy up more and more of the resources of the earth, including the labor of men and women. So today we increasingly are witnessing the growth of a rigid, soulless, master-slave society.

Even political democracy seems to be dying due to corruption and manipulation and with it the hopes of mankind for spiritual health, well-being and development.

The Worldwide Monetary Reform Movement

The worldwide monetary reform movement has come into existence to secure the benefits of control of the monetary supply by the community rather than monopolistic cliques exemplified by the Western banking system. While this is only one means of attaining economic democracy, it may be the most important one, because money as an instrument of law controls all commodities.

This is not to minimize the need for other reforms such as liberalization of property laws, fair systems of taxation on land and natural resources like oil, reopening the patent system to individual inventors vs. corporate interests, and assurance to communities of economic sustainability. This would involve laws favorable to community-based economic institutions such as cooperatives, commercial barter networks, family farms, savings banks and credit unions.

Reform should also involve a return to sane programs of national economic development, including protectionist trade policies where appropriate. National financial systems should also get back to supporting investment in productive enterprise rather than financial speculation. The last U.S. president to consistently support long-term economic development both for the U.S. and developing nations was John F. Kennedy, as described in Professor Donald Gibson's book about the Kennedy presidency, *Battling Wall Street*.[1]

But unless money-creation is also controlled by the democratically-constituted community at the national, regional and local levels, with credit being treated unequivocally as a public utility, the lending of money at interest will defeat all other reform measures.

Four specific types of monetary reform aimed at democratization of the monetary system have been discussed with increasing regularity over past decades within the U.S. and other nations. Astute commentators agree that we are in the midst of epochal changes in consciousness among humanity. Some see it reflected politically in a worldwide populist revolution. The concepts represented through the monetary reform movement reflect the best thinking of this revolution and give us hope for human-centered change in the decades ahead.

1. Nationalize the Monetary System

Within the U.S., proposals have ranged from complete takeover of the Federal Reserve System by the federal government to the replacement of fractional reserve banking and the debt-based monetary system by one where the government spends money directly into existence as was done through the 19th century U.S. Greenbacks.

The Greenback system, which provided up to a third of the U.S. money supply through 1900, was highly successful. The bankers opposed it because it meant fewer loans and less profits, but it worked so well that a Greenback Party was formed which ran candidates for president and elected members of Congress.

Such a system adapted to modern conditions has been proposed by the American Monetary Institute through its American Monetary Act. Since it was first drafted in 2003, the Act has been presented in meetings on Capitol Hill by AMI Director Stephen Zarlenga, author of the landmark book, *The Lost Science of Money*.[2]

Under the Act, instead of relying on taxes and deficits to raise revenue, the government would be authorized to spend money on tangible investments such as infrastructure, education and healthcare. The backing of this new money would be the enhanced economic health and productivity of the nation that would result.

Regarding the private banking system, the American Monetary Act would require that banks borrow the money they lend, over and above their reserves, from the U.S. Treasury. The banks could still lend, but the federal government would earn a portion of the revenues from lending rather than having it all going into the pockets of the private financiers. The government would also save huge amounts of money by no longer having to borrow from the banking system or private investors in order to operate.

The American Monetary Act presents a model that would work vastly better than the existing system – in fact it would be a monetary revolution – but would also be more democratic through giving control over the monetary system to the people's elected representatives. The Act would allow the government to fund and support the actual needs of the people rather than simply act as an enforcer of capitalist monopoly prerogatives.

Related to these reforms are other proposals that would recognize credit as a public utility such as state-owned and operated banks like the one in North Dakota that uses public funds as a reserve for lending.

2. Institute a National Dividend System

Early in the 20th century a British engineer named C. H. Douglas argued that a pervasive imbalance could be found within industrial economies whereby not enough consumer purchasing power was generated for a nation to consume what it was capable of producing. Douglas advocated a National Dividend – cash payments to individuals by the government without taxation or debt – in order to redress this imbalance. Douglas' ideas fueled a worldwide movement called Social Credit that was strongest in Great Britain, Canada, Australia and New Zealand.

The National Dividend was actually a method of monetizing societal savings, which British economist John Maynard Keynes advocated through the much more awkward means of government deficit spending, a system that ultimately played into the hands of the banks that lend governments much of their needed cash. While Douglas' system has not yet been implemented, it remains a treasure trove of creative thinking and is economically sound.

Douglas proved that the solution to poverty, trade wars, excessive bankers' control, etc., really is as simple as the government printing and giving away money – limited of course by a nation's capacity to produce. Because the money would go to individuals for them to utilize in whatever ways they saw fit, Social Credit may be viewed as a much more spiritually advanced system than one where economic power lies solely with big institutions, whether private financial institutions or the totalitarian state.

3. Enact a Basic Income Guarantee

Related to a National Dividend is the idea of a Basic Income Guarantee. The Basic Income Guarantee has been advocated by reformers, since the days of Thomas Paine and the American Revolution. Modern economic life is a vicious circle of greed and exploitation where those who cannot or don't want to play the game are vilified and perhaps left homeless or subject to starvation. A Basic Income Guarantee would allow everyone the minimal financial means to survive in some semblance of dignity.

The issue that a Basic Income Guarantee addresses is the right to economic security, a right capitalism has never even acknowledged. One answer to this blatant aspect of human folly has been socialism, perhaps in a modified form as the welfare state. In the 1960s, even economic conservatives were advocating a reverse income tax, which was expressed in the U.S. tax code, though in watered-down form, as the Earned Income Tax Credit. In Alaska, the state pays an annual dividend to all residents from its resource revenues. This is a type of Basic Income Guarantee, which in 2008 amounted to over three thousand dollars per individual.

Some advocates of the Basic Income Guarantee want to pay for it by cutting government military expenditures or raising income taxes. Others say a Basic Income Guarantee would result in greater economic production which would pay for some of the costs through increased tax revenues. Few are so bold as to advocate the print-and-distribute solution, though it would work and would also be an effective measure to reduce individual and family reliance on credit cards and borrowing from banks. The American Monetary Act contains a provision for a provisional cash dividend to individuals of this type.

The best sources of information about the Basic Income Guarantee are the U.S. Basic Income Guarantee Network, the Basic Income European Network, and writers such as Karl Widerquist and Stephen Shafarman.[3]

4. Allow and Encourage Local Currencies

The local currency movement has become worldwide with some small-scale successes to its credit. The overarching effect of capitalism on the world economy has been to destroy local economic self-determination. This started through the growth of the medieval European cities which turned the surrounding countryside into suppliers of raw materials and consumers of manufactured goods made by urban monopolies. The same principle was applied to the colonization of the world by the Western maritime powers, above all Great Britain.

A good example of how British conquest created wastelands was its destruction of the Bengali textile industry in India, laying the groundwork for the transformation of modern Bangladesh into an international "basket case".[4]

Local currencies could provide the medium of exchange for a revival of local economies anywhere that willing buyers and sellers could be found. But this would be anathema to the monetary controllers who have spent the past several centuries centralizing monetary systems in order to facilitate unequal currency exchanges among the have vs. have-not nations and to assure the total control of trade by the rich capitalist banks and corporations.

The best-kept secret of economics is how easy it is, or would be, for a community, nation, or group of nations, to create its own currency for internal trading needs. There is no reason other than economic control by financial interests, for example, that any political jurisdiction could not hire any designated number of people to perform useful work and pay them in vouchers that would be legal tender within the local trading system. The immediate result would be a renaissance in small business, local manufacturing and family farming on a scale sufficient for many of the necessities of life.

Change Is Possible Now

Given modern systems of administration and technology, democratic currencies can and must be brought into existence if humanity is to have a future. It is the financiers, who also control governments, the media, and the educational systems, who are determined that this does not happen.

One of the leading methods of keeping the public ignorant is to raise the bugaboo of "inflation". Actually, nothing is more inflationary than the bankers' debt-based monetary system that creates, then destroys, inflationary bubbles at will. This is done largely through the method of raising and lowering interest rates. Now and then, when a really big bubble is desired, access to credit is eased so more suckers are drawn in, as with the

TEXT BOX 18.1
"THE COOK PLAN"

The various aspects of monetary reform would come together under what this author has called "The Cook Plan." This would involve the payment by the government of one thousand dollars per month to all adult citizens who applied to receive it. The payment would be made from a national income security account not dependent on taxes or government borrowing. This account could be maintained at a central institution such as the Treasury Department or against interest-free bonds deposited at the Federal Reserve.

The payment could be subject to taxation so as not to unduly benefit the affluent. It could also be issued in the form of vouchers that would be spent for necessities such as food, shelter, clothing, transportation, communications, etc. The vouchers could then be deposited by vendors in the local branch of a newly-created system of community savings banks. The banks would use the vouchers as reserves to capitalize lending at low-rates of interest to individuals, students, small businesses and family farms.

No single person would get rich from "The Cook Plan," but it would transform communities that are today sucked dry of all available cash and resources by the financial system.

sub-prime mortgages written during the recent housing bubble that burst in 2008.

Since the Federal Reserve System came into existence in 1913, when Congress gave the bankers complete control over the monetary system, the dollar has lost over 95 percent of its value due to inflation. Since the late 1960s, when interest rates were allowed to start escalating to new heights that reached over twenty percent by 1981, inflation has become rampant, though it has been concealed by government manipulation of cost-of-living statistics. Prices have slipped somewhat during the current recession, but they will never return to anything close to their former levels. For persons invested in such high-priced homes, such deflation would be catastrophic, so deeply is everyone snared within this system.

Those who argue that a government-controlled currency a) printed and spent into circulation or b) given away as a National

Dividend or Basic Income Guarantee would be unduly inflationary are unnecessarily worried. Such measures would reduce inflation by eliminating unnecessary bank debt and its load of interest and fees that constitute financier profit. Meanwhile, many of the people who fear inflation but also see the need for reform have gotten on the gold standard bandwagon. While in the past, gold, silver and other commodities have been monetized, there never has been a true commodity currency in a modern industrial economy.

The real backing of a currency is the production of goods and services within a trading area and its availability to facilitate trade between buyers and sellers. It is the responsibility of government to provide such a currency to the community. But it is here that modern governments have most egregiously failed. Instead, they have turned the currency over to financial monopolists, and the world has groaned under the burden of this system of organized larceny ever since.

Monetary reformers know how the system can and should be changed. They see it as a social and moral imperative to work for such change. Millions of people around the world are waking up to see how they have been exploited and how completely unnecessary that exploitation is.

♦

NOTES

1. Donald Gibson, *Battling Wall Street: The Kennedy Presidency*, New York: Sheridan Square Press, 1994.
2. Stephen Zarlenga, *The Lost Science of Money*, New York: Robert Schalkenbach Foundation Edition, 1966.
3. Stephen Shafarman, *Peaceful Positive Revolution*, Tendril Press, 2008.
4. This and other international economic crimes by Great Britain and other Western nations are by Dr. J.W. Smith in his book *Economic Democracy*.

PART V

The Shadow Banking System

CHAPTER 19

Wall Street's Ponzi Scheme

Ellen Brown

When the smartest guys in the room designed their credit default swaps, they forgot to ask one thing – what if the parties on the other side of the bet don't have the money to pay up?

Credit Default Swaps

Credit default swaps (CDS) are insurance-like contracts that are sold as protection against default on loans, but CDS are not ordinary insurance. Insurance companies are regulated by the government, with reserve requirements, statutory limits, and examiners routinely showing up to check the books to make sure the money is there to cover potential claims. CDS are private bets, and the Federal Reserve from the time of Alan Greenspan has insisted that regulators keep hands off. The sacrosanct free market would supposedly regulate itself.

The problem with that approach is that regulations are just rules. If there are no rules, the players can cheat; and cheat they have, with a gambler's addiction. In December 2007, the Bank for International Settlements (BIS) reported derivative trades tallying in at 681 trillion dollars – ten times the gross domestic product of all the countries in the world combined. Somebody is obviously bluffing about the money being brought to the game, and that realization has made for some very jittery markets.

"Derivatives" are complex bank creations that are very hard to understand, but the basic idea is that you can insure an investment you want to go up by betting it will go down. The simplest form of derivative is a short sale: you can place a bet that some asset you own will go down, so that you are covered whichever way the asset moves.

Credit default swaps are the most widely traded form of credit derivative. They are bets between two parties on whether or not a company will default on its bonds. In a typical default swap, the "protection buyer" gets a large payoff if the company defaults within a certain period of time, while the "protection seller" collects periodic payments for assuming the risk of default. CDS thus resemble insurance policies, but there is no requirement to actually hold any asset or suffer any loss, so CDS are widely used just to speculate on market changes.

In one blogger's example, a hedge fund wanting to increase its profits could sit back and collect 320 000 dollars a year in premiums just for selling "protection" on a risky BBB junk bond. The premiums are "free" money – free until the bond actually goes into default, when the hedge fund could be on the hook for one hundred million dollars in claims. And there's the catch: what if the hedge fund doesn't have the one hundred million dollars? The fund's corporate shell or limited partnership is put into bankruptcy, but that hardly helps the "protection buyers" who thought they were covered.

To the extent that CDS are sold as "insurance", they are looking more like insurance fraud. That fact began to hit home with the ratings downgrades of the "monoline" insurers in January of 2008, followed by the collapse of Bear Stearns, a leading Wall Street investment brokerage, in March of the same year. The monolines are so-called because they are allowed to insure only one industry, the bond industry. Monoline bond insurers were at that time the biggest protection writers for CDS, and Bear Stearns was the twelfth largest counterparty to credit default swap trades.[1] These players were major protection sellers in a massive web of credit default swaps, and when the "protection" went, the whole fragile derivative pyramid was at risk of going with it. The bright side to that perilous situation was that major crises are major opportunities for change. The multitrillion dollar derivatives trade is the last supersized bubble in a 300-year Ponzi scheme, one that has taken over the entire monetary system. The nation's wealth has been drained into private vaults, leaving scarcity in its wake. It is a corrupt system, and change is overdue.

The Wall Street Ponzi Scheme

The Ponzi scheme that has been going bad is not just another misguided investment strategy. It is at the very heart of the banking business, the thing that has propped it up over the course of three centuries. A Ponzi scheme is a form of pyramid scheme in which new investors must continually be sucked in at the bottom to support the investors at the top. In this case, new borrowers must continually be sucked in to support the creditors at the top. The Wall Street Ponzi scheme is built on "fractional reserve" lending, which allows banks to create "credit" (or "debt") with accounting entries. Banks are now allowed to lend from ten to thirty times their "reserves," essentially counterfeiting the money they lend. Over 97 percent of the U.S. money supply (M3) has been created by banks in this way.[2]

The problem is that banks create only the principal and not the interest necessary to pay back their loans, so new borrowers must continually be found to take out new loans just to create enough "money" (or "credit") to service the old loans composing the money supply. The scramble to find new debtors has now gone on for over three hundred years – ever since the founding of the Bank of England in 1694 – until the whole world has become mired in debt to the bankers' private money monopoly. The Ponzi scheme has finally reached its mathematical limits: we are "all borrowed up."

When the banks ran out of creditworthy borrowers, they had to turn to uncreditworthy "sub-prime" borrowers; and to avoid losses from default, they moved these risky mortgages off their books by bundling them into "securities" and selling them to investors. To induce investors to buy, these securities were then "insured" with credit default swaps.

But the housing bubble itself was another Ponzi scheme, and eventually there were no more borrowers to be sucked in at the bottom who could afford the ever-inflating home prices. When the sub-prime borrowers quit paying, the investors quit buying mortgage-backed securities. The banks were then left holding their own suspect paper; and without triple-A ratings, there was little chance that buyers for this "junk" would be found. The crisis was not, however, in the economy itself, which was fundamentally sound – or would have been with a proper credit system to oil the wheels of production. The crisis was in the banking system, which could no longer cover up the shell game it had played for three centuries with other people's money.

The Derivatives Chernobyl

The collapse of Bear Stearns on March 16, 2008, was a major crack in the massive derivatives edifice. Bear Stearns had helped fuel the explosive growth in the credit derivative market, where banks, hedge funds and other investors had engaged in 45 trillion dollars worth of bets on the credit-worthiness of companies and countries. Before it collapsed, Bear was the counterparty to thirteen trillion dollars in derivative trades. On March 14, 2008, Bear's ratings were downgraded by Moody's, a major rating agency; and on March 16, the brokerage was bought by J.P. Morgan for pennies on the dollar, a token buyout designed to avoid the legal complications of bankruptcy.

The deal was backed by a 29 billion dollar "non-recourse" loan from the Federal Reserve. "Non-recourse" meant that the Fed got only Bear's shaky paper assets as collateral. If those proved to be worthless, JPM was off the hook. It was an unprecedented move, of questionable legality; but it was said to be justified because, as one headline put it, "Fed's Rescue of Bear Halted Derivatives Chernobyl."[3]

The notion either that Bear was "rescued" or that the Chernobyl was halted, however, was grossly misleading. The CEOs managed to salvage their enormous bonuses, but it was a "bailout" only for JPM and Bear's creditors. For the shareholders, it was a wipeout. Their stock initially dropped from 156 dollars to two dollars, and thirty percent of it was held by the employees. Another big chunk was held by the pension funds of teachers and other public servants. The share price was later raised to ten dollars a share in response to shareholder outrage, but the shareholders were still essentially wiped out; and the fact that one Wall Street bank had to be fed to the lions to rescue the others hardly inspired a feeling of confidence. Neutron bombs are not so easily contained.

The Bear Stearns hit from the derivatives iceberg followed an earlier one in January 2008, when global markets took their worst tumble since September 11, 2001. Commentators were asking if this was "the big one" – a 1929-style crash; and it probably would have been if deft market manipulations had not swiftly covered over the approaching catastrophe. The precipitous drop was blamed on the threat of downgrades in the ratings of two major monoline insurers, Ambac Financial Group and MBIA, followed by a 7.2 billion dollar loss in derivative trades by Société Générale, France's second-largest bank.

Like Bear Stearns, the monolines served as counterparties in a web of credit default swaps, and a downgrade in their ratings would jeopardize the whole shaky derivatives edifice. Without the monoline insurers' triple-A seal, billions of dollars worth of triple-A investments would revert to junk bonds. Many institutional investors (pension funds, municipal governments and the like) have a fiduciary duty to invest in only the "safest" triple-A bonds. Downgraded bonds therefore get dumped on the market, jeopardizing the banks that are still holding billions of dollars worth of these bonds. The downgrade of Ambac in January 2008 signaled a simultaneous downgrade of bonds from over one hundred thousand municipalities and institutions, totaling more than 500 billion dollars.[4]

Institutional investors wound up losing a good deal of money in all this, but the real calamity was to the banks. The institutional investors that formerly bought mortgage-backed bonds stopped buying them in 2007, when the housing market slumped. But the big investment houses that were selling them had billions' worth left on their books, and it was these banks that particularly stood to lose as the derivative Chernobyl imploded.[5]

A Parade of Bailout Schemes

Now that some highly leveraged banks and hedge funds had to lay their cards on the table and expose their worthless hands, these avid free marketers began crying out for government intervention to save them from monumental losses, while preserving the monumental gains raked in when their bluff was still good. In response to their pleas, the men behind the curtain scrambled to devise various bailout schemes; but the schemes were bandaids at best. To bail out a 681 trillion dollar derivative scheme with taxpayers' money was obviously impossible. As Michael Panzer observed on SeekingAlpha.com:

As the slow-motion train wreck in our financial system continues to unfold, there are going to be plenty of ill-conceived rescue attempts and dubious turnaround plans, as well as propagandizing, dissembling and scheming by banks, regulators and politicians. This is all happening in an effort to try and buy time or to figure out how the losses can be dumped onto the lap of some patsy (e.g., the taxpayer). [6]

The idea was evidently to be to keep the violins playing while the Big Money Boys slipped into the mist and manned the lifeboats. As was pointed out in a blog called "Jesse's Café Americain" concerning the bailout of Ambac:

It seems that the real heart of the problem is that AMBAC was being used as a "cover" by the banks which originated these bundles of mortgages to get their mispriced ratings. Now that the mortgages are failing and the banks are stuck with them, AMBAC cannot possibly pay, they cannot cover the debt. And the banks don't wish to mark these CDOs [collateralized debt obligations] to market [downgrade them to their real market value] because they are probably at best worth 60 cents on the dollar, but are being held by the banks on balance at roughly par. That's a 40 percent haircut on enough debt to sink every bank involved in this situation. Indeed for all intents and purposes if marked to market banks are now insolvent. So, the banks will provide capital to AMBAC... [but] it's just a game of passing money around... So why are the banks engaging in this charade? This looks like an attempt to extend the payouts on a vast Ponzi scheme gone bad that is starting to collapse.[7]

The likely result was that the banks would be looking for one bailout after another from the only pocket deeper than their own, the U.S. government's. But if the federal government were to acquiesce, it too could be dragged into the voracious debt cyclone of the mortgage mess. The federal government's triple-A rating was already in jeopardy, due to a gargantuan debt that was then at nine trillion dollars. Before the government agreed to bail out the banks, it would need to insist on some adequate quid pro quo. In England, the government had agreed to bail out bankrupt mortgage bank Northern Rock, but only in return for the bank's stock.

On March 31, 2008, *The Telegraph* (London) reported that Federal Reserve strategists were eyeing the nationalizations that saved Norway, Sweden and Finland from a banking crisis from 1991 to 1993. In Norway, according to one Norwegian adviser, "the law was amended so that we could take 100 percent control of any bank where its equity had fallen below zero."[8] If their assets were "marked to market," some major Wall Street banks could already be in that category.

Benjamin Franklin's Solution

Nationalization has traditionally had a bad name in the United States, but like in Europe, it could be the most efficient way to resolve the nation's economic dilemma. Turning bankrupt Wall Street banks into public institutions could allow the government to get out of the debt cyclone by undoing what got us into it. Instead of robbing Peter to pay Paul, flapping around in a sea of debt trying to stay afloat by creating more debt, the government could address the problem at its source: it could restore the right to create money to Congress, the public body to which that solemn duty was delegated under the Constitution.

The most brilliant banking model in our national history was established in the first half of the 18th century, in Benjamin Franklin's home province of Pennsylvania. The local government created its own bank, which issued money and lent it to farmers at a modest interest. The provincial government created enough extra money to cover the interest not created in the original loans, spending it into the economy on public services. The bank was publicly owned, and the bankers it employed were public servants. The interest generated on its loans was sufficient to fund the government without taxes; and because the newly issued money came back to the government, the result was not inflationary.[9] The Pennsylvania banking scheme was a sensible and highly workable system that was a product of American ingenuity but never got a chance to prove itself after the colonies became a nation. It was an ironic twist, since according to some historians, restoring the power to create their own currency was a chief reason the colonists fought for independence. The bankers' money-creating machine has had two centuries of empirical testing and has proven to be a failure. It is time the sovereign right to create money is taken from a private banking elite and restored to the American people to whom it properly belongs.

◆

NOTES

1. Naked Capitalism, "Credit Swap Worries Go Mainstream", *naked-capitalism.com*, 17 February 2008; Aline van Duyn, "CDS Sector Weighs Bear Stearns Backlash", *Financial Times*, London, 16 March 2008.

2. The Telegraph, "Feds Rescue Halted a Derivatives Chernobyl", http://www.telegraph.co.uk/finance/newsbysector/banksand-finance/2786816/Feds-rescue-halted-a-derivatives-Chernobyl.html, 23 March 2008.

3. Ellen Brown, "Dollar Deception: How Banks Secretly Create Money", *webofdebt.com/articles*, 3 July 2008.

4. Wikipedia, "Monoline Insurance", *Wikipedia.com*, http://en.wikipedia.org/wiki/Monoline_insurance.

5. Jane Wells, "Ambac and MBIA: Bonds, Jane's Bonds", *CNBC*, 4 February 2008.

6. Michael Panzer, "Amac: More Smoke and Mirrors?", *Seeking Alpha*, http://seekingalpha.com/article/66108-ambac-more-smoke-and-mirrors?source=feed, 26 February 26, 2008.

7. Jesse's Café Américain, "Saving AMBAC, the Homeowners, or the Banks?", http://jessescrossroadscafe.blogspot.com, 25 February 2008.

8. Ambrose Evans-Pritchard, "Fed Eyes Nordic-style Nationalisation of US Banks", *The Telegraph*, http://www.telegraph.co.uk/finance/newsbysector/banksandfinance/2787249/Fed-eyes-Nordic-style-nationalisation-of-US-banks.html, 31 March 2008.

9. Ellen Brown, *Web of Debt*, Third Millennium Press, 2008, Chapter 3.

CHAPTER 20

Securitization: The Biggest Rip-Off Ever

Mike Whitney

Is it possible to make hundreds of billions of dollars in profits on securities that are backed by nothing more than cyber-entries into a loan book?

It is not only possible; it has been done. And now those who cashed in on the swindle have lined up outside the Federal Reserve building to trade their garbage paper for billions of dollars of taxpayer-funded loans.

Where is the justice? Meanwhile, the credit bust has left the financial system in a shambles and driven the economy into the ground like a tent stake.

The unemployment lines are growing longer and consumers are cutting back on everything from nights-on-the-town to trips to the grocery store. And it's all due to a Ponzi-finance scam that was concocted on Wall Street and spread through the global system like an aggressive strain of Bird Flu. This is not a normal recession; the financial system was blown up by greedy bankers who used "financial innovation" to game the system and inflate the biggest speculative bubble of all time. And they did it all legally, using a little-known process called securitization.

Securitization is the conversion of pools of loans into securities that are sold in the secondary market, providing a means for massive debt-leveraging. The banks use off-balance sheet operations to create securities so they can avoid normal reserve requirements and bothersome regulatory oversight. Oddly enough, the quality of the loan makes no difference at all, since the banks make their money on loan originations and other related fees.

What matters is quantity, quantity, quantity; an industrial-scale assembly line of fetid loans dumped on unsuspecting investors to fatten the bottom line. And, boy, can Wall Street grind out the rotten paper when there's no cop on the beat and the Fed is cheering from the bleachers.

In an analysis written by economist Gary Gorton for the Federal Reserve Bank of Atlanta's 2009 Financial Markets Conference titled, "Slapped in the Face by the Invisible Hand; Banking and the Panic of 2007", the author shows that mortgage-related securities ballooned from 492.6 billion dollars in 1996 to 3 071.1 dollars in 2003, while asset backed securities (ABS) jumped from 168.4 billion dollars in 1996 to 1 253.1 dollars in 2006. All told, more than twenty trillion dollars in securitized debt was sold between 1997 and 2007.[1] How much of that debt will turn out to be worthless as foreclosures skyrocket and the banks' balance sheets come under greater and greater pressure?

Deregulation opened Pandora's Box, unleashing a weird mix of shady off-book operations (SPVs, SIVs) and dodgy, odd-sounding derivatives that were used to amplify leverage and stack debt on tinier and tinier scraps of capital.

It's easy to make money, when one has no skin in the game. That's how hedge fund managers and private equity sharpies get rich. Securitization gave the banks the opportunity to take substandard loans from applicants who had no way of paying them back, and magically transform them into Triple-A securities. "Abra-kadabra". The Wall Street public relations throng boasted that securitization "democratized" credit because more people could borrow at better rates since funding came from investors rather than banks. But it was all a hoax. The real objective was to turbo-charge profits by skimming hefty salaries and bonuses on the front end, before people found out they'd been hosed. The former head of the FDIC, William Seidman, figured it all out back in 1993 when he was cleaning up after the S&L fiasco. Here's what he said in his memoirs:

> Instruct regulators to look for the newest fad in the industry and examine it with great care. The next mistake will be a new way to make a loan that will not be repaid. [2]

That is it in a nutshell. The banks never expected the loans would be paid back, which is why they issued them to ninjas; applicants with no income, no collateral, no job and a bad credit history. It made no sense at all, especially to anyone who's ever sat through a nerve-wracking credit check with a sneering banker. Trust me, bankers know how to get their money back, if that's their real intention. In this case, it didn't matter. They just wanted to keep their counterfeiting racket zooming ahead at full-throttle for as long as possible. Meanwhile, Maestro Greenspan was extolling the virtues of the "new economy" and the permanent high plateau of prosperity that had been achieved through laissez faire capitalism.

Now that the securitization bubble has burst, forty percent of the credit which had been coursing into the economy has been cut off triggering a 1930s-type meltdown.

Fed chief Bernanke has stepped into the breach and provided a thirteen trillion dollar backstop to keep the financial system from collapsing, but the broader economy has continued its historic nosedive. Bernanke is trying to fill the chasm that opened up when securitization ground to a halt and gas started exiting the credit bubble in one mighty whoosh. The deleveraging is ongoing, despite the Fed's many programs to rev up securitization and restore speculative bubblenomics.

Bernanke's latest brainstorm, the Term Asset-Backed Securities Lending Facility (TALF), provides 94 percent public funding for investors willing to buy loans backed by credit card debt, student loans, auto loans or commercial real estate loans. It's a "no lose" situation for big investors who think that securitized debt will stage a comeback. But that's the problem; no one does. Attractive, non recourse (nearly) risk free loans have failed to entice the big brokerage houses and hedge fund managers. Bernanke has peddled less than thirty billion dollars in a program that's designed to lend up to one trillion dollars. It's been a complete bust.

To understand securitization, one must think like a banker. Bankers believe that profits are constrained by reserve requirements. So what they really want is to expand credit with no reserves; the equivalent of spinning flax into gold. Securitization and derivatives contracts achieve that objective. They create a confusing netherworld of odd-sounding instruments and bizarre processes which obscure the simple fact that they are creating money out of thin air. That's what securitization really is; under-capitalized junk masquerading as precious jewels. Here's how economist Henry CK Liu sums it up in his article "Mark-to-Market vs. Mark-to-Model":

> The shadow banking system has deviously evaded the reserve re-quirements of the traditional regulated banking regime and in-stitutions and has promoted a chain-letter-like inverted pyramid scheme of escalating leverage, based in many cases on nonexis-tent reserve cushion. This was revealed by the AIG collapse in 2008 caused by its insurance on financial derivatives known as credit default swaps (CDS)...
>
> The Office of the Comptroller of the Currency and the Federal Reserve jointly allowed banks with credit default swaps (CDS) insurance to keep super-senior risk assets on their books with-out adding capital because the risk was insured. Normally, if the banks held the super-senior risk on their books, they would need to post capital at 8% of the liability. But capital could be reduced to one-fifth the normal amount (20% of 8%, meaning $160 for every $10,000 of risk on the books) if banks could prove to the regulators that the risk of default on the super-senior portion of the deals was truly negligible, and if the securities being issued via a collateral debt obligation (CDO) structure carried a Triple-A credit rating from a "nationally recognized credit rating agen-cy", such as Standard and Poor's rating on AIG.
>
> With CDS insurance, banks then could cut the normal $800 mil-lion capital for every $10 billion of corporate loans on their books to just $160 million, meaning banks with CDS insurance can loan up to five times more on the same capital. The CDS-insured CDO deals could then bypass international banking rules on capital. [3]

The same rule applies to derivatives (CDS) as securitized instruments; neither is sufficiently capitalized because setting aside reserves impairs one's ability to maximize profits. It's all about the bottom line. The reason credit default swaps are so cheap, compared to conventional insurance, is that there's no way of knowing whether the dealer has the ability to pay claims. It's fraud, on a gigantic scale, which is why the financial system went into full-blown paralysis when Lehman Bros defaulted. No one knew whether trillions of dollars in counterparty contracts would be paid out or not. There are simply more claims on wealth than there is money in the system. Bogus mortgages and phony counterparty promises mean nothing. "Show me the money". The system is underwater, and it cannot be fixed by more of the Fed's presto liquidity. Here's what Gary Gorton says later in the same article:

> A banking panic means that the banking system is insolvent. The banking system cannot honor contractual demands; there are no private agents who can buy the amount of assets necessary to recapitalize the banking system, even if they knew the value of the assets, because of the sheer size of the banking system. When the banking system is insolvent, many markets stop functioning and this leads to very significant effects on the real economy.[4]

Indeed. The shadow banking system has collapsed, not because the market is "frozen" or because investors are in a state of panic after Lehman, but because derivatives and securitization have been exposed as a fraud propped up on insufficient capital. It's snake oil sold by charlatans. That's why European policymakers are resisting the Fed's requests to create a facility similar to the TALF to start up securitization again.

In Europe regulators still do their jobs and make sure that financial institutions have money before they create trillions of dollars in credit. They don't stick their heads in the sand while crooked bankers fleece the public. Bernanke's job is to step in and put an end to the hanky-panky, not add to the problems by restoring a credit-generating regime that transferred hundreds of billions of dollars from hard-working people to fatcat banksters.

◆

NOTES

1. Gary Gorton, "Slapped in the Face by the Invisible Hand: Banking and the Panic of 2007", *Yale School of Management, National Bureau of Economic Research (NBER)*, 9 May 2009: http://ssrn.com/abstract= 1401882.
2. Laurence Arnold, "William Seidman, Who Led Cleanup of S&L Crisis, Dies", *Bloomberg*, 13 May 2009.
3. Henry C. K. Liu, "Mark-to-Market vs. Mark-to-Model", *Henry C. K. Liu*, http://www.henryckliu.com/page191.html, May 25, 2009.
4. Gary Gorton, "Slapped in the Face by the Invisible Hand: Banking and the Panic of 2007", *Yale School of Management, National Bureau of Economic Research (NBER)*, http://ssrn.com/abstract=1401882, 9 May 2009.

Glossary of Acronyms

ABS – Asset Backed Securities
ADM – Archer Daniels Midland
AIG – American International Group
AMP – Asian Mode of Production
AoA – Agreement on Agriculture
ASRRS – Army Survival, Recovery and Reconstitution System
BAE Systems – British Aerospace Systems
BCT – Brigade Combat Team
BIS – Bank for International Settlements
BP – British Petroleum
CAC – Cotation Assistée en Continu, Paris Bourse
CBOT – Chicago Board of Trade
CBP – Central Bank of the Philippines
CCCE – Council of Chief Executives
CDS – Credit Default Swap
CEO – Chief Executive Officer
CFR – Council on Foreign Relations
CIA – Central Intelligence Agency
CINC-USNORTHCOM – Commander-in Chief, United States
    Northern Command
CLA – Council for Latin America
CME – Chicago Mercantile Exchange
CoA – Council of the Americas
COG – Continuity of Government
CONUS – Continuous United States
COOP – Continuity of Operations Program
CRS – Congressional Research Service
CSTO – Collective Security Treaty Organization
DARPA – Defense Advanced Research Project Agency
DHS – Department of Homeland Security
DJIA – Dow Jones Industrial Average
DoD – Department of Defense
ECB – European Central Bank
EEC – European Economic Community
EMI – European Monetary Institute
EPZ – Export Processing Zone

Fannie Mae – Federal National Mortgage Association
FAO – Food and Agriculture Organization
FCMD – Federal Contractor Mismanagement Database
FEMA – Federal Emergency Management Agency
FOIA – Freedom of Information Act
FRBNY – Federal Reserve Bank of New York
Freddie Mac – Federal Home Loan Mortgage Corporation
FSB – Financial Stability Board
FSF – Financial Stability Forum
FSMA – Financial Services Modernization Act
FTA – Financial Services Agreement
FTA – Free Trade Agreement
FTAA – Free Trade Area of the Americas
FY – Fiscal Year
G20 – Group of Twenty Major Economies
G7 – Group of Seven Countries
G8 – Group of Eight Countries
GAO – Government Accountability Office
GATS – General Agreement on Trade in Services
GATT – General Agreement on Tariffs and Trade
GCC – Gulf Cooperation Council
GDP – Gross Domestic Product
GEOINT – Geospatial Intelligence
GM – General Motors
GMO – Genetically Modified Organism
GNP – Gross National Product
GWOT – Global War on Terrorism
HAARP – High Frequency Active Auroral Research Program
IBRD – International Bank for Reconstruction and Development
IG Act – Inspector General Act
IMF – International Monetary Fund
IMINT – Imagery Intelligence
IMS – International Monetary System
IPE – International Petroleum Exchange
ISIS – Integrated Sensor Is Structure
JSF – Joint Striker Fighter
MAI – Multilateral Agreement on Investment
MBIA – Municipal Bond Insurance Association
NACC – North American Competitiveness Council
NAFTA – North American Free Trade Agreement
NAMA – Non-Agricultural-Market Access
NASDAQ – National Association of Securities Dealers Automated
    Quotations
NATO – North Atlantic Treaty Organization

NEC – National Economic Council
NGA – National Geospatial-Intelligence Agency
NGO – Non-Governmental Organization
NIC – National Intelligence Council
NIC – Newly Industrialized Countries
NRO – National Reconnaissance Office
NSSSM 200 – National Security Study Memorandum 200
NWO – New World Order
NYSE – New York Stock Exchange
OCC – Office of the Comptroller of the Currency
ODNI – Office of the Director of National Intelligence
OECD – Organization for Economic Cooperation and Development
OPEC – Organization of the Petroleum Exporting Countries
OSS – Office of Strategic Services
PNAC – Project for a New American Century
POGO – Project on Government Oversight
RAID – Rapid Aerostat Initial Deployment
RBS – Royal Bank of Scotland
RWE – Rheinisch-Westfälisches Elektrizitätswerk
S&P 500 – Standard and Poor 500
SAP – IMF/World Bank Structural Adjustment Program
SAP – Special Access Program
SCO – Shanghai Cooperation Organization
SDR – Special Drawing Rights
SDS – Strategic Defense Initiative
SEC – Security and Exchange Commission
SPP – Security and Prosperity Partnership
SSA – Security and Secrecy Agreement
TALF – Term Asset-Backed Securities Lending Facility
TARP – Troubled Assets Relief Program
TCC – Transnational Capitalist Class
TINA – There Is No Alternative
TNS – Transnational State
TRIPS – Trade-Related Aspects of Intellectual Property Rights
TUAC – Trade Union Advisory Committee
UAW – United Auto Workers
UNODC – United Nations Office on Drugs and Crime
USAFRICOM – United States African Command
USCENTCOM – United States Central Command
USSOCOM – United States Special Operations Command
USSOUTHCOM – United States Southern Command
WEF – World Economic Forum
WFP – World Food Program
WMD – Weapons of Mass Destruction
WTO – World Trade Organization

Index

The Globalization of Poverty and the New World Order
MICHEL CHOSSUDOVSKY
ISBN 09737147-0-0 (2003), 403 pages

In this new and expanded edition of Chossudovsky's international best-seller, the author outlines the contours of a New World Order which feeds on human poverty and the destruction of the environment, generates social apartheid, encourages racism and ethnic strife and undermines the rights of women. The result as his detailed examples from all parts of the world show so convincingly, is a globalization of poverty.

This book is a skillful combination of lucid explanation and cogently argued critique of the fundamental directions in which our world is moving financially and economically.

In this new enlarged edition – which includes ten new chapters and a new introduction – the author reviews the causes and consequences of famine in Sub-Saharan Africa, the dramatic meltdown of financial markets, the demise of state social programs and the devastation resulting from corporate downsizing and trade liberalization.

Award winning author and economics professor Michel Chossudovsky is Director of the Centre for Research on Globalization (CRG).

Seeds of Destruction: The Hidden Agenda of Genetic Manipulation
F. WILLIAM ENGDAHL
ISBN 978-0-937147-2-2 (2007), 341 pages

This skillfully researched book focuses on how a small socio-political American elite seeks to establish control over the very basis of human survival: the provision of our daily bread. *"Control the food and you control the people."*

This is no ordinary book about the perils of GMO. Engdahl takes the reader inside the corridors of power, into the backrooms of the science labs, behind closed doors in the corporate boardrooms.

The author cogently reveals a diabolical world of profit-driven political intrigue and government corruption and coercion, where genetic manipulation and the patenting of life forms are used to gain worldwide control over food production. If the book often reads as a crime story, that should come as no surprise. For that is what it is.

Engdahl's carefully argued critique goes far beyond the familiar controversies surrounding the practice of genetic modification as a scientific technique. The book is an eye-opener, a must-read for all those committed to the causes of social justice and world peace.

F. William Engdahl is a leading analyst of the New World Order and author of the best-selling book on oil and geopolitics, A Century of War: Anglo-American Politics and the New World Order.

America's "War on Terrorism"
MICHEL CHOSSUDOVSKY
ISBN 0-9737147-1-9 (2005), 387 pages

In this 2005 best-selling title, the author blows away the smokescreen put up by the mainstream media that 9/11 was an attack on America by "Islamic terrorists". Through meticulous research, the author uncovers a military-intelligence ploy behind the September 11 attacks, and the cover-up and complicity of key members of the Bush administration.

This expanded edition, which includes twelve new chapters, focuses on the use of 9/11 as a pretext for the invasion and illegal occupation of Iraq, the militarization of justice and law enforcement and the repeal of democracy.

According to Chossudovsky, the "war on terrorism" is a complete fabrication based on the illusion that one man, Osama bin Laden, outwitted the $40 billion-a-year American intelligence apparatus. The "war on terrorism" is a war of conquest. Globalization is the final march to the New World Order, dominated by Wall Street and the U.S. military-industrial complex.

September 11, 2001 provides a justification for waging a war without borders. Washington's agenda consists in extending the frontiers of the American empire to facilitate complete U.S. corporate control, while installing within America the institutions of the Homeland Security State. Chossudovsky peels back layers of rhetoric to reveal a complex web of deceit aimed at luring the American people and the rest of the world into accepting a military solution which threatens the future of humanity.

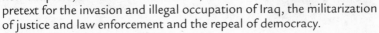

For prices and ordering details, visit our website at www.globalresearch.ca